THE NAHUA

IMS STUDIES ON CULTURE AND SOCIETY SERIES

VOLUME 1
*Symbol and Meaning behind the Closed Community: Essays in Mesoamerican Ideas*
edited by Gary H. Gossen

VOLUME 2
*The Work of Bernardino de Sahagún: Pioneer Ethnographer of Sixteenth-Century Aztec Mexico*
edited by J. Jorge Klor de Alva, H. B. Nicholson, and Eloise Quiñones Keber

VOLUME 3
*Ethnographic Encounters in Southern Mesoamerica: Essays in Honor of Evon Zartman Vogt Jr.*
edited by Victoria R. Bricker and Gary H. Gossen

VOLUME 4
*Casi Nada: A Study of Agrarian Reform in the Homeland of Cardenismo*
by John Gledhill

VOLUME 5
*With Our Heads Bowed: The Dynamics of Gender in a Maya Community*
by Brenda Rosenbaum

VOLUME 6
*Economies and Politics in the Aztec Realm*
edited by Mary G. Hodge and Michael E. Smith

VOLUME 7
*Identities on the Move: Transnational Processes in North America and the Caribbean Basin*
edited by Liliana R. Goldin

VOLUME 8
*Beware the Great Horned Serpent! Chiapas under the Threat of Napoleon*
by Robert M. Laughlin

VOLUME 9
*Indigenous Bodies, Maya Minds: Religion and Modernity in a Transnational K'iche' Community*
by C. James MacKenzie

VOLUME 10
*On Being Maya and Getting By: Heritage Politics and Community Development in Yucatán*
by Sarah R. Taylor

VOLUME 11
*Where Did the Eastern Mayas Go? Decolonizing Ethnography and the Historical, Relational, and Contingent Interplay of Ch'orti' Indigeneity*
by Brent E. Metz

VOLUME 12
*Pre-Mamom Pottery Variation and the Preclassic Origins of the Lowland Maya*
edited by Debra S. Walker

VOLUME 13
*The Nahua: Language and Culture from the Sixteenth Century to the Present*
edited by Galen Brokaw and Pablo García Loaeza

# THE NAHUA

*Language and Culture from the Sixteenth Century to the Present*

EDITED BY
Galen Brokaw and Pablo García Loaeza

UNIVERSITY PRESS OF COLORADO
*Denver*

© 2024 by University Press of Colorado

Published by University Press of Colorado
1508 North Logan Street, Suite 660
PMB 39883
Denver, Colorado 80203-1942

Institute for Mesoamerican Studies
Arts and Sciences
233 University of Albany, SUNY
1400 Washington Avenue
Albany, NY 12222

All rights reserved

 The University Press of Colorado is a proud member of the Association of University Presses.

The University Press of Colorado is a cooperative publishing enterprise supported, in part, by Adams State University, Colorado State University, Fort Lewis College, Metropolitan State University of Denver, University of Alaska Fairbanks, University of Colorado, University of Denver, University of Northern Colorado, University of Wyoming, Utah State University, and Western Colorado University.

ISBN: 978-1-64642-577-8 (hardcover) | ISBN: 978-1-64642-578-5 (paperback)
ISBN: 978-1-64642-579-2 (ebook) | https://doi.org/10.5876/9781646425792

Library of Congress Cataloging-in-Publication Data

Names: Brokaw, Galen, 1966– editor. | García Loaeza, Pablo, 1972– editor.
Title: The Nahua : language and culture from the sixteenth century to the present / edited by Galen Brokaw and Pablo García Loaeza.
Other titles: Language and culture from the sixteenth century to the present | Studies on culture and society.
Description: 1st edition. | Denver : University Press of Colorado, [2023] | Series: IMS Studies on culture and society | Includes bibliographical references and index.
Identifiers: LCCN 2023033194 (print) | LCCN 2023033195 (ebook) | ISBN 9781646425778 (hardcover) | ISBN 9781646425785 (paperback) | ISBN 9781646425792 (ebook)
Subjects: LCSH: Nahuas—Mexico—Social life and customs—History. | Nahuatl language—Study and teaching (Higher) | Nahuatl language—History. | Indians of Mexico—History.
Classification: LCC F1221.N3 N355 2023 (print) | LCC F1221.N3 (ebook) | DDC 972.0008997/452—dc23/eng/20230913
LC record available at https://lccn.loc.gov/2023033194
LC ebook record available at https://lccn.loc.gov/2023033195

This book will be made open access within three years of publication thanks to Path to Open, a program developed in partnership between JSTOR, the American Council of Learned Societies (ACLS), University of Michigan Press, and The University of North Carolina Press to bring about equitable access and impact for the entire scholarly community, including authors, researchers, libraries, and university presses around the world. Learn more at https://about.jstor.org/path-to-open/.

Cover illustration: detail from the *Codex Borbonicus*, p. 4. Wikimedia Commons public-domain image.

# Contents

List of Illustrations     vii

List of Tables     ix

Foreword
*Camilla Townsend*     xi

Preface     xiii

1. Nahua Studies, Past and Present
   *Galen Brokaw and Pablo García Loaeza*     3

2. The Early History of Nahua Languages in Mexico and Mesoamerica
   *Karen Dakin*     29

3. Naming the Space: Diphrases and the Cultural Construction of Place-Names
   *Mercedes Montes de Oca Vega*     55

4. Nahuatl from Southern Jalisco and Colima in Diachronic Perspective: Language Documentation and Variation
   *Rosa H. Yáñez Rosales*     85

5. Words in Revolution: How the Nahuas Disappeared from the State of Morelos and from the Historiography of the Mexican Revolution
    *Magnus Pharao Hansen*   115

6. The Vocabulary of Running in the Mexica World
    *John F. Schwaller*   133

7. Strategies for Confronting New Concepts in the Spanish-Latin Corpus of Ayer ms. 1478
    *Mary L. Clayton*   153

8. Fabián de Aquino's Nahuatl *Contemptus Mundi*
    *Ben Leeming*   179

9. Nahua Notaries of Jerusalem: Lucio Sestilio and His Partners in Crime
    *Louise M. Burkhart*   207

10. Nahua Curing through Graphic Communication: Ritual Paper Figures and Cosmic Balance
    *Alan R. Sandstrom and Pamela Effrein Sandstrom*   229

11. Five Centuries of Self-Determination: Indigenous Intellectuals and Nahuatl Language in Mexico
    *Kelly S. McDonough*   263

*Index*   287
*About the Authors*   295

# Illustrations

| | | |
|---|---|---|
| 2.1. | Map showing approximate location of the "Bajío" | 34 |
| 2.2. | Map showing the extent of Teotihuacan influence across central Mexico | 36 |
| 2.3. | A simplified version of Mason's and Whorf's classification of Nahuatlan | 41 |
| 4.1. | Map of western Mexico | 88 |
| 5.1. | Chrono-geographic map of the distribution of Nahuatl speakers in Morelos across the twentieth century | 124 |
| 5.2. | Diagram of Morelos census data including monolingual speakers of Nahuatl | 126 |
| 5.3. | Diagram of Morelos census data adjusted to allow for bilingual speakers of Nahuatl | 128 |
| 10.1. | Cirilo performing a cleansing-curing ritual for a client in September 1985 | 240 |
| 10.2. | Cirilo performing an elaborate cleansing-curing ritual | 241 |
| 10.3. | Cirilo chanting over an array in a cleansing-curing episode | 242 |
| 10.4. | Cleansing-curing ritual for a young female client with a chronic condition | 243 |
| 10.5. | A rendering of the variations in ritual specialist Encarnación (Cirilo) Téllez Hernández's standard arrays for cleansing and curing | 244 |

10.6. *Tlacatecolotl* and *tlacatecolotl cihuatl* — 247
10.7. *Miquiliztli ehecatl* — 248
10.8. *Miccatzitzin ehecatl* — 249
10.9. *Ehecatl* — 249
10.10. *Caruz ehecatl* — 251
10.11. *Tlalli ehecatl* — 251
10.12. *Atl ehecatl* — 251
10.13. *Miquiliztli ehecatl* — 252
10.14. *Tlacotontli* — 253

# Tables

| | | |
|---|---|---|
| 2.1. | Juan Hasler's dialect divisions (1954) | 42 |
| 2.2. | Juan Hasler's three proposed migration routes (1972) | 42 |
| 2.3. | Vowel changes from proto-Uto-Aztecan to Eastern and Western Nahua | 44 |
| 2.4. | Examples of pUA *$u$ > $i/e$ split | 44 |
| 2.5 | Southern Uto-Aztecan *$wa$ = 'past' clitic > introduced in Western and Central branches only | 45 |
| 2.6 | Examples of contrasts in reflexes of pUA initial **$p$ | 47 |
| 2.7. | Examples of dialect contrasts of proto-Nahua *$he$ | 47 |
| 4.1. | Lexical items from San Andrés Ixtlán, Tuxpan, and Suchitlán, according to Arreola 1934 | 93 |
| 4.2. | Lexical entries from San Andrés Ixtlán | 94 |
| 4.3. | Lexical entries from Tuxpan | 95 |
| 4.4. | Lexical entries from Suchitlán, Colima | 95 |

# Foreword

This book offers a fascinating history of a major phenomenon —yet most of the contributors are not historians. That is to say, readers will not find a collection of chapters by History PhDs. Instead, linguists, anthropologists, literary scholars, and historians all appear together in these pages to create a history of the Nahuatl—or "Aztec"—language. They express themselves clearly and without jargon so that people from other fields can understand them. What is valuable from each field shines, thus illuminating the work from other fields. If only all academic work were like this.

Perhaps the book coheres so well because the authors share not only a love for the Nahuatl language but also for people. They have called their volume not "Histories of the Nahuatl Language," as they might have done but, rather, *The Nahua: Language and Culture from the Sixteenth Century to the Present.* Thus, they maintain the focus not so much on Nahuatl, the language, as on the Nahua, the speakers of the language, and even in the title emphasize that it is the uses to which human beings have put their beloved language that these writers find compelling. It is the story of cultural survival—of change, adaptation, and resurgence—that they wish to document.

So it is that human beings of past and present emerge from the pages, often even in the midst of the linguistic examples. Some of these people are scholars' old friends—the Spanish friars, the European savants, the twentieth-century academics whose names we have long known. But other figures are new friends, Indigenous intellectuals who are finally gaining the recognition they deserve. We find them in sixteenth-century meetings of those who were putting together the *Historia tolteca chichimeca* and offering place names as beautiful diphrases; we see them in colonial-era libraries, where one man annotates a Spanish-Latin dictionary in Nahuatl, and another writes a devotional treatise that he never asked any Spaniard's permission to write. Several produce plays about the figure their communities loved to hate, the Native scribe (*escribano*); people in the early twentieth-century Morelos countryside speak in Nahuatl as they decide to support Emiliano Zapata's revolutionary cause; a late twentieth-century healer prays in Nahuatl as he teaches people how to maintain ancient glyphic traditions in the cutting of their ritual paper figures; the twenty-first-century director of a language center makes sure that the annual language workshops he convenes take place right in the middle of the local communities and that useful prizes (like food processors!) are given out to the winners of essay competitions. And these are only a few of the dozens of people whom readers will meet.

Yet if a reader is looking for a more traditional academic work, a clear and complete synthesis of what is known about different aspects of the history of the Nahuatl language, they will find that in these pages as well. The introduction by Galen Brokaw and Pablo García Loaeza is a tour de force, providing the kind of outline of each stage of the language's history that many of us have long wished existed. It will serve as a guide for many years. And this is followed by a piece authored by the historical linguist Karin Dakin explaining the latest understandings of Nahuatl's deep historical relationship to the Uto-Aztecan family as a whole, and of the subdivisions within the language brought about by migration. In numerous regards, this volume is effective in dispelling confusion as it may exist even among academics.

In short, this is a book worthy of the generous spirit and deep insight of Joe Campbell, the man who inspired it. Its authors and readers thank him for the precious greenstones that shine, the precious feathers that float in the air—for all the words he gave us over the years. As this book shows, they will continue to shine and float far into the future, for that is what words do, just as long as there is anybody left who cares about them.

*Camilla Townsend*
RUTGERS UNIVERSITY

# Preface

We dedicate this book to Joe Campbell. In 1962, during a University of Illinois summer graduate research trip to Morelos, Mexico, the renowned linguist Ken Hale encouraged Joe to study Nahuatl. In 1970 at Indiana University, Joe was asked to teach Nahuatl funded by a National Defense Education Act grant. This began a lifelong focus on the study and teaching of both modern and classical Nahuatl that has greatly enriched the Nahuatl studies community. Joe's Nahuatl research has focused on both modern dialects and what is commonly referred to as Classical Nahuatl. He has taken numerous field trips to communities throughout Mexico to record native speakers, and this allowed him to apply a comparative approach in his teaching of Classical Nahuatl. A pioneer in the digital humanities, in the 1970s Joe digitized the richest sources of data on Classical Nahuatl using computer punch cards: Alonso de Molina's sixteenth-century dictionaries and Bernardino de Sahagún's encyclopedic *Florentine Codex*. Joe periodically taught Nahuatl formally at Indiana University and other universities through the 1990s, and informally into the 2000s. He also partnered with Frances Karttunen to teach two National Endowment for the Humanities seminars on Nahuatl in 1989 and 1992, for which they produced the *Foundation Course in Nahuatl Grammar*, a textbook used widely both for formal classes and independent study. In these various Nahuatl courses, Joe trained scholars such as John Schwaller, Alan Sandstrom, Fran Karttunen, Elizabeth Boone, Barbara Mundy, Jong Soo Lee, and many others, including the editors of this volume.

But Joe's influence extends far beyond the students that he trained directly. Even before digital copies were accessible, the *Foundation Course* was made available to anyone who requested it simply for the cost of photocopies and postage, and many scholars and laypeople alike have used it to study Nahuatl on their own. Furthermore, Joe is well known throughout the Nahuatl studies community for his generosity in providing useful information drawn from his databases. All the contributors to this volume, who represent various disciplines and build upon the long tradition of Nahua studies, have benefited from this generosity.

THE NAHUA

# 1

## Nahua Studies, Past and Present

GALEN BROKAW AND PABLO GARCÍA LOAEZA

Nahuatl is a Uto-Aztecan language spoken mostly by communities in central Mexico with outliers in Durango in northern Mexico, Michoacán on the central Pacific coast, and Tabasco in southern Mexico. The Instituto Nacional de Lenguas Indígenas identifies what it calls thirty varieties of Nahuatl spoken by over 1 million people within Mexico. In addition, a variant of Nahuatl known as Pipil is spoken in El Salvador.

The extension of Nahuatl today results from its prominence and extension prior to the Spanish conquest. Jerónimo de Mendieta wrote that while different provinces had their own languages, Nahuatl functioned as a kind of lingua franca in Mexico like Latin in Europe (Mendieta 2017, 518 [libro 4, capítulo 44]; Wright 2007, 9). This may have been an exaggeration (see Wright and others), but Nahuatl was geographically more widespread than other Indigenous languages not only because it was the language of the dominant city-state of Tenochtitlan ruled by Moteuczoma at the time of the Spanish conquest but also because other Nahuatl-speaking groups had migrated to central Mexico and beyond prior to the rise of Tenochtitlan (Dakin, chapter 2 in this volume).

The prominence of Nahuatl in central Mexico, where the Spaniards established their administrative center by displacing the Indigenous one, inevitably required that the Spaniards engage with Nahuatl more than any of the other Indigenous languages spoken throughout Mexico. The Spanish administrators and priests who were charged with governing the Indians and converting them to Christianity learned many Indigenous languages, but Nahuatl received the most attention. The colonial administration incorporated Indigenous languages into the archive, and more documents were produced in Nahuatl than all other Indigenous languages combined (Sell 1999, 20). Nahua scribes typically produced these documents, but many Spaniards also learned Nahuatl. Spaniards were forced to either learn the language or rely upon others who became bilingual, whether through the interactions of quotidian life or through more formal study.

We know less about the language acquisition that took place in quotidian life because it left relatively little documentation. We know that it occurred both because that is what happens inevitably in such contexts and because Spanish and Indigenous individuals who informally learned Nahuatl and Spanish respectively show up in other contexts. Numerous Spaniards married Indigenous women, and the children of these unions often would have been raised speaking both Spanish and Nahuatl. At the same time, both Spanish and Nahua children developed a level of bilingualism through their daily interactions. Mendieta explains that Spanish priests attempted to learn Nahuatl by spending time with Native children and that these children learned Spanish (Mendieta 2017, 204). Likewise, Spanish children who came to New Spain with their parents or who were born there grew up exposed to Nahuatl, and they often acquired proficiency in the language naturally. The Franciscan Alonso de Molina and the Dominican Diego Durán, for example, came to Mexico as children and apparently learned Nahuatl on the street so to speak. Both colonial administrators and religious authorities sought out people like Molina to serve as translators and interpreters (León-Portilla 2004, xxv). But the nature and level of language acquisition varied by individual and context. Even though Molina learned Nahuatl as a child, it was not the language of his home life, and he did not consider himself a Native speaker (Molina [1571] 2004, "Prólogo").

Given the power dynamic, it was perhaps inevitable that more Nahuas would learn Spanish than Spaniards would learn Nahuatl, but from the very beginning the Spaniards exerted a consistent effort to learn and formally document the language. This formal study of Nahuatl is much easier to trace because it left a more direct documentary record.

In the sixteenth and seventeenth centuries, the Spaniards were motivated by a desire to convert the Indigenous population to Christianity, and whether to employ Spanish or the Indigenous languages was a topic of debate. The Franciscans believed that teaching and administering to the Native people in their own languages was the best way to convert them. In 1529, the Franciscan Pedro de Gante boasted that his missionary work had immersed him in the language so much that he spoke Nahuatl better than his Native Spanish (40). Franciscans such as Gante believed that Native terms and concepts could facilitate understanding and conversion, but others argued that employing Indigenous languages like Nahuatl ran the risk of perpetuating idolatrous beliefs and practices in the guise of Christianity.

In 1550, Carlos V sided with those who disapproved of the use of Native languages and ordered that the Indians learn Castilian as part of their indoctrination. The 1550 order explicitly identifies the purpose of the language instruction and alludes to the debate: "Haviendo hecho particular examen sobre si aun en la mas perfecta lengua de los indios se pueden explicar bien, y con propiedad los Misterios de nuestra Santa Fe Catolica, se ha reconocido, que no es posible sin cometerr grandes disonancias, e imperfecciones, y aunque estan fundadadas Catedras donde sean enseñados los sacerdotes, que huvieren de doctrinar a los Indios, no es remedio bastante, por ser mucha la variedad de lenguas" (Recopilación de leyes [1681] 1987, vol. 2, f. 190r [libro 6, título 1, ley 18]).[1] However, in 1565 Felipe II reversed his father's order and required the priests to learn the language of the Indians with whom they worked. Then, in 1570, he declared Nahuatl the official language of the Indians in New Spain (Heath 1972, 52–53). However, the policy changes announced in these edicts did not necessarily correspond to changes in actual practice. The 1570 order essentially recognized the fact that Nahuatl already served as a kind of lingua franca in New Spain, and missionaries had already been using it extensively even between 1550 and 1565.

Priests like Gante who arrived in the early years after the conquest had to learn the language on their own, but they also began writing grammars and dictionaries to facilitate language acquisition for others. At least thirty Nahuatl grammars were produced during the colonial period (A. León-Portilla 1972). Most of this documentation took place in the valley of Mexico. The initial work by the Franciscans Francisco Jiménez and Alonso de Rangel from around 1524 has been lost (Mendieta 2017, 515), but Andrés de Olmos, also Franciscan, may have built on their work for his *Arte para aprender la lengua mexicana*, which he completed around 1547. This was followed by Alonso de Molina's *Arte de la lengua mexicana y castellana* in 1571 (León-Portilla 2004), a companion to his monumental dictionary titled *Vocabulario en lengua castellana y mexicana* (1555, 1571 [Molina (1571) 2004]). By the end of the sixteenth century, the Jesuits had begun participating in this endeavor as well: Antonio del Rincón produced his *Arte mexicana* in 1595, and in 1645 Horacio Carochi composed the most detailed and sophisticated grammar of the colonial period: *Arte de la lengua mexicana* ([1645] 2001).

---

[1] "Having examined in particular whether even in the most perfect language of the Indians the Mysteries of our Holy Catholic Faith can be explained well and properly, it has been recognized that it is not possible without committing great inaccuracies and imperfections, and although classes have been created to teach the priests who will minister to the Indians, it is not a sufficient solution, because of the great variety of languages." Our translation.

These grammars document what is now called "Classical Nahuatl." It is commonplace to say that Classical Nahuatl was the form of the language spoken at the time of the conquest, but just like today numerous dialects were in use prior to the arrival of the Spaniards (Dakin, chapter 2 in this volume; Yáñez Rosales, chapter 4 in this volume). It is also important to keep in mind that the documentation of the language in the form of a grammar created the appearance of linguistic stability that did not necessarily characterize linguistic practice. Una Canger argues that Classical Nahuatl was a convergence of regional dialects spoken in the urban centers of Tlatelolco and Tenochtitlan (2011a).

Colonial grammarians who documented Indigenous languages often described their task as one of "taming" the language. This was not an infelicitous metaphor. The Spaniards felt like they had to "tame" Indigenous languages in two different ways. First, they had to alphabetize it to produce dictionaries and grammars in their own alphabetic script, and, second, they had to infer grammatical rules based on observed linguistic practices.

The Spaniards needed to subordinate Nahuatl to alphabetic script because they relied upon alphabetic writing to facilitate their own use of the language and to train Native scribes to help them in their evangelization efforts. It would be inaccurate to say that the Nahuas had no writing prior to the arrival of the Spaniards even if one defines writing narrowly as glottography, that is, the representation of linguistic elements (e.g., sounds, syllables, words). The Nahuas had an elaborate system of writing that incorporated both iconographic and glottographic practices (Whittaker 2021). However, these practices had not led to the kind of standardization that typically characterizes the writing of languages today. Even Spanish alphabetic literacy had not achieved such standardization in the sixteenth century, when Spanish priests began documenting Nahuatl. In principle, the use of alphabetic writing forces the writer to make decisions about how to represent individual sounds, something that Nahuatl glottography did not do, at least not in an extensively systematic way. When talking about sounds, modern linguists distinguish between phonemes, which are mental images of sounds, and allophones, which are the vocal articulation of phonemes. This distinction is necessary because one phoneme may be articulated differently depending on the context. For example, in English, in word final position the phoneme /s/ has two allophones, [s] and [z]. Plurality of nouns in English is signaled by use of the letter *s* which is a representation of the phoneme /s/, but it is pronounced as [z] when preceded by a voiced phoneme. Compare, for example, the difference between the words "cats" and "dogs." English speakers consider these to be the same sound, but the first is pronounced as an [s] and the second is pronounced as a [z]. Spanish and Nahuatl share many of the same, or very similar, sounds, but the set of phonemes and allophones of any given language generally do not coincide completely with those of any other. Carochi, for example, explains that Nahuatl "lacked" some of the letters of the Castilian alphabet such as *b, d, f, g, r, j*, and *ñ* ([1645] 2001, 18). His admirable description of the sound system of Nahuatl does not distinguish between sounds and the letters used to represent them, because he does not have recourse to the concepts of phoneme and allophone. But even more problematic than the lack of certain sounds was the fact that Nahuatl has sounds that Castilian does not. For the Spaniards, it was easy to transliterate sounds that were common to both languages (e.g., [k], [m], [n], [s], [t], etc.), but Nahuatl had at least two sounds that caused the Spaniards significant trouble: long vowels and a consonantal glottal stop.

In the case of the short-long vowel contrast, the word *chichi* with two short vowels, for example, means "dog" while *chīchi* with a long [ī] in the first syllable means "to suckle." This same contrast occurs with [a], [e], and [o] as well. Spanish has vowel phonemes with the same qualities, but the quantity of these vowels has no phonemic significance. Thus, the Spaniards would have had a hard time even perceiving the difference between short and long vowels. Nahuatl does not have a [u] probably because this sound is very similar to the long [ō]. In some cases, this similarity led the Spaniards to use the *u* to represent the long [ō] in Nahuatl, but they generally simply ignored vowel length.

The glottal stop, which colonial grammarians called *saltillo*, would have been easier to perceive because Spanish had no consonant similar enough that it might have interfered with its perception as a distinct sound. But this sound presented other difficulties. The glottal stop is not just a different sound; it is a different type of sound. It is produced by closing the airway with the glottis, and in Nahuatl it only occurs in syllable-final position. In Classical Nahuatl, the *saltillo* only appears within a word when the following syllable begins with another consonant. However, it also occurs at the end of words ending with a vowel, but in these cases, it has no phonemic value. No letter of the Spanish alphabet leant itself readily to representing this sound. Rincón ([1595] 1885, 63v) and Carochi ([1645] 2001, 22) actually describe the glottal stop as a feature of the vowel that precedes it. In most modern dialects, the "Classical" *saltillo* corresponds to an aspiration [h] represented by the letter *h*, but Rincón described aspirated versions of the *saltillo* in the sixteenth century as well (64r). Grammarians like Rincón and Carochi were sophisticated enough to understand the significance of the *saltillo*/aspiration, and they devised orthographic conventions to represent it. But their conventions were not widespread. Most colonial documents simply ignore glottal stops. As with the case of long vowels, the context usually disambiguated any confusion that this omission might have caused.

In addition to the alphabetization of the Indigenous languages, the Spaniards also had to create grammatical rules for them. This grammatical "taming" did not imply that these languages had no rules prior to this point. The Spaniards clearly based their work on what they perceived to be the normative linguistic practices of Native speakers. But they were employing grammatical concepts developed originally for Latin that were often ill suited to the nature of Indigenous American languages. We tend to universalize grammatical categories such as "noun," "verb," "adjective," and so forth. The functions that these categories serve may be universal, but all the categories themselves are not. Different languages perform some of these functions in different ways. The adjectival function, for example, works very differently in Spanish than it does in Nahuatl: Spanish has an independent class of words that function as adjectives, whereas Nahuatl performs this same adjectival function using stative verbs. This and other disparities made it difficult to make the reality of Nahuatl linguistic practice fit the preestablished paradigm of Latin grammar, and this difficulty contributed to the sense referred to by colonial grammarians that they were taming the language.

Furthermore, the formulation of grammatical categories and rules and the imposition of those rules through formal instruction are not simply a matter of reflecting the reality of language. The formal schooling that we receive from a young age makes it easy to pass over the fact that categories and rules have no real existence: they are abstractions induced by linguistic practices. There are at least two different ways to explain what gives rise to these abstractions: according to one theory, they are genetically programmed into our brains; according to another theory, they derive from the way in which we are embedded in our environment. Both theories posit certain universals, but the location of these universals and how they operate differ. Furthermore, whatever is universal regarding language does not manifest itself in a consistent way in actual practice. For example, even if one believes that on some deep level all humans think using a Subject-Verb-Object (SVO) syntax, in practice there are languages that fall under every possible word-order categorization: SVO, SOV, VOS, VSO, OSV, and OVS (Dryer 2013; Hammerström 2016, 25). Thus, regardless of the theory that one espouses, the communicative practices in which humans engage are not completely determined by whatever universals underlie language: an element of creativity is at work in the initial creation and negotiation of meaning.

This element of creativity inevitably becomes suppressed to the extent that we begin to follow preestablished rules or conventions. Every communicative practice operates on a continuum, one end of which corresponding to an absolutely rational, completely rule-governed practice with the other end being absolutely aesthetic, creative, and intuitive. Both extremes are theoretical; neither are possible in the absolute. All communicative practices have elements of both, but primordially they must originate from the creative, intuitive pole of the continuum. The primordial act of communication moves toward the rational, rule-governed side of the continuum for the sake of efficacy, but the extent to which it does so depends upon a variety of factors, perhaps the most influential being the institution of alphabetic literacy. Alphabetic writing transpositions linguistic utterances from the ephemeral medium of speech to the more enduring medium of pen or print. Modern societies have institutionalized this literacy through formal schooling, newspapers, publishing houses, and so forth; these institutions, in turn, produce prescriptive style guides and grammatical rules that attempt to control not only the way we write but also the way we speak. We distinguish here between prescriptive rules enforced by institutions of literacy and more descriptive conventions that characterize communicative practices. The fact that grammatical rules need to be taught and enforced attests to the primordially "unruly" nature of language. This is not to say that linguistic conventions cannot have considerable force absent institutional prescriptions, but generally speaking they are not rules in the same sense as those enforced by institutions of literacy. The very notion of a grammatical "rule" derives from prescriptions imposed by institutional authority. Repeated deviations from prescriptive rules often acquire the status of rule-like conventions, but they reveal the primordial creativity of linguistic communication. This creativity is as characteristic of Spanish or English (whether of the sixteenth century or of today) as it is of Nahuatl.

The formulation and enforcement of grammatical concepts and syntactic rules by institutions of literacy induce a regularity in the language that did not exist as such prior to this formulation and to which actual practice rarely conforms in any absolute way. Even the relatively limited institutionalized alphabetic literacy of the sixteenth century caused the Spaniards to think of language in alphabetic and formal grammatical terms. However, languages like Nahuatl whose syntax and lexical elements had not been subjected to an organic grammatical analysis do not always submit easily to rules and categories, and even less so to those developed for other languages, and this is why the Spaniards felt as if they were taming the language when they created grammatical rules for it.

The sense that Nahuatl and other Indigenous languages of the Americas are radically different has not diminished over time. Richard Andrews and James Lockhart both comment, for example, on the strange nature of Nahuatl nouns, which can take subjects like verbs (Andrews 1975: xiii, 143–144; Lockhart 2001a: x; 2001b, 1). As of this writing, the Wikipedia entry for "Classical Nahuatl Grammar" states that "Classical Nahuatl is a non-copulative language, meaning that it lacks a verb 'to be.'" But this is not actually true. The Nahuatl verb *ca* means "to be," but it is not always used. In his Nahuatl grammar, Michel Launey explains that the Nahuatl verb *ca* means "to be" only to express location like the Spanish *estar* (2011, 43). He states that in sentences that have nominal predicates such as "Mary is a woman,"

Nahuatl has no verb "to be." In such sentences "the noun itself serves as the predicate" (18). For this reason, Launey goes so far as to say that "to understand what a Nahuatl noun really signifies, we should consider that *mēxicatl* does not simply mean '(a) Mexica' but 'to be a Mexica.' Similarly, *cihuātl* is not just '(a) woman' but 'to be a woman,' and so on" (18). Lockhart and Andrews make similar arguments: Lockhart states that Nahuatl nouns are closer to what we call verbs (2001a: x; 2001b, 1), and Andrews claims that the word *chichi* is not the equivalent of the word "dog" but of the assertion "It is a dog" (2003, 112, 148).

I would argue, however, that these claims that Nahuatl nouns function essentially as verbs are based on a misunderstanding of the nature of language. The *ca* verb is used in the present tense like the Spanish verb *estar*, but as Launey himself explains, in the past tense, it is also used like the Spanish verb *ser* with nominal predicates (2011, 75). So it isn't that Nahuatl doesn't have a copulative verb. It is just that in the present tense, Nahuatl speakers dispense with the need for the copulative verb *ca* by attaching a subject prefix directly to a noun. This phenomenon has less to do with the nature of Nahuatl nouns than it does with the pragmatics of Nahuatl communicative practice. It is true that the Nahuatl verb *ca* is not used in the present tense with nominal predicates. But this practice—that is, the fact that Nahuatl nouns can take subjects like verbs—is not as odd as Andrews, Lockhart, and Launey seem to believe. The word *chichi* can mean "it is a dog," both because in practice no verb is necessary and because in Nahuatl the third-person subject is a null morpheme. A more illustrative example of how subject affixes attach directly to nouns would be *tichichi*, which literally translates as "you dog" but which Andrews and Launey would translate as "you are a dog." However, in some cases we do the same thing in English: "you dog" is a perfectly acceptable way of expressing the meaning "you are a dog."

Furthermore, the relationship between an utterance and the meaning that it conveys in a particular instance is not determined strictly by the nature of the words or even the grammatical structure itself. Linguistic utterances have no fixed, abstract referents. The nature of reference in practice cannot be reduced to the correspondence between a particular sentence much less a particular word like "dog" and an abstract referent like the idea of a dog. Even if one believes that a specific referent (e.g., dog) is essential to the nature of a specific word (e.g., "dog"), in actual practice it is not limited to that meaning. And this is true of all languages. A speaker of any language can use their term denoting dog to mean "it is a dog." But this term can also mean any number of other things, either in addition to or in place of its original, base meaning. In English, for example, "dog" can also mean "Watch out for the dog!" or "you filthy low-life." To give another example, if one adopts Andrews's perspective, the word "fire" in English or any other language can mean "There is a fire" or even "There is a fire; get the hell out of here!" But it can also mean "pull the trigger on your rifle!" or "give me a match" or more recently for many people "cool," "excellent," and so on. What this demonstrates is that meaning is not located solely in the word or utterance itself but also in the context of its use.

It is misleading to say that in Nahuatl *chichi* means "it is a dog," not only because this meaning depends on the context in which the word is expressed but also because it projects a linguistic structure onto an utterance that does not employ that structure. The claim that *chichi* means "it is a dog" assumes that full sentences underlie all linguistic utterances. But this idea only makes sense to a mentality that has been conditioned by conventions and stylistics such as those of modern alphabetic literacy that normativize full sentences (Brokaw 2021, 108; Linell 2005). At the time of the conquest, Nahuatl speakers had not been conditioned by this type of literacy. Nahuatl writing did employ glottography, which would have induced at least in Nahua scribes a higher degree of self-consciousness about the formal properties of the language, but the nature and extent of their glottography was very different from European alphabetic literacy. Nahuatl writing practices combined glottography and iconography, and even if one assumes that literacy in Nahua writing was widespread the fact that iconography constituted a much higher proportion of the written signs means that its cognitive impact would have been greater than that of the glottographic practices.

Writing systems—whether glottographic or iconographic—enter into a dialogic interaction with the language that they represent. Communication is a multidimensional activity that cannot be reduced strictly to verbal expression. The transpositioning of verbal language into any glottographic script disembodies it and divorces it from all the other elements that normally come into play in the communicative act (facial expressions, gestures, tone, context, etc.). The loss that occurs in this transpositioning results in a reduction of communicative efficacy. European writing systems attempt to compensate for this loss by introducing conventions specific to the medium (punctuation, word spacing, the normativization of full sentences, etc.) that help avoid the ambiguity and confusion that would be caused by a strict transcription of oral discourse (Brokaw 2021, 107).

The relatively rapid introduction of alphabetic writing in Nahuatl almost certainly led scribes to transposition Nahuatl oral discourse without adopting all the discursive conventions that Spanish had been developing for centuries in its dialogic interaction with alphabetic writing practices. What Lockhart calls the "verbless sentence" may have been more common in Nahuatl oral discourse, and this may even have been more in tune with an iconographic mode of thought that employs images to convey meaning, but it is not uncommon in the oral discourse of other languages. What makes the verbless sentence in Nahuatl seem so odd is at least in part the fact that it appears in written texts. The fact that Nahuatl linguistic practice does not require a verb in all instances does not mean that nouns therefore become verb-like. Rather, it means that Nahuatl linguistic practice relies upon pragmatics in such cases more than other languages do. This type of pragmatics is more characteristic of oral discourse than alphabetic discourse, and the documentation of Classical Nahuatl by colonial grammarians was based on oral practices that historically had not been conditioned by alphabetic writing. Even today, most Nahuatl speakers have remained outside of the institutions of alphabetic literacy.

However, from the beginning of the colonial period, the Spaniards also trained Indigenous nobles to write alphabetic Nahuatl as well as Spanish and Latin. In 1535, Carlos V ordered that the religious orders establish schools to educate Indigenous nobles; he reaffirmed this order in 1540, and Felipe II issued a similar order in 1579 (Heath 1972, 35). But even before these formal edicts, Spanish missionaries had already begun this endeavor. Pedro de Gante set up a primary school in Texcoco in 1523, just four years after the arrival of the Spaniards, and Martín de Valencia established one in Mexico City in 1525 (Baudot 1995, 105). In 1533, the Franciscan order began operating an institution of higher learning known as the Colegio de Santa Cruz de Tlatelolco, which was officially inaugurated in 1536. There has been some debate about whether the primary purpose of the school in Tlatelolco was to prepare the Indigenous students for ordination to the priesthood (Maxwell and Hanson 1992, 5), for participation in colonial governance (Laird 2014, 152), or for work as "native linguists" that would "reconcile cultural spheres" (Arencibia Rodríguez 2006, 264). Regardless of any intent, all these schools contributed to the creation of an alphabetically educated Indigenous ruling class and a cadre of Native Nahuatl speakers who assisted the priests in their research and evangelization efforts. Native Nahuatl speakers were instrumental, of course, in the investigations of the language itself, and they engaged in their own research for their own audience. Around 1540 a Native Nahuatl speaker produced a trilingual dictionary by copying Antonio de Nebrija's Spanish-Latin dictionary and adding Nahuatl definitions (Anonymous n.d.; Clayton 1989, 2003, and chapter 7 in this volume).

For the Spaniards, the study of the language was primarily a means to facilitate the governing and evangelizing of the Indigenous population. To this end, many Spanish priests studied Nahuatl, but they still needed the assistance of Native speakers in their multifaceted projects, particularly in the early colonial period. One of the first projects that newly alphabetized Native Nahuatl speakers participated in was the production of religious texts for use in evangelization. Pedro de Gante, for example, oversaw the production of a pictographic catechism ([1529] 1973) and a *Doctrina* in Nahuatl (1547). Other Nahuatl language religious texts included confessional guides (e.g., Molina 1565), sermons (Sahagún 1563), and plays (Sell and Burkhart 2004).

In addition to the study of Indigenous languages and the production of religious texts, the Spaniards studied the history and culture of the groups that they governed, and the students at the school at Tlatelolco and other schools were instrumental in these efforts as well. For the Spanish Crown, the history of Indigenous polities had implications, at least theoretically, regarding the justification of the conquest and the status of the Indigenous in the new colonial order. And for the priests of the Catholic Church to effectively convert the Nahuas and other Indigenous groups, they had to understand their history, their culture, and the concepts that informed their thoughts and behaviors.

In 1533, the president of the Real Audiencia in Mexico commissioned Andrés de Olmos to investigate the history and culture of the Indians. Olmos's initial research resulted in a work titled *Tratado de las antigüedades de México* containing sections on religion, history, calendrics, society, and language (Baudot 1995, 41). Unfortunately, this text was lost, but Olmos continued his investigations throughout his life. In addition to a *vocabulario* and a grammar, he collected a set of Nahuatl *huehuehtlahtolli* (discourses that convey moral instruction to Nahua youth), a series of sermons in Nahuatl, and several other texts. Olmos developed a method involving interviews with Native informants, the use of Indigenous iconographic texts, and the categorization of source data (Maxwell and Hanson 1992, 9), and he would have employed the students at Tlatelolco in compiling his earliest works.

Other priests adopted this same methodology, the most notable being Bernardino de Sahagún, who taught at the Colegio de Tlatelolco. Like Olmos, Sahagún studied the language, culture, and history of the Nahuas, and he produced several religious and ethnographic texts with the collaboration of students from the school at Tlatelolco. He is best known for the monumental twelve-volume *Historia general de las cosas de Nueva España* (Sahagún [1579] 1994), which covers religious, social, cultural, and historical topics. Sahagún had his assistants document the initial historical and ethnographic information in Nahuatl. The version of the *Historia* known as the *Florentine Codex* contains a thorough text in Nahuatl, iconographic elements, and Spanish glosses that summarize the Nahuatl text.

While primary schools and the school at Tlatelolco were training the first generation of alphabetically literate Nahuas, marriages between Spaniards and Indigenous women produced a Nahuatl-speaking mestizo class that also often received an alphabetic education. This education made it possible for the Indigenous nobility to participate in colonial government, but it also laid the groundwork for the creation of an intellectual culture based on Nahuatl alphabetic literacy. Initially, the Native intellectuals who emerged from this context during the first fifty years or so after the arrival of the Spaniards worked primarily alongside, and under the direction of, Spanish priests on projects that related in one way or another to evangelization (sermons, catechisms, confessional guides, etc.). But even in this period, in some cases Native authors began evincing a specifically Nahuatl intellectual culture. Ben Leeming has recently discovered two mid-sixteenth-century Antichrist plays by Fabián de Aquino that were produced outside of the supervision of the Spaniards and that demonstrate a uniquely Indigenous take on Christianity (2017, 2022, and chapter 8 in this volume). John Schwaller argues that this phenomenon becomes more prominent at the beginning of the seventeenth century, with works such as Juan Bautista's *Vida y milagros del bienaventurado San Antonio de Padua* and *Libro de la miseria* from the first decade of the century, Bartolomé de Alva's translation into Nahuatl of three Spanish Golden Age religious-themed plays (Burkhart 2008), and Luis Lasso de la Vega's *Huei Tlamahuizoltica* (the apparition of the Virgin of Guadalupe narrative) from 1649 (Sousa, Poole, and Lockhart 1998; Schwaller 1994).

This culture of Nahuatl literacy emerged even earlier in more secular texts produced by the first generation of Native and mestizo chroniclers such as Chimalpopoca (Alonso de Castañeda), Don Mateo Sánchez, Don Pedro de San Buenaventura, Hernando de Alvarado Tezozomoc, Diego Muñoz Camargo, Juan Bautista Pomar, and Juan de Tovar. These Nahua writers and intellectuals took an interest in researching the history and culture of the Nahuas in the sixteenth century at the same time as Spaniards such as Jerónimo de Mendieta and Diego Durán. All chroniclers from this period relied by necessity on Native informants and often Indigenous iconographic documents as well. But some, both Native/mestizo and Spanish, produced hybrid texts that employed both iconography and alphabetic writing (Chimalpopoca; Durán; Tovar), and others wrote in Nahuatl (Tezozomoc).

A second generation of writers born in the last decades of the sixteenth century further developed this alphabetic Nahuatl intellectual culture. Fernando de Alva Ixtlilxochitl, born around 1578, drew from Native sources to write extensively about the history of the Nahuas. Domingo Francisco de San Antón Muñón Chimalpahin, born in 1579, produced historiographic work in both Spanish and Nahuatl, thus continuing the tradition initiated by Sahagún's assistants and Tezozomoc. These efforts were not limited to religious and historiographic works. In the sixteenth century, an anonymous writer and Juan Bautista Pomar compiled the collections of Nahuatl poems known as *Cantares mexicanos* and *Romances de los señores de la Nueva España*, respectively (see Bierhorst 1985 and 2009). Regardless of whether one believes that these poems were originally composed in the precolonial or colonial period, their alphabetization reflects, and contributes to, the development of a culture of Nahuatl literacy.

In 1640–1641, another initiative involved the translation of three Spanish Golden Age plays into Nahuatl by Bartolomé de Alva. On the one hand, these translations of Spanish plays are derivative of Spanish culture; on the other hand, they are not strict translations. They adapt the plays to the Nahua context, as all translations must do. These plays had religious themes, but they also inscribed them within Nahua culture and put Nahuatl "on a par" with Spanish (Burkhart 2008, 48).

Bartolomé de Alva belonged to a group of Nahuatl-speaking intellectuals in the seventeenth century associated in one way or another with Horacio Carochi (Schwaller 1994). Angel María Garibay describes Alva's project of translating European dramas into Nahuatl as "broken flight" because it did not lead to a more institutionalized tradition (Garibay, *Historia II*: 340; cited in Schwaller 1994, 396). Even leaving aside the question of pre-Hispanic versus colonial origins, this notion of broken flight may be even more appropriate to the poetry of the *Cantares mexicanos* and the *Romances de los señores de la Nueva España* because the tradition to which they belong also died out.

These types of cultural productions reveal the way in which colonial domination never destroys Indigenous agency; it just induces it to redirect its energies. The extent to which these energies were directed to developing and preserving alphabetic literacy in Nahuatl depended, like all literacies, on institutions that perpetuate it. Evangelization efforts and the colonial administration drove many of the initiatives that led to the production of Nahuatl texts throughout the colonial period, but even in these contexts Native authors often disseminated a uniquely Nahua perspective. And numerous local institutions and private individuals engaged in their own religious and secular projects. Camilla Townsend observes that by around 1600, Indigenous intellectuals began producing historical texts to preserve traditional historical knowledge that they felt was in danger of becoming lost (2019, 13–14). In some cases, these chroniclers produced their works in Spanish (Fernando de Alva Ixtlilxochitl), but others such as Chimalpahin, Juan Buenaventura Zapata y Mendoza, and Don Miguel Santos wrote in Nahuatl (Townsend 2019, 175–225).

In the eighteenth century, this type of research diminished significantly; or if it continued to be produced, it appears less frequently in the archive. At this time, many of the Indigenous elite began to see the continued use of Nahuatl as an impediment to their participation in the colonial order. In 1728, a group of nobles petitioned the archbishop of Mexico requesting that the Colegio de Santa Cruz de Tlatelolco be reopened, and that the curriculum contain a rigorous program of Spanish instruction (Heath 1972, 78). Spanish priests continued to publish grammars, vocabularies, sermons, catechisms, and other religious texts in Nahuatl throughout the eighteenth century (Schwaller 1973), but the historiographic projects of the sixteenth and seventeenth centuries gave way to more strictly pragmatic endeavors of the present.

As Yáñez Rosales (chapter 4 in this volume) demonstrates, priests continued to study and publish on Nahuatl into the twentieth century, but the perspective of these studies changed in the mid-eighteenth century. Schwaller argues that starting around 1840, "works in and dealing with Nahuatl became more analytical and less creative. Production shifted from that of religious works, grammars, and dictionaries for clerics to linguistic studies and secular works for the educated and scientifically-oriented public" (Schwaller 1973, 70). In this period, the French scholars Joseph Aubin and Rémi Siméon spent time in Mexico, learned Nahuatl, and studied the Indigenous past. Aubin acquired an impressive number of iconographic and alphabetic documents, a portion of which had been collected in the seventeenth century by Lorenzo Boturini Benaducci, and he produced a study of what he called the "didactic painting" and "figurative writing" of the ancient Mexicans (Aubin 1885). For his part, Siméon, published the largest Nahuatl dictionary since that of Molina (Siméon 1885).

European scholars such as Aubin and Siméon were interested in Nahuatl and Nahua culture as objects of scientific study, and this perspective was consistent with a shift that was marked most clearly after 1821 in the nation-building projects of newly independent Mexico. As Kelly McDonough explains, these projects involved the subsumption of the "Indian" under the category "citizen." On the one hand, this homogenization of the population under this category ostensibly made everyone equal. On the other hand, it erased Indigenous culture, and this erasure allowed conservative governments to justify the dispossession and privatization of Indigenous communal lands (McDonough 2014, 89).

This may be at least in part why nineteenth-century Nahua intellectuals like Faustino Galicia Chimalpopoca spent more time negotiating the present than preserving the past. Chimalpopoca was a Native Nahuatl speaker and a devout Catholic who attended, and later taught at, the Colegio de San Gregorio. He was politically conservative, but he had a decidedly liberal perspective on Indigenous issues. He defended the preservation of communal lands, advocated for the use of Nahuatl in both religious and secular contexts, and taught the language at the Colegio de San Gregorio and later at the University of Mexico. He transcribed and translated many Nahuatl texts, and he produced works designed to teach Nahuatl and promote Nahuatl literacy (McDonough 2014, 111). According to Chimalpopoca, "the true history of Mexico is marked in her language, in Nahuatl" (cited in McDonough 2014, 108). Unfortunately, many of his contemporaries disagreed. The dominant perspective of this period saw Nahuatl as an impediment to modernization and to the unity of the Mexican nation. Thus, the ideology of modernization and Mexican nationalism created an environment that was not friendly to the preservation of Nahuatl. Chimalpopoca was an exception in that he was a nationalist who valued Nahuatl.

Unfortunately, Chimalpopoca's ideological stance lacked the institutional support that would have given it a chance at success. The cultural prestige and political dominance of Spanish in the colonial period naturally put Nahuatl in an inferior position. Like most cultural products and practices, language depends upon institutions that perpetuate it. Thus, the survival of Nahuatl depended upon the extent to which Indigenous individuals, families, and communities did not integrate into Spanish-speaking society. In the colonial period, the two-republic model, the training of Indigenous scribes who produced Nahuatl language documents, and the acceptance of these documents into the archive provided a certain level of institutional support for the preservation of the language. Even so, contact with Spanish and increasing bilingualism influenced the nature of Nahuatl linguistic practice. James Lockhart and Frances Karttunen have identified three stages in the development of Nahuatl after the conquest (Karttunen and Lockhart 1976), with a fourth phase added later (Lockhart 1994). In each phase, Nahuatl evinces progressively more Spanish influence because of increased levels of contact and bilingualism. Magnus Pharao Hansen (2016 and chapter 5 in this volume) explains that the implication of this model is that the process would eventually lead to the complete disappearance of Nahuatl in favor of Spanish, and this seems to be what happened in those areas where Nahuatl documents allow the process to be tracked. But Hansen points out that Nahuatl is still spoken in the communities that did not produce alphabetic documents. In other words, it seems that Nahuatl literacy went together with increased levels of bilingualism and contact with Spanish, which ironically undermined the continuity of Nahuatl in the long term.

Kelly S. McDonough traces the legacy of Nahuatl intellectuals from the colonial period through the present, but just as important she points out that the Nahua intellectual tradition did not depend upon alphabetic literacy (McDonough 2014, and chapter 11, this volume). Those of us who approach Nahuatl by way of alphabetic writing must always remind ourselves that the written language captures a particular instance of linguistic practice that is mediated by alphabetic script, and that a wealth of intellectual and "literary" traditions existed, and continue to exist, independent of this medium. For example, Jonathan Amith has documented a tradition of oral stories in Nahuatl from Guerrero (2009). Amith's volume and his larger project are appropriately titled "Ok nemi totlahtōl," which translates as "Our language still lives." Even many alphabetic activities may be historically invisible merely because they have not made it into the archive or because that archive has not been thoroughly explored.

The kind of scholarly engagement with Nahuatl described here occurred in one way or another, although with some differences related to changes in the sociopolitical context, throughout the seventeenth, eighteenth, nineteenth, and twentieth centuries. The nineteenth and early twentieth centuries saw the emergence of more formalized academic disciplines. In the mid-twentieth century, Robert Barlow acquired expertise in Nahuatl, taught at Mexico City College, and financed a short-lived Nahuatl language newspaper (McDonough, chapter 11 in this volume). Angel María Garibay contributed to the establishment of the study of Nahuatl language and culture as an independent discipline in Mexico through the creation of the permanent Seminario de Cultura Náhuatl at the Universidad Nacional Autónoma de México in 1956. This seminar produced generation after generation of scholars who have contributed to our understanding of Nahuatl language, culture, and history, including such luminaries as Miguel León-Portilla, Alfredo López Austin, Karen Dakin, José Rubén Romero, Jorge Klor de Alva, Thelma Sullivan, and Patrick Johansson. In 1959, Garibay and his most distinguished student and disciple, Miguel León-Portilla, founded the journal *Estudios de Cultura Náhuatl* to provide a venue for the publication of Nahua-related research. León-Portilla succeeded Garibay as director of the permanent seminar and editor of *Estudios de Cultura Náhuatl*. Like Garibay, León-Portilla not only encouraged the study of Nahuatl language but also actively promoted the recognition of the Nahua past as equivalent to classic Western antiquity—although to a large extent at the expense of the former's specificity. In numerous works, starting with *La filosofía náhuatl estudiada en sus fuentes* (1956), and until his death in 2019, León-Portilla passionately upheld the universal worth of ancient Nahua culture. León-Portilla's *Visión de los vencidos* (1959), a compilation of Indigenous sources on the Spanish conquest translated from Nahuatl, became extremely popular. The English translation, *The Broken Spears: The Aztec Account of the Conquest of Mexico*, appeared in 1962.

Around the same time in the United States, developments in linguistics, anthropology, and history had laid the groundwork for several scholars who began studying Nahuatl and using it in their research in the 1950s, 1960s, and 1970s. Charles Gibson demonstrated the importance of accessing the Indigenous perspective through Nahuatl language sources (1964). Charles Dibble and Arthur Anderson began a long-term project to translate and publish Sahagún's *Florentine Codex* (1970–1975). Arthur Anderson, Frances Berdan, and James Lockhart followed Gibson's lead in advocating for the use of Nahuatl documents in historical research (Anderson, Berdan, and Lockhart 1976; Lockhart 1994). Lockhart founded what he called the "New Philology," which studies ethnohistory using Native-language texts, and over many years at UCLA he trained numerous scholars who work with Nahuatl and other Native-language sources: for example, Susan Schroeder, Robert Haskett, John Tutino, Sarah Klein, Stephanie Wood, Matthew Restall, Kevin Terraciano, Rebecca Horn, Camilla Townsend, and John Sullivan. Other hubs of Nahuatl studies emerged at various universities in the United States. Joe Campbell taught a program intermittently at Indiana University from the 1970s through the 2000s. Yale University offered a summer program for many years. And the language has been taught at many other universities: the University of Chicago, Tulane, the University of Utah, and others.

Much of this academic study has focused on Classical Nahuatl, but it is important to keep in mind that Nahuatl continues to be a living language. The number of Nahuatl speakers has been in decline since the colonial period. In the twentieth century, the Mexican government began promoting bilingual education, but the purpose of this program was to Hispanicize the Indigenous population (Flores Farfán 1999, 37; Marcelín-Alvarado, Collado-Ruano, and Orozco-Malo 2021, 619–620). This tactic contributed to a further decline in the number of Native speakers. It also meant that language activism inevitably shifted from preservation to revitalization. However, in most cases, preservation and revitalization initiatives have been local endeavors that have not been fully documented in academic scholarship.

Beginning in the late 1980s but more intensely starting in the mid-1990s, largely in response to the Zapatista rebellion, the Mexican government began to acknowledge demands by Indigenous groups. The San Andrés Accords in 1996 represented a particularly productive negotiation in which the government agreed in principle to recognize Indigenous rights. The agreement was never fully implemented, but these and other events initiate an ideological shift in Mexican politics that is at least nominally sympathetic to Indigenous issues. Regarding education and Indigenous languages, this period marks a transition from bilingual to intercultural education, which in theory values and supports Indigenous languages (Marcelín-Alvarado, Collado-Ruano, and Orozco-Malo 2021).

Perhaps the most prominent manifestation of this transition was the establishment of Intercultural Universities in the early 2000s. These schools are in areas with large Indigenous populations, and inherent to their mission are language revitalization and community outreach and engagement (Casillas Muñoz and Santini Villar 2006, 19–23). Critics have pointed out that these universities actually perpetuate an ideology of integration (Marcelín-Alvarado, Javier Collado-Ruano, and Miguel Orozco-Malo, 2021, 621) and that they have not been effective at language revitalization (Sandoval Arenas 2016).

Around the same time that the Intercultural Universities were being formed, John Sullivan, who studied Nahuatl with James Lockhart in the 1990s, founded the nonprofit Instituto de Docencia e Investigación Etnológica de Zacatecas (IDIEZ; Zacatecas Institute for Teaching and Research in Ethnology). Justyna Olko and John Sullivan explain that Nahuatl is disappearing because intergenerational transmission has decreased dramatically in recent decades. This reduction is due to a variety of interconnected factors such as a negative language ideology and what we might call a lack of linguistic infrastructure (e.g., schooling in Nahuatl, written materials in Nahuatl, the production of literature in Nahuatl, etc.) (Olko and Sullivan 2014, 377–378). The goal of IDIEZ, now under the direction of Native speakers, is to address these underlying causes of language decline by creating the requisite linguistic infrastructure and promoting the use of Nahuatl as a language of instruction and knowledge production. To this end, in addition to teaching Nahuatl language and culture, they have produced a monolingual Nahuatl dictionary and several other texts in Nahuatl.

More recently, the Universidad Veracruzana Intercultural (UVI) has also begun implementing institutional measures to address structural obstacles inherent in the system and the problem of linguistic infrastructure. Carlos Sandoval, a language activist and professor at UVI, identifies the same issues as Olko and Sullivan, and he explains that UVI is taking steps to overcome them: the use of written Nahuatl with a standardized alphabet (although different from the one used by IDIEZ), the production of a bilingual magazine, the use of Nahuatl in public spaces, the use of Nahuatl as an academic language, and so forth (Sandoval Arenas 2016). The Universidad Veracruzana Intercultural has also created a master's program in Nahuatl language and culture delivered and administered completely in the language (Bernal Lorenzo and Figueroa Saavedra 2019). The initiatives at UVI primarily, but also others like it, are at least beginning to create the kind of institutionalization for which Chimalpopoca advocated in the nineteenth century.

Even researchers from outside Mexico have begun integrating traditional scholarship and community engagement that promote the revitalization of Nahuatl. This step marks a fundamental shift at a time when the field of Nahua studies has been expanding. The goals of community outreach and language activism naturally focus on contemporary issues, but Nahua studies continues to encompass all aspects and periods of Nahua language and culture. For academic researchers outside of Mexico who wish to specialize in Nahua studies or even colonial Mexico more broadly, it is now essential that they study Nahuatl or other Indigenous languages; instructional programs for non-Native speakers like those at Indiana University, UCLA, Yale, IDIEZ, and now UVI have made that possible. Many of the contributors to this volume have benefited from these programs.

The chapters in this book speak to the roots and resiliency of Nahua culture and language, highlighting the adaptations and changes it has undergone over the centuries. The first essay sets the stage by offering an overview of the linguistic development of Nahuatl. In chapter 2, Karen Dakin sheds light on the early history of Nahua languages in Mexico and Mesoamerica by considering the division into the so-called Western and Eastern varieties. After an overview of prevailing theories about Nahua language diversification, Dakin describes several linguistic variants that point to the historical origins of the split between the two groups and help establish the chronology for those specific features. Dakin's consideration of the development of the Nahua language and its variants adds to our understanding of the sociohistorical identity and changing position of what became Mesoamerica's lingua franca. As she notes, the existence of markedly different Nahua dialects indicates a changing history of political interaction among the region's multilingual societies.

The next three chapters showcase the place of Nahuatl in the linguistic and social geography that links ancient Anahuac, to colonial New Spain, to modern Mexico. In chapter 3, Mercedes Montes de Oca Vega considers the use of diphrases in pre-Hispanic Nahua place-names. Also known as semantic couplets, diphrases combine two or more terms to create an idea that is greater than the sum of its parts. Found in both graphic and textual sources, diphrases help conceptualize specific relationships through a selection of meaningful referents. This strategy is related to privileged speech, such as might be used to address revered ancestors, deities, and high-ranking individuals. In the case of toponyms, diphrases activate the landscape so that what might otherwise be generic spaces become specific places. Montes de Oca Vega's review of toponymic diphrases sheds light on the way the study of Nahuatl can yield important insights into Nahua cultural practices.

Next, in chapter 4, Rosa H. Yáñez Rosales addresses the evolution of Western Nahuatl, Nahuatl from southern Jalisco and Colima, a dialect whose documentation is rather scarce. Based on a review of published language samples and on her field research, Yáñez Rosales considers the dialectical peculiarities and the decline of Nahuatl in the region. In the town of Tuxpan, for example, the tradition of formally greeting distinguished visitors in Nahuatl lasted until the late twentieth century. On the other hand, in the town of Ayotitlán, the words that healers incorporate into the curing prayers they recite for the sick are barely recognizable as Nahuatl. Even so, these traditions are proof of the lasting symbolic value of the Nahua language. The distinctive features of the dialect spoken in western Mexico, Yáñez Rosales finds, can still be heard in the twenty-first century.

In chapter 5, Magnus Pharao Hansen examines the process of language shift in the state of Morelos. Hansen argues against the traditional account of a slow and gradual language shift from Nahuatl to Spanish. Instead, he proposes that the decline of the Nahuatl language accelerated sharply in the early twentieth century because of a shift in the state's demographics caused by the intense violence of the Mexican Revolution. According to Hansen, the revolutionary upheaval turned the Indigenous population of Morelos into a minority. Thus, the Nahuatl language lost ground as a regular means of communication among the Indigenous towns of the region. Hansen asserts that ethnohistorical, ethnographic, and ethnolinguistic considerations can help recover local histories that might otherwise be forgotten. Thus, Hansen's contribution exposes an event of genocidal proportions in recent Mexican history.

The focus next turns to Nahua cultural practices and intellectual work from the sixteenth century to the present to show that even as they have evolved, Nahua cultural expressions maintain a connection to pre-Hispanic antiquity. In chapter 6, John F. Schwaller investigates ritual running among cultures that belong to the Uto-Aztecan language family—including Mexica, the Rarámuri, and the Hopi—and considers the role of porters in pre-Hispanic Mexica society. The chapter pays particular attention to the terms used to describe running in Mexica religious rites, such as Panquetzaliztli, Ochpaniztli, and the New Fire ceremony, in the Nahuatl section of the *Florentine Codex*. Schwaller argues that the rich vocabulary associated with running, swiftness, and haste, along with the symbolic value of running, indicates the important role that runners and bearers—of news, goods, or even gods—played in Mexica religious and commercial life.

In chapter 7, Mary L. Clayton considers the Newberry Library's Ayer manuscript 1478, an undated and anonymous trilingual Spanish-Latin-Nahuatl dictionary, composed during the sixteenth century, based on Nebrija's *Vocabulario de romance en latín*. Clayton previously demonstrated that the Ayer manuscript is a copy of an earlier work containing all three languages and presented evidence that the author of the Nahuatl glosses was almost certainly a Native speaker of Nahuatl rather than Spanish. In this volume, she shows how the fact that the author was preparing a passive dictionary rather than an active one allowed him to employ strategies for confronting new concepts that were not available to Alonso de Molina in his dictionaries and gives examples that show his resourcefulness in squeezing meaning out of Nebrija's Spanish-Latin pairs in a variety of ways. In addition to devising fully Nahuatl equivalents and utilizing Spanish borrowings, he made use of hyperonyms and explanatory equivalents, taking hints from Nebrija's disambiguating glosses and his Spanish explanations for Latin equivalents. In some cases, he relied on Nebrija's Latin, with variable results. This variety of devices, along with his point of view as a Native Nahuatl speaker, gives the dictionary its distinctive character.

The translation of foreign concepts was nowhere more salient and consequential than in the religious sphere, owing to the systematic efforts of zealous Catholic missionaries who sought to master local languages to reshape Native belief. This translation was often done with the help of literate and indoctrinated Native speakers, such as the students at the Franciscan school in Tlatelolco. However, as Ben Leeming shows in chapter 8, not all religious texts composed by Nahua intellectuals were written under the stern eye of a wary friar. Leeming highlights the work of colonial Nahua intellectual Fabián de Aquino, who copied, adapted, and composed Christian religious texts in Nahuatl without necessarily having obtained the church's approval. The chapter focuses on Aquino's Nahuatl rendering of a popular genre of medieval European religious writing known as the *contemptus mundi*. Noting that

Aquino may have been influenced by the work of Fray Luis de Granada (1505–1588), Leeming argues that the former's creativity and masterful use of Nahuatl resulted in a unique expression of Nahua Christian religiosity. Aquino's *contemptus mundi* exemplifies how Christian devotional literature was received and reworked by literate Nahuas who were not directly associated with official evangelical efforts.

Beyond theological and metaphysical questions, the mundane details incorporated into religion-themed works also reflected Nahua ideas and concerns. In chapter 9, Louise M. Burkhart focuses on the role of the notary in Nahua religious dramas. The important role that notaries played in real life was mirrored on stage: they wrote and read the documents that sanctioned important events. In plays about the Passion of the Christ, Burkhart argues, the character of Escribano, possibly played by an actual notary, enhanced both the gravity and immediacy of events being portrayed. Even when the testimony was false and the result grievous, and even when they might sometimes serve unjust authorities, fictional notaries exhibited great discretion and fidelity, for in truth, in both the public and private spheres, much depended on a notary's accuracy and trustworthiness.

Chapter 10 shows that Nahua traditions continue to have important implications in the material and spiritual worlds. Alan R. and Pamela Effrein Sandstrom offer an anthropological study of cut-paper images used in a Nahua community for healing and spiritual cleansing. Based on many years of direct experience, the authors argue that these sacred paper cuttings are a living tradition linked to pre-Hispanic graphic conventions and religious beliefs. Cut by ritual specialists, the anthropomorphic images embody powerful spirit entities that must be bargained with to solve specific problems, such as a person's illness, and maintain order in nature. The chapter describes the various paper figures, the entities they represent, and the symbolism of their careful layout as part of an offering. The features of the cuttings and their arrangement constitute a contemporary expression of the highly sophisticated semasiographic writing system whose origins can be traced to Mesoamerica's earliest civilizations.

Along with traditional practices rooted in ancient lore, Nahua intellectual production has persisted through the centuries, continuing to adapt to new realities. In chapter 11, Kelly S. McDonough surveys Nahua intellectual activity from the sixteenth century to the present. She highlights how Nahuas were always able to adapt to changes, managing not only to preserve but also to assert their identity and cultural traditions against hegemonic forces that sought to undermine them. Starting in the sixteenth century, Nahuas quickly embraced alphabetic writing as a tool to defend their material and immaterial heritage. Crucially, they wrote in Nahuatl, which served as a mechanism and symbol of resistance and self-determination. McDonough posits that Nahuatl is particularly concerned with relationships, including those with the past and the ancestors, and among kin. Those connections have been preserved over many generations through the written work of Nahua intellectuals.

Ranging widely across several disciplines, from ethnohistory to literature, and from anthropology to philology and pure linguistics, the chapters included in this volume link their authors to a long series of Native and non-Native Nahuatl-speakers and observers going back centuries. The contributors highlight the continuity of Nahuatl as a vital language and cultural vehicle. Collectively, they speak to the origins of Nahuatl; its past and present evolution according to contemporaneous political, demographic, cultural, and economic pressures and changes; its rich literary and cultural heritage; and its prominent historical role in the history of precolonial, colonial, and independent Mexico.[2]

## REFERENCES

Amith, Jonathan, ed. 2009. *Ok nemi totlahtōl*. Vol. 1. *Estado de Guerrero*. Mexico City: Instituto Nacional de Lenguas Indígenas.

Anderson, Arthur, Frances Berdan, and James Lockhart. 1976. *Beyond the Codices: The Nahua View of Colonial Mexico*. Berkeley: University of California Press.

Andrews, Richard. 1975. *Introduction to Classical Nahuatl*. Austin: University of Texas Press.

Andrews, Richard. 2003. *Introduction to Classical Nahuatl*. Rev. ed. Norman: University of Oklahoma Press.

Anonymous. n.d. *(Vocabulario trilingüe)*. *Dictionarium ex hisniensi in latinum sermonem interprete Aelio Antonio Neprissensi*. Trilingual Spanish-Latin-Nahuatl manuscript dictionary. Ayer ms. 1478 [vault]. Newberry Library, Chicago.

Arencibia Rodríguez, Lourdes. 2006. "The Imperial College of Santa Cruz de Tlatelolco: The First School of Translators and Interpreters in Sixteenth-Century America." In *Charting the Future of Translation History*, edited by Georges L. Bastin and Paul F. Bandia, 263–275. Ottawa: University of Ottawa Press.

Aubin, Joseph Marius Alexis. 1885. *Mémoire sur la peinture didactique et l'écriture figurative des anciens mexicaines*. Paris: Imprimerie Nationale.

Baudot, Georges. 1995. *Utopia and History in Mexico: The First Chroniclers of Mexican Civilization (1920–1569)*. Translated by Bernard R. and Thelma Ortiz de Montellano. Colorado: University Press of Colorado.

Bautista, Juan. 1604. *Libro de la miseria y brevedad de la vida del hombre: y de sus quatro postrimerias, en lengua Mexicana*. Mexico City: Diego Lopez Davalos.

---

[2] We thank one of the volume's anonymous reviewers for these insights.

Bautista, Juan. 1605. *Vida y milagros del bienaventurado San Antonio de Padua*. Mexico City: Diego Lopez Davalos.

Bernal Lorenzo, Daisy, and Miguel Figueroa Saavedra. 2019. "Nueva oferta educativa universitaria con enfoque intercultural: El caso de la Maestría en Lengua y Cultura Nahua de la Universidad Veracruzana." *Revista Educación* 43 (2): 1–14.

Bierhorst, John, ed. and trans. 1985. *Cantares Mexicanos: Songs of the Aztecs*. Stanford, CA: Stanford University Press.

Bierhorst, Joh, ed. and trans. 2009. *Ballads of the Lords of New Spain: The Codex Romances de los Senores de la Nueva España*. Austin: University of Texas Press.

Brokaw, Galen. 2021. "An Integrational Approach to Colonial Semiosis." In *The Routledge Hispanic Studies Companion to Colonial Latin America and the Caribbean (1492–1898)*, edited by Yolanda Martínez-San Miguel and Santa Arias, 99–116. London: Routledge.

Burkhart, Louise M. 2008. "Nahuatl Baroque: How Alva Mexicanized the Spanish Dramas." In *Nahuatl Theater*. Vol. 3, *Spanish Golden Age Drama in Mexican Translation*, edited by Barry D. Sell, Louise Burkhart, and Elizabeth Wright, 35–49. Norman: University of Oklahoma Press.

Canger, Una. 2011a. "El náhuatl urbano de Tlatelolco/Tenochtitlan, resultado de convergencia entre dialectos. Con un esbozo brevísimo de la historia de los dialectos." *Estudios de Cultura Náhuatl* 42: 243–258.

Carochi, Horacio. (1645) 2001. *Grammar of the Mexican Language with an Explanation of Its Adverbs*. Edited and translated by James Lockhart. Stanford, CA: Stanford University Press.

Casillas Muñoz, María Lourdes, and Laura Santini Villar. 2006. *Universidad intercultural: Modelo educativo*. Mexico City: Secretaría de Educación Pública.

Clayton, Mary L. 1989. "A Trilingual Spanish-Latin-Nahuatl Manuscript Dictionary Sometimes Attributed to Fray Bernardino de Sahagún." *International Journal of American Linguistics* 55:391–416.

Clayton, Mary L. 2003. "Evidence for a Native-Speaking Nahuatl Author in the Ayer Vocabulario Trilingüe." *International Journal of Lexicography* 16 (2): 99–119.

Dryer, Matthew S. 2013. "Order of Subject, Object, and Verb." In *The World Atlas of Language Structures Online*, edited by Matthew S. Dryer and Martin Haspelmath, v 2020.3. Leipzig: Max Planck Institute for Evolutionary Anthropology. http://wals.info/chapter/81.

Flores Farfán, José Antonio. 1999. *Cuatreros somos y toindioma hablamos: Contactos y conflictos entre el náhuatl y el español en el sur de México*. Tlalpan, Mexico: CIESAS.

Gante, Pedro de. [1525–1528] 1970. *Catecismo de la doctrina cristiana*. Madrid: Ministerio de Educación y Ciencia.

Gante, Pedro de. [1529] 1973. "Carta de fray Pedro de Gante a los Padres y Hermanos de la Provincia de Flandes, 27 de junio de 1529." In "Fray Pedro de Gante, Maestro y civilizador de América," edited by Ernesto de la Torre Villar, 40–43. *Estudios de Historia Novohispana* 5: 9–77.

Gante, Pedro de. 1547. *Doctrina cristiana en lengua mexicana*. Mexico City: Casa de Juan Pablos.

Gibson, Charles. 1964. *The Aztecs under Spanish Rule: A History of the Indians of the Valley of Mexico, 1519–1810*. Stanford, CA: Stanford University Press.

Hammerström, Harald. 2016. "Linguistic Diversity and Language Evolution." *Journal of Language Evolution* 1 (1): 19–29.

Hansen, Magnus Pharao. 2016. "Nahuatl Nation: Language Revitalization and Indigenous Resurgence in 21st Mexico." PhD diss., Brown University, Providence, RI.

Heath, Shirley Brice. 1972. *La política del lenguaje en México: De la colonia a la nación*. Mexico City: Secretaría de Educación Pública / Instituto Nacional Indigenista.

Karttunen, Frances, and James Lockhart. 1976. *Nahuatl in the Middle Years: Language Contact Phenomena in Texts of the Colonial Period*. Berkeley: University of California Press.

Laird, Andrew. 2014. "Nahuas and Caesars: Classical Learning and Bilingualism in Post-conquest Mexico: An Inventory of Latin Writings by Authors of the Native Nobility." *Classical Philology* 109 (2): 150–169.

Launey, Michel. 2011. *An Introduction to Classical Nahuatl*. Translated by Christopher Mackay. Cambridge: Cambridge University Press.

Leeming, Ben. 2017. "A Nahua Christian Talks Back: Fabián de Aquino's Antichrist Dramas as Autoethnography." In *Words and Worlds Turned Around: Indigenous Christianities in Colonial Latin America*, edited by David Tavárez, 172–192. Boulder: University Press of Colorado.

Leeming, Ben. 2022. *Aztec Antichrist: Performing the Apocalypse in Early Colonial Mexico*. Albany: Institute for Mesoamerican Studies.

León-Portilla, Ascensión H. de. 1972. "Bibliografía lingüística nahua." *Estudios de Cultura Náhuatl* 101: 409–441.

León-Portilla, Miguel. 1956. *La filosofía náhuatl, estudiada en sus fuentes*. Mexico City: Instituto Indigenista Interamericano.

León-Portilla, Miguel. 1959. *Visión de los vencidos: Relaciones indígenas de la conquista*. Mexico City: Universidad Nacional Autónoma.

León-Portilla, Miguel. 1962. *The Broken Spears: the Aztec Account of the Conquest of Mexico*. Boston: Beacon Press.

León-Portilla, Miguel. 2004. "Introducción." In *Vocabulario en lengua castellana y mexicana y mexicana y castellana*, by Fray Alonso de Molina. Edited by Miguel León-Portilla. 5th ed. Mexico City: Porrúa.

Linell, Per. 2005. *The Written Language Bias in Linguistics: Its Nature, Origins, and Transformations*. London: Routledge.

Lockhart, James. 1994. *The Nahuas after the Conquest: A Social and Cultural History of the Indians of Central Mexico, Sixteenth through Eighteenth Centuries*. Stanford, CA: Stanford University Press.

Lockhart, James. 2001a. "Editor's Preface." In *Grammar of the Mexican Language with an Explanation of its Adverbs*, edited by Horacio Carochi and translated by James Lockhart, vii–xxii. Stanford, CA: Stanford University Press.

Lockhart, James. 2001b. *Nahuatl as Written: Lessons in Older Written Nahuatl with Copious Examples and Texts*. Stanford, CA: Stanford University Press.

Marcelín-Alvarado, María A., Javier Collado-Ruano, and Miguel Orozco-Malo. 2021. *Language and Intercultural Communication* 21 (5): 618–630.

Maxwell, Judith M., and Craig A. Hanson. 1992. *Of the Manners of Speaking that the Old Ones Had: The Metaphors of Andrés de Olmos in the Tulal Manuscript*. Salt Lake City: University of Utah Press.

McDonough, Kelly. 2014. *The Learned Ones: Nahua Intellectuals in Postconquest Mexico*. Tucson: University of Arizona Press.

Mendieta, Jerónimo de. 2017. *Historia eclesiástica indiana*. N.p.: Plaza Editorial.

Molina, Alonso. (1571) 2004. *Vocabulario en lengua castellana y mexicana y mexicana y castellana*. Mexico City: Porrúa.

Olko, Justyna, and John Sullivan. 2014. "Toward a Comprehensive Model for Nahuatl Language Research and Revitalization." *Proceedings of the Fortieth Annual Meeting of the Berkeley Linguistics Society*, edited by Herman Leung, Zachary O'Hagan, Sarah Bakst, et al., 369–397. Berkeley, CA: Berkeley Linguistics Society.

*Recopilación de leyes de los reynos de las Indias*. (1681) 1987. 5 vols. Mexico City: Escuela Libre de Derecho/Porrúa.

Rincón, Antonio. (1595) 1885. *Arte mexicana*. Mexico City: Secretaría de Fomento.

Sahagún, Bernardino de. [1579] 1994. *Historia general de las cosas de Nueva España*. Madrid: Club Internacional del Libro.

Sandoval Arenas, Carlos O. 2016. "Displacement and Revitalization of the Nahuatl Language in the High Mountains of Veracruz, Mexico." *Arts and Humanities in Higher Education* 16 (1): 66–81.

Schwaller, John F. 1973. "A Catalogue of Pre-1840 Nahuatl Works Held by the Lilly Library." *Indiana University Bookman* 11: 69–88.

Schwaller, John F. 1994. "Nahuatl Studies and the 'Circle' of Horacio Carochi." *Estudios de Cultura Náhuatl* 24: 387–398.

Sell, Barry D. 1999. "The Classical Age of Nahuatl Publications and Don Bartolomé de Alva's *Confessionario* of 1634." In *A Guide to Confession Large and Small in the*

*Mexican Language*, 1634, edited by Barry D. Sell and John Frederick Schwaller, with Lu Ann Homza, 17–32. Norman: University of Oklahoma Press.

Sell, Barry D., and Louise Burkhart. 2004. *Nahuatl Theater*. Vol. 1: *Death and Life in Colonial Nahua Mexico*. Norman: University of Oklahoma Press.

Siméon, Rémi. 1885. *Dictionnaire de la langue nahuatl ou mexicaine*. Paris: Imprimerie Nationale.

Sousa, Lisa, Stafford Poole, and James Lockhart. 1998. *The Story of Guadalupe: Luis Laso de la Vega's* Huei tlamahuiçoltica. Stanford, CA: Stanford University Press.

Townsend, Camilla. 2019. *Annals of Native America: How the Nahuas of Colonial Mexico Kept Their History Alive*. Oxford: Oxford University Press.

Whittaker, Gordon. 2021. *Deciphering Aztec Hieroglyphs: A Guide to Nahuatl Writing*. Berkeley: University of California Press.

Wright Carr, David Charles. 2007. "La política lingüística en la Nueva España." *Acta Universitaria de la Universidad de Guanajuato* 17 (3): 5–19.

2

# The Early History of Nahua Languages in Mexico and Mesoamerica

KAREN DAKIN

The early history of Nahua languages in Mexico and Mesoamerica is still somewhat open to conjecture, but this chapter will concentrate on an early division into two groups, which have been have called "Western" and "Eastern" in classification because of their distribution at the time of European contact. Using the evidence discussed by a number of historical linguists, archaeologists, and ethnohistorians working on the area, I find that it does seem that the early diversification of Nahua from other Uto-Aztecan languages took place first in western central Mexico. It has been proposed that Nahua and Corachol may have been a subgroup of the southern languages, but in any case the earliest division within the Nahua community was a split in which a first group of Nahuas moved out and migrated south and east into central Mexico—with some groups as part of early migrations that included movements through Teotihuacan—where some settlements were probably established. Linguistic evidence suggests that these early Eastern Nahua eventually moved through the central highlands and into La Huasteca, but one branch of the Eastern migration went down the Isthmus and into Central America. In this process they came into contact with other Mesoamerican linguistic groups that included Otomangueans, Tepehua-Totonacans, and further south Mixe-Zoqueans and Mayans, and perhaps other groups as well.

Later, with the political and economic changes that took place in the post-Classic and including the increasing role of the more militant, multiethnic Chichimec groups into the northwest, Nahua migrated down into central Mexico, establishing themselves in Tenochtitlan-Tlatelolco and settling into the surrounding central area, producing a situation of language contact between the earlier Eastern Nahua groups and the later Western Nahua arrivals. As a result, the central area shares features from both Eastern and Western branches, a situation that has been noted in different moments already by Juan A. Hasler ([1976] 2011) and more recently by Una Canger (1988, 2011, 2018), Gordon Whittaker (1988), Magnus Pharao Hansen (2014), and Jane Hill (2017) among others. This chapter provides linguistic evidence that describes the historical origins and identification in each case of the innovating variant for four features that distinguish Eastern and Western Nahuas from each other, and also helps establish the chronology for those same innovations.

## 0. INTRODUCTION

Consideration of the development of the Nahua language and its variants adds to our understanding of the sociohistorical identity and changing position of what became the dominant language not only of Tlatelolco-Tenochtitlan and the governing Mexica at the time of contact with the European world but also in relation to the variants of the language that the Europeans encountered on the Isthmus and the Gulf Coast and in the mountains to the northwest. As will be seen, in the multilingual societies of Mesoamerica the existence of sometimes notably differing variants of the Nahua language reflects a history of social and political interaction and change. In this chapter, some of the main theories about the diversification of the language from what we reconstruct as the variant of the first speakers will be summarized first. Following will be a description of the principal points of contrast that are the basis for the different theories. Also discussed will be the problems in some cases of contrasts between given forms and how judgments can be made as to which one represents the more innovative feature, since sharing the innovation is stronger proof of a common history.

These findings are interpreted in association with some of the recent archaeological and ethnohistorical theories related to those reconstructions, and a tentative linguistic history is offered to provide at least some of the comparative and historical bases for their differences. Recent work about variation in the language itself by Canger (1980, 1988), Hill (2017), Brígida von Mentz (2017), and Whittaker (1988), especially, is considered.

Although perhaps Joe Campbell's best-known contributions have been in relation to the extensive materials on the Colonial Central variants—in particular, those of Alonso de Molina and Bernardino de Sahagún—his interest in the language is much wider and includes a great number of topics. Campbell's own field materials include texts and an especially extensive lexicon that have been collected since the 1960s, which have been incorporated into his extensive digitalized databases. He has generously shared them to the great benefit of his colleagues and students. The materials that he has processed and analyzed are not limited to the Colonial documents drawn from the Central area but also include a long list of the different variants of the language he has gathered from the Nahua speakers he has worked with in documentation and teaching of modern Nahua variants. These variants are from both the Valley of Mexico and the Tepoztlan and Hueyapan areas of Morelos and from San Miguel Canoa, Puebla, and neighboring towns; a number of Guerrero dialects; and, in the last several years, La Huasteca areas as well. Also important to note are those in the Western Nahua variants from Michoacán, these last collected not in Mexico but in the state of Michigan. Campbell's digitally organized materials also include ordered treatments of comparative materials that show important dialect divisions. He has also been extremely generous in providing concordances when questioned about particular words, and his reverse dictionary and his organizations of semantic classes of Molina based on Charles F. and Florence M. Voegelin's Hopi domains have been basic tools for anyone working on morphological and semantic classes, whether it be for synchronic or historical purposes. His work has been a major contribution to our knowledge of dialect variants and understanding of the historical configuration of the Nahua language.

Section 1 of the chapter presents a summary based on a number of general hypotheses about the history of the Nahua diversification, beginning with their position in the Uto-Aztecan family. Section 2 briefly traces the history of some of the specific hypotheses, and section 3 provides arguments in support of these hypotheses based on the linguistic evidence. Section 4 refers to work that describes sociolinguistic features that are evidence of language contact in the Colonial period among distinct Nahua populations in the Basin of Mexico.

### 1. A BRIEF HISTORICAL CONSIDERATION OF NAHUATL IN UTO-AZTECAN

Nahua is the southernmost of the known Uto-Aztecan languages. There are various proposals for the classification of both branches of Uto-Aztecan and of Nahua within that family. Although Wick Miller (1984) and Mario Cortina-Borja and Leopoldo Valiñas Coalla (1989), both studies based on lexicostatistics, have shown that the mesh model for the relationships among the various languages and their variants may better reflect their history than the more traditional tree diagrams, it is helpful to briefly note the tree diagrams that have been proposed. On the higher level, representing the oldest divisions, the existence of a Northern Uto-Aztecan branch has been generally accepted. In the most conservative views, the southern languages should perhaps still be divided into branches (see Lamb 1964): Tepiman, Corachol, Guarijío-Tarahumara, Yaqui-Mayo (Cahita), Eudeve, Tubar, and Nahua (Dakin 1980). However, proposals have been made for the unity of a Southern Uto-Aztecan branch, in particular those by Cortina-Borja and Valiñas Coalla (1989), just noted, and also those by William Merrill (2013) based on specific phonological innovations, and by Brian Stubbs (2011) based on comparative phonology and lexicon.

The diversification of Nahua from Uto-Aztecan has been related as well with the social forces that led to migrations and the eventual separation of different groups from a core population, giving rise to language change and evolution from an older protolanguage. For that reason, work by archaeologists and ethnohistorians regarding the dispersal of different groups is important to understanding first the diversification of the Uto-Aztecan language community, and then that of Nahua and its variants. In this chapter particular reference is made to the work of archaeologists Christopher Beekman and Alexander Christensen (2003) and Christopher Beekman (2015), based on their research in western Mexico involving migrations from the northern edge of Mesoamerica and into central Mexico, a focus that has special bearing on the history of the development and diversification of Nahua.

We are not certain of the precise dispersal point or *homeland* for Uto-Aztecan languages. C. Fowler's important 1983 analysis of the biological territorial limits for cognates for reconstructible plant and animal species leads her to tentatively establish the location of a Uto-Aztecan dialect chain in what are now Southern California, Arizona, and Sonora and Chihuahua in Mexico. Hill describes an additional possibility, by her identification of parallel, if not necessarily precisely cognate, vocabulary, which supports a dispersal point that would be still farther south, in northern Mesoamerica, and on that basis she argues that Uto-Aztecans probably already must have had corn and pottery (Hill 2001, 2019), specific cultural developments found earliest in the archaeological evidence for Mesoamerica.

## 2. DISPERSAL POINT AND MOVEMENTS OF NAHUA POPULATIONS

The dispersal point for the Nahua language itself, the most southern of the Uto-Aztecan languages, has been generally accepted to have been from western Mexico, moving into the central area of Guanajuato. Dakin and Søren Wichmann (2000), Martha Macri and Matthew Looper (2003), and also Dakin (2003, 2010) have provided arguments, on the basis of various loanwords, that there were very probably earlier movements of Nahuas into the center and north into La Huasteca and that there were small groups moving to the south, arriving as far as Central América. Beekman (2015, 76) has noted that the evidence of the earlier migrations is still under debate:

> Confirmation comes from epigraphic data. Rebus writing interpreted as using Nahuatl occurs at the new central Mexican Epiclassic centers of Cacaxtla and Xochicalco (Berlo 1989; Dakin and Wichmann 2000:68; Hirth 1989; Wichmann 1998:302). There are also proposed Nahuatl loanwords in a handful of inscriptions in the Maya cities of Guatemala and southeastern Mexico that more precisely situate contact with Nahuatl speakers by ad 650–750 (Macri 2005; Macri and Looper 2003). Earlier than this, the evidence becomes significantly more controversial (Dakin and Wichmann 2000; Kaufman and Justeson 2007), and Nahuatl's arrival in central Mexico, should not have occurred much before this date.

On the basis of the model Beekman and Christensen described earlier (2003)—one that draws on evidence from biological research, ethnohistory, and linguistics, as well as from archaeology—Beekman (2015) has now proposed more specifically that the starting point for later Nahua migrations was probably centered in the Bajío area, to the south of Zacatecas and San Luis Potosí and east of Nayarit, in the lowlands of Jalisco, Guanajuato, Aguascalientes, and Querétaro, possibly as early as the sixth century CE in the late Classic period (figure 2.1). They treat Nahua migrations as "part of a longer-term process tying together Mesoamerica's northern periphery with its highland core" (Beekman and Christensen 2003, 111, 114, 135–136). Their proposal is very important for the problems of defining the movements of the different branches of Nahuatl, separately identified based on the linguistic isoglosses.

Other considerations related to the dispersal have merited increasing attention over the last several years. These have centered on the multilingual nature of pre-Hispanic societies and their patterns of language use, as pointed out, for example, by Leopoldo José Valiñas Coalla (1981, 2010), and with more specific documentation by Rosa Yáñez (2013, 2017), Yáñez Rosales and Álvaro Torres Nila (2018), and Medina García (2016) for the use of Nahua in contact with languages in western Mexico. The contact between Nahua variants and other languages has historical implications as well for the development of Central Nahua in the post-Classic and Colonial periods.

Of interest also in terms of the subgrouping for and development of Nahua are the proposal by Lyle Campbell and Ronald Langacker (1978) and a more recent one by Pharao Hansen (2017) for a Corachol-Nahua branch. Their proposals are based principally on shared phonological innovations, which include in particular that proto-Uto-Aztecan (pUA) \*\**p* became *h* in Cora and Huichol under certain

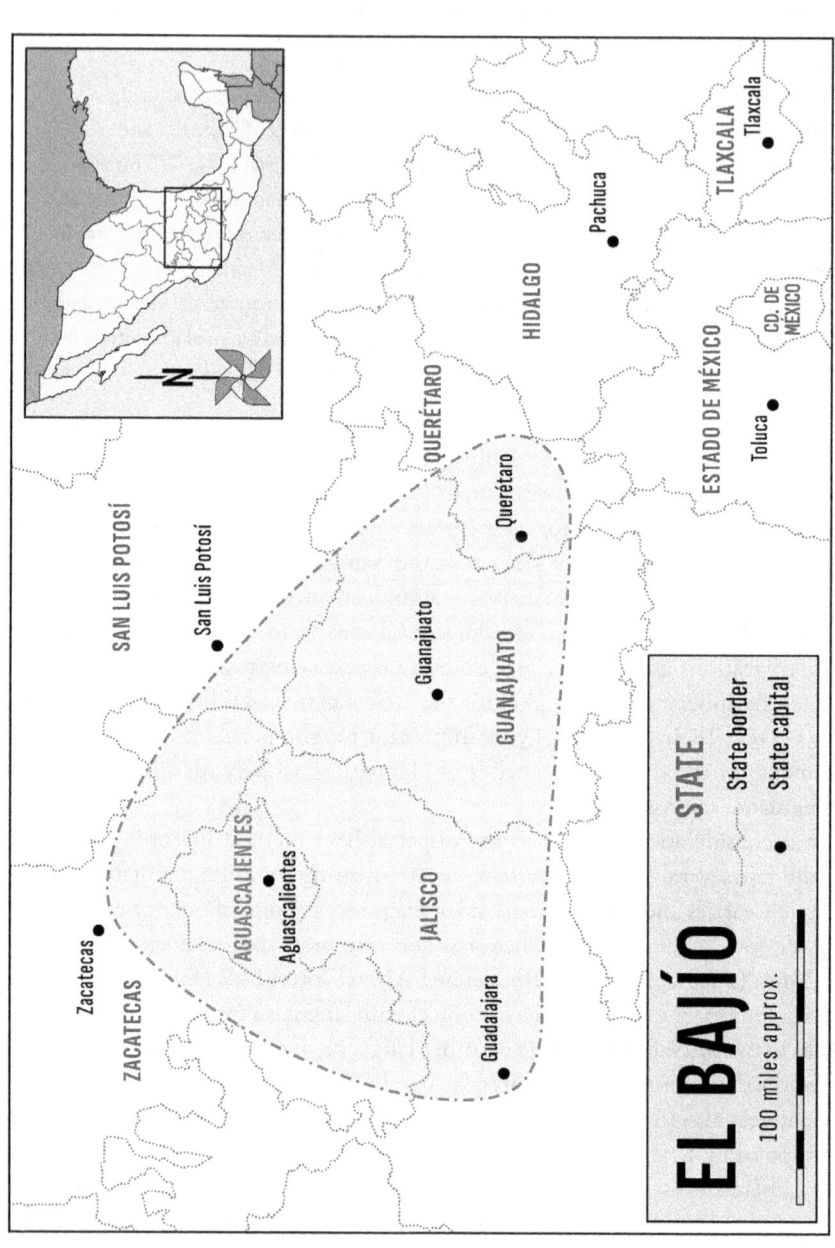

**Figure 2.1.** Map showing approximate location of the "Bajío."

conditions, a change shared initially with Nahua.[1] Other researchers have suggested that the shared features in support of a Corachol-Nahua branch are probably due more to language contact than to a shared immediate ancestor, since Eastern Nahua does not have them (Dakin 2017; Yáñez 2017).

The proposal giving weight to contact between Western Nahua and Corachol in particular would tie in with the idea of a mesh-like classification suggested by Miller (1984) and Cortina-Borja and Valiñas Coalla (1989). As discussed under "1. A Brief Historical Consideration of Nahuatl in Uto-Aztecan," their results suggest the need for different emphases in language classification, in many aspects lending more support to proposals for mesh as opposed to tree groupings for the southern languages. This would be expected given that more extensive contact across languages produces more mesh-like shared characteristics.

If Nahua is not part of a Corachol-Nahua subgroup, we would have the alternative proposal that the separate Nahua language group went through a first major split into two basic branches that Canger and Dakin (1985) refer to simply as Eastern and Western because of their locations at time of European contact, although other terms have been suggested for them. The linguistic evidence for this split is discussed in detail in section 3. According to this hypothesis, in this basic split, a group of speakers moved away from the area of the "homeland," as identified by Beekman and Christensen (2003), and migrated eastward, very probably during the Classic period, into areas in the central highlands, which would then have been under domination by Teotihuacan. They established at least some settlements in central Mexico but continued through to La Huasteca. Linda Manzanilla (1985, 75) includes a possible corridor connecting the two areas of central Guerrero and La Huasteca during the Classic and early epi-Classic periods in Teotihuacan (figure 2.2). Eastern Nahua influence from this migration also reached at least as far south as Guerrero, and linguistic similarities support the possibility that that was during the period these were under control by Teotihuacan.

La Huasteca Nahuas must also have been in greater contact with the central area during the period of Teotihuacan but especially with the central Guerrero towns, identified as the historical Coixca by Mentz (2017). The Guerrero and Huasteca Nahua variants share several constructions that are found in several Eastern Nahua variants, but a few appear to be more limited to just the Balsas region in central Guerrero and La Huasteca. Some of the most notable include the use of the agentive suffix *-ke-tl* as in Chicontepec, Veracruz, *tepahtiketl*, and Oapan, Guerrero,

---

[1] Hypothesized protoforms reconstructed to proto-Uto-Aztecan are indicated with a double asterisk (\*\*), while those reconstructed for a proto-Nahua language are shown with a single one (\*).

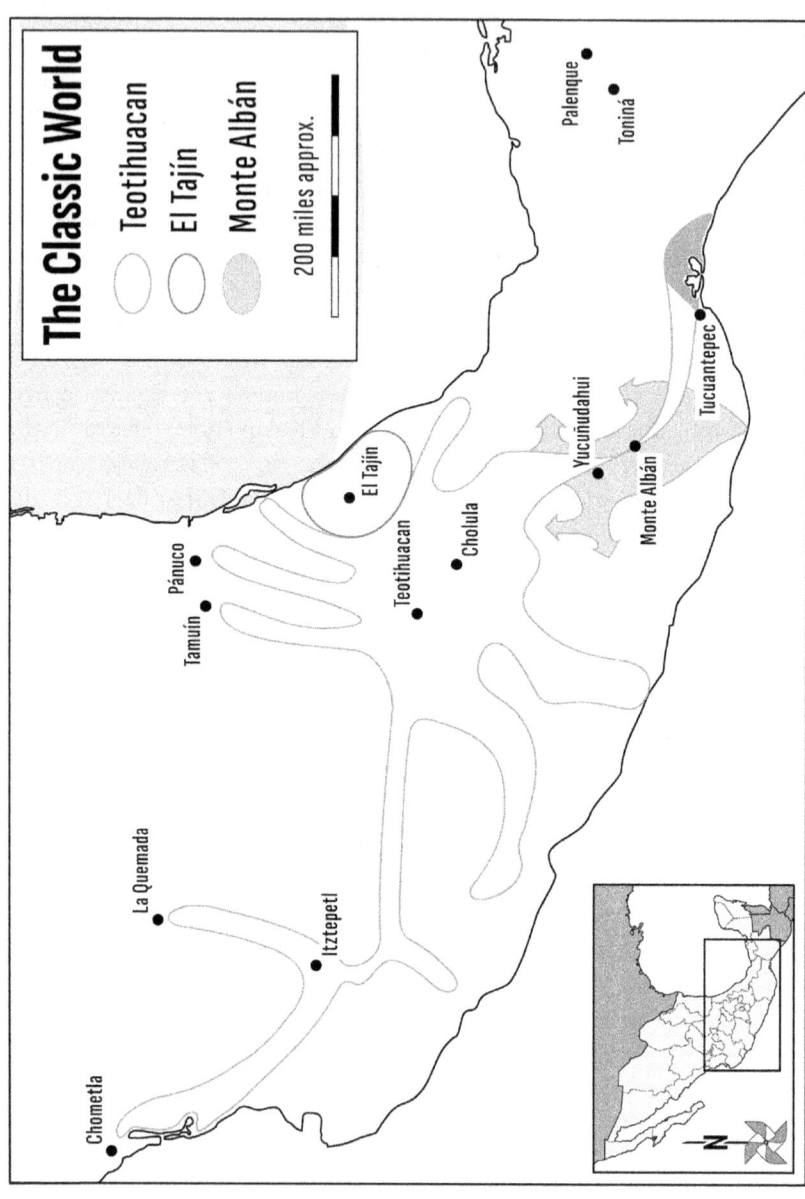

**Figure 2.2.** Map showing the extent of Teotihuacan influence across central Mexico and the possibility of the earlier connection of the central Balsas region of Guerrero and La Huasteca, based on Manzanilla (1985, 75).

*Tēpatikētl* (curer). Also, the Guerrero negative is *š-* in predicative constructions, and that of a number of Huasteca Nahua dialects is *aš-* or *š-*. The *š-* is very probably related to the central area *ay-* negative prefix, found attested in central and western dialects as in *aya:k* and the preconsonantal negative prefix *ah-*. However, in central Guerrero there are number of features due to a later layer of Western Nahua influence, probably the arrival of the Chichimecs in the post-Classic and the Mexica during the periods of domination by Tenochtitlan-Tlatelolco.

Mentz provides an explanation for the subsequent isolation of the Coixca variant of Eastern Nahua from that spoken in La Huasteca. She hypothesizes that speakers of what today is referred to as "Eastern" became partially disconnected from the highlands in the epi-Classic and post-Classic and remained divided in the seventh to ninth centuries by the villages that penetrated wedge-like into central Mexico from the east (as suggested by Xochicalco's and Cacaxtla's links to the Mayan world), and from the north (Toltec-Chichimecas). As a result, the same archaic Eastern variant in the Balsas region and La Huasteca became divided (Mentz 2017, 37).

It would seem that as the migration of this first group spread eastward, a branch of the migration separated from them, moving toward the south and continuing slowly through the Sierra de Puebla and down along the Gulf Coast and the Isthmus and farther into Central America. Sociohistorical evidence in the form of archaic place-names corroborates these movements, as pointed out also by Mentz (2017), who relates these two important trade routes. The earliest of these Eastern Nahuas to arrive in El Salvador, Honduras, and Nicaragua would have thus been in small groups of speakers, who in keeping with Mesoamerican patterns would have settled along the way in small communities neighboring those of speakers of other Mesoamerican languages. However, these first Nahuas also may have been responsible for some of the Nahua words found borrowed into other languages for important objects of exchange, such as cacao, *kakawa* (see Dakin 2003, 2010; Dakin and Wichmann 2000; Whittaker 1986). It was in the later epi-Classic that the migration of Pipil speakers came in, as documented by archaeological and ethnohistorical sources (Beekman 2015; Beekman and Christensen 2003; W. Fowler 1989;). These immigrants also introduced more loanwords and possibly borrowed some themselves from other languages into Nahua (Justeson et al.1985).

But a population of Western Nahua speakers stayed behind, some perhaps moving farther northwest, where they came into closer contact with the speakers of Coracholan languages. Western Nahua also developed several innovations, some perhaps because of the contact with Cora and Huichol.

Of more importance for Nahua dialectology, and contrary to what has been accepted for the grouping of Pochutec until now (see Campbell and Langacker 1978; Hill 2017, 137; Kaufman 2001;), recent comparisons support the conclusion that

Pochutec also shares several Western Nahua innovations with those Western variants of Nahua and should be considered part of that same branch. Given the kinds of correspondences, described in section 3, it can be seen that these are innovations that predate the separation of the Western Nahua Pochutec dialect, located on the southern coast of Oaxaca, when it was cut off from the rest of Western Nahua by the Mixtec conquest in the eleventh–twelfth centuries. The similarities also suggest that the theories that it was a completely separate branch from all the rest of Nahua can be explained more coherently by taking into account Pochutec's later isolation. As pointed out by Mentz (personal communication, 2018), in the sixteenth-century *Relaciones geográficas del siglo XVI: Antequera*, the respondents of Pochutla, Guatulco, and Tonameca all comment that "they are descendents of a generation of *chichimecas*, and thus, the language that they speak is disguised, corrupt *mexicana*" (original emphasis).[2] By the use of the term *disfrazada*, it may be that they referred to a basically Western Nahua variety with specific innovations. Also, in considering that at the time Franz Boas (1917) collected the limited data he could from the few speakers he was able to find, the variety would have been undergoing processes of language death. Although initial examinations of the data that Boas collected, particularly in terms of the vowels and vowel losses, create an impression of major differences within the family, a detailed comparison and reconstruction based on comparative recent data from the Western Nahuas collected by Valiñas Coalla (1979, 1981) and Yolanda Lastra de Suárez (1986), as well as in Colonial documents (Medina García 2016; Yáñez Rosales 2018), show regular sound correspondences with the Western Nahua variants; they also let us identify specific shared vocabulary and Western Nahua grammatical constructions (Dakin 1983, 2017).

Returning to the development of the Western Nahua groups as a whole, the following stage came when the interruptions and upheavals in the post-Classic began, apparently at least partially the result of climate changes, as well as of other factors, and the migrations of multiethnic Chichimec that included Western Nahua speakers began to move down into the central highlands again in search of more fertile areas to settle.

Beekman and Christensen (2003, 116–117) summarize their conclusions about both sixth-century Classic and later post-Classic waves of migrations into the central Mexico highlands:

> We conclude that the migrants responsible for the introduction of Nahuatl into the central highlands were previously sedentary refugees from north-central Mexico, who arrived long before the better-known migrants from the historical records.

---

2  "Que ellos descienden de generación de *chichimecas*, y, así, la lengua que hablan es *mexicana* corrumpida [*sic*], disfrazada."

Methodologically we find that the data sets do not all correlate neatly with one another, but that their divergences can help in interpretation. From a theoretical perspective, we find that important factors for migration include environmental instability, the fluidity of migrants' social organization, the shifting nature of ethnicity, prior contact and information flow, and the recursive link between migration and political stability.

The ethnohistoric sources help to further detail the mechanisms behind the Late post-Classic migrations, but also demonstrate that Nahuatl was already spoken in central Mexico when nomads like the Aztecs arrived. We draw upon a new biological analysis to support the broad conclusion that there was substantial gene flow from northwestern Mexico into the central basin of Mexico some time between the Formative and Late post-Classic periods.

## 3. EVIDENCE FOR DIVERSIFICATION IN LANGUAGE VARIATION

### 3.1. THE CREATION OF COLONIAL CENTRAL NAHUATL

In addition, as Hasler, Canger, Valiñas, and others have already emphasized, in contrast to a belief perhaps inherent in the use of the term "Classical" for the Colonial Central variant, it is important to point out that the Central Nahua represented in the colonial data was not the direct representative of a historical mother language from which the rest of Nahua dialects derived. Rather, the position of the Colonial Central dialect is a reflection of the history of the number of migrations at different points in time and of populations with diverse linguistic repertoires, beginning with the Eastern Nahua migration and followed by those of the Western Nahua speakers in the post-Classic. Their speakers have together created variants of a Central dialect spoken in a somewhat vaguely defined area in the central highlands that includes Tenochtitlan-Tlatelolco, Tetzcoco, the northern areas of Morelos, and also areas of central Puebla and Tlaxcala. Canger (1988, 65) and Whittaker (1988) provide more detailed information on the sociolinguistic variation notable in the same Central area evident in the Colonial materials.

### 3.2A. LINGUISTIC EVIDENCE FOR DIVERSIFICATION

#### 3.2A.1. EARLIER PROPOSALS

Understanding the conformation through dialect and language contact of Colonial Central Nahua, among the settlements by different groups coming in as described, is based on identifying the linguistic changes that have resulted in the diversification of the different Nahua dialects. It is possible also to posit some of the chronological sequence in which those changes must have occurred. These steps can be carried out with the tools of the comparative method that permit the ordering of morphophonological changes in particular. They provide evidence to identify the different groups and their stages of development. As noted in section 1, additional evidence is found in the sharing of vocabulary through lexical statistical comparisons, but it is harder to provide chronological ordering for it.

With our growing knowledge of the principal but contrasting variants still existing today, and to some degree from records of those that are now extinct, it has been possible, however, to formulate a number of hypotheses for the diversification of Nahua that underlie the Colonial and present-day dialect situations. The hypotheses are also based on reconstructions that let us identify at least the major linguistic innovations.

Both Canger (1980, 1988) and Pharao Hansen (2014) have provided more detailed summaries of the history of the theories that have been developed from the early twentieth century on and that are still going through changes as increasing evidence is acquired.

A first question that has been raised in the process of the expansion of older Nahua is, What linguistic evidence is there for a first basic split or basic splits in that diversification? A second related question, noted earlier, has to do with what we can reconstruct about the dialect situation of Pochutec Nahua as it represents older Western Nahua in relation to the other variants found in western Mexico, since initial proposals such as those of Juan Hasler (1954, 2011) and Campbell and Langacker (1978) had considered it a complete break from the rest of Nahua.

The history of our changing views of the sociohistorical nature of the Nahua language and the identification of the important variation it contains is interesting in itself, however. Its more scientific beginnings were in the first half of the twentieth century.

Canger (1988, 29–35) points out that Walter Lehmann (1920, 973), J. Alden Mason (1936), and Whorf (1946), in considering early observations about Nahua variants, suggest that the differences between Colonial Central Nahuatl and the variants in southern Mexico and Central America represent contrasts between the language spoken by the older Toltec migrations and later Aztec ones. Lehmann (1920, 790) also contrasts a variant he calls pre-Toltec both with the "Soconusco Pipil" and with Guatemalan and El Salvadorean Pipil and Nicarao Nahua variants. In addition, he notes that he is not clear about the relationship with the Pochutec variant, which Boas had described in 1911–1917, only shortly before Lehmann's work (1920, 212). Canger also cites Whorf's 1946 classification of Nahua dialects (figure 2.3).

For the more historical interests here, note that Whorf clearly expressed in his classification, in reference to the Nahua dialects without *tl*, or "Nahuat," that the

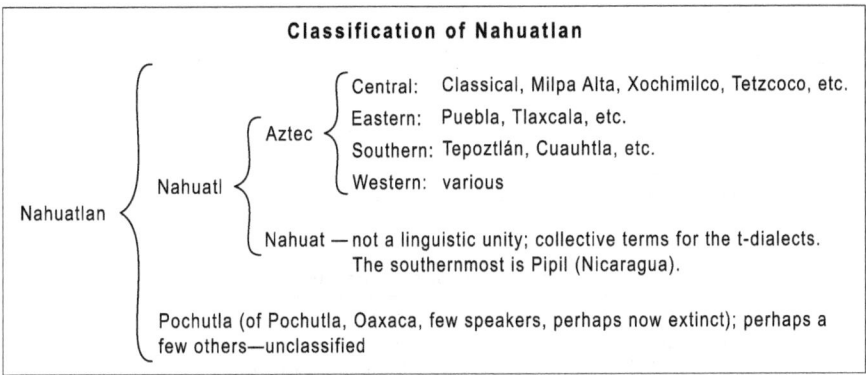

**Figure 2.3.** A simplified version of Mason's and Whorf's classification of Nahuatlan (Whorf 1946, 367).

latter are "not a linguistic unity and that Nahuat is the collective term for the t-dialects including the southernmost language, Pipil (Nicaragua)" (Whorf 1946, 367). He also does not attempt to classify the Nahua dialect of Pochutla, noting only that there were few speakers and that it was "now extinct."

However, a more detailed look at Nahua dialects was first made by Juan A. Hasler, using data from a wider range of variants, including those from his own additional work on those spoken in the Isthmus and some other areas as well. He developed a theory of the overall diversification and the history of the migrations of Nahua speakers. These ideas are developed in his publications and manuscripts beginning in the 1954 and continuing into the 1990s and the twenty-first century but are then included and in some cases revised and updated in two volumes published in 2011 and 2013, *Estudios nahuas* and *Estudios tuztecos y de la región olmeca*.

Hasler's aim is to offer a brief vision of the diversification process. For example, in speaking of the central highlands area, he notes the following, relevant to the relation of the speakers in western Mexico: "In migrating, not only have they separated into two groups [the Pochutec speakers and the Eastern groups], but also these separate from a third group, that of the Nahuas who remained in the mythical land of their origins, the Chicome-Óztoc of Arid America." In this way, Hasler takes the position that Pochutec was a completely separate branch: "The extinct Pochutec was the last survivor *of a modality or group of dialects descendants from the Nahua introduced by the first immigrants who had arrived from the north*" (italics added). Of the later migrations, he writes, "the Nahua Chichimec come [face] to face with Mesoamericanized groups" and "some go to the eastern Huasteca" (J. Hasler 2011, 103–105), so he seems to have considered the eastern Huasteca of Western rather than Eastern Nahua origins, probably because of the presence of the *tl* phoneme.

**TABLE 2.1.** Juan Hasler's dialect divisions (1954)

| |
|---|
| 1. Nahua septentrional (which later he changed to "nahua del norte" / "northern nahua") |
| 2. Central Nahua (the highlands of "Anáhuac" and Puebla) |
| 3. Western Nahua (the groups in both the Western and Southern Sierra Madre and in the state of Guerrero) |
| 4. Eastern Nahua (from the "Sierra de Puebla" to Central America) |

**TABLE 2.2.** Juan Hasler's three proposed migration routes (1972)

| |
|---|
| a. One that resulted in a chain of western dialects that he relates to a "Pochutec type" (His outline for this group was sketchy, but it was based on specific features, of importance among them, because of its contrast with Eastern dialects, the clitic $ō$ = for past [Hasler (1976) 2011, 119]). |
| b. A second route formed a "major eastern dialect chain, from the Sierra de Puebla to Central America" (Hasler [1976] 2011, 119). |
| c. The third refers to the conformation of the central area, and he notes clearly, "We suppose that they [Nahua migrants] brought successive states of the language during the stage of the migrations, the groups separated and their languages were becoming divergent." |

In his 1954 publication, Hasler had divided Nahua dialects into four groups, given in table 2.1.

In relation to the possible paths of the migrations that led to dialect diversification, in 1972, J. Hasler ([1976] 2011, 141–145) proposed three main routes that he considered the Nahuas followed in their movements from the western area south, listed in table 2.2.

Beginning in 1980 with the publication of Canger's book, additional points that relate to the identification of isoglosses and ordering for the stages of the diversification have been addressed and various proposals made. In part, these recent proposals have benefited from an increasing amount of information on a much wider range of Nahua variants. A major source for those data are the results of Lastra de Suárez's extensive survey (1986) and more and more descriptive materials slowly provided from other researchers. The particular interest here is on the work that has sought to develop a historical interpretation of the linguistic materials themselves, beginning with earlier hypotheses. These include Canger and Dakin (1985), Canger (1980, 1988), mentioned earlier, and Pharao Hansen (2014), as well as several other proposals relevant to particular points.[3] The main emphasis in the discussion in this chapter is limited, first, to a small number isoglosses that are the basis

---

[3] See Canger (2011, 2018), Cortina-Borja and Valiñas (1989), Valiñas Coalla (2010, 2017), and Yáñez Rosales (2013).

for distinguishing the early Western Nahua/Eastern Nahua split, and, then, to the ways that speakers of the different variants have come to coexist with the influx of Western Nahua Chichimec migrants into the Basin of Mexico (Canger 1988, 2011; Whittaker 1988).

### 3.2B. LINGUISTIC EVIDENCE: ISOGLOSSES
### 3.2.1 *TL

Perhaps the most well-known and obvious contrast in Nahua dialectology is that between those variants that have the lateralized affricate *tl* coexisting with a simple occlusive *t*, while others have only *t*, and also in a small number either of *l* or *t* or both realizations in different positions corresponding to the *tl*. Sapir reconstructed *\*tl* for proto-Uto-Aztecan simply because he could not identify any correspondences in other Uto-Aztecan languages that would have given origin to the *tl*. It was Whorf, in his well-known article from 1937, who argued that it was an innovation confined to *tl* dialects that occurred before a following *\*a*, either actually present or, according to his theories, reconstructible. Campbell and Langacker (1978) and Canger (1980) reconstructed *\*tl* for all Nahua, basing their reconstruction on the occurrence of -*l* correspondences to -*tl* found in some morphological structures in -*t* dialects. That reconstruction has been generally accepted for proto-Nahua.

However, Dakin has argued, in addition, that *tl* may have had its early origins in proto-Uto-Aztecan, not as a unit phoneme but in sequences of *\*t-\*l* and *\*l-\*t* that eventually developed through vowel loss to fuse as a lateral affricate. A number of cognate constructions found in final position in the formation of deverbal nouns or as remnants of the old case marker *\*t* and other affixes containing *\*l* can be identified in other Uto-Aztecan languages (Dakin 1995, 2017). In any case, the important point for historical subgrouping, if the reconstruction of *\*tl* for proto-Nahua is correct, is that it is possible to see that there are cases of groups of -*t* dialects, in which the loss of the lateral is a shared innovation, as found in the southern Eastern Nahua group, in contrast with the presence of a *tl*, a retention and reconstructible to the protolanguage. A perhaps more controversial proposal, related to the change of lateral affricate *tl* to a simple *t*, is included in 3.2.5, the last section on dialect innovations, in which arguments are given for tying the loss of the lateral feature in *tl* to a more general innovation that has affected other consonant clusters with *\*l*.

### 3.2.2. PUA **U > I,E

The second change discussed here is, we have argued (Canger 1988; Canger and Dakin 1985; Dakin 2017), the oldest change in the development of proto-Nahua

**TABLE 2.3.** Vowel changes from proto-Uto-Aztecan to Eastern and Western Nahua

| |
|---|
| \*\*a > \*a |
| \*\*o > \*o |
| \*\*iᵃ > \*e |
| \*\*i > \*i |
| \*\*u > i in Eastern Nahua<br>    > i, e in Western Nahua |

a. PUA \*\*i = e in all southern languages except for Tepiman.

**TABLE 2.4.** Examples of pUA *u > i/e split

| pUA | | pUA | Eastern Nahua | Western Nahua | 'Gloss' |
|---|---|---|---|---|---|
| \*\*u | /s_n | \*\*sun- | sin- | sen | 'corn' |
| | /t_s | \*\*tusV | tis- | tes | 'grind' |
| | /t_l | \*\*tulV | tlatil- | tlatel- | 'mound, hill' |
| | | \*\*mukV | miki | miki | 'die, suffer' |
| | | \*\*tsu | tsi | tsi | 'bone-' (lexical prefix) |

from proto-Uto-Aztecan, given that it divides the whole Nahua area and has its origins at the point in time when the five-vowel pUA system was a four-vowel system in Nahua variants: *a, *o, *e, and *i.[4] The important difference between Eastern and Western Nahua is clearly marked in the ways the two groups organized the changes in pUA **u.

What happened to pUA *u? In Eastern Nahua **u became i in all environments, a simple change fronting the back high vowel to a front high vowel. However, in Western Nahua, although in most environments **u was fronted to i just as in Eastern Nahua, there was one significant difference, where instead, under very specific conditions, it became the lower front vowel e. Examples of this change are given in table 2.4.

The distribution of the forms in the two principal dialects is very systematic. As a result, it is evidence for concluding that the Eastern Nahuas must have separated from Western Nahuas before pUA **u had completed the change, and following its separation, in Eastern Nahua, all **u > Eastern Nahua /i/. However, in Western Nahua, the change was different: **u > i in *almost* all cases, but in the specific

---

[4] Although phonetic realizations of **o in many dialects is [u], it is not a reflex of and does not correspond to pUA *u.

TABLE 2.5. Southern Uto-Aztecan *wa = 'past' clitic > introduced in Western and Central branches only

| *Western Nahua* | | |
|---|---|---|
| Pochutec (Boas) | e = quíz-c | |
| | /e = kis-k/ | 'he/she left' |
| | e = tém-c | |
| | /e = tem-k/ | 'it finished' |
| *Central Nahua* | | |
| Colonial Central Nahua | ō = quīz | |
| | /ō = kīs/ | 'he/she left' |
| Colonial Central Nahua | ō = tlan | |
| | /ō = tlan/ | 'it finished' |
| *Eastern* | | |
| Huasteca Nahua | kīs-ki | |
| | /kīs-ki/ | 'he/she left' |
| Huasteca Nahua (Hidalgo) | /tlan-ki/ | 'it finished' (Beller and Beller 1979) |

phonetic environment after *t or *s and before certain consonants, it became *e. In this case, then, there is a basic early split between Eastern and Western Nahua groups. Our proposal is now generally accepted.

Campbell and Langacker's 1978 proposal held that **u had a different reflex in Pochutec than in the rest of Nahua and should be a separate branch from what they called "General Aztec." However, this proposal was based on limited data, and because it does not distinguish the basic contrast between the noted reflexes of the same **u, it is incompatible with the Eastern/Western correspondences just shown as they hold for Pochutec. Dakin (2017) offers more detailed examples that are included to show the problems involved.

### 3.2.3. ō = , 'PAST'

There is a third important contrast between Western and Eastern Nahuas that also lets us establish a chronology for the sound changes involved (see table 2.5). The use of the preclitic ō = , 'past', is an innovation found only in Western Nahua and not in Eastern Nahua, and so can be interpreted as a change in its early history limited to the Western Nahua dialects. Part of the importance of the innovation of the ō = is that it is cognate with a *wa* = clitic in Huichol and Cora, one that also corresponds to *ga* = and *va* = in Tepiman and may have cognates in other Uto-Aztecan languages as well.

In Corachol, Nahua *ō* = corresponds to variants *a* = and *o* =. Its incorporation as *ō* = in Nahua is in keeping with the *wa* > *ō* change frequent in Nahua inflectional morphology, such as the imperative and future constructions of verbs derived with *-o(w)a*. Its absence in Eastern Nahua in contrast with its incorporation into Western Nahua can be explained as probably due to contact with Corachol languages in western Mexico but at a time point following the separation of Eastern Nahua.

This third contrast is of key importance for the grouping of Pochutec in Western Nahua because it is also found in all of Boas's examples of past-tense verbs in Pochutec as *e* =, which is the vowel that corresponds to the *a* = alternant of the Corachol and Nahua forms. Initial short *a* corresponds regularly to *e* in Pochutec Nahua in open syllables so that *e* = is the expected cognate form for the *ō* = clitic in Pochutec.

This use is good evidence that Pochutec was an integral part of Western Nahua, especially because it shared a feature that had to have developed after the separation of Eastern Nahua described earlier.

It would seem that it was with the movements of the Chichimec Nahua population into central Mexico in the post-Classic period that the *ō* = was introduced, since it is found described in Colonial Central Nahua grammars and texts. Both Canger (1980) and Launey ([1986] 1988) have described limited specific grammatical uses for the *ō* = clitic.

### 3.2.4. \*\**pi* > \**HE*

> *e-* in Eastern Nahua

> *ye-* in Western Nahua

There is a fourth, old contrasting feature between Western and Eastern Nahua, that of the reflexes of the proto-Uto-Aztecan sequence \*\**pi* when in initial position. Word-initial pUA \*\**p* underwent a change, weakening to \**h* in Huichol and Cora, which it also must have done in Nahua. However, in Nahua, what would have been an initial \**h* as in Corachol has in general now been lost, except in two cases. The first, in the forms derived from \**pVCV*, that have lost the following vowel, proto-Nahua has an *h* corresponding to initial pUA\*\**p* when that \**h* has been protected by an initial epenthetic vowel or other prefix, so that it was no longer initial (Dakin 1990), as shown in examples in table 2.6.

The \**h* from \*\**p* must have also been retained in proto-Nahua in the sequences with initial \*\**pi* under discussion, developing to a proto-Nahua \**he-*, as in table 2.7.

**TABLE 2.6.** Examples of contrasts in reflexes of pUA initial **p*

| *pVCV- | Corachol *hVCV | Nahua *(i)hCV |
|---|---|---|
| **pusa* 'wake up' > *hVsa > | Huichol *histi* 'awake' | Nahua *ihsa* 'wake up' |

*pVCV- > *(i)hCV**pa* 'water' and the instrumental applicative suffix *-wa-li-ya:*

| **pa-wa-li-ya* > *haw- > | Huichol *hawríka* 'to swim' | Nahua *ahwilia* 'to water' |
|---|---|---|
| | (McIntosh and Grimes 1954, 8) | (*GDN*: Carochi 1645) |

**TABLE 2.7.** Examples of dialect contrasts of proto-Nahua **he*

***piti* 'heavy' >

| Proto-Nahua | Eastern Nahua | Western Nahua |
|---|---|---|
| *heti-k | eti-k | yeti-k |

***piwa-* 'skin, husk'

| *hewa | ewa- | yewa- |
|---|---|---|

(cf. Nahua *xi-pēua /šipēwa/* 'to skin', in which the pUA ***p* is not initial); Mayo retains the **p*: *péute* 'is skinning' (Stubbs 2011, 333).

The importance of this change as an isogloss is that while in the Eastern dialects, the initial **h* from **p* was lost completely in all environments after separating from the Western Nahuas, the pUA sequence ***pi* became initial *ye* in Western Nahua, probably through the fronting of the old **he* to *ye-*, most likely in the Classic period. Dakin (2000, 2017) provides more specifics on the development of pUA **p* to *h* in those specific environments.

And if Beekman and Christensen's hypothesis that the Nahua homeland was actually in the Bajío is correct, it may have been that it was the Western Nahuas who moved farther west into Jalisco, Nayarit, and the coast of Michoacán, coming into more contact with Indigenous language speakers in that area.

### 3.2.5. LOSS OF -L- IN CONSONANT CLUSTERS

The fifth and last important dialect innovation under discussion, related to the changes discussed in section 3.2.1 of proto-Nahua **tl* to *t*, *has* not been studied as extensively as the changes in Western Nahua previously described, but it can also be considered to have featured in the change in at least some of the same dialects (Dakin 2015, 2016, 2020). Tentative analysis suggests that the loss of the lateral element in the change from *tl-* to *t-* is actually a more general change that occurs in consonant clusters formed historically with *l*, especially in the southern branch of

Eastern Nahua. Phonologically, and perhaps also in terms of the dialectology, the two changes may well be related to the same phonological process: loss of the lateral element in consonant clusters with -*l*-.

It was Canger (1980, 130) who first identified an applicative construction with an -*lw*- cluster, which she analyzed as an innovating metathesis for the forms for verbs in *\*-o(w)a*. Dakin (2006a, 2006b) developed a historical analysis for the verbs in Canger's -*oa* classification. She proposed that all -*oa* verbs were derived by adding *\*-li-wa suffix* to a verb root, and that the -*l*- was lost following certain consonants. If that reconstruction is correct, then the innovation in the applicative formations would be more on the part of dialects that do not have the -*lwia* applicative, in other words, that the change is the loss of an original -*l*- in the derivation -*\*li-wa-lia*, rather than a metathesis of the *w* and *l* in -*w(i)lia*. This proposal is based on the fact that the data for the distribution are limited and not completely clear but that the applicative without the -*lw*- sequence is found especially in a number of Eastern Nahua variants, suggesting that the original first -*l*- has been lost in these forms. Examples Canger includes show that the -*l*- of the suffix is retained in Colonial Central Nahua and that in the Huauchinango area, which is North Puebla, all dialects that also have *tl* keep the *l*:

*pachihui* /pačiwi/, *vi*, 'to cover' and *tlapoa* /tlapowa/, *vi*, 'to open'
  Western Nahua
    Colonial Central Nahua
    *ki-mo- pači- l- wi- lia* / 'he covers himself (HON)'
30.def-refl-verb—nom-vi-apl
    North Puebla
      a. -*pachilhuilia* / *pačilwilia*-
      b. -*tlapo-l-wi(li)a* /tlapo-l-wi-(li)a/ 'to open (for)'

In contrast, although the data are not complete, in at least some *t dialects*, including Mecayapan (Gulf Isthmus), central Guerrero Nahua (Xalitla/Ameyaltepec), and northeast highland Puebla, we find -*wi-lia*.

Eastern Nahua (*[ɬ]*-showing position of *l* lost)
  Sierra of Puebla (northeast highland Puebla [Cuetzalan, Tacuapa]):
    a. *něch-pacho[ɬ]-wi-lia* 'she covers me' (Amith 2018)
    b. *tlapo-[ɬ]wi-lia*

A number of other characteristic contrasts that have been shown to vary along the lines of "Eastern" or "Western" are commented on by Canger (1988, 2011, 2018),

Lastra de Suárez (1986), and Pharao Hansen (2014), and also by A. Hasler Hangert (2011).

The changes discussed in this chapter were chosen because they provide evidence of particular processes of change and support the existence of the Eastern Nahua–Western Nahua split and the change of *tl* to /t/ in the southern Eastern dialects.

### 4. COLONIAL CENTRAL NAHUA: EASTERN INNOVATIONS

In their 1988 publications, Gordon Whittaker describes in detail and Canger also provides examples of variation in the language of Colonial Central Nahua documents that give evidence of the presence of distinct Nahua populations in contact in the Basin of Mexico. Canger (2011) has used the term "Urban Nahua" in her description of that variation and in explanation of the particular sociolinguistic features associated with both language contact and the existence of different chronological layers. Whittaker (1988) proposes tying features of variation in Colonial documents to specific different Nahua groups in Tenochtitlan-Tlatelolco, the Acolhuaca, Eastern Aztec, and Western Aztec in contrast with the Xochimilca, while Canger notes evidence of the existence of both Eastern and Western Nahua speakers in the Colonial period, for instance, in Molina's inclusion of both *cintli* and *centli* and the other pairs that show the Eastern-Western *i/e* variation. Her summing up of the situation follows:

> The considerations presented here have tried to identify the early divisions and features of those dialects, and then to give some idea of the ways in which the layering of language variants one on another provides us with a more precise idea of the conformation of the population, homogeneous in some ways, but representing a number of different dialects who had come together in Tlatelolco-Tenochtitlan, and evidence that can be found in documents and grammars for the coexistence of the early and later Nahua populations (1988, 63–66)

The aims of the present chapter have been, on the one hand, to give a background setting for the diversification of the Nahua language and, on the other hand, to argue for linguistic chronological evidence of the innovations in both Eastern and Western Nahua branches that provide clear proof of their early separation and the importance of both in the early, perhaps Teotihuacan, era and later Chichimec migrations into the central area, where they developed the variants of the Central Nahua dialects described in the Colonial period and present in the area today.

## REFERENCES

Amith, Jonathan D. 2018. "Nahuatl of the Sierra Nororiental de Puebla: Dictionary, Mesolex, Lexicosemantic resources for Mesoamerican languages (under construction)." https://staging.mesolex.org.

Beekman, Christopher S. 2015. "Causes and Consequences of Migration in Epiclassic Northern Mesoamerica." In *Migration and Disruptions*, edited by Brenda J. Baker and Takeyuki Tsuda, 73–96. Gainesville: University Press of Florida.

Beekman, Christopher S., and Alexander F. Christensen. 2003. "Controlling for Doubt and Uncertainty through Multiple Lines of Evidence: A New Look at the Mesoamerican Nahua Migrations." *Journal of Archaeological Method and Theory* 10 (2): 111–164.

Beller N., Ricardo, and Patricia Cowan de Beller. 1979. "Huasteca Nahuatl." In *Modern Aztec Sketches*, edited by Ronald W. Langacker, 199–306. Dallas: Summer Institute of Linguistics and University of Texas at Arlington.

Boas, Franz. 1917. "El dialecto mexicano de Pochutla, Oaxaca." *International Journal of American Linguistics* 1: 9–44.

Campbell, Lyle, and Ronald W. Langacker 1978. "Proto-Aztecan Vowels." *International Journal of American Linguistics* 44: I, 85–102; II, 197–210; III, 262–279.

Canger, Una. 1980. *Five Studies Inspired by Nahuatl Verbs in -oa*. Travaux du Cercle Linguistique de Copenhague 19. Copenhagen: Lingvistkredsen.

Canger, Una. 1988. "Nahuatl Dialectology: A Survey and Some Suggestions." *International Journal of American Linguistics* 54 (1): 28–72.

Canger, Una. 2011. "El náhuatl urbano de Tlatelolco/Tenochtitlan, resultado de convergencia entre dialectos: Con un esbozo brevísimo de la historia de los dialectos." *Estudios de cultura náhuatl* 42: 243–258.

Canger, Una. 2018. "La primera escisión básica dialectal de la lengua nawatl otra vez: Invitación a discusión." Paper presented to the Friends of Uto-Aztecan Annual Meeting, Universidad de Guadalajara, Guadalajara, June 27.

Canger, Una, and Karen Dakin. 1985. "An Inconspicuous Basic Split in Nahuatl." *International Journal of American Linguistics* 54: 258–261.

Cortina-Borja, Mario, and Leopoldo Valiñas C. 1989. "Some Remarks on Uto-Aztecan Classification." *International Journal of American Linguistics* 55 (2): 214–239.

Dakin, Karen. 1980. "Commentary on Wick Miller's 'The Internal Classification of Uto-Aztecan Based on Lexical Evidence.'" Symposium on Uto-Aztecan Historical Linguistics, Linguistic Institute, Albuquerque, June.

Dakin, Karen. 1983. "Proto-Aztecan Vowels and Pochutec: An Alternative Analysis." *International Journal of American Linguistics* 49: 196–203.

Dakin, Karen. 1991. "Raíces en *ih-* y *ah-* en el náhuatl y la \*\*p protoyutoazteca." *Estudios de cultura náhuatl* 20: 261–280.

Dakin, Karen. 1995. "Contribuciones de las fuentes coloniales a la lingüística yutoazteca histórica." *La "découverte" des langues et des écritures d'Amérique*, edited by Duna Troiani. *Amerindia* 19–20: 211–222.

Dakin, Karen. 2000. "Proto-Uto-Aztecan \*p and the *e-/ye-* Isogloss in Nahuatl Dialectology." *Uto-Aztecan Structural, Temporal, and Geographic Perspectives, Papers in Memory of Wick R. Miller*, edited by Eugene H. Casad and Thomas L. Willett, 213–220. Hermosillo: UNISON and the Summer Institute of Linguistics.

Dakin, Karen. 2003. "Uto-Aztecan in the Linguistic Stratigraphy of Mesoamerican Prehistory." In *Language Contacts in Prehistory. Studies in Stratigraphy*, edited by Henning Andersen, 259–288. Philadelphia and Amsterdam: John Benjamins.

Dakin, Karen. 2006a. "Aspectos históricos de la evolución de la clase de verbos nahuas en *-oa*." *V Encuentro Internacional de Lingüística en Acatlán*, edited by Pilar Máynez and María Rosario Dosal G., 425–440. Mexico City: Facultad de Estudios Superiores Acatlán, Universidad Nacional Autónoma de México.

Dakin, Karen. 2006b. "Verbos nahuas en \*-li-wa: Una interpretación histórica de los verbos en *-oa*." *Memorias del VIII Encuentro Internacional de Lingüística en el Noroeste*, vol. 2, edited by Rosa María Ortiz Ciscomani, 217–230. Hermosillo, Mexico: UniSon.

Dakin, Karen. 2010. "Linguistic Evidence for Historical Contact between Nahuas and Northern Lowland Mayan Speakers." In *Astronomers, Scribes, and Priests: Intellectual Interchange between the Northern Maya Lowlands and Highland Mexico in the Late Post-Classic Period*, edited by Gabrielle Vail and Christine Hernández, 217–240. Washington, DC: Dumbarton Oaks.

Dakin, Karen. 2015. "New Phonemes from Consonant Clusters in Uto-Aztecan Nominalizations: Evidence from the Development of Resultatives." II International Congress of Mesoamerican Linguistics, California State University–Los Angeles, March.

Dakin, Karen. 2016. "Conformación del náhuatl central: Hipótesis sobre sus variaciones y sobre la cronología de las isoglosas, Conferencia magistral." XI Coloquio de Lingüística en la ENAH, April.

Dakin, Karen. 2017. "Western and Central Nahua Dialects: Possible Influences from Contact with Cora and Huichol." In *Language Contact and Change in Mesoamerica and Beyond*, edited by Karen Dakin, Claudia Parodi, and Natalie Operstein, 263–300. Amsterdam: John Benjamins.

Dakin, Karen. 2020. "Grupos consonánticos y la palatalización morfológica en el naua: el papel de la disimilación." In *Lenguas yutoaztecas: historia, estructuras y contacto lingüístico. Homenaje a Karen Dakin*, coordinated by Rosa H. Yáñez Rosales, 37–58. Guadalajara: Universidad de Guadalajara.

Dakin, Karen, and Søren Wichmann. 2000. "Cacao and Chocolate: A Uto-Aztecan Perspective." *Ancient Mesoamerica* 11: 55–75.

Fowler, Catherine S. 1983. "Lexical Clues to Uto-Aztecan Prehistory." *International Journal of American Linguistics* 49: 224–257.

Fowler, William R., Jr. 1989. *The Cultural Evolution of Ancient Nahua Civilizations: The Pipil-Nicarao of Central America*. Norman: University of Oklahoma Press.

*Gran Diccionario Náhuatl (GDN)* [en línea]. Universidad Nacional Autónoma de México [Ciudad Universitaria, México D.F.]: 2012 [ref del 28-07-2023]. http://www.gdn.unam.mx.

Hansen, Magnus Pharao. 2014. "The East-West Split in Nahuan Dialectology: Reviewing the Evidence and Consolidating the Grouping." Paper presented to the Friends of Uto-Aztecan Annual Meeting, Universidad Autónoma de Nayarit, Tepic, Nayarit, June 20.

Hansen, Magnus Pharao. 2017. "The Relation between Nahuatl, Cora and Huichol: Initial Thoughts." *Nawatl Scholar* (blog), July 6. http://nahuatlstudies.blogspot.mx/2017/07/the-relation-between-nahuatl-cora-and.html.

Hasler, Juan A. 1954. "Los cuatro dialectos de la lengua Mexicana." *Revista mexicana de estudios antropológicos* 14: 145–146.

Hasler, Juan A. (1972) 1976. "La situación dialectológica del pochuteco." *International Journal of American Linguistics* 42 (3): 268–273.

Hasler, Juan A. (1976) 2011. *Estudios nahuas*. Xalapa: Universidad Veracruzana.

Hasler, Juan A. 2013. *Estudios tuztecos y de la región olmeca*. Xalapa: Universidad Veracruzana.

Hasler Hangert, Andrés 2011. *El nahua de la Huasteca y el primer mestizaje: Treinta siglos de historia nahua a la luz de la dialectología*. Mexico City: Centro de Investigaciones y Estudios Superiores en Antropología Social and Publicaciones de la Casa Chata.

Hill, Jane H. 2001. "Proto-Uto-Aztecan: A Community of Cultivators in Central Mexico." *American Anthropologist* 103: 913–934.

Hill, Jane H. 2017. "The Languages of the Aztec Empire." In *The Oxford Handbook of the Aztecs*, edited by Deborah L. Nichols and Enrique Rodríguez-Alegría, 129–142. Oxford: Oxford University Press.

Hill, Jane H. 2019. "How Mesoamerican Are the Nahua Languages?" In *Migrations in Late Mesoamerica*, edited by Christopher S. Beekman, 43–65. Gainesville: University Press of Florida.

Justeson, John S., William N. Norman, Lyle Campbell, and Terrence Kaufman. 1985. *The Foreign Impact on Lowland Mayan Language and Script*. Middle American Research Institute 53. New Orleans: Tulane University.

Kaufman, Terrence. 2001. "The History of the Nawa Language Group from the Earliest Times to the Sixteenth Century: Some Initial Results." Manuscript. https://www.albany.edu/pdlma/Nawa.pdf.

Lamb, Sydney M. 1964. "The Classification of the Uto-Aztecan Languages: A Historical Survey." *University of California Publications in Linguistics* 34: 106–125. Berkeley: University of California Press.

Lastra de Suárez, Yolanda. 1986. *Las áreas dialectales del náhuatl moderno*. Mexico City: Instituto de Investigaciones Antropológicas, Universidad Nacional Autónoma de México.

Launey, Michel. (1986) 1988. *Catégories et opérations dans la grammaire nahuatl*. PhD diss., Université Paris-Sorbonne. Lille: Atelier National de Reproduction des Thèses.

Lehmann, Walter 1920. *Zentral-Amerika. I. Teil: Die Sprachen Zentral-Amerikas in ihren Beziehungen zueinander sowie zu Süd-Amerika und Mexiko*. Berlin: Dietrich Reimer.

Macri, Martha J., and Matthew G. Looper. 2003. "Nahua in Ancient Mesoamerica: Evidence from Maya Inscriptions." *Ancient Mesoamerica* 14: 285–297.

Manzanilla, Linda. 1985. "El mundo clásico mesoamericano." In *Atlas histórico de Mesoamérica*, edited by Linda Manzanilla and Leonardo López Luján, 74–76. Mexico City: Larousse.

Mason, J. Alden. 1936. "The Classification of the Sonoran Languages." In *Essays in Anthropology Presented to Alfred L. Kroeber*, edited by Robert H. Lowic, 183–198. Berkeley: University of California Press.

McIntosh, Juan B. and José Grimes. 1954. *Vocabulario huichol-castellano, castellano-huichol*. Mexico City: Summer Institute of Linguistics and Dirección General de Asuntos Indígenas.

Medina García, Ricardo. 2016. "Nahuatl-Language Petitions and Letters from Northwestern New Spain, 1580–1694." PhD diss., University of California Los Angeles.

Mentz, Brígida von. 2017. "Topónimos y cronología: Notas sobre una puerta distinta al estudio del pasado." *Historia mexicana* 67 (1): 7–59.

Merrill, William L. 2013. "The Genetic Unity of Southern Uto-Aztecan." *Language Dynamics and Change* 3: 68–104.

Miller, Wick R. 1984. "The Classification of the Uto-Aztecan Languages Based on Lexical Evidence." *International Journal of American Linguistics* 50: 1–24.

Molina, Fray Alonso de. (1571) 1970. *Vocabulario en lengua castellana y mexicana y mexicana y castellana*. Facsimile edition. Mexico City: Porrúa.

*Relaciones geográficas del siglo XVI: Antequera*, 1984. Edited by René Acuña. 2 vols. Mexico City: Instituto de Investigaciones Antropológicas, Universidad Nacional Autónoma de México.

Stubbs, Brian D. 2011. *Uto-Aztecan: A Comparative Vocabulary*. Blanding, UT: Rocky Mountain Books and Publications.

Valiñas Coalla, Leopoldo José M. 1979. "El náhuatl en Jalisco, Colima y Michoacán." *Anales de Antropología* 14: 325–344.

Valiñas Coalla, Leopoldo José M. 1981. "El náhuatl de la periferia occidental y la costa del Pacífico." Tesis para el título de licenciado en antropología con especialidad en lingüística, Mexico City. Escuela Nacional de Antropología e Historia.

Valiñas Coalla, Leopoldo José M. 2010. "Historia lingüística: Migraciones y asentamientos. Relaciones entre pueblos y lenguas." In *Historia Sociolingüística de México*, vol. 1, ed. Rebeca Barriga Villanueva and Pedro Martín Butragueño, 97–160. Mexico City: Colegio de México.

Valiñas Coalla, Leopoldo José M. 2017. "La negación en el náhuatl del centro de Guerrero." *Cuadernos de Lingüística de El Colegio de Mexico* 4 (1): 49–101.

Whittaker, Gordon. 1986. "The Mexican Names of Three Venus Gods in the Dresden Codex." *Mexicon* 8 (3): 56–60.

Whittaker, Gordon. 1988. "Aztec Dialectology and the Nahuatl of the Friars." In *The Work of Bernardino de Sahagún, Pioneer Ethnographer of Sixteenth-Century Aztec Mexico*, edited by José Jorge Klor de Alva, H. B. Nicholson, and Eloise Quiñones Keber, 321–372. Albany and Austin: University of New York at Albany and University of Texas.

Whorf, Benjamin L. 1937. "The Origin of Aztec tl." *American Anthropologist*. 39: 265–274.

Whorf, Benjamin L. 1946. "The Milpa Alta Dialect of Aztec." In *Linguistic Structures of Native America*, edited by Harry Hoijer, 367–397. New York: Viking Fund Publications. [Reprinted by Johnson Reprint Company Limited, 1963.]

Yáñez Rosales, Rosa. 2013. *Ypan altepet monotza san Antonio de padua tlaxomulco, "En el pueblo que se llama San Antonio de Padua, Tlajomulco," Textos en lengua náhuatl, siglos XVII y XVIII*. Guadalajara: Instituto de Cultura, Recreación y Deportes, Gobierno Municipal de Tlajomulco de Zúñiga and Prometeo Editores.

Yáñez Rosales, Rosa. 2017. "Nahuatl L2 Texts from Northern Nueva Galicia: Indigenous Language Contact in the Seventeenth Century." In *Language Contact and Change in Mesoamerica and Beyond*, edited by Karen Dakin, Claudia Parodi, and Natalie Operstein, 237–262. Amsterdam: John Benjamins.

Yáñez Rosales, Rosa, and Álvaro Torres Nila. 2018. "¿Náhuatl y coca en contacto? Documentos coloniales del sur del obispado de Guadalajara." In *Lenguas en contacto en el México colonial y contemporáneo: Español y lenguas indígenas*, edited by Saúl Santos, 5–21. Tepic: Universidad Autónoma de Nayarit.

# 3

## Naming the Space

*Diphrases and the Cultural Construction of Place-Names*

MERCEDES MONTES DE OCA VEGA

### 1. INTRODUCTION

Naming places is not always a straightforward process; it is necessary to identify the naming patterns in specific cultures. As Anthony Webster says, "places do not only exist out there to be named, rather they are socially, morally, and politically constituted" (2000, 230), and I would add another important aspect: they are culturally motivated.

The aim of this chapter is to expose the way diphrases, which are important linguistic structures in institutional discourses, construe and define spaces of various kinds, such as geographic, mythic, and conceptual. Diphrases employed in naming spaces build spatial representation schemes.

So let us begin by reviewing the definition of diphrases, also known as semantic couplets. A diphrase is a linguistic structure that by means of the juxtaposition of two (or more) terms constructs a different meaning from the one portrayed by the lexemes that integrate it.

While this is the definition of full or prototypical diphrases, as the one that refers to war.

| *in teōātl* | *in tlachinōlli* |
| the sea | something burnt |

there is another type, whose constituents do build their meaning through a compositional reading. In the same conceptual space as war, the next example belongs to this second type of semantic couplet:

> *in chīmalli*   *in tlahuiztli*[1]
> Shield        weapons

Lexical or semantic relations between the terms of the couplet are of diverse type: synonymy, similarity, opposition, antonymy, contrast, hyponymy, complementarity, part-whole relationship, parasinonymy, interdependency, and genre-specific (Montes de Oca 2013, 12, 39).

There has been some controversy regarding the number of terms that can compose a couplet. Some researchers have proposed that three, four, or more lexical items can form couplets (Dehouve 2009; Tedlock 1985). My stance on this matter stems from several corpora I have built through the search for diphrases or couplets in colonial sources. I have found that the most pervasive pattern is to have two lexical units forming a couplet;[2] frequent variation of this pattern involves having a third member with the very precise semantic function of reinforcing or exposing the meaning of the couplet. Also, if more terms are paired, there is a high chance that the result is a diphrastic chain, two or more adjacent diphrases that appear in the same textual context (Montes de Oca 2013, 82). These lexical structures were of great importance not only in alphabetic texts; they also appear on diverse visual media, including pre-Hispanic codices. Scholars have reported the widespread presence of diphrases on stone, paper, and ceramics in central Mexico (Alcina Franch 1995; Baena 2014; Davis 2015; León Portilla 1996; Mikulska 2008).

Certain types of ritual-institutional discourses are privileged contexts in which diphrases seem to be a frequent lexical item. Because of their ubiquitous presence, they appear to be a lexical obligatory trait in the construction and textual organization of such discourses; it could also be a feature of their oral character. The main function of diphrases, among others, is designation. The use of couplets in specific contexts gives the referent an honorific or relevant status. We may also say that the use of diphrases indicates a selection of special referents in discourse. Not all referents can be designated with a couplet. So, we have the habitual way of referring to things, persons, and places in general in contrast with a more significant or

---

[1] *In mitl* 'the arrow' *in chīmalli* 'the shield' is a prototypical diphrase, and it also refers to war. For all the different diphrases included in the conceptual field of war, see Montes de Oca (2013, 196–200).

[2] This is not a surprising pattern; many languages in the world share the same pattern in relation to semantic couplets (see Montes de Oca 2013, esp. 15–20).

special way of naming using diphrases. For example, the common word for woman is *cihuātl*, but semantic couplets are employed to highlight diverse aspects of being a woman: they can (a) portray a sexual- and gender-related perspective, (b and c) focus on a woman's ability to prepare food, or (c) refer to the weaving task that women carried out in pre-Hispanic times.[3]

| | |
|---|---|
| *(a) in cuēitl* | *in huīpīlli* |
| the skirt | the blouse |
| *(b) in ātl* | *in metlatl* |
| Water | grinding stone |
| *(c) in cōmitl* | *in caxitl* |
| the pot | the plate |
| *(d) in malacatl* | *in tzōtzopāztli* |
| Spindle | weaving stick |

In this chapter, I will be reviewing certain diphrases that designate different types of spaces, so I will treat all names mentioned as place-names. There can be many ways of dissecting or approaching the topic of space, distinguishing, for example, between geographic, mythic, and conceptual places. I will emphasize the interaction of language and cultural motivations in naming spatial locations by diphrases.

Perhaps one of the reasons there are diphrases that designate places is related to one of the functions of these structures, that of privileged communication. Diphrases were an essential element in the communication with gods, ancestors, and dignitaries of high rank. In the same sense, Keith Basso reports, Apache people give a special status to place names because "Apache placenames might be heard by those who use them as repeating verbatim—actually quoting—the speech of their early ancestors" (1996, 10). I could add that using a place-name made up of diphrases sets up a privileged communicative path with the ancestors and other relevant personages. Place diphrases give a unique vantage point from which to perceive and recognize a specific site and the landscape thus activated.

## 2. NAMING THE SPACE

In dealing with how a language names spaces, it is essential to look into the linguistic means for doing this. In Classical Nahuatl, locative expressions can be achieved through morphological or syntactic processes: "A locative can be a nominal modifier, an argument of a motion verb or a verbal modifier" (Sasaki 2011, 5).

---

[3] For details of the semantics of these couplets, see Montes de Oca (2013, 117–120).

I will focus mainly on the linguistic codification of place-names that are basically words with a locative status. The main grammatical resources to express a spatial relationship are morphological suffixes that attach to nominal or verbal roots. Among locative suffixes, the main suffix is *-c(o)*, which is added to inanimate nouns.[4] Another productive suffix added to nouns is *-pan*, a suffix that implies contact with a surface; it can be translated as 'on' or 'by.' Besides being a locative suffix, *-pan* is also considered a relational noun in a possessive paradigm. Other suffixes employed to construct place-names are *-cpac* (over, on top), *-tlān* or *-titlan* (with, near, under), *cān* (place, where), and *-tzālan* (between). There is also a locative suffix used exclusively with verbal forms, *-yān*, and it is highly productive with toponyms.

Not all nouns have the status of place-names in the sense of being proper nouns, but there are also common nouns that refer to different types of locations and have the same linguistic codification. In this sense, we may also consider them place-names. Assessing how pre-Hispanic peoples designated or expressed space through diphrases provides insight into how they conceptualized different types of spaces.

### 3. GEOGRAPHICAL SPACES

Toponyms are proper names given to specific geographic locations. There are different patterns of naming a geographic space, but the focus here is on names constructed with couplets. Toponyms constructed with two lexemes provide sociocultural and historic information besides describing physical characteristics of the landscape. This naming procedure is not special or particular, since cultures around the world use the same naming pattern to denominate geographical referents. For example, in Sumba, an island in eastern Indonesia,

> Weyéwa toponyms may be described as falling into three broad categories: (1) simple, (2) complex, and (3) couplet. A simple toponym is a name which cannot be analyzed into other constituents . . . A complex toponym, by far the most common in Weyéwa, is one that can be decomposed into at least two separate constituents, typically consisting of a noun followed by an adjective modifier . . . Many of the place names of the two types just mentioned are linked to a third kind of name, a couplet name, most often used in ritual contexts as an expansion of or supplement to one of the other names. (Kuipers 1984, 457)

Diphrases that designate place-names have what Eugene Hunn calls "descriptive force," meaning that "place names may indicate some perceptible feature or

---

[4] Launey argues that this is the only real locative suffix, since the others are locative noun suffixes (2011, 116).

meaningful association of the sites named and thus reveal facets of indigenous world view" (1996, 4).

Two significant features of the cultural and geographical landscape appear in the naming process of toponyms in pre-Hispanic times. For example, the couplet *in ātl in tepētl* (the water, the mountain) designated human settlements and is thus translated as *pueblo* (town). Perhaps a more basic couplet speaking in terms of a geographical landscape is *in ātl in tlālli* (the water, the land), which appears in a manuscript from *Izhuatán*, Guatemala, and perhaps in earlier documents:

1. *ce quitemoua yecti tali yecti at. (Dakin 2008)*
    good land is sought, good water is sought.

In the various sources I reviewed, I was not able to find this couplet. However, there is an anthroponym that recovers an archaic locative suffix, *-chi*, which is a derived form of the couplet *in ātl in tlālli*.[5]

2. ā-qui-i-āch                    tlāl-chi-i-āch
   water-LOC-POS-chief/first/elder    land-LOC-POS-chief/first/elder[6]

The complete names of the lords of the Olmeca-Xicalanca that in turn are diphrases were

3. *yn tlalchiyach tizacozque*        *yn aquiyach amapane. (Kirchhoff, Odena Güemes,*
                                                *and Reyes García 1989, 149)*[7]

   the elder of the land              the elder of the water
   the one who has a necklace of      the one who has paper flags
      chalk

Diego Muñoz Camargo recorded these names and their translation in a modified form: "The first advance was made through the side of Cholula where two gentlemen called *Tlaquiach* and *Tlalchiac* ruled and reigned, and those who succeeded in this command were always called by these names, which mean the elder of the high

---

[5] I thank Karen Dakin for bringing to my attention the couplet *tlālchiāch āquiāch* and its locative origin.

[6] LOC = locative, POS = possessive.

[7] In a note, an element in the name glyph of *Tlalchiach* is identified as a black liquid coming out of the personage's head and is interpreted as water (Kirchhoff, Odena Güemes, and Reyes García 1989, 149n2). I think that the material depicted in the name glyph is black soil (*tlālli*).

and the elder of the low ground."⁸ So I believe the trajectory of this naming pattern was from a toponym to an anthroponym and then to a title or military rank. The translation given by Muñoz Camargo regarding the concepts of "high" and "low" is obscure; the one proposed here is "the first [or elder] in the land" and "the first [or elder] in the water."⁹

The few mentions of the diphrase *in ātl in tlālli* contrast with the numerous occurrences of *in ātl in tepētl*, which is a pervasive and important couplet in the configuration of place-names. This can be seen in iconographic records, where the figure of a hill and water coming out from it represent the generic elements that convey the idea of town, and which are present in many toponymic glyphs. The word *āltepētl*, the lexicalized form of the couplet, which Molina translated as "pueblo o rey" (1977, 14r), became an administrative title for settlements that had certain characteristics in terms of population and political power.¹⁰ This diphrase appears in early texts and without restrictions of dialectal variety, as in this example from *Izhuatán*, Guatemala:

4. *chicnauhtepet chicnavi oztoc chicnavi at. (Dakin 2008)*
    nine mountains, nine caves, nine waters

Although toponyms are considered proper names, some common names can refer to a specific geographical site. When they establish a univocal relationship with a certain place, they lose the ability to designate random references. It is worth bearing in mind that the distinction between common and proper nouns does not always hold.

Place-names can have a direct connection or meaning as common nouns, but other place-names are less transparent as to the object they are naming. Consider, for example, *Mēxi'co Tenōchtitlan* and *ācatzalan tōltzalan*. Although both diphrastic

---

⁸ "La primera entrada que se hizo fue por la parte de Cholula donde gobernaban y reynaban dos señores que se llamaban *Tlaquiach* y *Tlalchiac* que siempre los que en este mando sucedían eran llamados deste nombre, que quiere decir el mayor de lo alto y el mayor de lo bajo del suelo" (Muñoz Camargo 1892, 208).

⁹ This meaning could signify recognition or assertion of primacy in the occupation or perhaps in the possession of land and water.

¹⁰ The lexicalization of a couplet reduces the lexical pair to a single structure and as such is used in habitual contexts of speech. The lexicalization of the word *āltepētl* occurred early and coexisted with the ritual couplet *in ātl in tepētl*. For more information about *āltepētl* as a sociopolitical concept that designates a geographic and social entity in charge of leading and administrating justice, see Lockhart (1992). For other aspects involved in the making of the diphrase *in ātl in tepētl*, see Dehouve (2016).

names refer to the same geographical location, they do so in different ways. The first one, *Tenōchtitlan* is a symbolic or conceptual unit whose translation is unnecessary because it is a known name, even if its meaning is not transparent. On the contrary, the meaning of *ācatzalan tōltzalan* has greater transparency, but its translation is necessary because its degree of conventionality and its relation to the named space are not totally fixed. *Ācatzalan tōltzalan* is an alternate way of naming *Tenōchtitlan* that describes geographical features of the landscape, specifically two types of plants, *tōlin* 'rushes' and *ācatl* 'reeds'.

In example 5, the word *Tenōchtitlan*, as the third term of the couplet, gives the meaning of this particular diphrase that functions as a toponym:

5. *Calli xihuitl 1325 ypan in yn acico ynic mocentlallico* **yn toltzallan**
                                          **acatzallan Tenochtitlan**
*yn teochichimeca huehuetque mexica. (Chimalpáin 2012, 238)*[11]
In the year 1325 the old Mexica Teochichimecas came to settle **among the rushes**,
                                            among the reeds in
                                            Tenochtitlan.

Another way to describe this same feature of a real or imaginary landscape appears in the introductory paragraph of the *Crónica mexicáyotl*:

6. *in atl ihtic yn tultzallan*
    *in acatzallan, yhuan mitohua*
        *motenehua tolli ycoyocayan*
            *acatl ycoyocayan. (Crónica mexicáyotl 2021, 78)*
    Inside the water, among the rushes
        among the reeds and it was said
            it was named the place where the rushes blow
                the place where the reeds blow.

In the history of the migration of the Aztec people, there are myriad places that do not correspond to the naming pattern of a single word, starting with the very point of departure:

---

[11] The organization and disposition of textual fragments in a terrace-like manner constitute a personal proposal that highlights parallelism, discursive markers, and particles.

7. *Chicōmoztōc*                      *Aztlān*
the place of the seven caves      the place of the wing / big feather[12]

The name is sometimes composed of three terms, *Quinehuayān Chicōmoztōc Aztlān* (*Crónica mexicáyotl* 2021, 108).[13] The double word pattern also characterizes the final point of arrival:

8. *Chapultepec*                  *Cuitlapilco. (Sahagún 1992, bk. 3, 29)*[14]
at the hill of the grasshopper     at the tai

It is meaningful that the place where the migration starts, *Aztlān*, shares the root *a'aztli* with the first term of the diphrase *in a'aztli in cuitlapilli*,[15] whereas the name of the place of arrival *Cuitlapilco* shares the root *cuitlapilli* with the second term.

9. *in a'ztli*                         *in cuitlapilli*[16]
the wing                              the tail

---

[12] The most recognized meaning for the word *Aztlan* is "place of herons," but this is problematic because it should read *Aztatlan*. A more plausible root seems to be *a'ztli*, attested in Book 11 of the *Florentine Codex*, which refers to the feathers of the eagle: *in jatlapal:itoca ahaztli yoan hapalli yoan mamaztli* (Sahagún 1992, bk. 11, 40). There are also several occurrences as a diphrase, e.g., *in mahaz in mocuitlapil* (your wing, your tail) (Sahagún [1577] 1976, bk. 6, 58). Dakin (2010) relates it to the eagle through the identification of a special type of feather, *ahaztli*, and provides the linguistic arguments for this etymology.

[13] The etymology of *Quinehuayān* proposed by Dakin (2021) is as follows: "In *Quineuayan* place-name, the instrumental element qui-, / ki—/, 'between teeth' enters into composition with a morpheme that is probably an archaic intransitive verb, with variation between -naua/ nawa and -neua / newa, and that surely is related to a verb naua /nawa, 'to speak'." Perhaps this meaning stresses the fact that in the beginning there was not a clear form of communication between the dwellers of the seven caves.

[14] This toponym is also present in the *Crónica mexicayotl* (2021, 124), although *cuitlapilco* is generally translated as "at the back of," the correct locative form for this translation would be -*cuitlapan* or -*tepotzco*.

[15] This couplet referred to common people, or *mācēhualli*, who were responsible for sustaining society; the image portrayed by the wing and the tail is that of a bird, highlighting the parts that enable it to stay in the air and fly.

[16] *In cuitlapilli in a'tlapalli* is more frequent, and the order in which the terms appear is fixed. However, in all occurrences of *in a'aztli in cuitlapilli*, the term for wing always comes first (Sahagún 1992, bk. 6, 23, 58, 137).

As the couplet in 9 designated common people, it is possible that the symbolism of the place of origin and the arrival of the migration of the Mexica people is present in the meaning of the diphrase.[17]

Cholula is another location with alternate names built by diphrases:

*10. Chollolan Tlachiualtepetl Ycatcan. (Kirchhoff, Odena Güemes, and Reyes García 1989, 142)*
    Cholula where the hand-made hill stands.

As I have demonstrated in earlier examples, a common convention to compose place-names throughout Mesoamerica was to use *tepētl*, the word for 'hill':. In the nominal compound, the first noun, *tlachīhualli* (creation, accomplishment, offspring [Karttunen 1992, 254]), stresses the fact that it is a constructed hill, in fact a man-made hill, because it refers to the Great Pyramid that was a sacred center of the town.

Cholula was an important city that achieved notoriety as a sacred city in the Tlaxcallan and Puebla region, so it received the denomination of Tōllān, which described great cities like Teotihuacan and Tula (Rivera 2009, 60).[18] Since the name *Tlalchihualtepetl* was also a designation of Cholula, there are three terms forming the toponym *Tollan Cholollan Tlachihualtepetl*. The ceremonial center of Cholula was synonymous with the Great Pyramid; Tollan Cholollan Tlachihualtepetl was "Cholula city of the man-made mountain" (McCafferty 1996, 12). In the account of the migration of the Tolteca Chichimeca entering the land of the Olmeca-Xicalanaca, the city of Cholula is mentioned several times with other ways of naming the city. Moreover, the name Cholula appears to be the lexicalized form of one of the terms of a diphrase. Ursula Dyckerhoff reports two toponyms in the Huejotzingo area: *ātl īcholoayān ātl īmēyayān* (cited in García Bernal 2006, 252). It is possible that these two terms were joined in a single place-name on the basis of the semantic relatedness of the verbs *choloa* (gush out)[19] and *mēya* (water flowing) and that one of the terms remained as the toponym in a lexicalized form:

---

[17] To read more about the ways in which diphrases acquire meaning, see Montes de Oca (2013).

[18] The name *Tollan* was a metaphoric denomination for places that had certain characteristics of a great city, such as power, a large population, and economic importance. López Luján and López Austin (2007, 44) call attention to the iconographic representation of Tollan in the glyphs that designate the sacred cities.

[19] This meaning is given to the inanimate form of the verb *choloa*, and it applies to a liquid (Wimmer 2007).

11. *Cholo-l-lān*
   gush out-water-LOC

Cholula, then, is highlighted by a diversity of toponyms that name this *āltepētl* explicitly, and I want to propose that the naming convention in this sequence follows the pattern of pairing two predications to designate this geographical space.[20] The origin of these names is not clear nor are the historical or mythic motivations behind this kind of designation.[21] The structural pattern is clear: a locative suffix attached to a nominal or a verbal root. Toponyms of this kind are complex constructions and function as predicates. Thus, in *Historia tolteca chichimeca* the toponyms arranged in a sequence appear to be joined at the semantic level, but it is not clear whether it is a pattern of two or more terms.

12. *in atl yayauhcan*
   the place where the water darkens

   *in iztaquauhtli ytlaquayan*
   the place where the white eagle eats

   *in xochatlauhtli ypilcayan*
   the place where the flowery canyon hangs

   *in quetzaltototl yhicacan*[22]
   the place where the quetzal bird stands

   *in iztac zolin ynemomoxouayan*[23]
   the place where there is scratching of the white quail

   *yn apechtli yyonocan*
   the place where the waterbed lies

---

[20] Reyes asserts that all are names for Cholula, repeated in several paragraphs but not in the exact same way, and should probably be read in groups of four terms (Kirchhoff, Odena Güemes, and Reyes García 1989, 160).

[21] These toponyms have been translated elsewhere; see Rivera Domínguez (2009) and García Bernal (2006). There is variation in some of the translations, and some are problematic. Here I provide my own translation.

[22] Apache place-names have a very similar way of describing the landscape in long toponyms like "big cottonwood trees stand spreading here and there" (Basso 1984, 36).

[23] Translation of this toponym is complicated because the only verb that comes close is *momotzoa* 'to scratch' or 'to claw'. The quails are birds which are more terrestrial, and, apparently, they go on scratching the soil to look for food.

| | |
|---|---|
| *in ecoztlan*[24] | *yn temamatlac* |
| at the arrival | on the stone staircase |
| *yn couatl ypilhuacan* | *yn calmecac* |
| the place where the serpent reproduces | in the corridor |
| *yn atliztac ymancan* | *yn ozomacouatl yn euimollocan*[25] |
| the place where the white water spreads | the place where the monkey-serpent's skin is drawn |
| *yn iztac tollin yxeliuhcan* | *yn iztac xalli yyonocan* |
| the place where the white reeds divide | the place where the white sand spreads. (Kirchhoff et al. 1989, 179) |

Two other important places, Colhuacatepec and Cuauhtinchan, have similar consecutive placenames in *Historia tolteca chichimeca*. For Colhuacatepec Chicomoztoc,[26] the naming pattern consisting of two nouns is clearer:

| | |
|---|---|
| *13. coliuhquitepetl ycatcan* | *atl xoxouhqui ymancan* |
| the place where the curved hill is | the place where the blue water spreads |
| *iztac tollin ymancan* | *iztac acatl ymancan* |
| the place where the white rushes spread | the place where the white reeds spread |
| *iztac uexotl yhicacan* | *iztac axali ymancan* |
| the place where the white willow stands | the place where the white sand spreads |

---

[24] Robelo argues that *e'coztli* is "the name that they also gave to the month called *Paxtontli* and *Teotleco*. It derives from the verb *eco* to arrive and it means arrival" ([1905] 1982, 168). If there is really an association between *e'coztli* and *temamatlac*, perhaps this name is specifying a particular region of the stone staircase, or perhaps it is stressing the function of this staircase. Another possible translation is "yellow bean," but in the context of the stone staircase it is difficult to connect both.

[25] The word *huimoloa* can be translated as draw, trace (Joe Campbell, personal communication).

[26] Reyes identifies these toponyms of Chicomoztoc in a footnote; however, he doesn't pair them in the way done here, and he doesn't provide a translation, which here is my own.

    *tlapapalichcatl yyonocan*      *tlapapalatlacuezonan yyonocan*
    the place where the red cotton lies    the place where the red water lily lies
    *nauallachtli yyonocan*      *yn zaquan miztli*[27] *ymancan*
    the place where the sorcerer ball    the place where the zacuanmiztli spreads.
    court lies

Source: Kirchhoff, Odena Güemes, and Reyes García (1989, 160).

In its turn, Cuauhtinchan is called:

*14. Quauhtli (y)chan*      *ocellotl ychan*[28]
    the house of the eagles      the house of the ocelotl
    *Tlatlauhqui*      *tepexioztoc*[29]
    in the red boulder      in the (the red) cave
    *yn teyocan*[30]      *yn machiyocan*
    the place of the fame      the place of the sign
    *yn auixco*      *yn tepeixco*
    in front of the water      in front of the mountain

The same couplets are used in a different context and not in consecutive order:

*15. Oncan in tlauelmatque yn Chichimeca yn quautli*
                                   *yn ocellotl ychan*
    *yn tlatauhqui tepexioztoc yn teyocan*
                       *yn machiyocan ynic tlatocamaco yn auixco*
                       *yn tepeixco. (Kirchhoff, Odena Güemes, and Reyes García 1989, 197)*
There the Chichimeca were happy in the house of the eagle
                                   (the house) of the ocelotl

---

[27] This term must refer to a type of feline which has some quality of a *zacuan*, a bird of yellow feathers; it could be a cougar.

[28] The toponyms appear in two subsequent pages with slight variations. In the first, there are other place-names like *yn tepetl cotoncan, yn petlazolmetepec, yn tzouac xillotepe*; although note 3 on page 193 states that "this paragraph mentions six place names that apply to the site occupied by the *quauhtlinchantlaca*," in the next page they appear as successive places that the Chichimecas crossed in their migration journey.

[29] Perhaps these were originally two words, *tepexic oztoc*, and should be read this way, so I have translated it taking this possibility into account.

[30] It should read *tenyocan,*

in the red boulder (the red) cave, in the place of the fame
in the place of the sign, government was given
in front of the water
in front of the mountain

The toponyms presented here are constructed in a special way. They employ diphrases because they are vital to link the narrative tissue. As Joel Kuipers points out, "there are in the historical sources lists of toponyms that accompany the narratives of migration stories, place names that appear in lists as points of an itinerary function in a metaphoric way to link narrative events" (1984, 460). Maybe all these long toponyms are telling a story that we have yet to discover.

Another example of a toponym formed by a pairing of two, and in this case three, names is *Chalchiuhmomozco Amaquemecan Chalco* (Chimalpáin Cuauhtlehuanitzin 1991, 91n162). This toponym appears several times in Chimalpáin's *Memorial breve acerca de la fundación de la ciudad de Culhuacan*. The first of the three terms refers to a ritual name given to a shrine in honor of the goddess *Chalchiuhmatlalatl*. This shrine was located in a place designated by a diphrase:

*16. in ayauhithualco*         *in xochithualco.* (Chimalpáin Cuauhtlehuanitzin
                                1991, 90)
in the yard of the fog          in the yard of the flowers

The univocality of both names is explained in Chimalpáin Cuauhtlehuanitzin (1991, 91): *Yn quitocayotique chalchiuhmomoztli yn tepetzintli yn axcan ye itoca Amaqueme* (they called 'jade shrine' to the little mountain that now its name is Amaqueme).[31] There is a frequent variation with the pairing of just two terms, *Chalchiuhmomozco Amaquemecan* or *Amaquemecan Chalco*.

Although many toponyms are apparently composed of two names, it is not easy to establish if they are designating a unique region or if one (or two) of the terms expresses a relation of subordination or some other type of political or administrative link. For example, in trying to elucidate the meaning of three toponyms, the following consideration is made: "The main idea Chimalpáin offers us is of a dominion with a main ruling center called Tenanco Texocpalco Tepopollan; which leads us to ask whether Tenanco Texocpalco and Tepopollan are two different towns

---

[31] It is important to consider the historicity of toponyms as well as the way in which they can change or remain fixed over a certain period due to political, social, or administrative factors. Names that could have originated as a diphrase could have changed to exhibit a whole part relationship between both terms of the pair.

(*tlayacatl*) of the same unit (*altepetl*) or a single *cabecera*" (Monterrosa Desruelles and Pineda Santa Cruz 2006, 143).[32]

I believe that the following list may contain toponyms that have a diphrastic pattern to name a single geographic space, but it is difficult to be certain. In the *Crónica mexicayotl* some toponyms seem to be paired: *Chalco-Atenco, Itztlacoçauhcan-Amaquemecan Chalco, Michhuacan-Chiuhcnahuapan, Pantitlan-Atlixicco, Ayotzinco-Atenco, Atlauhtlan-Tenanco, Tzacualtitlan-Tenanco-Amaquemecan* (Chimalpáin 2012, 75, 210, 220, 224, 226).

## 4. CONCEPTUAL SPACES

By conceptual space,[33] I mean a set of nouns that can be connected by similarity and because they share certain properties. Some places can be grouped in domains[34] or conceptual spaces[35] in which the quality "dimension of danger" involves the conception of spaces as specific geographic landscapes that involve threatening or malignant situations. To account for dangerous spaces, one can posit a simple question: How can a space be conceptualized as dangerous? This is a very culturally mediated consideration, for in pre-Hispanic central Mexico, one of the main parameters of a dangerous place was a polar opposition between center and periphery. Central places tend to be represented by a habitat built by humans and, therefore, its main characteristic is to be a populated space. On the contrary, forests, canyons, crags, ravines, roads, and more specifically crossroads were peripheral spaces where people could be harmed.[36] They were uninhabited spaces that lacked control, and therefore security was compromised.

---

[32] "La idea principal que nos ofrece Chimalpáin es la de un señorío con un centro rector principal llamado Tenanco Texocpalco Tepopollan; lo que nos lleva a preguntar si Tenanco Texocpalco y Tepopollan son dos pueblos distintos (tlayacatl) de una misma unidad (altepetl) o una sola cabecera" (Monterrosa and Pineda 2006, 143).

[33] Some of the ideas in this section were first articulated in Montes de Oca (2013).

[34] I use "domain" in the sense proposed by Langacker (2008, 44): "Any kind of conception or realm of experience." The size or determination of the domain depends on the objective of the research.

[35] According to Gärdenfors, "A conceptual space consists of a number of *quality dimensions* . . . The dimensions are taken to be cognitive and infra-linguistic in the sense that we (and other animals) can represent the qualities of objects, for example when planning an action, without presuming an internal language in which these qualities are expressed" (1994, 104–105).

[36] For a more detailed description of the entailments of danger in peripheral settings, see Burkhart (1989).

The diphrases that can be grouped in the conceptual domain of danger are the following:

*17. in ātlān*         *in oztōc*
   in the water        in the cave
   *in ātōyāc*          *in tepe'xic*
   in the river          in the cliff
   *in texcalli*         *tepe'xitl*         *in ātlauhtli*
   crag                     cliff                    canyon
   *in cencuahuitl*   *in cemixtlāhuatl*
   woodland            plain
   *in cuauhtla'*       *in zacatla'*
   forest                    grassland
   *in o'tlamaxalli*   *in nextepēhualli*
   the crossroads     spread ashes

The association of water and caves has a mythological and religious explanation since the cave is seen as an axis mundi as a place where the owners of the water and of the mountain live; it is a place of communication between the underworld and the earth (cf. Montes de Oca 2013). Caves were seen as places of origin (cf. Durán [1581] 1995; Kirchhoff, Odena Güemes, and Reyes García 1989); they were probably places of worship where rituals were carried out. Caves were also conceptualized as an entrance to the underworld and into the darkness. Water, when associated with the cave, is seen as a negative force. Thus, the diphrase *in ātlān in oztōc* (in the water, in the cave) refers both to a dark, undefined place with an excess of water and humidity. Although one might think that there is ambivalence in the consideration of caves, they have a wider semantic spectrum as a place of origin or as an entrance to the underworld. Some couplets have a dual meaning, as is the case of *in ātlān in oztōc*, which can be seen as a dangerous place as is shown in the following example, where there is a contextualization through the adjacency to couplets that designate spaces where there are risks or threatening situations. This diphrase also designates *Mictlan* or 'the place of the dead.'[37]

---

[37] As we will show later the contextualization of *atlan oztoc* as a name for *Mictlan* is also carried out through similar diphrases or an explicit reference to underworld themes.

18. *ca nonoma nonnotlaça*
   *nonnomaiavi: in atlan*
      *in oztoc in tepexic*
         *in atoiac.* (Sahagún [1557] 1976, bk. 6, 10)
   I throw myself
      I cast myself in the water
         in the cave in the canyon
            into the river.

The hill, the river, the forest, the grassland, the plain, and the desert all share the characteristic of being uninhabited and peripheral places with respect to a center, and as such they were considered dangerous because space was not controlled (Montes de Oca 2013, 185). The dangers of the river and the cliff also appear in a narrative in which *Titlacahuan* ordered all the Toltecs to sing and dance, and he invited other groups to do the same. He then collapsed a stone bridge, and since there were many people and they were behaving in a drunk fashion, as if they had lost their mind, they fell into the river gorge turning into stones (Sahagún 1992, 200).

Crossroads were also conceived as dangerous places because they were the sites where the *tzitzimime coleletin* appeared. These were fearsome beings believed to descend to earth at crossroads on certain nights to harm pregnant women and children (Klein 2000, 27). The only occurrence of this couplet in the *Florentine Codex* is on the last pages of Book 6, and Sahagún includes a moral observation about "bad women" or "vicious men" that does not follow the Nahuatl text. Thus, it is possible that "the crossroads" and "the spread ashes" were resemanticized in evangelization discourse to denote bad behavior, and it is understandable that its use is far more productive in evangelization texts.

19. *nextepehualli*
   *otlamaxalli nicnonantia*
      *nicnotatia.* (Sahagún [1557] 1976, bk. 6, 247)
   I take as mother
   I take as father the crossroads
      the spread ashes.

Another conceptual space—though not a conceptual domain—is one related to generation. Two body parts, the womb (*xillāntli*) and the throat (*tozquitl*), are used in an exclusively locative form to designate a place where there is creation of people and things such as words, which are seen as having a certain degree of liveliness. It is not strange to link words and discourse with *tozquitl*, because this was also the word for voice. Both words as body parts are necessarily possessed and are functionally asymmetric; they are not part of the same topographic region, and therefore the objects that come out of or are located in these body parts are asymmetric as well: persons and words.

This is one of the "metaphors" explained by Sahagún in Spanish: "This wording means: It came out of the entrails and the throat. And metaphorically it means: A generous person who comes from illustrious people, it also means the talk or prayer that the speaker makes, which comes from the entrails and the throat" (Sahagún [1557] 1976, bk. 6, 247).[38] Both body parts represent the generative force that produces human beings as well as discourses, but contexts of the couplet, in Book 6, also establish this location as a place of return, where resting can take place in the womb, in the throat of *Tonatiuh Tlaltecuhtli*, and it is also a place where the eagle and ocelot warriors are received:

20. *Auh in axcan tlacatle*
  *totecoe titlacaoane ma ivian*
    *iocoxca yxillan*
      *itozcatlan*
  *imacochco ommoteca in tonan*
 *in tota in tonatiuh*
  *in tlaltecuhtli ma qujoalmanjli*
    *ma qujoalmocelili.* (Sahagún [1577] 1976, bk. 6, 13)

And now Tlacatle
  Totecoe
  Titlacahuane may he stretch calmly
    peacefully in the womb
      in the throat
  in the lap of our mother
    our father in Tonatiuh
   in Tlaltecuhtli may he welcome him (the warrior)
    may he receive him (the warrior).

## 5. MYTHICAL SPACES

In this section, I will deal with places that are not located geographically but instantiated by narratives or oral accounts of imaginary or legendary events.

---

[38] "Esta letra quiere dezir. Salio de las entrañas y de la garganta. Y por metaphora quiere dezir. Persona generosa que viene de personas ylustres: quiere dezir tambien. La platica o oración que haze el orador, que le sale de las entrañas y de la garganta."

The couplet *in mātlālātl in toxpalātl* gives identity to a cave where Tenochtitlan was founded and from which flowed a stream of green-blue water and a stream of yellow water.[39] There was another cave from which the waters that flowed were described as 'fiery' (*tleātl*) and as 'burning waters' (*ātlatlayān*). Even more, besides being primordial waters, the blue-green and yellow waters embody a greater symbolism because they are a way of purifying people through the act of bathing. One of the functions of the *tla'toāni* that derived directly from the exercise of his functions was to be the depository of these types of water, whose symbolic value was very high, due to the possibility of purification that was achieved through the act of washing and bathing people (Montes de Oca 2013, 144).

21. *in petlapan*
 *in jcpalpan in vncan motepapaqujlitica in vncan manj in matlalatl*
  *in toxpalatl*
  *in vncan moteahaltilitica.* (Sahagún [1577] 1976, bk. 6, 19)

 In the place of the mat
 in the place of the seat where people are washed, there where the blue water
   the yellow water lay
  where people are bathed.

Not only the *tla'toāni* but also the midwife bathed the newborn baby to purify him. This diphrase is constructed through a metaphorical trajectory, in which the features of water as a cleansing element, as well as its symbolic value as primordial water, are reconstructed in the domain where the *tla'toāni*, the gods, or the midwife purify common people with this water.

The sea is equated with the green-blue water and the yellow water. In this place, the god *Tloque Nahuaque* also had the power of bathing and purifying people:[40]

22. *ma axcan*
 *ma njcan xicmahaltili*
  *xicmopâpaqujli:*
 *ma ontemo ma xocommaqujli in matlalapan*
  *in toxpalapan in jlvicaapan*
   *in axoxovilco*

---

[39] Heyden proposed that Tenochtitlan inherited material and ideological elements from Teotihuacan and that "the streams of red and blue interlacing waters that surround the Tepantitla painting" serve as evidence (2002, 178–179).

[40] *Tloque nahuaque* is also a diphrase but in this case is an anthroponym by which the god Tezcatlipoca was known (Montes de Oca 2021, 84, 85).

*in vncan timotepapaquilia*
*in vncan timoteahaltilia. (Sahagún [1577] 1976, bk. 6, 30)*
Now
here cleanse him
   bathe him
May you come down and put him in the green-blue water
               in the yellow water in the sea
                              in the deep water,
there you wash the people
   you bathe the people.

One of the factors to which caves owe their importance was being located on these waters:

23. *Auh niman oquittaque nepaniuhticac yn texcalli, yn oztotl ynic ce in texcalli, in oztotl tonatiuh iquiçayan ytztoc, ytoca tleatl, atlatlayan. Auh ynic ome yn texcalli in oztotl mictlampa ytztoc, ynic nepaniuhtoc ytoca matlallatl yhuan ytoca toxpallatl. (Crónica mexicáyotl 2021, 152)*[41]

*Mictlān* 'the place of the dead' is another place designated by diphrases that foreground diverse features of this location. They can be gathered in a conceptual domain:

| 24. *in mictlān* | *in ilhuicac* | |
| the place of the dead | in the sky | |
| *in mictlān* | *Yohuayān* | |
| the place of the dead | the place of darkness | |
| *in a'pōchquiyāhuayo'cān* | *in a'tlecallo'cān* | |
| the place where there is no exit for smoke | the place where there are no chimneys | |
| *in ātlān* | *in ōztōc* | |
| in the water | in the cave | |
| *quēnami'cān* | *in xīmōhuayān* | *in huīlōhuayān* |
| the place of the quenami | the place of dwelling | the place of arrival |

---

[41] "Luego vieron que estaban juntos [dos] peñas y [dos] cuevas: en la primera peña y cueva que miraba hacia el oriente, se hallaba la llamada 'agua de fuego donde arden las aguas' y en la segunda peña y cueva, que miraba hacia el norte, se mezclaban el agua azul y el agua amarilla" (translated by Rafael Tena in Chimalpáin Cuauhtlehuanitzin 2012, 73).

*in tēma'māuhti'cān*    *in itze'ecatica*
the place where people    the place of the obsidian wind
    are frightened

*tocenchān*    *tocempo'polihuiyān*
our common home    our common place of disappearance

Examples of couplets in context:

25. *Cujx tiqujtozque in otechmocnelili in tloque*
                              *naoaque*
    *ca çan oc techmocnelilizinequj ipampa ca oc mjctlan*
                              *ca oc iooaian in tontlatoa. (Sahagún [1577] 1976,*
                              *bk. 6, 154)*

Perhaps we say that Tloque
                Nahuaque had done us good
that he only is going to favor us because in the land of the dead,
                          in the night we go speaking about.

26. *ca oqujnmotoptemjli*
    *ca oqujnmopetlacaltemjli in totecujo ca oiaque*
                          *ca omotecato in tocenchan in apuchqujiaoaiocan*
                                    *atlecallocan*
    *ca ie qujcevitoque in jtloc*
        *in jnaoac in tonan*
                *in tota in mjctlan tecutli. (Sahagún [1577] 1976 bk. 6, 152)*

Our lord has filled the box with them[42]
has filled the coffer with them. They have gone
                they went to lie down in our home
the place with no smoke exits
the place with no chimneys. They already went to rest near
                          close to our mother
                          our father Mictlantecuhtli.

---

[42] The subjects referred to are "*in vevetque in jlamatque in tzoneque in izteque in aoaiooque in vitziooaque in coltin in citi*" (the old men, the old women, those who have the hair, those who have the nails, those who have the thorns, those who have the spines).

*27. in vevetque*
 *in jlamatque in oqujnpolo*
  *in oqujntlati in totecujo in oiaque*
   *in omotecato in atlan*
    *in oztoc*[43]
     *in omotecato in mjctlan. (Sahagún [1577] 1976, bk. 6, 136)*

Totecuyo destroyed
 hid the old men
  the old women
   they have gone
    they went to lie down in the water
     in the cave
      they went to lie down in the land of the dead.

In Book 3 of the *Florentine Codex*, there is another couplet that designates Mictlan: *in quenamican in ximohuayan in huilohuayan*.[44] This diphrase is next to two couplets that also designate this space: *in apochqujiaoaiocan in atlecalocan* and *tocenchan tocempopolihuiyan*. The first term, *quēnami'cān*, has traditionally been translated as an interrogative form: "like what?" or "of what nature?" (Launey 2011, 271). Dibble and Anderson translate it as "the place of mystery" (Sahagún [1577] 1976, bk. 3, 42). Another etymology has been proposed by Karen Dakin (2021) related to the *quinametzin*, mythical giants that lived in ancient times. In that case, the translation would be "the place of the *quenami/quinami*." In turn, *Ximohuayan* has been translated as the place of the unfleshed, but Dakin (2021), based on observations by Thelma Sullivan, has proposed that the verb *ximi* (to remain, to dwell) is the root of this toponym. This meaning makes sense with *huilohuayan* (the place of arrival). The meaning of the diphrase would be a place where one arrives, stays, and returns to a place of origin that goes back to the first inhabitants of Anahuac.

*28. Auh in axcan ca omitzalmanili in mjctlan tecutli*
 *in Aculnaoacatl*
  *in Tzotemoc yoan in Mjctecacihoatl*
*ca omitzalmotetzonti*

---

[43] This couplet belongs to the conceptual domain of danger and designates *Mictlān* through contextualization.

[44] The translation of this diphrase composed of three terms and sometimes of two has been problematic, but Dakin (2021) has proposed a new translation that gives sense to the meaning of the couplet.

> *ca omjtzalmocpalti ca nel vmpa tocenchan*
> *vmpa tocenpopolivjian vmpa tlatlalpatlaoa*
> *ca oiccen onquiz ca otonmovicac in quenamjcan*
> *ximooaian*
> *in vilooaian in apochqujiaoaiocan*
> *in atlecalocan.* (Sahagún [1577] 1976, bk. 3, 41)

> And now Mictlantecuhtli
> Acolnahuacatl
> Tzontemoc and Mictecacihuatl
> have come to offer you (the dead person) a foundation
> a seat.
> There it is in truth our common home
> there is our common place of disappearance. There the earth widens
> where it comes out as one.
> You have come to the place of the quenami
> to the place where one dwells
> to the place where one arrives, the place with no smoke exits
> the place of no chimneys.

The diphrase *ōmeyōcān chiucnāuhnepaniuhcān* instantiates the frame of another mythical place, *Ōmeyōcān*, where *Ometecuhtli, Omecihuatl,* and other gods like *Tonacatecuhtli* and *Tonacacihuatl, Citlallatonac, and Citlalicue* lived (Mikulska 2015, 125). The second term specifies the location of the *Ōmeyōcān*, "where nine paths are joined together or assembled." *Ōmeyōcān* has traditionally been translated as "the place of duality," which is problematic. Another proposal identifies *ome/omi* as the root for "bone" (Dakin 1996; Haly 1992). In its turn, the usual translation for *chiucnāuhnepaniuhcān* is "nine floors," perhaps due to a misunderstanding of the word *sobrado*, which referred to the highest place of the house such as a rooftop or a loft. Carochi translates *calnepaniuhqui* as "casa de un sobrado *calnēnepaniuhqui* casa de mas de uno: no tiene saltillo por auer orden en los sobrados" (Carochi [1645] 2001, 274). The sense of *nepaniuhqui* should be understood as an "assembly of spaces," a junction; perhaps it could be thought of as a kind of wrap. This interpretation follows Cecelia Klein's suggestion that "at least some Mesoamericans conceived the universe in terms of cords and fabric" (1982, 29).[45]

*Ōmeyōcān* is also a place of origin of children, as can be noted from the words that the midwife addressed to the newborn:

---

[45] For a detailed discussion of the ethnohistorical and visual contexts of the term *chiucnāuhnepaniuhcān*, see Díaz (2015) and Mikulska (2015).

29. *Cozcatl*
>*quetzalli chalchivitl*
>>*maqujztli*
>>>*teuxivitl otijocoloc in vmeiocan*
>>>>*in chicunauhnepanjuhcan omjtzima*
>>>>>*omjtziocux*

*in monan*
*in mota in vme tecutli*
>*in vme cioatl in jlvicacioatl.* (Sahagún [1557] 1976, bk. 6, 176)

Necklace
precious feather, jade
>bracelet
>>turquoise, you were created in the place of bones
>>>in the place of the nine junctions

your mother
your father Ometecutli
>Omecihuatl ilhuicacihuatl have shaped you
>>have created you.

In the greetings dispensed to the firstborn by their grandparents, there is the same expression of a place of origin with a very similar text:

30. *Noxviuhticatzine tlacatle*
>*totecoe tlaçotzintle*
>>*tlaçotitlacatle chalchiuhtle maqujztle*
>>>*quetzalle teuxivitle*

*tzontle*
*iztitle oticmjhijovilti*
>*oticmociavilti otijoculoc in vmeiocan*
>>*in chicunauhnepanjuhca omjtzpitz*
>>>*omjtzmamal*

*in monan*
*in mota in vme tecutli*
>*in vme cihoatl. (Sahagún [1557] 1976, bk. 6, 183)*

My grandchild, man
>our lord, appreciated one
>>appreciated man, jade
>>>precious feather, bracelet
>>>>turquoise, hair.
>>>>>nail

> you have suffered
> you have been fatigued, you were formed in the place of bones
> > in the place of the nine junctions.
> you were blown
> you were perforated[46] by your mother
> > by your father Omecihuatl
> > > Ometecuhtli

The diphrase *Tlīllān Tlapallān* is the locative form of *tlīlli* 'black ink' *tlapalli* 'red ink', a well-known diphrase that refers to two materials, the black and the red inks used for drawing codices. There is another meaning construed by a metaphoric extension to also refer to wisdom and knowledge of the ancients, the ancestors. The symbolic value of this place lies in the fact that it is where Quetzalcoatl went to die as it is stated in *Anales de Cuauhtitlan*.

> 31. *1 Acatl Yn ipan xihuitl yn mic Quetzalcoatl.*
> > *Auh mitoa çan ya in Tlillan*
> > > *Tlapallan ynic ompa miquito. (Anales de Cuauhtitlan 2011, 42)*
> > 1 Reed, in this year Quetzalcoatl died.
> > It is said that he went to the place of the black ink,
> > > the place of the red ink and there he went to die.

> 32. *Niman yc ya in quetzalcoatl, moquetz quincennotz yn itecpoyohuan quinchoquili.*
> > *Niman yaque ompa tlamattiaque yn tlillan*
> > > *tlapallan*
> > > *yn tlatlayan*
> *Auh nohuian quitztia moyeyecotia aca tlahuelittac. (Anales de Cuauhtitlan 2011, 48)*
> > Then Quetzalcoatl, gets up, summons his assistants, and cries with them.
> > Then they head calmly to the place of the black
> > > the place of the red,
> > > the place of the burning.
> > He looked everywhere, tried, but he did not like anything.

A geographical reference is assigned in some historical accounts in which *Tlapallan* is considered a place in the east, situated somewhere along the coast of Veracruz. In this type of account, no mention is made of *Tlillan*.[47] The narrative of Quetzalcoatl's

---

[46] The terms of the couplet *pītza* 'blow-cast-melt' *mamali* 'drill' referred to the fabrication of jewels, and by analogy the meaning of the couplet alluded to the birth of a human being with the connotation of preciousness.

journey on his way to the place where he is supposed to die is linked to the place called *Tlillan Tlapallan*. Accordingly, this place-name worthy of being remembered is a diphrase in its own right and is not seen just as a mere derivation of the couplet *in tlīlli in tlapalli*.

Another mythical place designated with a diphrase is *in tlālxīcco in xiuhtetzacualco* 'in the navel of the earth,' 'in the turquoise enclosure,' and it was the place that the god *Huehueteotl* inhabited.

33. in teteu innan
    in teteu inta in veveteutl in tlalxicco maqujtoc
                               in xiuhtetzaqualco monoltitoc. (Sahagún [1557] 1976, bk. 6, 19)
    The mother of the gods
    the father of the gods *huehueteotl* lies into the navel of the earth,
                    he settled in the turquoise enclosure.

There is a variation of the first term of the diphrase that refers to fire and not to earth or soil: *in tlexicco in xiuhutetzacualco* (in the navel of the fire, in the turquoise enclosure). Both terms joined in a conceptual unit specify the dwellings of the god *Huehueteotl*, known also as *Xiuhtecutli*.

34. Auh in qujtlatenqujxtilizque in motechiuhcauh in teteu inna
                               in teteu inta in veueteutl in tlexicco
                               in xiuhtetzaqualco maqujtoc
                               in xiuhtecuhtli. (Sahagún
                               [1557] 1976, bk. 6, 41)
    Those who will speak for your creator, the mother of the gods
                    the father of the gods *huehueteotl* who lies
                    in the navel of the fire
                    in the turquoise enclosure *xiuhtecuhtli*.

## 6. CONCLUSION

Diphrases represent natural and cultural processes as well as different types of experiences that contribute to the meaning of place-names that are thus seen as linguistic and cultural constructs. The heterogeneity of spaces that can be accounted for in terms of a diphrastic way of naming includes geographical, mythical, and

---

[47] In the *Florentine Codex* the place-name recorded is *Tullan Tlapallan*. A. M. Garibay has a note in his edition in which he states that this is probably a mistake and should read *Tlillan Tlapallan*; that is also my opinion (Sahagún 1992, 197).

conceptual places. Not only can geographical locations be named using two terms, but also narratives trigger the need to focus on mythical spaces whose names also have a mnemonic function when they activate the narrative in which they are inserted. As for conceptual spaces, the use of diphrases highlights the sociocultural scheme.

By reviewing the register of semantic couplets to name spatial locations, we can access a feature of the Nahuatl language, which is pervasive to this day, offering insights of the rich universe in which symbolic, cultural, and geographic spaces are constructed.

## REFERENCES

Alcina Franch, José. 1995. "Lenguaje metafórico e iconografía." *Anales del Instituto de Investigaciones Estéticas* 66: 7–44.

*Anales de Cuauhtitlan*. 2011. Paleography and translation by Rafael Tena. Mexico City: Consejo Nacional para la Cultura y las Artes.

Baena, Angélica. 2014. "Metáforas, metonimias y digrafismos en la parte central del Códice Borgia (29–32)." *Itinerarios* 20: 199–224.

Basso, Keith. 1984. " 'Stalking with Stories': Names, Places, and Moral Narratives among the Western Apache." In *Text, Play and Story: The Construction and Reconstruction of Self and Society*, edited by Edward M. Bruner, 19–55. Prospect Heights, IL: Waveland.

Basso, Keith. 1996. *Wisdom Sits in Places: Landscape and Language among the Western Apache*. Albuquerque: University of New Mexico Press.

Burkhart, Louise. 1989. *The Slippery Earth: Nahua-Christian Dialogue in Sixteenth-Century Mexico*. Tucson: University of Arizona Press.

Carochi, Horacio. (1645) 2001. *Grammar of the Mexican Language*. Translated by James Lockhart. Stanford, CA: Stanford University Press.

Chimalpáin Cuauhtlehuanitzin, Domingo de San Antón Muñón. 1991. *Memorial breve acerca de la fundación de la ciudad de Culhuacan*. Edited and translated by Víctor. Castillo. Mexico City: Universidad Nacional Autónoma de México.

Chimalpáin Cuauhtlehuanitzin, Domingo de San Antón Muñón. 2012. *Tres crónicas mexicanas: Textos recopilados por Domingo Chimalpáhin*. Paleography and translation by Rafael Tena. Mexico City: Consejo Nacional para la Cultura y las Artes.

*Crónica mexicáyotl*. 2021. *Obra histórica de Hernando de Alvarado Tezozómoc, editada por Domingo Francisco de San Antón Muñón Chimalpáin Cuauhtlehuanitzin, con fragmentos de Alonso Franco*. Gabriel K. Kruell (introductory study, paleography, translation, notes, Calendaric appendix, and index). Mexico City: Instituto de Investigaciones Históricas, Universidad Nacional Autónoma de México.

Dakin, Karen. 1996. "Huesos en el náhuatl: Etimologías yutoaztecas." *Estudios de Cultura Náhuatl* 26: 310–325.

Dakin, Karen. 2008. "Análisis dialectal de un documento náhuatl de Izhuatán, Guatemala." Primer Coloquio Internacional Lenguas y Culturas Coloniales, Instituto de Investigaciones Filológicas, September 4–5.

Dakin, Karen. 2010. "Etimologías y migraciones nahuas: Perspectivas yutoaztecas." Keynote address, XI Encuentro Internacional de Lingüística en el Noroeste, Universidad de Sonora, Hermosillo, Mexico, November 17.

Dakin, Karen. 2021. "Consideraciones sobre paradigmas y topónimos nahuas: Los casos de *Ximohuayan* y *quinehuayan*." In *Estudios lingüísticos y filológicos en lenguas indígenas mexicanas, Celebración por los 30 años de Seminario de Lenguas Indígenas*, edited by Francisco Arellanes and Lilián Guerrero, 33–66. Mexico City: Universidad Nacional Autónoma de México, Instituto de Investigaciones Filológicas.

Davis, Caitlin. 2015. "Ritualized Discourse in the Mesoamerican Codices: An Inquiry into Epigraphic Practice." MA thesis, Leiden University, Leiden, Netherlands.

Dehouve, Danièle. 2009. "El lenguaje ritual de los mexicas: Hacia un método de análisis." In *Image and Ritual in the Aztec World. Selected papers of the "Ritual Americas" Conferences*, edited by Sylvie Peperstraete, 19–33. Oxford: Archaeopress.

Dehouve, Danièle. 2016. "*Altepetl*: El lugar del poder." *Americae*. https://americae.fr/dossiers/altepetl/altepetl-lugar-poder/.

Díaz, Ana. 2015. "La pirámide, la falda y una jicarita llena de maíz tostado: Una crítica a la teoría de los niveles del cielo mesoamericano." In *Cielos e inframundos: Una revisión de las cosmologías mesoamericanas*, edited by Ana Díaz, 109–174. Mexico City: Universidad Nacional Autónoma de México and Fideicomiso Teixidor.

Durán, Diego. (1581) 1995. *Historia de las Indias de Nueva España e islas de tierra firme*. 2 vols. Mexico City: Consejo Nacional para la Cultura y las Artes.

García Bernal, María Elena. 2006. "Tu agua, tu cerro, tu flor. Orígenes y metamorfosis conceptuales del altepetl de Cholula, siglos XII y XVI." In *Territorialidad y paisaje en el altepetl del siglo XVI*, edited by Federico Fernández Christlieb and Ángel Julián García Zambrano, 231–349. Mexico City: Fondo de Cultura Económica and Universidad Nacional Autónoma de México.

Gärdenfors, Peter. 1994. "Frameworks for Properties: Possible Worlds vs. Conceptual Spaces." *Sémiotiques*, no. 6–7: 99–120.

Haly, Richard. 1992. "Bare Bones: Rethinking Mesoamerican Divinity." *History of Religions* 31: 269–304.

Heyden, Doris. 2002. "From Teotihuacan to Tenochtitlan: City Planning, Caves and Streams of Red and Blue Waters." In *Mesoamerica's Classic Heritage: From Teotihuacan to the Aztecs*, edited by David Carrasco, Lindsay Jones, and Scott Sessions, 165–184. Boulder: University Press of Colorado.

Hunn, Eugene. 1996. "Columbia Plateau Indian Place Names: What Can They Teach Us?" *Journal of Linguistic Anthropology* 6 (1): 3–26.

Karttunen, Frances. 1992. *An Analytical Dictionary of Nahuatl*. Norman: University of Oklahoma Press.

Kirchhoff, Paul, Lina Odena Güemes, and Luis Reyes García, eds. 1989. *Historia tolteca chichimeca*. Mexico City: Centro de Investigaciones Superiores del Instituto Nacional de Antropología e Historia.

Klein, Cecelia. 1982. "Woven Heaven, Tangled Earth: A Weaver's Paradigm of the Mesoamerican Cosmos." In *Ethnoastronomy and Archaeoastronomy in the American Tropics*, edited by Anthony F. Aveni and Gary Urton, 1–35. Annals of the New York Academy of Sciences 385. New York: New York Academy of Sciences.

Klein, Cecelia. 2000. "The Devil and the Skirt: An Iconographic Inquiry into the Prehispanic Nature of the *Tzitzimime*." *Ancient Mesoamerica* 11 (1): 1–26.

Kuipers, Joel. 1984. "Place, Names and Authority in Weyéwa Ritual Speech." *Language in Society* 13 (4): 455–466.

Langacker, Roland. 2008. *Cognitive Grammar: A Basic Introduction*. New York: Oxford University Press.

Launey, Michel. 2011. *Introduction to Classical Nahuatl*. New York: Cambridge University Press.

León Portilla, Miguel. 1996. *El destino de la palabra: De la oralidad y los glifos mesoamericanos a la escritura alfabética*. Mexico City: Fondo de Cultura Económica.

Lockhart, James. 1992. *The Nahuas after the Conquest*. Stanford, CA: Stanford University Press.

López Luján, Leonardo, and Alfredo López Austin. 2007. "Los Mexicas en Tula y Tula en México-Tenochtitlan." *Estudios de Cultura Náhuatl* 38: 33–83.

McCafferty, Geoffrey. 1996. "Reinterpreting the Great Pyramid of Cholula, Mexico." *Ancient Mesoamerica* 7: 1–17.

Mikulska, Katarzyna. 2008. *El lenguaje enmascarado: Un acercamiento a las representaciones gráficas de deidades nahuas*. Mexico City: Universidad Nacional Autónoma de México and University of Varsovia.

Mikulska, Katarzyna. 2015. "Los cielos, los rumbos y los números: Aportes sobre la visión nahua del universo." In *Cielos e inframundos: Una revisión de las cosmologías mesoamericanas*, edited by Ana Díaz, 109–174. Mexico City: Universidad Nacional Autónoma de México.

Molina, Alonso de. (1571) 1977. *Vocabulario en lengua castellana y mexicana y mexicana y castellana*. Facsimile edition. Mexico City: Porrúa.

Monterrosa Desruelles, Hervé, and Edgar Pineda Santa Cruz. 2006. "Estudio de los topónimos Tenanco Texocpalco Tepopolla y Acxotlan Calnahuac Cochtocan: Un altepetl y un tlayacatl de la región Chalco-Amaquemecan." *Estudios de Cultura Náhuatl* 37: 139–169.

Montes de Oca, Mercedes. 2013. *Los difrasismos en el náhuatl de los siglos XVI y XVII*. Mexico City: Instituto de Investigaciones Filológicas, Universidad Nacional Autónoma de México.

Montes de Oca, Mercedes. 2021. "Los difrasismos, términos apelativos en el náhuatl clásico." In *Estudios lingüísticos y filológicos en lenguas indígenas mexicanas: Celebración por los 30 años del Seminario de Lenguas Indígenas*, edited by Francisco Arellanes and Lilián Guerrero, 67–100. Mexico City: Instituto de Investigaciones Filológicas, Universidad Nacional Autónoma de México.

Muñoz Camargo, Diego. 1892. *Historia de Tlaxcala*. Edited by Alfredo Chavero. Mexico City: Oficina Tipográfica de la Secretaría de Fomento.

Rivera Domínguez, Ligia. 2009. "La montaña sagrada de Cholula y su entorno sobrenatural." PhD diss., Facultad de Filosofía y Letras, Universidad Nacional Autónoma de México.

Robelo, Cecilio. (1905) 1982. *Diccionario de mitología nahua*. Mexico City: Porrúa.

Sahagún, Bernardino de. (1577) 1976. *Florentine Codex. General History of the Things of New Spain*. Translated by Arthur J. Anderson and Charles. E. Dibble. Santa Fe, NM: School of American Research and the University of Utah.

Sahagún, Bernardino de. 1992. *Historia general de las cosas de Nueva España*. Edited by Ángel María Garibay. Mexico City: Porrúa.

Sasaki, Mitsuya. 2011. "Classical Nahuatl Locatives in Typological Perspectives." *Tokyo University Linguistic Papers* 31: 287–316.

Tedlock, Dennis. 1985. *Popol Vuh: The Mayan Book of the Dawn of Life*. New York: Simon and Schuster.

Webster, Anthony. 2000. "The Politics of Apache Place Names: Or Why 'Dripping Springs' Does Not Equal 'Tónoogah.'" *Texas Linguistic Forum* 43: 223–232.

Wimmer, Alexis 2007. *Dictionnaire de la langue Nahuatl classique*. www.malinal.net/nahuatl.page.html.

# 4

## Nahuatl from Southern Jalisco and Colima in Diachronic Perspective

*Language Documentation and Variation*

ROSA H. YÁÑEZ ROSALES

### 1. NAHUATL IN WESTERN MESOAMERICA

There is no doubt that Nahuatl, among others, was one of the languages of western Mesoamerica. Its presence is recorded in the very first report we have on the area: the "Visitación que se hizo en la conquista" (1937). Written in 1525, the text records that there are towns where "Nahual" and "Otomí" are spoken.[1] A few decades later in the territory called "Nueva Galicia," it became clear that "Otomí" was not a language from the region, but the term Spaniards used to refer to a non-Nahuatl language. Mainly thanks to the *Relaciones geográficas* (Acuña 1987) and to Antonio de Ciudad Real's report (Ciudad Real [ca. 1582–1587] 1976) both written in the 1580s, specific names of western languages were recorded, such as *Coano, Tecozquín, Coca, Tepecano, Zayahueco, Zacateco, Guachichil*, and others. These languages were not documented in any way that we know of or used by religious or administrative authorities. After the middle of the seventeenth century, their names were no longer registered; Nahuatl remained as the language used for Christianization and for administrative and legal documentation in the territory.

The colonial administration strengthened the status of Nahuatl as a lingua franca in the region by promoting its use in both administrative and ecclesiastical contexts. The fact that Nahuatl literacy in central Mexico was already developed by

---

[1] This report is not surprising since it is known that, for example, Tenochtitlan had Otomí, Nahuatl, and Zapotec speakers.

1530 fostered, in a way, its rapid adaptation in other areas. And the proliferation of scribes inevitably accompanied the development and imposition of the colonial administration throughout Mexico. As far as the available texts allow us to state, the use of written Nahuatl was spread out to regions where it may not always have been the first language of the people, but it frequently was a vehicular language used by town councils, individuals, confraternities, and so on, to report a theft or the invasion of a piece of land, to write a will, and other events.[2]

After 1530, in western colonial Mexico, there were several demographic changes due not only to massive death from war and diseases but also the migration of allied warriors who accompanied the Spanish captains and administrators who settled in the region. Many of them were Nahuatl speakers from central Mexico *altepetl*, such as Chalco, Tlatelolco, and Tlaxcala.[3] This migration initially created a situation in which different dialects coexisted, but over time dialectal differences naturally diminished. How all the varieties of Nahuatl that were in contact (local western Nahuatl, and those from central Mexico) leveled is still something we know little about (see Yáñez Rosales and Schmidt-Riese 2017). Leveling usually refers to a process that results in a reduction of variation between dialects in contact. Multiple factors play a role in the process, such as the number of speakers, the intensity of communication among them, and the migration of speakers to or from the region under analysis. The fact is that in the sixteenth century, daily life was taking place simultaneously in different Nahuatl varieties in western Mexico; this coexistence gave rise to a "new" Nahuatl dialect, that is, the language was "leveled," probably because of intense contact (Thomason 2001) among the Nahuatl-speaking groups.[4]

---

[2] Although Nahuatl is one of the languages of the western region, in fact it was the vehicular language for groups who were not Nahuatl speakers, since literacy in Nahuatl was favored by both religious and administrative representatives. See Torres Nila (2020a), where he transcribes and translates a letter written in Nahuatl by Francisco Nayari, a Cora leader, to bishop of Guadalajara Juan Ruiz Colmenero, in 1649. The Nahuatl used reveals that Nahuatl was not Nayari's native language. See also Medina García (2016), about petitions written in Nahuatl in the region.

[3] *Altepetl* is the Nahua word for "city," "town." Usually, it is understood as an independent political unit. "Central Nahuatl" does not refer to a smooth, uniform dialect region. The dialect area is named in that way due to shared isoglosses between the many towns comprised under such a name, but there are observable differences as well. It comprises the core area of Mexico City, Tlatelolco, Azcapotzalco, Puebla-Tlaxcala, southeast Puebla, and central and southern Guerrero. See Lastra de Suárez (1986, 212, ff.).

[4] Intense contact usually leads to convergence of both dialects and languages. Thomason (2001, 66) and Winford (2003, 13; 23), review such cases. Mufwene (2006, 178–179) on the other hand, highlights the importance of competition and selection of the linguistic features in the formation of a new dialect.

It is possible to observe the changes in western Mexico, through the tracking of linguistic features in notarial texts in Nahuatl,[5] the production of which lasted approximately 200 years (1557–1765). One of the effects of this process involved a change from the systematic presence of *tl* in all the word contexts (beginning, middle, suffixes) in sixteenth-century notarial texts to the emergence in the second decade of the seventeenth century of its variations *t* and *l*: this phoneme shows up as *t* in northern Nueva Galicia, from Tlajomulco (Jalisco) in its southernmost point, to San Pedro Lagunillas (Nayarit), and Juchipila (Zacatecas), its northernmost points (see figure 4.1); *l* is found in southern Nueva Galicia, where Tlajomulco lies as its northernmost point and Colima and surrounding towns as its southernmost point. This does not mean that *tl* completely disappeared in western Mexico. We find it in many place-names—such as Ocotlán, Tepatitlán, Jalostotitlán, Zapotlán, and so on—and in colonial texts, as part of greeting formulas—for example, . . . *myxpantzinco otinecico yntitlatohuani sr alde mayor* . . . We come before you, ruler, sir, mayor . . .—since the formulas of a text for addressing an authority were very fixed. Occasionally, we find *tl* in other sections of a text: *Au huel ompa timotlatoquililo tomilpan ya yxquich cahuitl tocolhuan catca* . . . (And over there we have well planted our corn, all the time, since our grandparents were alive . . .) (Apango 1658; emphasis added; cited in Yáñez Rosales 2022, 184–185).

It is likely that the first scribes who produced texts in western Mexico were trained at the Colegio de Santa Cruz de Tlatelolco and were sent to different towns in New Spain to carry out tasks as scribes and as interpreters who aided the Catholic Church's representatives. The oldest extant texts written in the region, one from Tuxpan in southern Jalisco, in 1557, and one more from Tecomán, in the Colima area, in 1576, exhibit central Nahuatl traits (Barlow 1949; Yáñez Rosales 2022, 55–77).

The Indigenous scribes from Mexico City most likely stayed in the towns to which they were sent, and then they trained local people to become scribes. It probably became a family profession and was transmitted from parents to children, within a closed circle. As decades and centuries went by, the various linguistic traits that defined western Mexico Nahuatl began to appear in the texts produced by scribes in this region. Besides the presence of *t* in northern Nueva Galicia, and of *l*, mainly in southern Nueva Galicia and Colima,[6] we have

---

[5] Regarding notarial Nahuatl and indigenous notaries or scribes, see Haskett (1991); Restall, Sousa, and Terraciano (2005); Mentz (2008); for western Mexico in particular, see Yáñez Rosales (2013).

[6] Colima was part of Nueva España, not of Nueva Galicia. I found *l* as an absolutive suffix in a document written in Amacueca, southern Jalisco, as early as in 1630. From then on, it appears in such function continuously in the southern region of Jalisco. See Cortés y Zedeño (1765); Yáñez Rosales (2022, 162–166); and Yáñez Rosales and Schmidt-Riese (2017, 180–181).

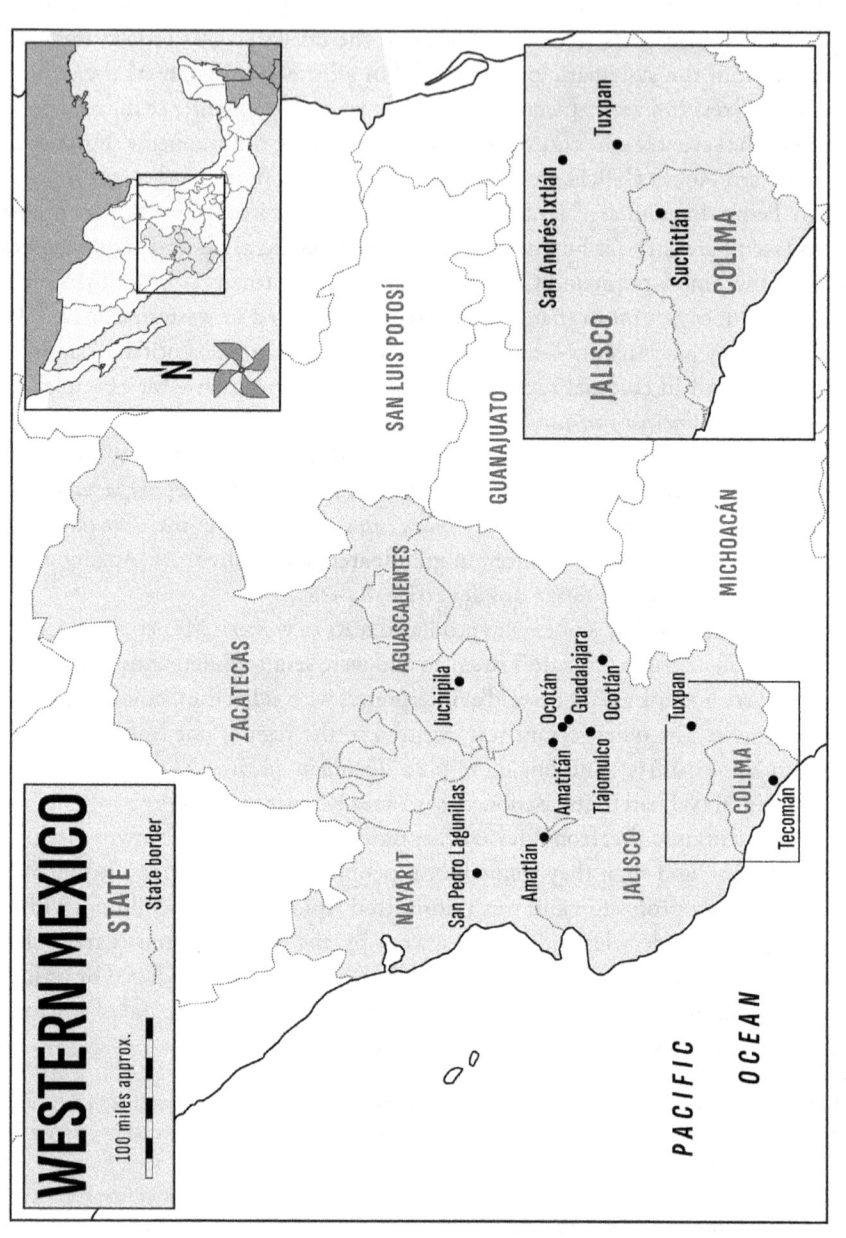

**Figure 4.1.** Map of western Mexico. Map drawn by Pablo García Loaeza.

- -the suffix *-lo*, added to the present tense plural verb, for example, *ti-choka-lo*, "we cry," whereas in central Nahuatl, we would expect *ti-choka-j*;
- -the use of reflexive pronoun *-mo* for all the grammatical persons, for example, *ni-mo-paka*, "I wash myself," *ti-mo-paka-lo*, "we wash ourselves," whereas in central Nahuatl we would expect *ni-no-paka, ti-to-paka-j*;
- -retention of absolutive suffix in nouns, regardless of possessive prefix, for example, *no-kal-li*, "my house," *to-altepe-t*, "our hometown," whereas in central Nahuatl we would expect *no-kal, to-altepe-uh*;
- -the use of *exot*, or *exol* for "bean," instead of *etl*;
- -the use of *texuxti* for "fire," instead of *tletl*.[7]

During the colonial period, these and other traits (Yáñez Rosales 2013, 126–127) gradually appeared in texts, such as wills, transfers of power, land measurements, and others. However, it is a process that is better documented in some areas than in others. For example, I have still not found documents written in Nahuatl after 1654 in the Colima region. The latest one is from Acautlán and has predominantly central Nahuatl traits. There is a text from Macuilli, Alima, Aquila, and Ostula from 1634 (see Yáñez Rosales 2022, 167–170)., which already exhibits *-lo* suffix for present tense plural verbs, and in the twentieth century, traits from western Nahuatl were recorded as part of the dialect from Suchitlán and from Ixtlahuacán, Colima. I will return to this topic in section 3. My guess is that the leveling process in the Colima area was taking place in the seventeenth century or maybe later, although not as early as in Nueva Galicia, but there are very few colonial documents that allow us to track it.

The town or area that seems to mark the boundary between the *t*-dialect and the *l*-dialect is Tlajomulco, which is located about twenty kilometers south of Guadalajara. It is interesting to observe that the texts produced there show it as the place where the dialects converge and where the dialect that in the twentieth century was called western peripheral Nahuatl (N-WP) is focalized. By 1765, all the traits were distinguished by Gerónimo Thomas de Aquino Cortés y Zedeño (1765) in his *Arte*, or grammar.[8] In the alphabetical lexicon section, he recorded the following entries:

---

[7] The lexical items and phrases listed have been taken from Cortés y Zedeño (1765). See note 12.

[8] Cortés y Zedeño spoke Nahuatl as his mother language. He was the brother of an Indigenous cacique from Tlajomulco, and somehow he managed to enter the Jesuit seminary in Puebla, where in 1765, his *Arte* was published (Torres Nila 2016, 13–15). By 1768 Cortés y Zedeño was back in his home region, teaching Nahuatl in Guadalajara and translating documents.

Agua, *At, vel Al.*          "Water, *At*, or *Al*" (Cortés y Zedeño 1765, 55).

Whereas in central Nahuatl, we would expect *Atl*. For "fire," he recorded:

Lumbre, *Texuxti*          "Fire, *texuxti*" (Cortés y Zedeño 1765, 93), not *tletl*.[9]

I have not found materials in Nahuatl written during the nineteenth century. The only information we have is that it continued to be taught within the realms of the church (see "2. Linguistic Fieldwork in Southern Jalisco and Colima"). Language policies in independent Mexico did not favor the continuity of Indigenous languages: on the contrary, in the first decades of the twentieth century, after the Mexican Revolution, when the national education system was founded, there was no intention to develop a bilingual educational project that allowed the knowledge and maintenance of the mother language and Spanish, nor any intention to promote the Indigenous languages to be used for written, as well as oral, expression. We know there were some isolated efforts, and it is known that many of the materials, either of pre-Hispanic or colonial origin, began undergoing translation. But interest in history, anthropology and archaeology followed its own track.

Going back to the western region, we find that Nahuatl in the northern part of Guadalajara must have been completely substituted with Spanish by the end of the nineteenth century or before. We know that Tepecano, a language from northern Jalisco, mainly in the Bolaños area, was registered with no vitality as a spoken language by Alden Mason (1917). Years later, Dávila Garibi made a great effort to document what must have been the Coca language spoken near the lake areas, that is, Chapala, Cajititlán, and Sayula, as well as in Tonalá and Tlajomulco (Dávila Garibi 1935). He was able to collect some lexical items and prove that Coca is part of the Uto-Aztecan family. Let us now look closer at the Nahuatl materials collected in the twentieth century.

---

[9] The question arises why the isogloss takes place in Tlajomulco. We do not have enough information about this *altepetl* in pre-Hispanic times. For the early colonial period, we know that before 1550, during the decades of conquest (1530s) and repression of the Mixton War (1540–1542), Tonalá, Tlajomulco, and the nearby Pueblos de Ávalos had to provide warriors, foodstuff, and *tamemes* (porters, carriers). People from northern Jalisco and Zacatecas, the core region of the Mixton rebellion, were displaced from their original towns and taken southward, in an intent by the vice-royal authorities to dismantle the focal points of the rebellion. So, there were migration movements from and to Tlajomulco, a fact that must have favored both language and dialect contact. By 1587, Ciudad Real reports that the Coca language is spoken there; nonetheless, the people understand Nahuatl and they represent the play *The Three Kings* in Nahuatl. Ciudad Real emphasizes the fact that it is the Nahuatl language the participants use (Ciudad Real [ca. 1582–1587] 1976, t. II: 99–103). A more detailed explanation of how the Nahuatl dialects could have become leveled in the region is provided in Yáñez Rosales and Schmidt-Riese (2017, 172–175).

## 2. LINGUISTIC FIELDWORK IN SOUTHERN JALISCO AND COLIMA (1919–1968)

The Nahuatl variety spoken in southern Jalisco and Colima became known only in 1934, when José María Arreola, a priest and scientist from Ciudad Guzmán, published three vocabulary lists in *Investigaciones Lingüísticas*.[10] Arreola collected this data in 1919 in San Andrés Ixtlán (281 lexical items and expressions), Tuxpan (168 words and phrases), and Suchitlán (124 words). The following year (1935), Father Melquiades Ruvalcaba republished in the same journal the list of words from Tuxpan that Arreola had recorded, adding what he considered the "correct" version of the Tuxpan list. This achievement is amazing in terms of what we would expect of *curas de pueblo* (small town priests) working in these towns.[11] It is even more amazing in the case of Ruvalcaba, since it reveals his interest and updated knowledge of the linguistic world in Mexico, to the point where he felt compelled to correct for the readers of *Investigaciones Lingüísticas* what he considered to be misleading information about the Nahuatl variety of Tuxpan.

Later, in the 1940s, Jean B. Johnson visited part of the state of Jalisco and recorded some Nahuatl words in a few towns.[12] In 1968, Ruvalcaba published his *Manual de gramática náhuatl*, a huge achievement accomplished by a cura de pueblo.

It must be noted that Arreola and Ruvalcaba were priests, and that it was their work that put them in contact with Nahuatl speakers. Although it is known that the priesthood seminary of Guadalajara preserved the Nahuatl chair during the nineteenth and early twentieth centuries,[13] it was mainly their position as priests that led them to learn the language. Arreola's particularly profound scientific curiosity

---

[10] Ciudad Guzmán is also known as Zapotlán el Grande. *Investigaciones Lingüísticas* was the first linguistics journal published in Mexico.

[11] According to Arreola's biographer, Juan Nepote (personal communication), Arreola visited these towns when he had already resigned from being a priest, which must have happened around 1914. It was his scientific curiosity that led him to get involved in documenting the Nahuatl language spoken in southern Jalisco.

[12] His notes were preserved by linguist Yolanda Lastra; they were reviewed and cited by Valiñas (1981).

[13] In the letters that went back and forth in the eighteenth century between Friar Antonio Alcalde and the Spanish authorities so that the Real y Literaria Universidad de Guadalajara (its first name) would be founded, it was clearly stated that the lectures the seminary held would pass on to the *universidad* (Razo Zaragoza 1980, 63). Among them was the Lengua Mexicana class. However, when the universidad started its lectures in 1792, Nahuatl was not part of them. At some point in the nineteenth century, the lecture at the seminary was closed. In 1869 it was reopened in the seminary, and Agustín de la Rosa was the lecturer. He remained in that position at least until 1895. See Torres Nila (2020b).

led him to be in contact with scholars who were doing research in Teotihuacan in the 1920s. The contact with Nahua culture lent further support to his knowledge about the language.

It is not clear how in 1934 Arreola decided to send to *Investigaciones Lingüísticas* the three vocabularies he collected in 1919. I assume that the three vocabulary lists were printed in the order he sent them to the journal, First, I will discuss the three vocabulary lists, and then I will focus on the one from Tuxpan.

The three towns where the lexicons were collected are relatively close to each other. San Andrés Ixtlán is about thirty-five kilometers north of Tuxpan, and Tuxpan is about eighty kilometers north of Suchitlán, Colima (see figure 4.1). At the time, traveling was done by train or by car on dirt roads, and probably on horseback. The three towns in fact share some cultural traits. For example, in Tuxpan and San Andrés there are groups of dancers who call themselves *paixtles*. They cover their face with a wooden mask, and their body with a heavy cape made of *paixtle*, a type of hay that grows after the rainy season on holm oaks. They also share the celebration of San Sebastián, which in Tuxpan is the most celebrated saint both in terms of participants and of the duration of the celebration.[14]

Regarding the lexicons, it is necessary to make some remarks. Unfortunately, Arreola does not say how he collected them. At first glance it seems as if he asked one or two speakers in each town, whose fluency it is impossible to rate, to provide a series of phrases and terms. It does not seem that he followed a list organized in an identifiable manner. Rather, it must have been what the speaker considered useful for Arreola: greetings, farewells, and phrases such as "How much is this?," "Where are you going?," "What are you doing?," and "did you light the candles?" Regarding lexical items, the lists include terms for persons and relatives, body parts, plants, animals, vegetables, house tools, and so forth. The Tuxpan list begins naming persons, relatives, and the responsibilities of the organizers of celebrations that take place in Tuxpan, whereas the San Andrés list starts with greetings and daily life questions and answers. The list from Suchitlán starts naming relatives, goes on to body parts, and then some animal names.

There is only partial agreement in terms of content among the lexicons. For example, only in a limited number of cases is it possible to find the same entry in the samples. Some of these entries are the words "bean," "corn," "fire." However, there are others recorded only in one or two of the lexicons (see table 4.1).

---

[14] San Sebastián is celebrated in Tuxpan on January 20 and 27 and on February 2. There are three main images that belong to different families, and they are not kept in a specific church. It has been like that since the times of the Cristero War (1927–1930). Many images of saints were never returned to the churches but instead kept in private homes, just in case the "government" tried to shut them down again.

**TABLE 4.1.** Lexical items from San Andrés Ixtlán, Tuxpan, and Suchitlán, according to Arreola 1934

| Lexical item in English and Spanish | Equivalent from | | |
|---|---|---|---|
| | San Andrés Ixtlán | Tuxpan | Suchitlán |
| Bean/frijol | Exotl | Ixol | Exol |
| Black/negro | Lile | Tlil | Lili |
| Corn/maíz | Tlayule | Tlayol | Layule |
| Deer/venado | | | Mazal |
| Fire/fuego | Tlexuchtle | Tlel | Tlixochtle |
| Flower/flor | | Xochitl | |
| Green/verde | | Xuxo | |
| Land/tierra | | Tlal | La'li |
| Mud/lodo | Zucuil | Zocuel | |
| Paper/papel | Amal | | Amalt |
| Salt/sal | Ystal | | Ystal |
| Squash/calabaza | Ayutli | Ayol | Ayoctle |
| Star/estrella | Ixtlalli | Lizarem | |
| Stone/piedra | Tel | Telt | Tel |
| Tortilla/tortilla | Tlaxcale | Tlaxcal | |
| To make tortillas / tortear | Laxcaloa | | |
| Water/agua | Al | | Atl |
| Wind / viento, aire | Yjecatl | | Ajecal |

*Note*: In all cases I have transcribed every term the way it is written in Arreola's article.

Arreola was knowledgeable enough about the Nahuatl language to write down what the speaker must have said. In the case of Tuxpan, the presence of a lateral *l* was recorded, along with *tl*, and a vibrant *r*, which we can see in the word for "star," *lizarem*.[15]

There are some remarks regarding the spelling of Nahuatl words that must be mentioned. There is a frequent problem with the spelling of *tl* in the Tuxpan and Suchitlán vocabularies. We do not know if the mistakes that appear in the Tuxpan

---

[15] Valiñas also registered a vibrant *r* in Tuxpan. When talking about lateral phonemes, he states: "La lateral sonora *l* aparece solo al final de palabra y entre vocales... Tiene un alófono vibrante sonoro *r* el cual aparece en ciertos contextos. Los casos de '¡siéntate!' *šimołatare* y 'dulce' *soperik*, son la muestra" (1981, 48–49). (The voiced lateral *l* appears only at the end of words and between vowels... It [Tuxpan Nahuatl] has a vibrant voiced allophone *r* which appears in certain contexts. The cases of 'sit down!' *Šimołatare* and 'sweet' *soperik*, are examples; translation mine).

**TABLE 4.2.** Lexical entries from San Andrés Ixtlán

| Lexical item in English and Spanish | Term from San Andrés Ixtlán | Central Nahuatl[a] |
|---|---|---|
| Basket/canasta | *Chiquihuil* | *Chiquihuitl* |
| Buzzard/buitre | *Zopilol* | *Zopilotl* |
| Flesh/meat/carne | *Nacal* | *Nacatl* |
| Hen/gallina | *Totol* | *tototl, totolin* |
| Owl/tecolote | *Tecolol* | *Tecolotl* |
| Paper/papel | *Amal* | *Amatl* |
| Scorpion/alacrán | *Colol* | *Colotl* |
| Snake/serpiente | *Coal* | *Coatl* |
| Water/agua | *Al* | *Atl* |

*Source*: Arreola (1934).
[a] Central Nahuatl entries are transcribed according to Molina 1555–1571 *Vocabulario* . . .

and Suchitlán lexicons have to do with Arreola's transcription or with the printing process. Some of the "mistakes" are

| Tuxpan | reed | *Aca**lt*** |
|---|---|---|
| | guayaba | *Xoco**lt*** |
| Suchitlán | water | *a**lt*** |
| | paper | *ama**lt*** |

Definitely, the examples that record final *-l* are numerous and abundant in the three samples as can be seen in tables 4.2 through 4.4:

The number of phrases that potentially reflect parts of a conversation is higher in the San Andrés word list. With regard to why there are such differences in the number of items collected, one can only speculate about who the interviewees were, their fluency as speakers, their memory, their interest in informing Arreola, and so on. Some of the phrases collected in San Andrés Ixtlán are

| ¿*Quen amotlanelzi?*[16] | Good morning. |
|---|---|
| ¿*Domingo campa tia?* | On Sunday, where do you go? |

---

[16] *Quena* seems to be a shortened form of *quenamih*, "how"? Literally, "How was / is your morning / your coming to light?" "In what mood did you wake up?" Arreola recorded it twice, with different word segmentation; the reflexive pronoun *mo* is usually written with the verb, as one word: *motlanelzi, monotza*. I have transcribed it as it is in the original. Canger recorded a variation of this phrase in Mexicanero from Durango: "¿*Kinán ttanés*? ¿Cómo amaneciste?" (2001, 51–52).

TABLE 4.3. Lexical entries from Tuxpan

| Lexical item in English and Spanish | Term from Tuxpan | Central Nahuatl |
|---|---|---|
| Bean/frijol | Exol | Etl |
| Black/negro (color) | Tlil | Tlilli |
| Carnation (small) / clavellina | Xiloxochil | Xiloxochitl |
| Fire/fuego | Tlel | Tletl |
| Hail/granizo | Tecihuil | Tecihuitl |
| Mud/lodo | Zocuel | Zoquitl |
| Palm leaf / hoja de palma | Zoyal | Zoyatl |
| Squash/calabaza | Ayol | Ayotl |
| Sun, the light of / luz, claridad del día | Tonal | Tonalli |
| Water/agua | Al | Atl |

Source: Arreola (1934).

TABLE 4.4. Lexical entries from Suchitlán, Colima

| Lexical item in English and Spanish | Term from Suchitlán, Colima | Central Nahuatl |
|---|---|---|
| Bean/frijol | Exol | Etl |
| Black/negro (color) | Lili | Tlilli |
| Deer/venado | Mazal | Mazatl |
| Fire/fuego | Tlexuchtle | Tletl |
| Grass/pasto | Zacal | Zacatl |
| Land/tierra | la'li | Tlalli |
| Reed/carrizo | Acal | Acatl |
| Salt/sal | Yztal | Iztatl |
| Shaft of the corn cob / olote | Olol | Olotl |
| Snake/culebra | Cohual | coatl/cohuatl |
| Stone/piedra | Tel | Tetl |

Source: Arreola (1934).

| | |
|---|---|
| *Ya pozontica al.* | The water is boiling. |
| *Notatzi amo nechnequi.* | My father does not love me. |
| *Oyac nopiltzin.* | My son is gone. |
| *¿Quenamonotza?*[17] | ¿What is your name? |
| *¿Tleca choca?* | ¿Why does she/he cry? |
| *Axca ya tiolac* | Now it is already late. |

Some of the phrases from Tuxpan are

| | |
|---|---|
| *Ne nió nocha.*[18] | I go home. |
| *Nio tlacuazo.* | I am going to eat. |
| *Ne tlacuazquia.* | I was eating. |
| *Quemi*[19] *tetlanez.* | Good morning. |
| *Ixtataca chihua ce poso.* [sic] | Dig to make a well. |
| *Tzatzihuala.* | He/she comes shouting. |

Whereas examples from Suchitlán are

| | |
|---|---|
| *Ya lanezi.* | It is dawn already. |
| *¿Quinami tilanezi?*[20] | How are you this morning? |
| *Nehual nicnique*[21] *nicochiz.* | I want to sleep. |
| *Nehua nihuala de Colima.* | I come from Colima. |
| *Nic[h]uicatica adobes para no callé.* | I am carrying adobe for my house. |

Let us now look at the "Observaciones" (Remarks) Ruvalcaba made to Arreola's Tuxpan lexicon.[22] Ruvalcaba sent his remarks to the same journal where the lexicons were published the year before: *Investigaciones Lingüísticas*. Both samples, Arreola's and Ruvalcaba's, appeared in two columns side by side, Arreola's list on the left-side column and Ruvalcaba's remarks on the right-side one.

How can we interpret Ruvalcaba's interest in Nahuatl, also known by its speakers as Mexicano? In those years, it was probably not easy to stay up to date on what was

---

[17] Literally: "How are you called?"
[18] Literally: "I go to my house"
[19] *Quemi* seems to be another shortened form of *quenamih*, "how."
[20] Literally: "How has the dawn of the day been to you?"
[21] In central Nahuatl, it would be *nicnequi*. See section 3.
[22] Father Melquiades Ruvalcaba arrived in Tuxpan ca. 1930. The title of his contribution is "Vocabulario Mexicano de Tuxpan, Jal."

being published in Mexico City regarding linguistics. It was probably by chance that Ruvalcaba became aware of Arreola's publication; or maybe he had been seeking information about Tuxpan Nahuatl and noticed inconsistencies between what he knew and what was written. When he sent his remarks to *Investigaciones Lingüísticas*, his intention was to provide a more accurate description of the Tuxpan Nahuatl. It is insightful to read his commentaries about Arreola's recording of pieces of conversation. The following are some examples:

*Arreola, 1934*
*Toteco*. Nuestro Señor [Our Lord].
*Ioquich*. Marido [Husband].
*No mamai*. Mis brazos o manos [My arms or hands].
*No metzmetz*. Mis piernas [My legs].
*Huala*. Venir [To come].
*Mahuala*. Ven [Come].

*Ruvalcaba, 1935*
*Está correcto*. [It is correct.]
*Está exacto y por lo general con esa palabra se entiende todo varón*. [It is accurate, and with that term it is generally understood any male.]
*No está bien. "No mazozopaztli" llaman a los brazos y "no imahuan" a las manos*. [It is not right. They say *No mazozopaztli* to refer to arms and *no imahuan* to refer to hands.]
*Está bien*. [It is correct.]
*Este verbo solo es del varón; la mujer dice: "huitz" ¿Campa tihuitz? ¿De dónde vienes?* [This verb is used only by males; women say *"huitz" ¿Campa tihuitz?* Where do you come from?]
*Mahuala es: dígnate venir. El ma suaviza la orden*. [*Mahuala* is: please come. *Ma* softens the order.]

Beyond providing what Ruvalcaba considered to be a more accurate description, mainly in terms of pronunciation, his contribution lies in its provision of more detail in terms of usage. The fact that Ruvalcaba distinguishes between what men and women say is very enriching. This feature was recorded in colonial times by Andrés de Olmos (1547), and in central Mexico's sixteenth-century Nahuatl by Alonso de Molina (1555–1571), but we had no news about such difference in other regions.

Further on, Ruvalcaba provides some phrases that are used by males. If men used the expressions women were expected to use, it would be considered effeminate. It would be equally inappropriate the other way around. Let us look at the examples:

In the morning, males say,

- -¿*Kiemi titlanez?*[23]
- -**Cualli**, *pampa Dios*
- -¿*Ti chicauhticac?*[24]
- -*Nichicauhticac,*[25] pampa Dios
- How has the dawn been to you?
- Good, thank God.
- Are you healthy?
- I am healthy, thank God.

whereas women say,

- ¿*Kimi titlanez?*
- *Yec, pampa Dios.*
- How has the dawn been to you?
- Good, thank God.

The rest of the phrases are the same for both men and women (213–214; emphasis added).

The difference Ruvalcaba recorded is the use of *cualli* by men and *yec* (*yectli*) by women. These two adjectives are translated with the same meaning, according to Molina (1555–1571), as "something good." The Franciscan does not state any further difference. In fact, both words can be found in complementary distribution in a couplet:

Ma yectia, ma cualtia, ma chipahuac in iyollo. (Sullivan 1983, 92)

May he become good, may he become fair, may his heart become pure.

Both verbs, *yectia* and *cualtia*, mean basically the same, "to become a good person," "to become a goodhearted person." There is no clear reason for the difference. It must be the usage, which according to Ruvalcaba is very "precise." At the end of the phrases, he points out:

---

[23] Two remarks about *kiemi* must be stated. First, the use of letter *k* is unexpected; it only appears in these examples, not in the rest of the lexicon, although the same sound is registered in many other vocables, as *cualli, yectli*, etc. Second, Ruvalcaba does not comment on the *i* of the first syllable. It is not possible to know whether this is really the way men pronounced the word *quemi*, "how," or is just a typographical error.

[24] *Chicauhticac* is derived from the verb *chicahua*, "to be strong," "to be robust." Ruvalcaba translates it as *con salud*, "with health" or "healthy."

[25] Although both *ti chicauhticac* and *nichicauhticac* are basically the same construction, the first syllable being the semipronoun *ti*, "you," and *ni*, "I," the first one is detached from the adjective; the second, as most likely would be expected, is not.

They [the people from Tuxpan], have another beautiful greeting when a person is visited or when someone oversees taking something important to someone; but I leave it out, limiting myself to the vocabulary. (Ruvalcaba 1935, 214).[26]

This comment may refer to a speech act that formed part of a practice of greeting visitors to the community that was documented in the early twentieth century. When I started doing fieldwork in Tuxpan in 1988, I asked whether the interviewee knew someone who spoke Mexicano. One of the answers I received was "There was a woman at the beginning of the century, she welcomed Porfirio Díaz in Mexicano; he inaugurated the train station." I was able to interview the granddaughter of the sister of the woman who was at the train station that day. The name of the lady who gave the speech was Rafaela Villanueva.[27] Sometime later, I found a printed version of what happened on January 5, 1909. President Porfirio Díaz was at the Tuxpan train station in order to open the recently built Guadalajara-Manzanillo Railroad. During such an important occasion, Rafaela Villanueva delivered a speech in Mexicano to welcome the visitor. It is not possible to know when it became usual that a woman, wearing the traditional attire in an official event, would stand in front of the government or church representative and greet the visitor in Nahuatl. The greeting acts as an opening ceremony in which the visitor waits for his turn to speak once the greeting has been concluded. The most that the visitor could have said is "thank you," in Spanish. Most likely, he had no hint of what he was being told. However, for the community, it was their turn to have a voice and speak. And for sure, it was a demonstration of politeness too.

Rafaela Villanueva, and other women afterward, continued greeting in Nahuatl those visitors who called for the gathering of people. President Lázaro Cárdenas visited Tuxpan in 1935, although I have not found references about a greeting delivered to him. In 1969, presidential candidate Luis Echeverría visited Tuxpan. He was welcomed in Nahuatl by Paulina Bautista; the speech was recorded in a newspaper published in Guadalajara.[28] In Tuxpan, it was known that a polite way to receive a visitor was to greet him in Mexicano. Most of the time, a woman dressed in her traditional garment oversaw delivering the speech.

After Ruvalcaba's remarks were published, he kept on studying and practicing the Mexicano language. He even in 1968 published a grammar book, which partially

---

[26] Translation of "Tienen otro saludo hermoso, para cuando se hace una visita o para cuando se lleva alguna comisión; pero lo omito, concretándome sólo al vocabulario" (translation mine).

[27] Rafaela's sister, Jesusita, continued providing the greeting for some years. It is her granddaughter I interviewed. In order to honor Rafaela Villanueva, there is a kindergarten in Tuxpan that bears her name.

[28] *El Informador*, December 8, 1969.

records the Tuxpan variety. It seems to be a reproduction of Franciscan Juan Guerra's *Arte*, published in 1692 (1900),[29] except for the fact that he adds some "exercises" for practicing the language. These exercises comprise sentences and tales, or brief narratives told by real speakers. They seem authentic. Ruvalcaba did not continue publishing texts that recorded the variety from Tuxpan. This is why his 1935 remarks are so valuable. They were written right from the heart of a cura de pueblo, a priest who was learning the language, preaching in the language, and mediating within the community using the language, and he felt that he had enough knowledge and authority to question another priest, who by that time was dedicated to scientific observation and writing.

In the late 1980s, Ruvalcaba was remembered as having been a fluent speaker who would even perform the ritual of asking a father for his daughter's hand in marriage, taking confession in Mexicano, and encouraging people to speak the language.[30]

If we look back at what Arreola and Ruvalcaba collected, their lexicons are valuable in several ways:

a. Although the number of phrases and lexical items collected in each town is rather small, they reveal the vitality of the language in its everyday uses and functions.
b. Considering later fieldwork carried out by Valiñas (1979, 1982), and Yáñez Rosales (1988–1996), it was during the first decades of the twentieth century when Nahuatl's transmission to the younger generation was halted. Very likely, the language was being substituted with Spanish, or Spanish was used from the beginning in some of the new social environments that emerged after the Mexican Revolution, for example, the school system and the new system of land possession.
c. In terms of the sociolinguistic features recorded, speech variation between women and men, each group using different lexical items in some communicative exchanges, is a very valuable cultural distinction.
d. Regardless of the fact that there seem to be spelling mistakes, both Arreola and Ruvalcaba documented some of the linguistic traits of the Nahuatl variety still spoken in southern Jalisco and Colima. The features that can be identified as "western" regarding lexicon are the terms for "fire," and "bean"; regarding phonology, there is the systematic presence of *l* in contexts where in central Nahuatl *tl* would be expected.

---

[29] Guerra's was the first *Arte* to record western Nahuatl features. Ruvalcaba must have had access to a copy and made some adaptations. He probably thought that the content of Guerra's *Arte* was more "correct" than the Nahuatl spoken in Tuxpan.

[30] I met several people who were acquainted with him. In a way, the vitality of the language was vanishing in parallel with his actions and lifetime. He was buried in the curacy of the main church of Tuxpan.

## 3. NAHUATL IN SOUTHERN JALISCO: TUXPAN AND AYOTITLÁN, 1978–2010

In the 1970s, as part of a larger project whose goal was to record Nahuatl variation, Yolanda Lastra and Jorge Suárez at UNAM prepared a questionnaire with more than 400 test items designed to examine vowel length, synonymy, and other aspects of the language across the Nahuatl-speaking regions. Leopoldo Valiñas traveled throughout the western part of Mexico and gathered data using this questionnaire. His findings were reported in four works—published in 1979, 1981, 1982, 1994—and in Lastra de Suárez's 1986 comprehensive book. Valiñas's visits to Tuxpan and other towns in Jalisco, Nayarit, Colima, and Michoacán yielded the most consistent results in terms of documenting the local Nahuatl varieties. In terms of continuity, he predicted that the language would only survive through the year 2020 in those Nahuatl-speaking towns located in coastal Michoacán (Valiñas 1979, 340).

At the end of the 1980s, I started my own fieldwork in Tuxpan, and later, in 2010, in Ayotitlán, in the municipality of Cuautitlán de García Barragán (CGB). I will focus on the material from Tuxpan collected by Valiñas as they are presented in his 1982 article, in some of the brief dialogue exchanges I collected between 1988–1996,[31] and in the very scarce material from Ayotitlán in the municipality of CGB (Ayotitlán/CGB), collected by Rosa Yáñez Rosales et al. (2016) and Yésica Higareda Rangel (2018).[32]

Valiñas (1982) consulted two elderly women, Paulina Bautista and Balbina González, who provided enough material to describe the dialect (45–55); he confirmed some of the prior statements made by Ruvalcaba (1935), as well as some of the lexical entries registered in Cortés y Zedeño (1765). But he also found differences that had not been recorded and that make the dialect different from its neighbors (Valiñas 1982, 45–46).

Besides the questionnaire Valiñas applied, he elicited utterances of some speech acts. Paulina Bautista told him a few greetings, a song, a legend, and two brief tales. The greetings can be identified as part of the tradition Ruvalcaba referred to in 1935. Valiñas indicates that they were used to welcome people such as the bishop, a government authority, or the teachers (1982, 56–58). There is one more greeting used

---

[31] It is the first time I transcribe some of the brief Nahuatl data I collected. As mentioned, I started fieldwork in 1988. By 1989 it was clear that those who grew up speaking Nahuatl as a first language, or were in very close contact with speakers such as their parents or grandparents at the beginning of the twentieth century, had a dormant or latent knowledge of the language (Campbell and Muntzel 1989, 181; Vallejos 2016, 147).

[32] Valiñas (1979) visited a town also called Ayotitlán, which is within the municipality of Tecolotlán, Jalisco.

when a person from Tuxpan travels to Guadalajara, the capital city of the state of Jalisco, apparently to ask for a favor.

The greetings are straightforward and rather modest. There is no usage of honorific forms, as politeness in general has been characterized (Hill and Hill 1986; Karttunen 1990) or as shown in the *huhuehtlahtolli*, "sermons of the old people" (Ramírez Celestino and Flores Farfán 2008), or in the elegant register used in prayers (Serafino 2015), both collected in the state of Guerrero. However, a continuation in the greeting speech act can be identified. I will transcribe the greeting to a teacher and the translation provided by Paulina Bautista, which Valiñas documented (1982, 58–59):

> Kemi čikawaʔ kʷeyihme temaštenihmeʔ kampa inwariahke momaštatke ye inwariaskeʔ
> Ma teon meskawa senyores miek šuwil. (Valiñas 1982, 59)

> I have come to greet you and at the same time to thank you for the great benefit that you have done. You have come to educate great generations. May God protect you for many years.[33]

Approximately fifty years later, the initial greeting formula has not changed very much. Ruvalcaba recorded,

> Kiemi titlanez, tichicahuac?

> How has the dawn been to you? Are you healthy? (see earlier examples),

whereas Valiñas registered:

> Kemi čikawaʔ

The latter could be translated more literally as "How healthy are you?," although in Paulina's translation a more pragmatic than literal version is provided.

Both greetings, the first one recorded in 1935 and the second in 1982, reveal that a manifestation of courtesy is to show concern about the other person's health. It is the opening formula of the speech act. Another greeting that Paulina Bautista told

---

[33] Translation of "He venido a saludarlo y al mismo tiempo a darle las gracias por el gran beneficio que ha hecho. Ha venido a enseñar grandes generaciones. Que Dios lo guarde muchos años" (translation mine). Valiñas transcribed the texts using the phonetic alphabet. There are probably typographical errors. For example, the final *n* in the word *teo*, "God," does not make sense. The translation he recorded is the one Paulina Bautista gave him. As he commented, there is no correspondence between the number of the object, singular and plural (1982, 59n2).

Valiñas was the one used when a person traveled to Guadalajara:

Wehkałali tewalkiske
Ikampa šočil motemaka'
tewariahke temiščikawako ika moči toyolo'
manáč iškiše de latenteloya.

We have come from far away territories
where flowers are grown.
We have come to greet you [to ask you about your health], from the depth of our heart.
[We hope] that my brother is released from prison.[34]

The fact that Paulina Bautista overtly entitled these four utterances as *saludos* (greetings) is insightful. It seems like she saw herself as an expert in this speech act. In fact, it was she who welcomed candidate Echeverría to Tuxpan in 1969 (see earlier note 31).

The greetings also show us that such a speech act probably remained the best-known manifestation of the Nahuatl or Mexicano language toward people who visited Tuxpan. In the 1980s, the greeting had been shortened to *Kemiz tlanez huey lakal* (How has the dawn been to you, great man?).[35]

Valiñas recorded a conversation between Paulina Bautista and Alfredo Ramírez, a Nahuatl speaker from Xalitla, Guerrero, with the aim of finding out about the intelligibility between the dialects. At the beginning of the conversation, it seems like they will not reach comprehension. Paulina Bautista clearly says, "There, I don't understand." However, Ramírez, who besides being a Nahuatl speaker was a linguist,[36] made some adaptations and after a few exchanges the speakers understood each other regarding the basic content of the dialogue (Valiñas 1982, 61). The conversation is very straightforward. It is Paulina who, upon Alfredo's request, talks about her activities. She grows flowers and sells them, although sometimes she also gives them away. The fact that she grows flowers is reflected in the text of the song she shared with Valiñas, as well as in the greeting she expresses when she travels to Guadalajara (see earlier quotation).

---

[34] My translation of "De lejanas tierras hemos venido / de donde se producen las flores / Hemos venido a saludarlos de corazón / que a mi hermano lo saquen de la prisión" (Valiñas 1982, 56).

[35] *Kemiz* seems to be another shortened form of *quenamih*, "how," whereas *tlanez* is the preterit form of *tlaneci*, "for the day to break," "to get light" (see Karttunen 1983, 284).

[36] The transcription of the conversation was also published in the 1982 article (61–67). Alfredo Ramírez Celestino worked as a linguist at the Instituto Nacional de Antropología e Historia. He passed away in 2016.

Yáñez Rosales (1988–1996) collected brief exchanges uttered by four elder women. They were between seventy-seven and ninety-two years old at the time. The four women had learned the language in their childhood with their parents or grandparents. In terms of the grammatical information Valiñas published in 1982, my findings were basically the same. I will transcribe data I collected, and I will also refer to other authors' work about other dates and regions within western Mexico, to have some regional perspective about the Tuxpan dialect.

As Ruvalcaba registered, the use of *yectli* by women, to mean "good," was confirmed in my data. It was registered at the beginning of a dialogue between Concepción Figueroa (CF) and Maximiana Reyes (MR). Other terms not mentioned before are *ue* for "yes," *tle* meaning "no," and *tlako*, "what." None of these terms are registered in Cortés y Zedeño (1765), or in Una Canger's work on Mexicanero (2001), although Valiñas registers *tle* and *tlako*. Let us look at the brief dialogue:

CF: *¿Kemis tlamate?*
"How is the day going?" [Good afternoon]

MR: *Yee, pampa Dios.*
"Good, thank God."

CF: *¿Tlako tekchihua? ¿se mantiris?*
"What do you do? A tablecloth?"[37]

MR: *Ue*
"yes"[38]

CF: *¿Teknamakaso?*
"Will you sell the work [when you finish it]?"

MR: *Ue, ue neknamakaso*
Yes, yes, I will sell it. (Yáñez Rosales, fieldwork, 1988–1996)

The future morpheme that is added to a verb is *-so*, whereas in central Nahuatl we would expect *-s*. It was recorded in Ruvalcaba's work (1935, 213) and in Valiñas's as well (1982, 53). On the other hand, Valiñas states that vowels *e* and *i* exhibit free variation mainly in the pronominal prefixes (50). This variation can be seen in the

---

[37] *Mantiris* looks like a Spanish loan, *mantel*, tablecloth, or "napkin," made with embroidery.
[38] This term for "yes" is used by MR consistently.

last utterances of both women. However, these vowels are recorded in other terms and word positions too. The following is reported speech by Catarina Osorio (CO). She is narrating when Father Ruvalcaba (MRU) went to her house to ask for her hand in marriage:

CO: *Šiuala*, le dijo mi papá, y dijo el padre:
"Come [to the mother], said my dad, and [then] the father said:"

MRU: *Neuala neka, tekpia se šuwapil.*
I come here, [because] you have a young lady [daughter].

CO: No, le dijo mi mamá: *Amo nešpia šuwapil. Nešpia se iškuin.*
No, my mother told him: I don't have a daughter, I have a dog.[39] (Yáñez Rosales, fieldwork, 1988–1996)

In another dialogue between Balbina González (BG) and Concepción Figueroa (CF), BG says:

BG: *Temačtiani keneke łajtoa. ¿Temačtiani o temačtia?*
"The teacher (referring to RY) wants to speak. [What is the word?] Teacher or to teach?"[40]

CF: *Temačtiani.*
"Teacher."

BG: *Ye motemačtiso.*
"She is going to learn." (Yáñez Rosales 1988–1996)

There is an *e* in verbs usually ending in *-ki*, as in *neke* (preceding), and in the following:

BG: *łe tenečkake ... Nepake*
"You don't hear me ... I laugh."[41] (Yáñez Rosales 1988–1996)

---

[39] The narration reveals an attempt at denying the possibility of a daughter becoming engaged to marry a man.

[40] It was frequent when the women started a conversation, upon my request, that after a couple of minutes one of them would ask, "How do you say ... ?" It is clear that the lack of communicative functions of the language had affected the fluency considerably. Literally, Spanish had taken up even those spaces that could be intimate, since these women were close friends.

[41] Balbina González provided the translation. Usually *paki* is translated as "to be happy," "to be cheerful."

There are some traits from western Nahuatl mentioned earlier that are not found in Tuxpan. For example, there is no usage of suffix -*lo* to indicate present plural subject, as was found in the colonial documentation. On the other hand, there are shared traits found in other regions. Canger (1986, 283–284) believes that there must be some historical relationship between northern Guerrero and western Mexico traceable to a point before the sixteenth century. A lexical item shared between northern Guerrero and Tuxpan Nahuatl is the use of *aman*, to indicate "now," instead of *axcan*. *Aman* is reported in Pérez's 1713 *Arte*, which documents some lexical items from northern Guerrero Nahuatl, and *amantzin*, "right now" (*ahorita*) is in Cleofas Ramírez Celestino and Karen Dakin (1979, 113). *Tlexochtli* is the word for "fire" in northern Guerrero very similar to what it is in western Nahuatl, *texuxti*, whereas in Tuxpan the word is *lel*.

Let us now talk about the scant materials from Ayotitlán/CGB. In 2010, together with a group of four graduate students in linguistics from the University of Guadalajara, I started to visit the town along with other tiny settlements, *rancherías*, and small groups of dwellings that are part of Ayotitlán, as a larger unit: not the head of the municipality, but the head of the towns that acknowledge Ayotitlán as an ancient and important community.[42] The dialect was not documented at all, nor had "systematic research on language shift and loss, linguistic attitudes toward Nahuatl, or about the symbolic presence of this language ... been done in the region prior to 2010" (Yáñez Rosales et al. 2016, 113).

In the first 2010 elders' council meeting attended, one of the representatives, when asked if there were Nahuatl speakers in Ayotitlán, answered that he himself was one, and started reciting a prayer. When saying the prayer, among other things, he uttered several words portraying the absolutive suffix *l*.

Some of the vocabulary we found in Ayotitlán that exhibits -*l* as suffix talking to the healer and to some of the elders is:

| | |
|---|---|
| *suči-l* | "flower" |
| *naka-l* | "meat" |
| *te-l* | "stone" |
| *nejua-l* | "I" |

We found no speakers, only rememberers (Campbell and Muntzel 1989, 181). However, it was clear that the language plays an important symbolic role, and the elders overtly requested some project that would revitalize the language. In fact, there are two reclamation projects currently in progress (Yáñez Rosales et al. 2016, 127–132).

---

[42] The linguistics students are Paulina Lamas Oliva, Dana K. Nelson, Melissa Niño Santana, and Rodrigo Parra Gutiérrez.

As in Tuxpan, where the greeting in Nahuatl was maintained as an important speech, healing prayers have been maintained in Ayotitlán. In 2018, biologist Higareda Rangel published the corpora of prayers she collected between 1998 and 2001 among healers from Ayotitlán. Her fieldwork was aimed to learn about plants and their usage in healing practices. Thanks to her work (Higareda Rangel 2018), we learn about the role of the healer and their knowledge about plants in a context where the environment is very rich in terms of botanical diversity, but we also realize how important the ritual of saying a healing prayer is, since those who cure are important and reliable persons in their community. It must be underscored that access to medical doctors is scarce and the towns or cities where *centros de salud* (health care centers) can be found are far away, so the traditional healer performs a necessary and respected role within the several towns grouped together with Ayotitlán.

Higareda collected prayers told by nine healers: eight men and one woman. Thanks to these prayers we have more data on Ayotitlán Nahuatl. The prayers consist of a few loose words, many of which are impossible to recognize. The healer must have memorized them orally from someone else, and the whole speech act is very much embedded in the healing performance itself.

The most recognizable term is *jecal*, "wind." In Higareda's corpora, it was uttered many times; in Ayotitlán it is believed that the wind is the "lord of the hills," of the mountains, and since Ayotitlán lies in the sierra there are hills and mountains everywhere. *Jecal* exhibits a couple of variants: *ajecal* (singular), and *jecame*, and *eecame* (plural). In central Nahuatl, we would expect *ehecatl*, "wind." Molina (1555–1571) does not record the plural possibility. However, other dialects do (see De Wolf 2003; Karttunen 1983). Cortés y Zedeño recorded *ehecat*, *ehecal* (1765, 56). *Ajecal* is also recorded by Arreola as the term used in Suchitlán (see table 4.1), which fits perfectly in the Nahua Jalisco-Colima region.

Other recognizable Nahuatl terms found in the prayers are

Novaso de mezcalsúchil

"my glass of blooming mescal," "my glass of mescal flower."[43]

Tegual cempasúchil

"you are marigold"

---

[43] It should be noticed that the possessive is expressed in Nahuatl, *no*, and that the Spanish preposition "de," is already part of the language. Cortés y Zedeño (1765) included numerous expressions that by the time he finished his book, already had *de* as part of fixed phrases, for example: "de cerca," *de amohuecca*; "de algún lugar," *de ten lugar*; "de dentro de la casa," *decalictic*, etc.

Copalsúchil sigual

"incense flower, come" (Higareda Rangel 2018, 132–133).[44]

Tel jacalguey, tel jacal tepichi, san lloque melagua . . .

"Great stone hut, small stone hut, in this manner it is true . . ." (Higareda Rangel 2018, 137)

## CONCLUSIONS

These are the Nahuatl materials from southern Jalisco and Colima recorded over the last 100 years. By the time they were collected, the dialect was already severely threatened.

The samples are limited in many ways. By just looking at Arreola's lexicons, it is impossible to know how the language was spoken by children and teenagers, who usually perform most of the changes in a language and are an indicator of its vitality. Most likely, both Arreola and Ruvalcaba asked adults to provide the lexical items and phrases they collected. These were speakers whose age was, it is my guess, more than thirty. By the time Ruvalcaba published his "Observaciones," children were already listening to more Spanish than Nahuatl. Thanks to Valiñas's materials, we have a linguistic description of the southern Jalisco and Colima dialect, its phonological inventory, and a speech act performed by women during those occasions when an important visitor traveled to Tuxpan. The greeting is as important as a *huhuehtlahtolli*, or a healing prayer. We have greetings that would be said to four different recipients, although they were recorded at the request of the linguist rather than in a natural context.

Regarding the presence of *-l* in southern Jalisco and Colima, Valiñas is cautious. After enumerating the Western Nahuatl isoglosses, he refers to *-l*: "It is important to state, that it is not so much the realization of /t/, but of /l/, which is considered a western innovation." Then he adds: "To this moment, the only thing that can be stated for sure is, I insist, the presence of /l/" (Valiñas 1994, 148, 150).[45]

---

[44] It is not clear whether the prefix of *siguala*, *si*, is the equivalent of *xi*, the imperative prefix added to verbs, in this case, *huallauh*, "to come."

[45] My translation of "Es importante señalar que no es tanto la realización de /t/, sino la de /l/, la que se considera una innovación occidental." A page further down he writes: "Hasta el momento, lo único que se puede plantear como seguro es, insisto, la presencia de la /l/."

As mentioned at the beginning of this chapter, it is still an area of inquiry as to whether in western Mexico, particularly in southern Jalisco and Colima, *tl* changed to *l* at some point in the past, since the earlier texts found in the region exhibit not only central Nahuatl phonological traits but also the elegant style of what was known as classical Nahuatl.[46] This has led me to consider whether the earliest scribes who produced documents in the region originally came from central Mexico, and whether it was only afterward, in the seventeenth century, that the scribes, probably born and raised in western Mexico, wrote texts using the dialect of this region. Some of the western Nahuatl traits appear in the 1618 file from Jalostotitlán (Jalisco) (Sullivan 2003).[47] As time went by, there was every-increasing text production in the western region, and western Nahuatl traits appeared more consistently. It does not matter how large or small a town was; there was a scribe who took responsibility for listening to the dictation of a will, a complaint, a lawsuit, the minutes of an election, and the like. The largest number of extant documents in Nahuatl were written in the seventeenth century, and they clearly exhibit the features of western Nahuatl. The few extant documents written in the eighteenth century confirm the traits of the dialect, among other things that *t*, in all the possible contexts, is distributed from Tlajomulco northward and *l*, in all possible contexts as well, from Tlajomulco southward.

The concern for language documentation and revitalization has existed for some decades already. There are many questions that arise due to the multiple contexts and factors that have caused the substitution of a language in favor of another. At the same time, there are several reclamation and revitalization processes in progress, which also vary in terms of the vitality of the language, whether there is some documentation, if there were one or more fluent speakers, and so on (see Santos García, Carrillo de la Cruz, and Verdín Amaro 2016). Rosa Vallejos (2016) calls our attention to the fact that in the case of languages that are rapidly falling into disuse, dramatic structural changes take place, but these are not clear (144). They may change from language to language depending on the context, the number of speakers, the functions and spaces in which the language was spoken, or other types of factors.

---

[46] See the document from Tuxpan, 1557 (Yáñez Rosales 2022, 55–77), which, besides having the presence of *tl*, is filled with honorifics, like those described by Olmos ([1547] 2002); these honorifics were not used in western Nahuatl documents after 1590.

[47] The file is an accusation against the priest who oversees seven small towns. The fact that there are seven towns where the denunciation is registered is part of the richness of the file. The priest is accused of sexual harassment, beating up the *alcalde* or *mayordomo*, the *prioste* of the brethren, etc. [*alcalde* refers to the mayor, an administrative authority, while *mayordomo* and *prioste* refer to the persons in charge of the religious celebrations organized by the brethren]; he is a very abusive person.

In the case of the elderly women I consulted from Tuxpan, it was very difficult for them to hold a conversation in Nahuatl for more than five minutes. On one occasion, BG went on uttering some phrases, but she had problems finding the words (*temachtiani* or *temachtia*?), and her interlocutor, CF, provided the right word; CF did not say much, mostly she nodded or said *ue*, "yes." On a different occasion, BG displayed her knowledge of the language more fluently, teaching me different phrases and terms—such as "today," "tomorrow," "the day after tomorrow," and "yesterday"—and telling me how to say hello in the morning, in the afternoon, and so forth. The first task implied not only uttering phrases but taking turns, following up what the other person said, putting together meanings and words in a spontaneous manner. In the second one, she was in total control of the content's selection; most of it were fixed phrases. In a different meeting, CF and MR started to talk upon my request. CF always supplied the input, and she tried different topics; however, MR could not follow up.

In the case of Ayotitlán, the prayers contain sentences that look very much like Nahuatl but are not understandable. It could be that the linguistic structure has eroded, in terms of its textual cohesion; the grammatical pattern seems modified. The healers are Spanish speakers and they memorized prayers that were probably composed in Nahuatl, but after decades of not listening to the language, of not practicing it on a regular basis, its healing power no longer resides in the morphology, semantics, or structure of the prayer as a text composed in Nahuatl but rather in the Nahuatl and Spanish words and phrases, which together with the healer's performance make it a believable text.[48]

It is uncertain when the Tuxpan dialect diverged from other western dialects. Cortés y Zedeño (1765) recorded *-l* as absolutive suffix, coexisting with *-t* in terms where in central Nahuatl *-tl* would be expected, and *-ti* (*texuxti*: "fire") where *-tli* would be expected. Valiñas states that the same suffixes have dropped the vowel; that is, *-li* and *-tli* became *-l* and *-t* (1982, 52). There is not enough information to hypothesize when this variation took place: perhaps in the nineteenth century, since Arreola records some cases (*tlaxcal* vs. *tlaxcalli*, "tortilla"; *tonal* vs. *tonalli*, "light,"; 1934, 437). Finally, we have evidence that the Nahuatl dialect from Ayotitlán shared the *l* phoneme that is salient in Nahuatl from southern Jalisco and Colima.

What happened in Tuxpan and Ayotitlán could be the story of many towns where the native language was substituted by another one. In Ayotitlán, the mining

---

[48] One example of this is the following (I have highlighted the recognizable Nahuatl words in boldface, but I have no way of identifying the word order): **Ajecal** pata agua **cualque** lamentica tilo chija los pilite llanos, / pañique laderas: la **temo tigualas**, / carimboro **tigualas**, / carimboro **tigualas** in santo ángel de la guarda, / in santo ángel de su espíritu, < / in santo ángel de su nombre . . . (Higareda Rangel 2018, 132).

industry, legal and illegal, as well as other factors, disrupted the social cohesion of the communities. The strength that Nahuatl communities in southern Jalisco and Colima built during centuries was severely eroded during the first decades of the twentieth century. If I were asked what has remained, I would answer that the language is there and can be identified in the words, in greetings, and in healing prayers; the dialect is also there, since there is a clearly uttered phoneme, *l*, mainly as a suffix, that reveals it is part of southern Jalisco and Colima Nahuatl.

### REFERENCES

Acuña, René 1988. *Relaciones geográficas: Nueva Galicia*. Mexico City: Universidad Nacional Autónoma de México.

Arreola, José María. 1934. "Tres vocabularios dialectales del mexicano." *Investigaciones Lingüísticas* 2: 428–443.

Barlow, Robert. 1949. "Las salinas de Tecomán y otros documentos colimenses del siglo XVI." *Tlalocan* 3: 42–52.

Campbell, Lyle, and Martha C. Muntzel 1989. "The Structural Consequences of Language Death." In *Investigating Obsolescence: Studies in Language Contraction and Death*, edited by Nancy C. Dorian, 181–196. Cambridge: Cambridge University Press.

Canger, Una. 1986. "Los dialectos del náhuatl de Guerrero." In *Primer Coloquio de Arqueología y Etnohistoria del Estado de Guerrero*, 281–292. Mexico City: Instituto Nacional de Antropología e Historia and Gobierno del Estado de Guerrero.

Canger, Una. 2001. *Mexicanero de la Sierra Madre Occidental*. Archivo de las Lenguas Indígenas de México 24. Mexico City: El Colegio de México.

Ciudad Real, Antonio de. (ca. 1582–1587) 1976. *Tratado curioso y doto de las grandezas de la Nueva España*. Edited by Josefina García Quintana and Víctor Manuel Castillo Farreras. 2 vols. Mexico City: Universidad Nacional Autónoma de México.

Cortés y Zedeño, Gerónimo Thomas de Aquino. 1765. *Arte, vocabulario y confesionario en el idioma mexicano como se usa en el Obispado de Guadalajara*. Imprenta del Colegio Real de San Ignacio de la Puebla de los Ángeles.

Dávila Garibi, J. Ignacio. 1935. "Recopilación de datos acerca del idioma coca y de su posible influencia en el lenguaje folclórico de Jalisco." *Investigaciones Lingüísticas* 3: 248–302.

De Wolf, Paul. 2003. *Diccionario español-náhuatl*. Mexico City: Universidad Nacional Autónoma de México, Universidad Autónoma de Baja California Sur, and Fundación Teixidor.

Guerra, fray Juan. (1692) 1900. *Arte de la lengua mexicana según la hablan los indios del Obispado de Guadalajara y parte de los de Durango y Mechoacán*. 2nd ed. Edited by Alberto Santoscoy. Guadalajara: Imprenta Ancira y Hno. A. Ochoa.

Haskett, Robert. 1991. *Indigenous Rulers: An Ethnohistory of Town Government in Colonial Cuernavaca*. Albuquerque: University of New Mexico Press.

Higareda Rangel, Yésica. 2018. *El arte de curar: Los nahuas del ejido de Ayotitlán, Jalisco*. Guadalajara: STAUdeG.

Hill, Jane H., and Kenneth C. Hill. 1986. *Speaking Mexicano: Dynamics of a Syncretic Language in Central Mexico*. Tucson: University of Arizona Press.

Karttunen, Frances. 1983. *An Analytical Dictionary of Nahuatl*. Norman: University of Oklahoma Press.

Karttunen, Frances. 1990. "Conventions of Polite Speech in Nahuatl." *Estudios de Cultura Náhuatl* 20: 281–296.

Lastra de Suárez, Yolanda. 1986. *Las áreas dialectales del náhuatl moderno*. Mexico City: Universidad Nacional Autónoma de México.

Mason, J. Alden. 1917. *Tepecano, a Piman Language of Western Mexico*. New York: Annals of the New York Academy of Sciences.

Medina García, Ricardo. 2016. *Nahuatl Language Petitions from Northwestern New Spain, 1584–1695*. PhD Diss., University of California Los Angeles.

Mentz, Brígida von. 2008. *Cuauhnáhuac 1450–1675: Su historia indígena y documentos en "mexicano." Cambio y continuidad de una cultura nahua*. Mexico City: Porrúa.

Molina, Fray Alonso de. (1555–1571). 1977. *Vocabulario en lengua castellana y mexicana y mexicana y castellana*. Mexico City: Editorial Porrúa.

Mufwene, Salikoko S. 2006. "The Comparability of New-Dialect Formation and Creole Development." *World Englishes* 25 (1): 177–186.

Olmos, Fray Andrés de. (1547) 2002. *Arte de la lengua mexicana*. Edited by Ascensión Hernández de León-Portilla y Miguel León-Portilla. Mexico City: Universidad Nacional Autónoma de México.

Pérez, Fray Manuel. 1713. *Arte de el Idioma Mexicano*. Mexico City: por Francisco Rivera Calderón.

Ramírez Celestino, Cleofas, and Karen Dakin. 1979. *Vocabulario náhuatl de Xalitla, Guerrero*. Mexico City: Centro de Investigaciones y Estudios Superiores en Antropología Social.

Ramírez Celestino, Cleofas, and José Antonio Flores Farfán. 2008. *Huehuetlatolli náhuatl de Ahuehuepan: La palabra de los sabios indígenas hoy*. Mexico City: Centro de Investigaciones y Estudios Superiores en Antropología Social.

Razo Zaragoza, José Luis. 1980. *Crónica de la Real y Literaria Universidad de Guadalajara y sus primitivas constituciones*. Guadalajara: Universidad de Guadalajara.

Restall, Matthew, Lisa Sousa, and Kevin Terraciano, eds. 2005. *Mesoamerican Voices: Native-Language Writings from Colonial Mexico, Oaxaca, Yucatan and Guatemala*. Cambridge: Cambridge University Press.

Ruvalcaba, Melquiades. 1935. "Vocabulario Mexicano de Tuxpan, Jal." *Investigaciones Lingüísticas* 3: 208–214.

Ruvalcaba, Melquiades. 1968. *Manual de gramática náhuatl*. Guadalajara.

Santos García, Saúl, Tutupika Carrillo de la Cruz, and Karina Ivett Verdín Amaro. 2016. "The Revitalization of Wixárika: A Community Project in the Midwest Región of Mexico." In *Language Documentation and Revitalization: Latin American Contexts*, edited by Gabriela Pérez Báez, Chris Rogers, and Jorge Emilio Rosés Labrada, 81–108. Berlin: Walter de Gruyter.

Serafino, Gregorio. 2015. "Las plegarias en náhuatl de La Montaña de Guerrero: Testimonios y recopilaciones." *Estudios de Cultura Náhuatl* 50: 329–353.

Sullivan, Thelma D. 1983. *Compendio de la gramática náhuatl*. Ciudad de México: Universidad Nacional Autónoma de México.

Sullivan, John, ed. 2003. *Ytechcopa timoteilhuia yn tobicario (Acusamos a nuestro vicario): Pleito entre los naturales de Jalostotitlán y su sacerdote (1618)*. Zapopan: El Colegio de Jalisco.

Thomason, Sarah G. 2001. *Language Contact: An Introduction*. Edinburgh: Edinburgh University Press.

Torres Nila, Álvaro J. 2016. "Noticias breves sobre la vida del bachiller Gerónimo Thomas de Aquino Cortés y Zedeño, 1724–1786." In *El náhuatl del Obispado de Guadalajara a través de las obras de los autores fray Juan Guerra (1692) y Gerónimo Cortés y Zedeño (1765)*, edited by Ricardo Medina García, Álvaro J. Torres Nila, and Rosa H. Yáñez Rosales, 11–40. Guadalajara: Universidad de Guadalajara and Biblioteca Pública del Estado de Jalisco Juan José Arreola.

Torres Nila, Álvaro J. 2020a. "Francisco Nayari hace una petición al obispo Juan Ruiz Colmenero (1649): Análisis y traducción de una carta escrita en náhuatl por un hablante de cora." *Tlalocan* 25: 343–385.

Torres Nila, Álvaro J. 2020b. "Agustín de la Rosa: La enseñanza del náhuatl en el Seminario de Guadalajara durante la segunda mitad del siglo XIX." In *Lenguas yutoaztecas: historia, estructuras y contacto lingüístico. Homenaje a Karen Dakin*, edited by Rosa H. Yáñez Rosales, 413–454. Guadalajara: Universidad de Guadalajara.

Valiñas, Leopoldo. 1979. "El náhuatl en Jalisco, Colima y Michoacán." *Anales de Antropología* 16: 325–344.

Valiñas, Leopoldo. 1981. *El náhuatl de la periferia occidental y la costa del Pacífico: Tesis de licenciatura en Lingüística*. Mexico City: Escuela Nacional de Antropología e Historia.

Valiñas, Leopoldo. 1982. "El náhuatl actual en Jalisco." *Tlalocan* 9: 41–69.

Valiñas, Leopoldo. 1994. "Transiciones lingüísticas mayores en occidente." In *Transformaciones mayores en el occidente de México*, coordinated by Ávila Palafox, 127–165. Guadalajara: Universidad de Guadalajara.

Vallejos, Rosa. 2016. "Structural Outcomes of Obsolescence and Revitalization: Documenting Variation among the Kukama-kukamirias." In *Language Documentation and Revitalization. Latin American Contexts*, edited by Gabriela Pérez Báez, Chris Rogers, and Jorge Emilio Rosés Labrada, 143–164. Berlin: Walter de Gruyter.

"Visitación que se hizo en la conquista, donde fue por capitán Francisco Cortés." 1937. In "Nuño de Guzmán contra Hernán Cortés, sobre los descubrimientos y conquistas de Jalisco y Tepic, 1531." *Boletín del Archivo General de la Nación* 8 (4): 556–572.

Winford, Donald. 2003. *An Introduction to Contact Linguistics*. Malden-Oxford: Blackwell Publishing.

Yáñez Rosales, Rosa H. 1988–1996. Fieldwork in Tuxpan, Jalisco. Journal, notes, and recordings. Guadalajara, Jalisco.

Yáñez Rosales, Rosa H. 2013. *Ypan altepet monotza san Antonio de padua tlaxomulco*. "En el pueblo que se llama San Antonio de Padua, Tlajomulco." *Textos en lengua náhuatl, siglos XVII y XVIII*. Estudio, paleografía y traducción. Guadalajara: Instituto de Cultura, Recreación y Deporte de Tlajomulco/<t>Prometeo Editores.

Yáñez Rosales, Rosa H., ed. 2022. *Escribiendo desde el occidente colonial: Paleografía, traducción y vocabulario de 20 documentos en náhuatl, 1557–1737*. Guadalajara: Universidad de Guadalajara.

Yáñez Rosales, Rosa H., Dana Kristine Nelson, Melissa Niño Santana, Rodrigo Parra Gutiérrez, Paulina Lamas Oliva, Agustín Vega Torres, and Rocío Rojas Arias. 2016. "Reclamation Initiatives in Non-speaker Communities: The Case of Two Nahua Communities in the South of Jalisco State, Mexico." In *Language Documentation and Revitalization: Latin American Contexts*, edited by Gabriela Pérez Báez, Chris Rogers, and Jorge Emilio Rosés Labrada, 109–141. Berlin: Walter de Gruyter.

Yáñez Rosales, Rosa H., and Roland Schmidt-Riese. 2017. "Procesos de nivelación en la historia del náhuatl: Consideraciones apoyadas en documentos del antiguo Obispado y Audiencia de Guadalajara." In *Lenguas en contacto, procesos de nivelación y lugares de escritura*, edited by Rosa H. Yáñez Rosales and Roland Schmidt-Riese, 169–199. Guadalajara: Universidad de Guadalajara.

# 5

## Words in Revolution

*How the Nahuas Disappeared from the State of Morelos and from the Historiography of the Mexican Revolution*

MAGNUS PHARAO HANSEN

### 1. INTRODUCTION

Today, the Nahuatl language is spoken in only a handful of towns in the Mexican state of Morelos by a population of some 15,000–20,000 people.[1] We know that at the arrival of the Spanish invaders in 1519, Nahuatl was the primary language spoken in the Morelos valley, which was probably inhabited by some 600,000–800,000 people (Smith 1994). But we do not really know much about the process that led to the disappearance of the Nahuatl language in Morelos. Accounts of the history of Indigenous culture and language in Mexico have tended to assume a slow and

---

[1] I share a special connection to the town of Hueyapan and to the Nahuatl-speaking communities of the state of Morelos with Joe Campbell, to whom I am grateful for his support, inspiration, and friendship. This chapter was first presented in November 2015 as a conference paper; then it became part of a chapter of my 2016 dissertation. Talks with Eric van Young and Gerardo Rios at UCSD helped me develop the argument during this time. The essay was next prepared as a manuscript for an edited volume, which finally did not materialize. In the meantime, historian Baruc Martínez Díaz wrote his dissertation about the Nahuatl language in the chinampa region of Tláhuac, south of Mexico City, and he also argued for a central role of ethnic Nahua people in the Zapatista movement (Martínez Díaz 2022a). In a popularized version of his central argument published in the online magazine *Tierradentro* (Martínez Díaz 2022b), he cites the draft version of this chapter, but essentially we have arrived at the same conclusion independently from each other. I am also grateful to Pablo García Loaeza for redrawing the figures, and to the late Leila Monaghan for her generous support and comments on earlier drafts of the chapter.

gradual process of *mestizaje*, in which Indigenous people peacefully adopted the dominant culture and its language, Spanish. Such accounts have tended to assume that the Nahua population was already a small minority by the end of the colonial period in the early nineteenth century.

In this chapter, I analyze what we know about the process of language shift in Morelos. Based on this analysis, I argue that the traditional account of a slow language shift is wrong. Rather, I propose, the data in fact suggest that the process of Nahuatl language decline accelerated sharply in the early twentieth century, and that instead of the decline being a slow and gradual process, the intense violence of the Mexican Revolution abruptly shifted the population dynamics in Morelos. The turmoil of the revolution converted the Indigenous population of Morelos into a minority and made the Nahuatl language obsolete as a general vehicle of communication among the Indigenous towns of the region.

In this way, I claim that by attending to language history it is possible to uncover what is in essence a genocidal event that took place in recent Mexican history but that has nonetheless been erased in the historiography of the period. The reason for this erasure, I argue, is that Indigenous history of the nineteenth and twentieth centuries has figuratively fallen into the crack between two traditions of Mexican historiography: The ethnohistory tradition privileges local and Indigenous viewpoints but primarily works with the colonial period and its many documents written in Indigenous languages. In contrast, political historiography of nineteenth- and twentieth-century Mexico works primarily with Spanish-language documents and privileges attention to national-level political processes and explanatory models. I suggest that by combining ethnohistorical, ethnographic, and ethnolinguistic methods and modes of attention, it is possible to recover local histories that have been otherwise submerged. Consequently, I argue that anthropologists and linguists continue to have a particular role to play in writing local, Indigenous, and other small histories. Language and processes related to language provide an important index of other sociocultural markers in historical contexts, and by studying the histories of language, we may uncover aspects of the past that would otherwise remain submerged.

I begin section 2 by reviewing what historians of the ethnohistorical school of historiography have written about the process of de-indigenization in Mexico and about the process that has led to the gradual disappearance of the Nahuatl language (and other Indigenous languages). Then, in section 3, I review specifically the literature on the Mexican Revolution in Morelos, focusing on the debates about the role of Indigenous peoples in the Zapatista rebellion. In section 4, I go on to present new evidence for the process of language loss in Morelos—I combine a dialect survey from 1897 with archival materials from Indigenous-language education program in the 1940s, and a 1970s dialect survey, to map the contraction of the Nahua speech community in Morelos over the twentieth century. Next, in section 5, I review the Mexican censuses, which have been used by historians to provide a picture of the ethnolinguistic demography of Morelos in the nineteenth and twentieth centuries. I demonstrate that a basic misreading of the census evidence by historians has erased the presence of tens of thousands of Indigenous Nahuatl-speaking people in Morelos in the decade before the revolution. In the final section, I conclude with a discussion of how attention to language and the social context of language in historiography may contribute to rediscovering past social processes that will otherwise remain out of the historian's view.

## 2. LANGUAGE SHIFT AND THE END OF THE COLONY IN THE NEW PHILOLOGY ETHNOHISTORY TRADITION: WHAT HAPPENED WHEN THE INDIANS STOPPED WRITING?

The bulk of historiography regarding Nahuatl in general and Nahuas of Morelos in particular has been carried out within the broad ethnohistorical tradition and especially by members of the historiographic school often called New Philology. The New Philology approach to ethnohistory was developed by James Lockhart based on his recognition of the immense value of colonial documentary records in Indigenous languages as a window into the complex cultural, social, and political dynamics of Mexican colonial society. Working together with linguist Frances Karttunen, James Lockhart particularly noted that it was possible to trace the history of intensifying contact between Spaniards and Nahuas through the documentary record. Different document types corresponded to different periods of colonization, and gradually the effects of bilingualism resulted also in modifications in the structure of written Nahuatl, making written Nahuatl of the early sixteenth century noticeably different from that of the late eighteenth century. This insight led Karttunen and Lockhart (1976) to propose a three-stage model in which changes in the form of written Nahuatl could be considered diagnostic for different levels of intensity of contact. In the first stage, few loanwords entered Nahuatl from Spanish, and when they did they were mostly related to European cultural items, and Spanish borrowings were still phonologically acculturated to the phonology of Nahuatl. In the second stage, large numbers of borrowings entered the Nahuatl language but mostly nouns and simple lexical material. In stage three, the grammar of Nahuatl began to experience restructuring under the influence of Spanish. In each case, Lockhart argued, the main factor of change was the intensity of language contact as administratively independent "Indian Republics" were gradually flooded with Spaniards, and Native people were gradually forced to work and live alongside speakers of Spanish through colonial policies such as *repartimiento* (labor service) and *congregación* (forced resettlement). In the context of Morelos, different stages of this process have been described by some of Lockhart's students: S. L. Cline (1993) translated and published a collection of very early testaments from Tepoztlán in northern Morelos, and Robert Haskett (1991) described the development of the Indigenous political institutions in western Morelos from the conquest and until independence.

The three-stage model has the implied assumption that the final stage of the process of colonization is a complete language shift from Indigenous languages to Spanish. This assumption is justified in many, perhaps even most, cases, because we know that the communities in which Indigenous language documents were produced are now monolingual Spanish "mestizo" communities. By the beginning of the nineteenth century only very few Indigenous language documents were produced, seemingly marking the end point of the three-stage model. But the problem with this analysis is that the Indigenous languages are still here. While indeed many of the main Indigenous administrative centers of the colonial period are now hispanophone communities, the Indigenous languages continue to be spoken in other towns and regions throughout Mexico. But generally, though with some exceptions such as Tepoztlán, the towns where the Indigenous languages are spoken today did not produce any Indigenous language documents in the colonial period, and frequently they have not used Indigenous languages in writing until recently—if at all. For example, from those regions where Nahuatl vitality today is the strongest—such La Huasteca, the Zongolica highlands in Veracruz, the Puebla highlands around Cuetzalan, central Guerrero, and southeastern Puebla—there are no major collections of colonial documents in Nahuatl. There are more colonial documents in Nahuatl from central Oaxaca, a region that was never Nahuatl speaking, than from the Huasteca region, where today around half a million Nahuatl speakers live.

This finding presents us with the curious paradox that the geographical distribution of Indigenous languages in Mexico in the colonial period as it is visible to the ethnohistorian and the distribution of Indigenous languages today as it is visible to the ethnographer or linguist are almost non-overlapping. Or stated in another way, the Nahuatl language disappeared first in exactly the same places where literacy was strongest and text-production most intensive in the colonial period.

This paradox of course does not mean that Karttunen and Lockhart were mistaken in seeing the intensity of contact as a significant factor in the disappearance of Nahuatl—after all, it is reasonable to assume that the intensity of contact was in fact stronger precisely in the administrative centers where texts were produced. On the other hand, the non-correspondence between current and historically documented Nahuatl speech communities demonstrates that we must not think that the documentary record is a faithful guide to the vitality of spoken languages. Outside of the administrative centers, the languages may have, and in many cases have, continued to be spoken long after they ceased to be used as written languages in the larger towns and cities. Therefore, the ethnohistorical methods of New Philology, which rely on the presence of written records in Indigenous languages, cannot give us adequate information about the process of language shift. While the last administrative documents in Nahuatl from Morelos are from the late eighteenth century, we must look for other sources if we want to know how and when Nahua people stopped using the languages as their everyday form of communication among themselves.

### 3. THE MORELOS REVOLUTION IN NATIONAL HISTORIOGRAPHY: WAS ZAPATA AN INDIGENOUS OR AN AGRARIAN LEADER?

Mexican national historiography has produced a fairly set account of the process that turned Mexico from an Indigenous to a "mestizo" majority nation. The Laws of Cádiz and the subsequent constitution of independent Mexico abolished the *casta* system, and "Indians" were converted into Mexican citizens without any special status. This change in official status made Indigenous people somewhat invisible to documentary history until the revolutionary *indigenismo* pulled them back into national consciousness and into the records. Nonetheless, the nineteenth century was also characterized by violent conflicts, in which Indigenous people and communities played significant roles (Brewster 2003; Mallon 1995; León-Portilla and Mayer 2010; Reina 1980; Van Young 2001). Generally, such Indigenous struggles have been understood in relation to the gradual development of Mexican national consciousness and the rapid development of private industry and of the institutions of the Mexican state.

In the context of Morelos, there are few references to the history of Indigenous communities in the nineteenth century; exceptions are references to the participation of Indigenous people in the independence struggle by E. Van Young (2001) and the descriptions of the gradual encroachment of haciendas on Indigenous landholdings that provide the background for many analyses of the motivation behind the Zapatista movement—was Zapatismo a part of a wider agrarian political movement or part of the tradition of Indigenous movements and rebellions?

In the literature, this question has often been treated as a question of Emiliano Zapata's own ethnicity, and different historians writing in different periods have emphasized either the Indigenous aspects of his identity such as his role as a local community leader, or his participation in national electoral politics prior to the outbreak of the revolution. Samuel Brunk (2008) shows how quickly after the assassination of Zapata, his image was incorporated into a wide range of different political causes, making it hard to separate the man from the various myths and the functions they have served. Brunk argues that Zapata was effectively indigenized as he was recruited as an icon by the dominant *indigenista* ideology of the postrevolutionary state. Perhaps the earliest example of this sort of indigenist historiography of Zapatismo is Jesús Sotelo Inclán's 1943 *Raíz y razón de Zapata* ([1943] 1970), the first biography of Zapata. Sotelo presents an interpretation of Zapata as an Indigenous community leader who fought primarily for the land rights of his own community, and secondarily for the rights of other Indigenous agriculturalists to the lands that the hacienda owners had usurped. Subsequent historians have reacted to this interpretation by inserting Zapata and his movement into the wider perspective of the agrarian movement as a reaction to the excesses of the hacienda system, noting the absence of ethnically inflected rhetoric in Zapata's discourse.

This reaction was exemplified in John Womack's 1969 biography, which simply dismissed in a footnote the possibility that the Morelos revolution had a significant Indigenous element, citing a 1962 UNAM master's thesis in geography (Holt-Büttner 1962) that analyzes census data in Morelos from 1900 to 1950 to the effect that Nahuatl speakers only made up 9.29 percent of the population of Morelos at the time the revolution broke out (Womack 1969, 71). Womack also cites an anecdote from Sotelo Inclán, which describes that Zapata's travels to the village priest in Tetelcingo to get his help in deciphering the ancient Nahuatl titles of Anenecuilco, as evidence that Zapata did not know a word of Nahuatl (apparently ignoring or ignorant of eyewitness accounts of Zapata speaking Nahuatl such as that of Luz Jiménez) (Horcasitas and Jiménez 1968). Luz Jiménez's eyewitness account has also been supported by the publication of the Zapata manifestos in Nahuatl aimed at the Nahuas of the Malinche region in Puebla (León-Portilla 1996). More recent work by historian Gerardo Ríos identified Zapatista propaganda aimed at local populations in Morelos and northern Guerrero that bluntly states, "El Zapatismo es la Revolución del Indio, no peleara [*sic*] por la Presidencia" (Zapatism is the Revolution of the Indian, it will not fight for the presidency) (Ríos 2019). Here, the Zapatistas clearly identify their movement as an ethnoracial one, aiming at land and freedom for Indigenous communities but uninterested in national politics.

Apart from Luz Jiménez, other contemporaries also recognized a significant Indigenous element in the revolutionary base in Morelos. A man who probably all would agree was qualified to assess the ethnic categorizations of Indigenous Mexicans was Manuel Gamio, the father of Mexican anthropology. As a young man, Gamio had lived on his parents' hacienda by the Río Hondo in the Zongolica region, and there he had learned Nahuatl speaking with the workers. Gamio's well-known foundational treatise of Mexican Nationalism is *Forjando Patria* (Gamio [1916] 2010), which was written in the Federal District in 1915 while Zapata and his men were fighting the Carrancistas fewer than 100 kilometers to the south. In his book, Gamio lists three "Nationalist problems" that must be solved to successfully "forge the nation." Each of them is a group that has a history of militantly resisting incorporation into the nation: Yaquis of Sonora, known for their protracted struggle with Porfirio Díaz's regime; the Maya of Yucatán, who had only recently become reincorporated into the nation after the Caste War; and the "Population of Morelos." Gamio analyzes the problem of Zapatismo, breaking it into three kinds of issues: "The first of these is simple banditry, which in Morelos, as in other parts of the republic, often hides behind the face of revolution. Second, there are surviving elements of the previous regime that have taken advantage of the eternal disorientation of the Indian and sent him off on nefarious adventures. Lastly, there is the legitimate Zapatismo, which could better be called Indianism. Zapatismo is a localist and temporary denomination that is bound to disappear, whereas Indianism has persisted vigorously in Mexico since Cortés placed his standard on the sands of Villa Rica" (Gamio [1916] 2010, 158). In this way, Gamio equates Zapatismo (of the "legitimate" kind) with Indian resurgence. Gamio, writing in close proximity to Morelos and with intimate knowledge of Nahuatl and Nahua culture, considered the Morelos revolution to be a primary example of the "Indian problem" and to be fueled by the legitimate grievances of Indigenous communities against the process of colonization and the Mexican national state.

Despite Gamio's contemporary identification of the Morelos rebellion as an Indigenous rebellion, Alan Knight (1986, 1990) also downplays the role of local Indigenous ethnic sentiment as a force in the revolution, distinguishing between "serrano" and "agrarian" rebellions and counting the Morelos revolution among the latter. Choosing the term *serrano* (highlander), instead of "Indigenous," to describe localist rebellions in rural areas, Knight seems almost at pains to avoid hints of ethnic categories in his analysis. Another Zapata biographer, Roberto Millón (1969), explicitly rejects the idea of an Indianist revolution, citing Zapata's dress style and parentage as evidence that he, and by extension his followers, were not Indigenous but "mestizo" (whatever that means). The gradual turn away from indigenism in Mexican national historiography also created a new vision of Zapata as a politician and military commander, more than as a leader of a social movement or as an Indigenous leader.

The writing of history is not only a question of "what actually happened." The indigenista era produced indigenista history, and the subsequent wave of political materialism in history produced histories of peasants and agrarian politics. Whoever tells history tells the story from the perspective of their particular interests, concerns, and epistemological commitments. Hence, it will always be necessary to have as many perspectives as possible in order to reveal the areas of omission of each historian and school of historiography (see Neutel 1978 on the importance of "ethnic archives" in order to become able to approach what "actually happened"). In telling the histories of Indigenous peoples, it is necessary to not only listen to their voices, as ethnohistorians would agree (von Mentz 2008), but also to find ways to recover voices that have not been recorded in writing.

Perhaps today, in the light of the Mexican neo-indigenism currently sweeping through Mexican cultural politics, it is time to reevaluate the ethnic and Indigenous element of the Mexican Revolution. In the next sections, echoing Miguel León-Portilla's similar critique (1996, 40–44), I will argue that Womack and Millon's arguments for seeing Zapata as an essentially mestizo farmer and the Zapatista rebellion as a mestizo agrarian movement are weak when we actually study the ethnic composition of Morelos at the time of the revolution. Womack and subsequent historians have been all too willing to accept the conclusion that Indigenous people were a small minority, and the kinds of sources that they have used for their histories—namely, official documents from the archives, which are of course all in Spanish—have given them no reasons to question this narrative. When we look at the history of the Nahuatl language in the state of Morelos, reasons to reconsider the role of the Nahuas in the Zapatista revolution emerge.

## 4. CONTRACTION OF NAHUATL IN MORELOS IN THE NINETEENTH AND TWENTIETH CENTURIES: A SURVEY OF THE SURVEYS

Today Nahuatl is spoken in six communities in Morelos: *Cuentepec* (Temixco municipality), *Hueyapan* (Hueyapan municipality), *Tetelcingo* (Cuautla municipality), *Santa Catarina* (Tepoztlán municipality), *Xoxocotla* (Puente de Ixtla municipality), and *Tenextepango* (Ayala municipality). Of these, Cuentepec is the only town where the language is spoken by all generations and by most of the inhabitants; in Santa Catarina and Xoxocotla only a few elderly persons speak the language. Tenextepango is located in the municipality of Ayala, where Zapata's hometown of Anenecuilco is also located, but as far as I have been able to ascertain all the speakers there are part of a community that migrated from Guerrero in the second half of the twentieth century. The Instituto Nacional de Estadística, Geografía e Informática (INEGI; Mexican institute of Geography and Statistics) 2020 census counts 24,617 speakers in the state out of a total population of some 1.97 million, and this figure may be rising due to current efforts to revitalize the language in several of the state's communities (https://cuentame.inegi.org.mx/monografia/informacion/mor/poblacion/diversidad.aspx?tema=me&e=17).

I have found three sources of information that give clues about the distribution of Nahuatl in the state of Morelos in the nineteenth and twentieth centuries: (1) an

1897 dialect survey in recording instances of language use in fifteen communities in the state; (2) a 1941 list of Nahuatl language teachers showing the language existing in four additional communities; and (3) a 1974 dialect survey by Karen Dakin and Diane Ryesky showing the language in eight communities (Dakin 1974). I compared these materials with the current state of the language: it is spoken in only six communities (one of which is a recent migrant community of speakers from Guerrero). This historical data about speaker populations are represented in figure 5.1.

When the valley of Morelos fell under Spanish colonial rule in the 1520s, Nahuatl was the main language spoken in the state. Through the colonial period, Spaniards arrived, establishing themselves mainly in the two main cities, Cuernavaca and Cuautla, creating sugar haciendas and mining operations and bringing in enslaved Africans to work them alongside the Indigenous workers who were levied through the encomienda and later *repartimiento* systems. By the end of the colony, Morelos's population was clearly more mixed than before, but we do not actually know how the impact of the hacienda system had affected the Indigenous language, and we do not have any data for how many speakers of the language were in the state, or where they were concentrated. Brígida Von Mentz (2010) cites a petition from eight communities around Jojutla in southwestern Morelos from 1812, in which the community requests that a local man be instated as the authority because he speaks the Nahuatl language. If nothing else, this petition shows the continued relevance of Nahuatl as a language also of political communication in the Morelos valley at the end of the colony.

A more systematic view of the distribution of Nahuatl in the nineteenth century comes from an 1897 dialect survey by Antonio Peñafiel, who collected words in Nahuatl across Morelos and other states. He noted words from fifteen different communities throughout the state, in a survey that actually covered the state's entire territory. Nahuatl was clearly widely spoken in the state, including in the tropical zone owned mostly by the haciendas at the end of the nineteenth century. The first clear indications that the language is on the wane are from 1941, when anthropologist Robert Barlow was looking for language teachers to teach Nahuatl literacy. Barlow was heading a project of Nahuatl language education in Morelos, and in his records found at the Barlow papers at the Universidad de las Américas in Cholula, we see that he interviewed potential Native-speaking teachers from several locations, including three towns not among the locations surveyed in 1897. Barlow in fact interviewed a Nahuatl-speaking teacher in Zapata's birth town Anenecuilco, showing us that the language was still spoken there a few decades after Zapata's death. In 1972, linguists surveyed the language in the state and found remnant elderly speakers in eleven communities but only children speaking in three (Cuentepec, Santa Catarina, Hueyapan). This data clearly fix the main

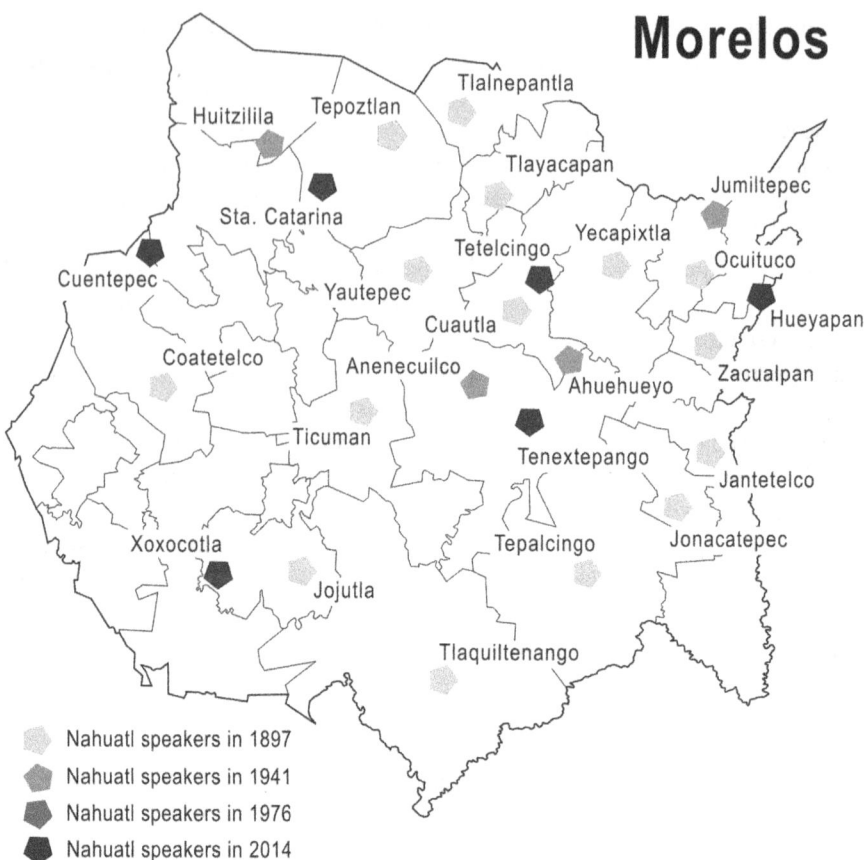

**Figure 5.1.** Chronogeographic map of the distribution of Nahuatl speakers in Morelos across the twentieth century. Each pentagonal-shaped point indicates a location where Nahuatl is known to have been spoken at some time between 1897 and 2014. Tenextepango is the only place where we know that the current Nahua population is a recent arrival; elsewhere we can assume that a place that has Nahua speakers currently also had speakers in the past.

moment of retraction of Nahuatl in Morelos to the period between 1897 and 1941. Notably, the 1940s saw a trend of urbanization across Mexico depopulating many of the country's rural communities, a process that could have affected the vitality of Indigenous languages, but it seems that the turn away from Nahuatl in Morelos predated the main period of rural-to-urban migration in the state. When we compare the places where Nahuatl was spoken at the beginning of the twentieth century and where it is spoken now, we see that the surveys found Nahuatl speakers in the main valley, the most densely populated part of the state. It is here that the sugar-producing haciendas, requiring a significant labor force, were located. We can see that today, the Nahuatl-speaking towns are found on the mountainous northern edge of the state—and in the three valley communities of Tetelcingo, Xoxocotla and Tenextepango. The community in Tenextepango arrived from Guerrero exactly to work as day laborers in the cane fields when the industry reconstituted itself in the second half of the twentieth century. In Tetelcingo and Xoxocotla (and also Hueyapan and Santa Catarina in the highlands), it seems that specific local political circumstances made communities rally around their Indigenous language and identity as they competed with more powerful mestizo *cabecera*-communities. The picture is clear: between 1900 and 1950 the Nahuatl language almost disappeared entirely from the Morelos valley floor, disappearing from the agricultural communities closest to the major sugar haciendas.

## 5. LANGUAGE AND DEMOGRAPHIC HISTORY: THE MEXICAN CENSUSES 1900–1930

A second set of sources are the official national censuses, which were collected every ten years beginning in 1900. They include language data, incorporating information about speakers of Indigenous languages. The censuses can be found online at the website of the INEGI. I looked at language data in the Mexican censuses of 1900, 1910, 1921, and 1930 to get a better idea of the demographic processes at play in this period.

In 1900 the national census surveyed the linguistic landscape of Morelos and gave a figure of 16.9 percent speakers of Indigenous languages in Morelos; in the 1910 census this number had fallen to 9 percent. The 1921 census carried out while the revolution was still ongoing did not include data on Indigenous languages and has been widely criticized as unreliable (McCaa 2003). But the 1930 census did collect language data and gave a figure of 14 percent of the total population. If read at face value, this figure suggests that the Indigenous population loss during the revolution was roughly proportional with the overall population loss in the state. Figure 5.2 gives a diagrammatic representation of the population composition in the four censuses using the crude numbers of speakers of Indigenous languages and speakers of Spanish. The dark part of each column represents the speakers of Indigenous languages counted in each census as portion of the entire population—as can be seen, discounting the 1921 census, the number appears more or less constant from 1900 to 1930 at around 20,000 Nahuatl speakers, only slightly higher than the current number.

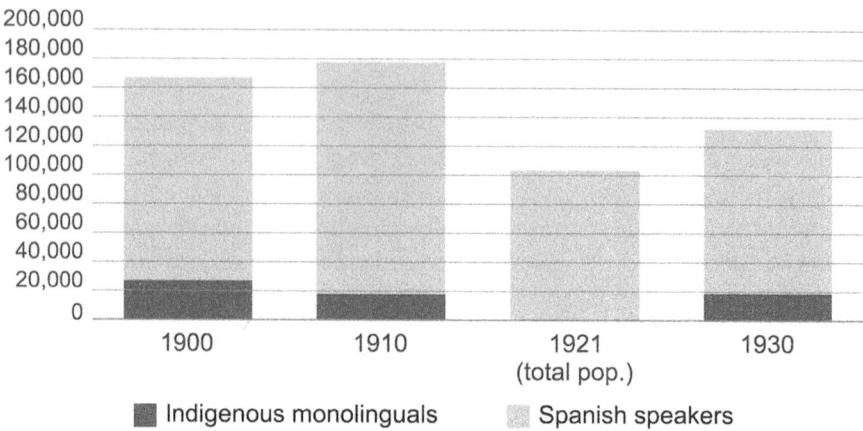

**Figure 5.2.** Diagram of census data for the four censuses; the dark part of each column is the number of counted speakers of Nahuatl, including only monolingual speakers.

When we looked chrono-geographically at the data in section 4, we saw that the most radical language shift in Morelos, the contraction of the language away from the valley floor, must have taken place in the period between 1900 and 1930 precisely the period of the Mexican Revolution. Yet the percentage numbers of Nahuatl speakers relative to the entire population in 1900 and 1930 are almost the same—17 percent and 14 percent, respectively. These figures would suggest that there was no major overall decrease in the Indigenous population between 1910 and 1930, neither in relative, nor in absolute, numbers. This is the assumption that underlies Womack's claim that the Zapata movement was primarily a mestizo movement. But how could speaker numbers remain steady while Nahuatl disappeared from the Morelos valley?

To understand the discrepancy between the speaker data and the census data, I enlisted the survey instruments used by the national census to see what exactly they were counting—the original survey instruments are also available at INEGI's website (http://www.inegi.org.mx/est/contenidos/Proyectos/ccpv/cpv1900/doc/1900_c.pdf).

The 1900 Mexican census questionnaire collected data about Indigenous languages spoken, providing a field with the title "Idioma nativo o lengua hablada" (Native or spoken language). The instructions to the person administering the census stated clearly the procedure for filling out the field: "the name of the native or commonly spoken language, such as Spanish, French, English, etc., should be noted on column 11a. Or also the name of the Indigenous language, such as Mexicano or Nahuatl, Zapotec, Otomí Tarascan, Maya, Tzeltal, Huastec, Totonac etc. *For the person who speaks Spanish and an Indigenous language such as Otomí, Mexicano, or any other, Spanish will be noted preferably*" (my emphasis and translation).[2] These instructions meant that for bilingual persons *only* Spanish should be noted, which in turn means that the percentage figure given for speakers of Nahuatl includes only *monolingual* Nahuatl speakers, whereas bilingual Nahuas (and any ethnic Nahuas who did not speak the language) are counted as Spanish speakers. In 1900, using this way of counting, the number of speakers of Indigenous languages given in the survey was 16.9 percent *monolingual* Nahuatl speakers in Morelos. But of course, in almost any society with a minority and a majority language spoken side by side, most of the speakers of the minority language are bilingual and hence would not figure in the survey.

For the 1930 census, the questionnaire gave the possibility of recording two languages, first whether the respondent spoke the national language or not and then, in the second slot which other language they spoke. This means that for 1930 the figure of 14 percent Nahuatl speakers includes *both* monolingual and bilingual speakers—whereas the figure for 1900 (and 1910, which used the same questionnaire) includes *only* monolingual speakers, counting bilinguals as Spanish speakers. So, in fact, the 1910 and the 1930 censuses counted completely different categories of speakers, and hence the percentages compared and used by Womack as his evidence for the small significance of Indigenous people in the Morelos revolution are not in fact comparable. To compare the numbers, they must first be made comparable by factoring the presence of bilingual speakers of Nahuatl into the population. This can be done by some informed guesswork based on our knowledge of ratios between monolinguals and bilinguals today.

Today, there are few communities anywhere in Mexico with percentages of monolingual speakers of Indigenous languages as high as 16 percent, and in those communities the vast majority of inhabitants tend to speak Nahuatl as a first language and Spanish as a second language. Towns with similar numbers of monolinguals are found, for example, in the Zongolica region of Veracruz. In the municipality of Tehuipango, Veracruz, there are estimated some 15 percent monolingual Nahuatl

---

[2] "En la columna 11*a* debe escribirse el nombre de la lengua nativa ó hablada comunmente, como castellano, francés, inglés, etc., ó bien el nombre del idioma indígena, como por ejemplo el mexicano ó nahuatl, el zapoteco, el otomí, el tarasco, el maya, el tzendal, el huasteco, el totonaco, etc., etc. *A la persona que hable el castellano y un idioma indígena, como el otomí ó el mexicano ó cualquier otro, se le anotará de preferencia el castellano.*" Census survey questionnaire from 1900 census accessed at https://www.inegi.org.mx/contenidos/programas/ccpv/1900/doc/1900_c.pdf.

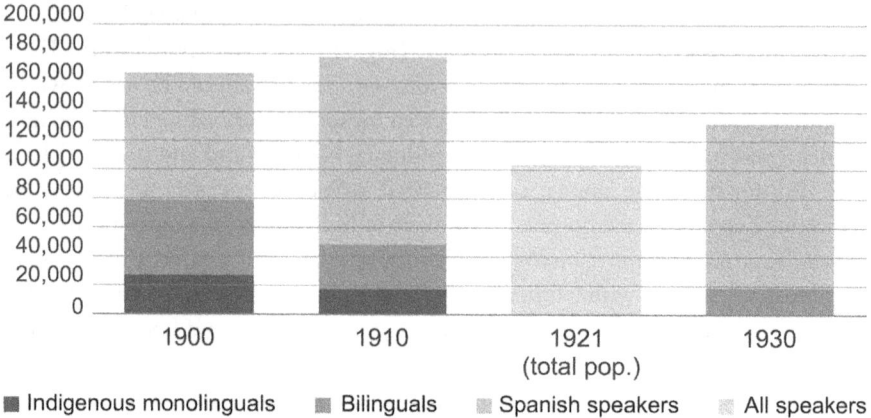

**Figure 5.3.** Diagram of population figures in the four censuses, adding a conservative estimate of the number of bilingual speakers in 1900 and 1910.

speakers, and virtually everyone else is a Nahuatl bilingual, except for people who have moved to the town from outside. The total percentage of Nahuatl speakers in Tehuipango is above 90 percent, the vast majority of them bilingual. If we assume that Morelos in 1910 had a similar demographic breakdown as municipalities like Tehuipango, we would arrive at an estimated population breakdown of 10 percent monolingual Nahuatl speakers, 10–20 percent monolingual speakers of Spanish, and 70–80 percent Spanish/Nahuatl bilinguals. Given that the state of Morelos had 161,000 inhabitants in 1900, that would suggest a composition with approximately 16,000 monolingual Nahuatl speakers, and probably at least 100,000 bilingual Nahuas in the state.

In 1930, the total population of Morelos was 130,000, 30,000 less than before the revolution. Of this population, based on the percentages of Nahuatl speakers, we can estimate the Indigenous population of Morelos at approximately 50,000 in 1910. These corrected numbers are given in figure 5.3. The corrected numbers show that after the war, the total Nahuatl-speaking population may have been reduced from approximately 50,000 to less than 20,000 (also including both mono- and bilinguals).

Given the relatively modest decline in the total population from 1910 to 1930, this proposed figure of an 80 percent Indigenous population loss may seem exaggerated. But the loss is hidden in the censuses because they don't take into account the influx of out-of-state people in the seven years following the revolution. The fact that Indigenous population loss was much greater than what the raw population figure suggests is also shown by cohort analyses that show that the people counted in 1910 are not the same as those counted in 1930. For example, of the 90,000 women counted in Morelos in 1910, only 35,000 were counted again in 1930 (McCaa 2003). This difference points to a drastic decline in Native-born (mostly Nahuatl-speaking) Morelenses and their replacement of people from other states during and after the war.

In figure 5.3, the corrected speaker numbers are given, calculating the monolingual/bilingual ratio for 1900 and 1910 in the following way: bilinguals = 2 × monolinguals (subtracted from the total number of Spanish speakers). The estimate of a 2:1 ratio of bilinguals is conservative compared to municipalities with large numbers of monolingual Nahuatl speakers today, allowing for the possibility that there were a higher percentage of Nahuatl monolinguals in Nahua communities 100 years ago. One would expect the bilingual Nahuatl-speaking population to grow slightly as the monolingual population declines, suggesting that the bilingual percentage for 1910 should be a little larger than that for 1900, but these figures assume a stable 2:1 ratio between 1900 and 1910. There is also a remarkable drop in Nahua population between 1900 and 1910 (of almost 11,000 persons). This drop in Indigenous populations was found all across Mexico in the 1910 census and may be explained by differences in the way the census was carried out. Perhaps rural areas were less thoroughly surveyed in 1910; or, alternatively, the increased reach of public education was taking effect, resulting in fewer monolingual youths (in this case the ratio of bilinguals to monolinguals should likely be higher). Nonetheless, the most dramatic drop of more than 50 percent clearly occurred between 1910 and 1930, the period affected by the death toll of the revolution, and the Spanish flu. This drop only becomes visible once we realize that the Nahuatl-speaking population did not grow by 2,000 people in that period but that the numbers are in fact not directly compatible, since the 1930 figure includes bilinguals and the 1910 figure does not. Between 1900 and 1930, the total Nahuatl-speaking population seems to have dropped from around 80,000 people to fewer than 20,000—close to the number found today. It seems, then, that the Nahua population of Morelos decreased by a massive 75 percent over thirty years.

### 6. CONCLUSION: THE ACCIDENTAL ERASURE OF A GENOCIDE?

The Nahuatl-speaking Indigenous populations of Morelos did not suddenly disappear when they stopped writing official documents in their Indigenous languages in the eighteenth century, or when they were suddenly reclassified as Mexican citizens after independence at the beginning of the nineteenth. They persisted through all this and continued to speak their languages. But spoken languages leave few traces of the sort that a historian finds useful, and even when they do one needs to actually decide to attend to languages, and to the social and cultural contexts in which they live to interpret these traces. The linguistic and demographic evidence and analysis here suggest strongly that at the beginning of the revolution the majority of the population of Morelos spoke Nahuatl—not just in the mountain villages and rural hamlets but throughout the countryside. Then what caused the precipitous drop in Nahuatl-speaking population between 1900 and 1930?

There are two probable causes of the disappearance of Nahuatl speakers between 1900 and 1930: one, is the onslaught of the Spanish flu pandemic of 1918, which has been estimated to have cost several hundred thousand lives in Mexico (Alexander 2019). The Spanish flu was particular in killing mostly people in the prime of life, rather than children and the elderly, but there is little reason to think that it would be biased against Indigenous people, though it may have been harsher for the communities of poor and starving peasants, who were predominantly Indigenous, than for urban dwellers.

The other likely reason is the exceptionally violent tactics of Francisco I. Madero, Victoriano Huerta, and Venustiano Carranza in dealing with the population of Morelos. They deployed General Juvencio Robles with the specific mission of carrying out a scorched-earth tactic, of the type that he had first used against the Yaqui rebellion in Sonora and that in turn made Morelos experience the most intense violence and the largest death toll during the revolution (McCaa 2003). These tactics are documented by Womack, who quotes Robles and Huerta for statements that directly express an intent to violently depopulate Morelos. Womack quotes a 1913 speech by Huerta announcing the beginning of military action in Morelos, in which he tells a group of Morelos hacienda owners that he would use "extreme measures, for the government is so to speak going to depopulate the state, and will send to your haciendas other workers" (Womack 1969, 165). Huerta also warned them not to be surprised if "something abnormal happens, because the state of things demands procedures that are not sanctioned by law . . ." (165). He cited General Robles himself for saying that he is trying to clean up beautiful Morelos, and "What a nice place it will be, once we get rid of the Morelenses. If they resist me, I shall hang them as earrings to the trees" (168).

If we believe, as Womack did, that Morelenses, were ethnically and culturally identical to the majority population, these comments may be draconic, but once we realize that a significant portion of the rural proletariat, perhaps even the majority, was Indigenous, we may understand the dehumanizing discourse in a different light. When constitutionalist authorities spoke of the "Morelenses" as a mass of troublesome bandits to be deported, pacified, hanged, and cleansed, this classification in fact implied a sense of ethnic and racial otherness.

Paco Ignacio Taibo II (2013) has argued that Porfirio Díaz's tactics against the Yaqui rebellion were in fact genocidal, and the erasure of the participation of Yaquis in the Mexican Revolution has been described as a form of historical "ghosting" (Serrano 2019). It seems that this argument applies also to the Nahuas of Morelos, where the counterinsurgency campaigns in Morelos during in the revolution appears to have had a racial motive and a genocidal impetus, and that this violence is at the root of the disappearance of Nahuatl as the main spoken language of Morelos.

**REFERENCES**

Alexander, R. M. 2019. "Spanish Flu and the Sanitary Dictatorship: Mexico's Response to the 1918 Influenza Pandemic." *Americas* 76 (3): 443–465.

Brewster, K. 2003. *Militarism, Ethnicity, and Politics in the Sierra Norte de Puebla, 1917–1930*. Tucson: University of Arizona Press.

Brunk, Samuel. 2008. *The Posthumous Career of Emiliano Zapata: Myth, Memory, and Mexico's Twentieth Century*. Austin: University of Texas Press.

Cline, Sarah L. 1993. *The Book of Tributes: Early Sixteenth-Century Nahuatl Censuses from Morelos*. Los Angeles: UCLA Latin American Center Publications, University of California Press.

Dakin, Karen. 1974. "Dialectología náhuatl de Morelos: Un estudio preliminar." *Estudios de cultura náhuatl* 11: 152.

Gamio, Manuel. (1916) 2010. *Forjando Patria: Pro-nacionalismo*. Edited and translated by Fernando Armstrong Fumero. Boulder: University Press of Colorado.

Haskett, Robert. S. 1991. *Indigenous Rulers: An Ethnohistory of Town Government in Colonial Cuernavaca*. Albuquerque: University of New Mexico Press.

Holt-Büttner, Elizabeth. 1962. *Evolución de las localidades en el estado de Morelos según los censos de población, 1900–1950*. Mexico City: Facultad de Filosofía y Letras, Universidad Nacional Autónoma de México.

Horcasitas, Fernando, and Luz Jiménez. 1968. *De Porfirio Díaz a Zapata: Memoria náhuatl*. Mexico City: Universidad Nacional Autónoma de México.

Karttunen, Frances, and James Lockhart. 1976. *Nahuatl in the Middle Years: Language Contact Phenomena in Texts of the Colonial Period*. Los Angeles: University of California Press.

Knight, Alan. 1986. *The Mexican Revolution, vol. 1. Porfirians, Liberals, and Peasants*, 82–91. Lincoln: University of Nebraska Press.

Knight, Alan. 1990. "Racism, Revolution, and Indigenismo: Mexico, 1910–1940." In *The Idea of Race in Latin America, 1870–1940*, edited by Richard Graham, Thomas E. Skidmore, Aline Helg, and Alan Knight, 71–113. Austin: University of Texas Press.

León-Portilla, Miguel. 1996. *Los manifiestos en náhuatl de Emiliano Zapata*. Mexico City: Instituto de Investigaciones Históricas, Universidad Nacional Autónoma de México.

León-Portilla, Miguel, and A. Mayer. 2010. *Los indígenas en la Independencia y en la Revolución Mexicana*. Mexico City: Instituto de Investigaciones Históricas, Universidad Nacional Autónoma de México.

Mallon, F. E. 1995. *Peasant and Nation: The Making of Postcolonial Mexico and Peru*. Los Angeles: University of California Press.

Martínez Díaz, Baruc. 2022a. "La chinampa en llamas: Conflictos por el territorio y zapatismo en la región de tláhuac (1894–1923)." PhD diss., Universidad Nacional Autónoma de México.

Martínez Díaz, Baruc. 2022b. "El Movimiento Zapatista y su relación con la lengua Náhuatl." *Tierradentro*. https://www.tierraadentro.cultura.gob.mx/el-movimiento-zapatista-y-su-relacion-con-la-lengua-nahuatl/.

McCaa, Robert. 2003. "Missing Millions: The Demographic Costs of the Mexican Revolution." *Mexican Studies* 19 (2): 392–393.

Millón, Robert P. 1969. *Zapata: The Ideology of a Peasant Revolutionary*. New York: International Publishers.

Neutel, Walter. 1978. "Geschichte Wie Es Eigentlich Gewesen or the Necessity of Having Ethnic Archives Programmes." *Archivaria* 1 (7): 104–109.

Reina, Leticia. 1980. *Las rebeliones campesinas en México (1819–1906)*. Mexico City: Siglo Veintiuno.

Ríos, Gerardo. 2017. "'Por la Patria Chica': Indigenous Rebellion and Revolution in the Oriente Central de México, Tlaxcala, and Puebla, 1853–1927." PhD diss., University of California, San Diego.

Serrano, C., 2019. "Ghosting Indigenous Cultures: Yaquis' Near Absence in Literature of the Mexican Revolution." *Journal of the Southwest* 61 (4): 788–820.

Smith, M. E. 1994. "Economies and Polities in Aztec-Period Morelos: Ethnohistoric Introduction." In *Economies and Polities in the Aztec Realm*. Vol. 6, edited by Mary G. Hodge and Michael E. Smith. Boulder: University Press of Colorado.

Sotelo Inclán, José. (1943) 1970. *Raíz y razón de Zapata*. Mexico City: Comisión Federal de Electricidad.

Taibo, Paco Ignacio, II. 2013. *Yaquis: Historia de una guerra popular y un genocidio en México*. Mexico City: Planeta.

Womack, John, Jr. 1969. *Zapata and the Mexican Revolution*. New York: Alfred Knopf.

Van Young, E. 2001. *The Other Rebellion: Popular Violence, Ideology, and the Mexican Struggle for Independence, 1810–1821*. Stanford, CA: Stanford University Press.

von Mentz, Brígida. 2008. "¿Podemos escuchar las voces de los grupos subalternos en los archivos?" *Desacatos* 26: 143–150.

von Mentz, Brígida. 2010. "Bases sociales de la insurgencia en las regiones mineras y azucareras del sur de la capital novohispana (1810–1812)." *Desacatos* 34: 27–60.

# 6

## The Vocabulary of Running in the Mexica World

JOHN F. SCHWALLER

Running had an important place in both the ceremonial and everyday life of the Mexica.[1] Several of the festivals of the Mexica *xiuhpohualli*, or vague solar year, saw the use of ceremonies that involved running. Indeed, the signature ritual of the Mexica festival of Panquetzaliztli involved a priestly runner who carried an amaranth dough image of Huitzilopochtli on a course in the capital of Tenochtitlan and adjoining regions of the Central Basin of Mexico for over twenty miles (thirty-three kilometers). This run was only one small part of a series of rituals that marked the end of Panquetzaliztli. Other festivals saw groups of warriors running from one point to another carrying trophies of one sort or another. The important New Fire ceremony also featured runners who distributed the newly lit flames to every village and town in the Central Basin of Mexico. Running was a very distinctive-yet-essential element to many Mexica ritual celebrations. Looking at the ceremonies scattered throughout the year, it is clear that running played an important life in the ritual life of the Mexica. In addition to the practice of running in various Mexica rituals, the larger commercial and economic entity of the Triple Alliance depended on courier, porters, and others whose occupation depended on their feet. Running was associated, as will be seen, with carrying both goods and messages. Thus, porters

---

[1] This work is based partially on the massive morphological index to the corpus of works written by Sahagún, developed by R. Joe Campbell, to whom I express my profound thanks. He was my first Nahuatl professor and has remained a close friend and colleague for nearly fifty years.

and bearers were frequently grouped with the fleet messengers. Needless to say, the vocabulary of running among the Mexica and related nations manifested these discrete functions. One can gain an appreciation for the use of the various words for running as they appear in Nahuatl version of the *Florentine Codex*. Looking at these elements, one sees that running and the carrying of burdens were central to the religious, political, and commercial life of the Mexica.

## I. RUNNING AMONG THE MEXICA

Nearly all significant studies on the Mexica rely on works by Fray Diego Durán and Fray Bernardino de Sahagún as their point of departure. In addition, Spanish accounts of the conquest and other sources provide information regarding running and runners. Hernán Cortés, in his letters to the Spanish crown, explained that the *huey tlahtoani*, Moteuczoma,[2] maintained a corps of fast runners to carry messages from one part of the empire to another. As a result of these couriers, when the Spanish finally landed on the Gulf Coast at a site they would call La Villa Rica de la Vera Cruz (The Noble Town of the True Cross), since they had landed on the feast of Good Friday, within hours emissaries dispatched by Moteuczoma greeted them. Cortés claimed that the runners had carried information 260 miles in less than a day (Sahagún 1975, bk. 12, chaps. 2–4, and 6:724–727, 728).

These couriers of the Mexica fulfilled a variety of purposes. Clearly one was to communicate quickly and efficiently with far-flung parts of the empire. More than carrying news and information, they also brought rare and exotic goods from great distances for the delight of the ruler. Items mentioned include ice and snow from nearby volcanoes to seafood and other coastal delights. Some colonial writers explained that Moteuczoma enjoyed fresh seafood brought up from the coast by the messengers on a regular basis. By using a relay system, a corps of messengers could cover 200 to 350 miles a day. The runners were stationed at approximately 2-league distances (5.2 miles).[3] Some of the sources report that a team of runners could cover 4–5 leagues (10.4 to 17.5 miles) in an hour (Hassig 1975, 32; Torquemada 1975–1983, 4:320–321 [bk. 14, chap. 1]). Individual marathon runners in modern times run at about six miles an hour on average, for a 26.3-mile run (9.5–10 minutes per mile).

---

[2] *Huey tlahtoani* is the Nahuatl term for the ruler of the collective polity later known to Europeans as the Aztecs. The term means "great speaker." The ruler of the empire at the time of the arrival of the Spanish was Moteuczoma, whose name is rendered in Spanish as Moctezuma and in English as Montezuma.

[3] The Spanish league at the time was a somewhat flexible measurement of length. The range was 4.2–5.5 kilometers, or about 2.6–3.5 miles.

One of the Nahuatl words for these runners was *titlantli*, generally glossed as a "messenger"; the other was: *paina*, "swiftness."⁴ While there was a special group of fleet runners who served as messengers, and who were called *titlantli*, this word was also applied generally to messengers and ambassadors. From the literature it seems that the runners as couriers consisted of two different types. One was the *tequipan titlantli* (victory messenger). The other was the messenger used to send regular communications from one part of the empire to the other, perhaps to carry small items as quickly as possible. This latter group may have included those were called simply either *titlantli* or *paina* and who carried messages or goods along a fixed route.

The victory messengers were young men of marriageable age who traveled with the Mexica troops to military engagements. When the Mexica began to take prisoners, and it seemed that victory was in their grasp, the messengers would be sent back to notify the *huey tlahtoani* (Sahagún 1950–1982, bk. 8, 72–73). These couriers wore a colored ribbon in their hair, which indicated the progress of the war. A white ribbon signified that victory was either at hand or had been achieved. The messengers wore the traditional cloak tied at one shoulder, but in order to run faster they belted it around their waist. They also carried messages written on paper in pictographs to provide the same information. If they were reporting victory, they carried a *chimalli* (round shield) in their left hand and a *maquahuitl* (war club edged with obsidian) in their right. When the courier had to report a defeat, he left his hair untied and disheveled.⁵

Runners also participated in certain important ceremonies, such as the New Fire ceremony. The ceremony was also known as the Binding of the Years, since it marked the completion of one 52-year cycle and the beginning of the next. In anticipation of the end of one age and the beginning of another, all fires throughout the realm were extinguished. On the appointed night, a special victim was sacrificed on a hilltop in the eastern basin of the Central Basin of Mexico called Huixachtlan/Huixachtepetl (Place/Hill of the Thorn Tree).⁶ The priests who specialized in the ritual of lighting fires ignited one in the chest of the sacrificial victim using a fire drill. Priests who gathered around would light their torches from the flame. The

---

⁴ Molina (1970, f. 113v); Torquemada (1975–1983, 4:320–321). A fuller discussion of the words used to describe running and their frequency in the *Florentine Codex* can be found in section 3.

⁵ Torquemada (1975–1983, 4:320–321 [bk. 14, chap. 1]). Torquemada calls the club a *macana*, which is a Taino word adopted by the Spanish in the Antilles early in the colonial period and then applied elsewhere. Clavijero (1958–1959, 211–212 [bk. 7, chap. 12]).

⁶ The Huizache is a type of acacia tree (*Vachellia farnesiana*).

priests then passed the fire to special runners who would carry this "new" fire to all locations in the basin. The most important of these runners sped directly to the Templo Mayor, the major structure within the sacred precinct in Tenochtitlan, where he first illuminated the image of Huitzilopochtli and put fire to the incense offered to the god. The fire was then passed to the priests of the sacred precinct and on to the rest of the city. In describing the runners, Sahagún wrote that these messengers were chosen from among the warriors who were both valiant but who also were fast. They were called *in painani, in tlaczani* (the fleet, the swift), using two of the common words for running, *paina* and *tlacza* (Carrasco 1999, 96–112; Read 1988, 124–127; Sahagún 1950–1982, bk. 7, 29–30).

While little else is known of the messengers, it is possible that the office was either hereditary or at least limited to a small number of well-trained individuals. Future couriers were chosen when still quite young. They trained under the supervision of the priests of the sacred precinct. In order to strengthen their legs and to build endurance, the boys were required to run repeatedly to the top of the Templo Mayor. Each trip was a total of 113 steps. To encourage them and to provide incentive, prizes were given to the winners of these sprints (Clavijero 1958–1959, 212 [bk. 7, chap. 12]).

## 2. BEARERS AND PORTERS

The couriers were associated with bearers and porters because of the similarity of their social and economic functions in aiding communication and trade. The couriers and porters used the same roads and stopping places and were frequently considered one group. The principal difference among them was speed. Indeed, one of the services of the messenger was to carry small items quickly over long distances. Other persons who carried larger loads over long distances were also essential in the trade system of the Mexica. In the absence of beasts of burden, all long-distance trade had to occur through the agency of human bearers and porters. These people were known generically as *tlamama* (he/she/it carries something).[7] Some evidence indicates that the porters and the couriers might have used the same way stations, since porters also were expected to carry burdens four to five leagues before being relieved, the distance reported between messenger stations.[8] While in the case of the runners this was the distance that could be covered in about an hour, for the porters this was

---

[7] The verb "to carry something" is *mama*. The particle *-tla-* is a direct object pronoun signifying "something." Thus, *tlamama* means "he/she/it carries something." In the colonial period this word appeared in several different variants, including *tlameme, tameme* and *tamama*. The plural form was *tlamamahqueh*. See Hassig (1985, 28); and Karttunen (1992, 134).

[8] Hassig (1985, 32). In all likelihood, the interval also represented the distance a porter could be expected to cover in one day.

the distance that could be covered in a day. If the gangs of porters only covered certain stretches along a given route, merchants would have had to contract with a series of labor providers to seamlessly transfer goods across a long distance.

The *tlamama* used a *mecapalli* (tumpline) and frame to carry their burdens on their backs (Nicholson 1966, 135–148). A tumpline is a rope that attaches to a carrying frame and then passes over the back and shoulders, across the forehead, and down the back to the other side of the frame. In the case of the Mexica, goods were normally carried either in wooden boxes or baskets, depending on what was being carried, which were attached to the carrying frame (Hassig 1985, 28). Consequently, the carrying frame and tumpline became symbolic of bearers.

The term *mecapalli* served also as part of a diphrase along with *huictli* (digging stick) to connote man's labor or servitude. Sahagún, in discussing the deity Cihuacoatl, wrote that "mitoaia, huictli mecapalli, quitemacaya, ic temotlaya ca" (Indeed it is said: the digging stick, the tumpline, she gives them, she forced men [to work]).[9] This diphrase also came to serve as a reference to a servant or even slave, as seen in the phrase *tehuic temecapal* (his digging stick, his tumpline). This indicated that rather than being a free person who could exercise self-determination, man became like a tool, a tumpline or digging stick, to be used by a master (Molina 1975, f. 72; Sahagún, *Florentine Codex* 1950–1982, bk. 4, 5; Simeón 1985, 267).

The *tlamamahqueh* served in the town or region where they lived and were subject to the jurisdiction of the local ruler, *tlahtoani*, according at comments from the conquest period and practices in the early colonial period. It is not clear whether third parties could contract the porters directly without the intervention of the local lord. As with couriers, porters might have been a clan or hereditary group within each polity. The *Codex Mendoza* shows young priests and youths serving as porters, using the tumpline, thus suggesting that other groups of porters prepared for service from a young age. Elsewhere in the *Codex Mendoza*, a five-year-old boy is depicted learning how to carry burdens in a shawl or blanket draped from his forehead like a tumpline (Berdan and Anawalt 1997, 128–129, 120–121; Castillo 1972, 110–113; Hassig 1985, 36).

Long-distance trade was an essential feature of the life of the empire and an area in which the *tlamamahqueh* played a central role. The *pochtecah* or *oztomecah*[10] (commercial traders and merchants) based in Tenochtitlan used hundreds of

---

[9] Sahagún (1950–1982, bk. 1, 3). (Nahuatl has been standardized; translation based on Dibble and Anderson.)

[10] The singular form for these words is *pochtecatl* and *oztomecatl*. The plural is formed through dropping the *-tl* and replacing it with a glottal stop, represented in the ACK system with the letter *h*. The ACK system draws upon the work of J. Richard Andrews, R. Joe Campbell, and Frances Karttunen.

bearers on their journeys, taking articles from the core to the periphery and vice versa. Since local lords controlled the *tlamamahqueh*, the merchants would have to contract for porters in each district. Indeed, the evidence seems to indicate that the *pochtecah* maintained ties to sources well outside of the Aztec sphere of influence, well beyond areas controlled by local Mexica or Nahua lords.

For some of the long-distance trade, the *pochtecah* employed a corps of specialized porters, based in Tenochtitlan and its twin city, Tlatelolco. Yet using this service was an expensive proposition. Bringing porters with them to distant lands, the traders incurred costs that might not necessarily be recouped by sales along the way. Bearers were paid only when on the road. During markets and trading opportunities, porters would not be paid. On the return trip, the merchants might be expected to be transporting more goods than on the outward leg. Thus, the number of porters used on the return trip would need to outnumber those on the outbound one, since there would be more to carry. It would thus be reasonable that merchants contracted for additional porters for the return trip to Tenochtitlan, dealing with local lords as needs dictated (Hassig 1985, 123–126; Hirth 2016, 242–243). The roles of the runners and long-distance merchants intersect as participants in the Panquetzaliztli celebrations.

Bearers also played an important ritual and symbolic role. In the legends of the Mexica migration, the 200 years of wandering after the Nation left Aztlan before it arrived in the Central Basin of Mexico, a bearer known as the *teomama* (god-carrier) carried their particular god, Huitzilopochtli. Just as the *tlamama* carried his burden on his back with a tumpline and carrying frame, so the *teomama* bore the god in a bundle on his back, using a cloak serving as a tumpline. In the *Tira de la Peregrinación*, four nobles are shown leading the nation, with the god-bearer in first place. Three of the leaders were men, but one is most clearly a woman, Chimalma, identified by her typical hairdo and garb.[11] In the religious festivals of the Mexica calendar, the priest who carried an image of a god was called a *teomama*.

Other burdens might also be carried using something like the tumpline. In the *Codex Mendoza*, the artist devotes part of a page to describing a marriage ceremony. A woman described as an *amanteca* carries the bride to the ceremony. The bride sits facing forward while seated in a large shawl or blanket that is looped over her bearer's forehead. The system is identical in all aspects to the shawl or blanket used to carry the deity.[12]

---

[11] Museo Nacional de Antropología de México, *Tira de Pregrinacón*, f. 2; Alvarado Tezozomoc, *Crónica mexicayotl*, p. 19. Alvarado Tezozomoc gives the leaders names as Iztac Mixcoatzin, Apanecatl, Tetzcoatl, and Chimalma. All are designated as *teomama*.

[12] Berdan and Anawalt (1997, 126–127). The term *amanateca* merely signifies "artisan," which in this context was suggested to mean physician in the Spanish gloss.

Not only was Huitzilopochtli pictured as being carried during the Mexica migration, but different gods were also envisioned as carrying their responsibilities on their backs. The gods had the duty to see that the calendar continued to move in a regular order. Because of the organization of the various calendars, the gods were thought of as moving time along. Sahagún discusses the god One Rabbit in this role: "One Rabbit. It is said [that this was] the year sign and year counter of the south. For thirteen years it carried, set on its path, took with it, bore the burden [of the year]" (Read 1988, 92; Sahagún 1950–1983, bk. 7, chap. 7, 21). Thus, by association, serving as a porter or bearer could be interpreted as an occupation with both divine and ritual associations. The deities carried their burdens; the leaders of the nation carried the deity; a ritual specialist carried a woman to her marriage; and priests had the duty to carry figurines of deities in other feasts and rituals.

### 3. THE LANGUAGE OF RUNNING IN THE *FLORENTINE CODEX*

Within the corpus of the *Florentine Codex* there are four Nahuatl words that convey the idea of running: *pāina*, *tlaloā*, *totōca/tōtoca*, and *tlacza*, several of which have already been seen.[13] To better understand these words, one can look to Fray Alonso de Molina, who composed a Spanish–Nahuatl vocabulary in the mid-sixteenth century.[14] All of these words function as verbs in Nahuatl. In general, verbs are either intransitive, which means that they do not take an object, or transitive, which do take objects. To better understand the use of these words, at least among early colonial Nahuatl speakers, modern scholars benefit from having several texts that were elaborated in the sixteenth century by Spanish observers collecting what is essentially ethnographic information about the Nahua, such as those outlined earlier.

*Pāina* and its variants appear eleven times in the *Florentine Codex*, mostly concentrated in Book 2, "The Ceremonies." It has the basic meaning of "to run fast." Molina glosses the word as to run lightly, "correr ligeramente" (1970, f. 79). The word *pāina* is particularly important because one of the Mexica gods took his name from that word: Painal or Paynal. The name of this god might be translated

---

[13] The diacritical markings convey some important linguistic features of Nahuatl. They are a more modern convention, absent in Molina. First developed in the early seventeenth century by the Jesuit Horacio Carochi, the signify vowel length. This is not what one encounters in English where the letter *a* can be pronounced differently in the words "fat" and "fate." Rather, the vowel is actually held longer in time. The long vowel length is denoted with the macron over the vowel in question, e.g., *ā*. I thank Frances Karttunen for her work in developing *An Analytical Dictionary of Nahuatl* (which provides vowel length for words [1992]).

[14] My deepest thanks go to R. Joe Campbell and his lifelong work with the Molina and Sahagún texts for having provided me with the data set from which this analysis is derived. Molina (1970, f. 30v).

as "Runner" or "Swiftness." The Mexica associated him with their principal deity, Huitzilopochtli. Sahagún describes the relationship between the two deities in this manner: "Paynal was 'the delegate,' 'the substitute,' 'the deputy'" because he represented Huitzilopochtli when there was a procession. He was given the name Paynal, because "he pressed on, he urged them ahead" (*quitototzaya, quimotlalochtiaya*) (Sahagún 1950–1982, bk. 1, 3[1]). The god was also referred to with the honorific, Paynaltzin, "Honored Paynal" (bk. 2, 175), and the diminutive, Paynalton, "Little Paynal" (bk. 9, 65–66). All of the occurrences of "Little Paynal" described a physically small image of the god, in ritual celebrations practiced by the merchants.

Looking at the distribution of the various words for running within the *Florentine Codex* reinforces the predominance of running images in the description of the different festivals and celebrations of the *xiuhpohualli*. The word *pāina* and its variants appear mostly in descriptions of rituals, in particular during Panquetzaliztli, when a priest ran carrying an amaranth dough image of the deity. In addition, over twenty instances refer to the god Painal/Paynal, who featured prominently in the running ritual of Panquetzaliztli and several other feasts.

Another word with the general value of "run" was *tlaloā*. The word means to run or to run away. Molina glosses the word as to run or flee, "correr o huir" (Molina 1970, f. 124). In the *Florentine Codex*, *tlaloā* was used ninety-one times, in all possible variations, with the form *motlaloā* appearing most frequently, some thirty-seven times, commonly in a compound form with one of the other words for running. It was distributed among several books, including Book 2 and in the descriptions of various festival ceremonies. As in the case of *pāina*, there are various instances of *tlaloā* in the descriptions of the rituals of Panquetzaliztli, some twenty occurrences. *Motlaloā* also appears frequently in Book 12, a section that mostly narrates the history of the conquest of Mexico by the Spanish. An example of its use is "When the people of Tenochtitlan who dwelt in Zoquipan saw this, they then fled (*motlaloa*); in fear they fled (*momauhcatlaloa*)" (Sahagún 1950–1982, bk. 12, 84).

The word *totōca/tōtoca* and other forms appeared sixty-eight times. Unfortunately, Nahuatl orthography of the early colonial period rendered the two words (*totōca/ tōtoca*) as the same: *totoca*. Prior to the early seventeenth century, Spaniards did not mark vowel length (see also note 14). It was only with the work of Horacio Carochi, a Florentine Jesuit, that vowel length began to be represented in Spanish-based texts. The *totōca* form is intransitive and means to run or to hurry or for an illness to worsen (Karttunen 1992, 247). It also has the somewhat related meaning of to flow, such as the flowing of water or other liquids, the flow of air, or even to have a pestilence (Molina 1970, f. 150). The other form, *tōtoca*, clearly is transitive and has a similar meaning: to run after someone or something, or to go along fighting with someone (Karttunen 1992, 248). *Tōtoca* is a reduplicated version of the verb *toca*, which means to follow or pursue someone.[15] It seems to be coincidental that the two words, *totōca* and *tōtoca*, have such similar meanings. There were twenty-eight instances of the words in the *Florentine Codex* that carry the meaning of run. Since the orthography of the *Florentine Codex* did not mark vowel length, it is not possible on the surface to determine which word was actually being used, except that one is transitive and the other is intransitive. The bulk of these occurrences (thirteen) appear in Book 12, the conquest of Mexico. These instances generally described battle scenes where troops were running to a battle: "O Mexicans, hasten there! (*huallatotoca*)" (Sahagún 1950–1982, bk. 12, 2). It seems that *totōca/tōtoca* were not the preferred terms to describe ritual running.

The fourth word under consideration is *tlacza*, an intransitive verb that means to run or move fast (Karttunen 1992, 259; Molina 1970 f. 116, tlacça). It is related to the verb *icza*, a transitive verb that means to step or trample on something (Karttunen 1992, 96). *Icza*, in turn, derives from the word for foot, *icxitl*. In reality, the meaning of the word *tlacza* as "to run" is not that common. Of the more than 800 times the base morpheme was used in the *Florentine Codex*, it only had the meaning of run in three instances, and two of these had to do with running in retreat (Sahagún 1950–1982, bk. 1, 42; bk. 2, 156; bk. 4, 63). Most of the time it carried the meaning of "to step, trample, or stride." In one instance it was paired with *paina*, and *tlaloa* when a situation called for choosing the fastest and swiftest runner: "in painani, in tlaczani, in iuhqui hecatoca is motlaloa" (the fleet, the swift, who could run like the wind; bk. 7, 29).

Nahua oratorical tradition appreciated the use of multiple words with similar meanings. In this way the speaker piled image upon image to develop a complex, yet nuanced description. As a result of this, there were several instances in the *Florentine Codex* in which forms of several of these four words, all of which mean run, appeared in juxtaposition. An example of this is "painani, totocani," "it is an easy runner, a runner" (Sahagún 1950–1982, bk. 11, 12). Juxtapositions including the other words were also fairly common: "cenca motlaloa, cenca paina," "much did they run, much did they hasten" (bk. 2, 120); "in huel paina, in huel totoca," "they [truly] would run, they [truly] would hasten." (bk. 2, 146). A slightly different instance is this: "motocayotia painal: ipampa ca cenca, quitotozaya," "he was given the name of Runner, because they pressed him on quickly" (bk. 1, 3). In this latter example, one sees the juxtaposition of the name of the god Painal, with a description of why he had that name. Although *totōca/tōtoca* was fairly common, it was seldom used on combination with other words for running, just a total of seven

---

[15] In Nahuatl there is a process called reduplication, in which the first syllable is repeated. It usually signifies motion or multiples of an item.

times, and in two of those it was with reference to the deity Painal. There were three instances of oratorical repetition: "huel totoca, motlaloa" (indeed they ran, the fled), "painani, totocani" (it is an easy runner, a runner), and "cenca motlaloa, cenca totocohua" (they ran hard, they ran fast; bk. 12, 88; bk. 11, 12; bk. 2, 125).

A significant number of instances of these words for running come from descriptions of ceremonies and rituals in Book 2 of the *Florentine Codex*, in particular those associated with Panquetzaliztli. One can see that the Nahuatl vocabulary for running appeared in two general contexts in the *Florentine Codex*. Perhaps the more prevalent was the description of ceremonies and rituals, in particular the running ritual of Panquetzaliztli. The other had to do with the conquest by the Spanish, when both parties were rushing from place to place in the heat of battle. This section has provided a small linguistic overview to the place of running words in the largest corpus of Nahuatl texts recorded within a generation of the conquest that have reached the modern day.

### 4. RUNNING IN FESTIVAL CEREMONIES

The feast of Ochpaniztli was the eleventh of the Mexica months. In the rituals for this month, running also played an important role. As part of the larger series of ceremonies honoring the goddesses *Teteo inan*, also known as *Toci* and *Tlazolteotl*, a young woman impersonated the goddess in a series of ritual dances and skirmishes. Eventually she was sacrificed and then flayed. A priest, who became a god-impersonator, wore her skin for the remainder of the twenty-days. A large piece of skin from her thigh was handed to a runner, who carried it to Pochtlan, the neighborhood of the merchants. There, another god-impersonator waited. He represented her son, Cinteotl. The skin was placed on his face as a mask.

While the thigh skin was being carried to Pochtlan, the priest who had worn the skin of the god-impersonator, now himself a god-impersonator named Teccizquacuilli, descended from the temple. Nobles and warriors waited at the bottom, and they then began to run, beating their shields, and engaging in a ritual of mock warfare in a ceremony called *çacacali* (*zacacalli*), "they fight with grass." In addition to shields, they carried grass brooms with which they beat one another, causing many small cuts and tears of the skin. In the end participants were covered with blood, their own and that of their mock enemies. Finally, the god-impersonator and her entourage confronted the warriors and drove them away (Sahagún 1950–1982, bk. 2, 120–121).

Later in the cycle of ceremonies for Ochpaniztli, the god-impersonator of Cinteotl ran away from Tenochtitlan in order to deposit the thigh-skin mask in enemy territory. Strong and agile warriors accompanied him. They ran to a region considered to be enemy territory on the slopes of *Iztac tepetl* (white mountain), a place called *Popotl temi* (full of straw). If they encountered enemies, they would fight. Upon the god-impersonator and warriors' arrival at the place, the skin was stretched on a wooden frame and left on display in commemoration of the event. In all likelihood, this ritual symbolized the birth of Cinteotl from his mother. The thigh-skin mask was symbolic of his emergence from her womb. It was taken to enemy land just as the umbilical cord of newborn boys was to be buried on a battlefield to give them strength in battle.[16] As the month of Ochpaniztli continued, other rituals involving running also took place. In particular, at one point the warriors blazed a path for the god-impersonator of Toci by running from the sacred precinct to the place called Tocititlan, "the place beside Toci" (Sahagún 1950–1982, bk. 2, 125). The ceremonies of this month have been considered to be expiatory and having to do with the rejection of filth and the maintenance of balance (DiCesare 2009, 98–99).

The running ceremony associated with the festival of Panquetzaliztli was known as Ipaina Huitzilopochtli (The Swiftness of Huitzilopochtli). As noted, it consisted of a priest carrying an *tzoalli* (amaranth dough) image of the god along a circuit in the Central Basin of Mexico. The priest ran from the Templo Mayor to the divine ball court within the sacred precinct. There, two people were sacrificed. The runner then proceeded to Tlatelolco, the twin city of Tenochtitlan located just to the north. From there he ran along the causeway toward Tlacopan, stopping in Tlaxotlan and Popotlan. From Tlacopan the running procession went to Izquitlan, passing just to the east of the outcropping of Chapultepec. Sacrifices were made at Izquitlan. The runner continued south to Coyohuacan and Huitzilopochco, where more sacrifices occurred. He then ran up the causeway to Acachinanco and eventually back to the Templo Mayor. The route of travel was symbolic of the original migration of the Mexica, which had taken them from Aztlan to Tenochtitlan. Moreover, the events that occurred at the Templo Mayor after the return of the priest and deity figurine recapitulated the elements of the birth of Huitzilopochtli. Thus, in the month of Panquetzaliztli, running was used to recall the Mexica migration and the birth and apotheosis of Huitzilopochtli as a solar deity, since the ceremony roughly corresponded to the winter solstice (Schwaller 2019).

In the seventeenth month, Tititl, there was a very minor running ceremony. In this instance, priests congregated at the base of the Templo Mayor. The ritual involved running up the temple as quickly as possible, grabbing flowers arrayed atop it, and then descending, dropping the flowers into the sacred vessel where grain had

---

[16] Berdan and Anawalt (1997, f. 56v., 171–173); Sahagún (1950–1982, bk. 2, 122–123); Carrasco (1999, 216–217). What was *iztac tepetl* (White Mountain) for the Mexica is now called Iztaccihuatl (White Woman).

also been deposited and was burning. This ritual accomplished, the priests simply left as quickly as they had appeared (Sahagún 1950–1982, bk. 2, 15).

## 5. RUNNING IN A LARGER CULTURAL CONTEXT

Among the Mexica in particular, and Nahuatl speakers in general, there was a well-developed vocabulary of words for running, swiftness, and haste. Within Mexica society, runners and bearers occupied an important place. They helped the cohesion of the far-flung polity. The messengers carried information long distances in relatively short periods. The network of couriers assisted the rulers of Tenochtitlan in knowing what was happening hundreds of miles away. It was the messengers who first informed the rulers about the arrival of the Spanish. But the bearers also provided for cohesion in the empire by serving as the beasts of burden for the commercial ties that helped to link the very different ethnic groups together into one loose empire.

Deities too were envisioned as bearers within the calendrical system. They moved the mechanisms of time and space. One of the key aspects of Mexica sacrificial system was to ensure the continued movement of the calendar, of the sun, moon, and planets. Consequently, gods as bearers formed the very heart of the Mexica conception of the universe. While there is no representation of deities carrying time elements in pictorial manuscripts, there are textual descriptions of them doing so.

In the origin legends, Huitzilopochtli was carried on the back of one of the leaders as the Mexica migrated from the semiarid regions of northwestern Mexico into the well-watered region of central Mexico. Rather than a simple bearer, *tlamama*, this priest was a god-carrier, *teomama*. In short, just as the gods bore the burden of the celestial mechanism, so humans, the Mexica, bore the god and were responsible for seeing that the god was propitiated, to ensure the continued movement of time and space.

Running ceremonies occupied important places in the Mexica ritual calendar. The three most important occurred in Ochpaniztli, in Panquetzaliztli, and in the New Fire ceremony. In these rituals running was largely a symbolic act. In Ochpaniztli, it referred to the strength of warriors running into battle. In Panquetzaliztli, running served to recapitulate the Mexica national story: of their migration and of the birth and triumph of Huitzilopochtli as a representation of the solar disk. In the New Fire ceremony, running was a bit more practical, allowing the sacred fire kindled in the chest of the sacrificial victim in the first minutes of the new era to be spread throughout the polity. Thus, running in these celebrations was symbolic of the vigor of the society as a whole. But the festivals themselves focused on the cosmic forces of light and dark, hot and cold, water and dryness, good harvests, prosperity, and success in war.

## 6. A CODA: THE ETHNOLOGY OF RUNNING AMONG RELATED PEOPLES

The Mexica, as Nahuatl speakers, were part of a much larger cultural family associated with the Uto-Aztecan language. As a group, Nahuatl speakers have their cultural origins in the northwestern and north central regions of modern-day Mexico along with other related ethnic and linguistic groups such as the Hopi, Ute, Paiute, and Tarahumara—all members of the Uto-Aztecan language family. Among Uto-Aztecans, at least two groups have rituals that involve running: the Hopi and the Tarahumara. Of these, the Tarahumara, also known as the Rarámuri, have gained recognition for long-distance running. At the same time, we must remember that the Mexica were separated from these other Uto-Aztecan groups for at least two centuries, and in all likelihood much more, as well as by at least 1,600 miles. We simply cannot look at these later cultures and draw definitive conclusions about the Mexica or even relationships between the Native groups without risking the *post hoc ergo propter hoc* fallacy. These observations are merely designed to indicate that the use of running in rituals is not uncommon among Native groups of Mesoamerica, by focusing on one large cultural group related by language.

The Norwegian scholar Carl Lumholtz made the first ethnographic descriptions of the Rarámuri. Working at the end of the nineteenth century, Lumholtz, after having first studied the Aboriginals of Australia, spent some twenty years investigating the Rarámuri, and other peoples of western and northern Mexico, under the auspices of the American Museum of Natural History. He collected his observations in his book *Unknown Mexico*. In that work, Lumholtz, who called them the "Tarahumare," noted that

> No doubt the Tarahumares are the greatest runners in the world, not in regard to speed, but endurance. A Tarahumare will easily run 170 miles without stopping. When an Indian is sent out as a messenger, he goes along at a slow trot, running steadily and constantly. A man has been known to carry a letter in five days from Guazapares to Chihuahua and back, a distance of nearly 600 miles. (Lumholtz 1902, 1:276–294; see also Irigoyen-Rascón 2015, 89–91)

Lumholtz further noted that the very name the Tarahumara used for themselves was *Rarámuri*, which he translated as "foot runners."[17] Thus, the very name of the group is associated with being fleet of foot. During races, the runners would sustain themselves with a gruel made from toasted cornmeal mixed with water. The dish was called *pinole* and is similar to what in central Mexico is generally known by its

---

[17] Subsequent investigations have cast some doubt on this interpretation: see Acuña Delgado (2006, 61).

Nahuatl name, *atole* (*atolli*). In addition to long-distance running, the Rarámuri also engaged in types of competitive running along shorter courses in which participants kicked along small balls, made of bones or stones, as they ran. Rather than kick objects, women would carry and toss woven rings or plaited balls to one another while running, catching them with a forked stick.

Following Lumholtz's initial studies of the Rarámuri, other scholars have focused on various aspects of the culture. In recent years, even popular nonfiction works have appeared describing the running culture of the Rarámuri, including one that is widely used as a first-year common reader in many colleges and universities (McDougall 2009). Scholars in recent decades have continued to look at the cultural aspects of running. Several authors have provided vivid descriptions of the races.[18]

The historical origins of the foot-racing culture are unclear. A missionary of the late eighteenth century placed its origins as much as a century earlier, that is, the seventeenth century. Rarámuri legends, however, recount that the races began shortly after the creation of people. Lumholtz believed that the races had an ancient origin. Other scholars questioned that fact and posited that Jesuit missionaries might have introduced racing in the eighteenth century as a positive substitute for the ancient Mesoamerican ball game *ulama* (Acuña Delgado 2006, 61–62; Pennington 1970, 27–35; 1963, 173). Indeed, the ball game, known as *tlachtli* among the Nahua, was a centrally important ritual common among many Mesoamerican cultures from as early as the Olmec, including both the Maya and Mexica, and which persists in western Mexico in a modified form. Like the Rarámuri running competition in which runners kick balls forward, in *ulama* or *tlachtli* competitors try to launch a rubber ball into a goal, without the use of hands, or possibly feet. Yet other scholars see the races as something quite internal to the Rarámuri. Since the running rituals among the Rarámuri are used to enhance internal social cohesion and to exclude persons of mixed Native and Spanish ancestry (mestizos), these scholars have held that it is an Indigenous ritual and not imposed from the outside (Kummels 2001, 75).

Recent scholarship has held that the contests are important religious rituals, providing a means of social arbitration and cohesion, and also simply sources of pleasure, even when no larger social consensus is reached. The Rarámuri have races involving children, with a distance of some 10–30 kilometers; for women, with distances of 50–100 kilometers; and for men, with distances of as many as 100–200 kilometers. While races may be organized for special commemorations, such as the death of an important leader, most of them occur in late spring and summer, May–September. As noted, the men race by kicking a small ball along the course. The object is to kick the ball some 40–50 meters along the course, keeping it under

---

[18] Zingg (2001, 82–85). This work was based on fieldwork from the late 1930s and 1940s.

control, since if the ball leaves the path, precious time would be spent in recovering it. Women run along their course with a plaited hoop that they toss forward using a curved stick. The principle is the same as with the men: to toss the hoop along the path, preferably rolling along, so that it can be recovered and tossed again. If the hoop falls over or leaves the path, it will take time to recover it. Essentially, these are races of endurance, not speed, although the victor is the first runner to complete the race trajectory. The exceptional distances and the skill required to move the token (ball or hoop) along the course compromise the overall speed (Acuña Delgado 2005, 134–137; Kummels 2001, 79–80).

A ritual framework surrounds the races. Blessings are sought before the race and upon successful completion. The races are also marked by copious consumption of alcoholic beverages and wagering. Because large amounts of money might be wagered on the races, there is significant reallocation of wealth in the community. Moreover, goods acquired in mestizo villages are frequently exchanged in the betting, allowing truly rural Rarámuri to gain access to manufactured goods. Thus, the races exist in a complex network wherein ritual, social structures, and simple enjoyment all play important parts (Acuña Delgado 2005, 165–171; Kummels 2001, 78–80). The races are seen as a means of keeping in contact with the divinity and a manifestation of cultural identity. They bind disparate villages of Rarámuri into a coherent community. Participants, both runners and observers, see the races as a means of manipulating powerful supernatural forces (Acuña Delgado 2005, 141–142; 2006, 194–201).

The Rarámuri are not the only Uto-Aztecans to have running games and rituals. The Hopi of Arizona also use running in their ritual life. Within the complex Hopi religion, running occupies an important place. It is considered one of the six modes of prayer. As a type of compulsive magic, at the end of a day of work in the fields, Hopi men will engage in footraces. There are two types: one is a very fast run over a short distance; the other is a longer, slower race over long distance. Both are seen as a prayer for the growth of crops. The short, fast race encourages crops to grow quickly, whereas the long, slow race attempts to slow the sun in its course to delay winter, thus prolonging the growing season. In both instances, the act of running contains two important elements: One is supplication, a wish for rain and an attempt to exact pity from the gods. The other is literally participation—that through their own physical exertion rain will come forth. In essence the running prayer is a wish and a will manifested through a single ceremonial act (Loftin 1986, 194).

Within Hopi rituals, there are other forms of ritual, prayerful running. One of the most important of these occurred in August. A layman first participated in a water ceremony in which all the members of the village would go to a sacred spring. That accomplished, the layman would initiate the ritual, prayerful race. This water fetcher called on his fellows to race with joy. He carries two ritual implements, not unlike the items carried by the Rarámuri. One is a prayer stick, which had an object called a "rain wheel" on the end. The wheel was often adorned with duck feathers, because of that bird's link to water. The rain wheel itself was made of the leaves of a cattail, a plant also associated with water. The other object was a clay ball made to look like a stone smoothed by the action of water in a riverbed. The race was a prayer for rain. As racers reached the water fetcher, he handed over the ritual objects, in a type of relay. Like the Rarámuri, the Hopi also raced kicking a ball made from pine pitch and fur from a rabbit or horse. These balls are symbolic of river pebbles and rocks being pushed down draws and gullies during heavy summer rains. To the outside observer, the prayerful running and the implements used (balls, sticks, and wheels or hoops) imply a degree of association between the Hopi and the Rarámuri.

The Hopi races that involved the greatest number of participants occurred in the late spring and summer.[19] In these races various men dressed up like the gods, Kachinas. These god-impersonators ran after their fellows, whipping them with yucca blades. The purpose of the race again was to bring forth clouds and have the nourishing rain run down the arroyos. The Kachina impersonators symbolized the clouds. If they whipped many boys, there would be much rain. If the impersonators could not catch the runners, they threw mud at them. If they hit the runners, it signified a forthcoming heavy rain. In these races, the Kachinas were the very clouds that bring rain (Loftin1986, 195–197).

Some research has indicated that the Nahua, as a result of the expansion of corn agriculture and extensive Mesoamerican trading networks, influenced some aspects of Hopi culture and religion. Some scholars have concluded that the Hopi religion could accommodate external influences, as seen in the period following the Pueblo Revolt of 1680, when other cultural groups joined the Hopi, bringing along some of their own gods and adding them to the pantheon of Kachinas. There are cognates in Hopi religion to Nahua ceremonies at the winter solstice urging the sun to return from the winter darkness, and some Kachinas can be linked to Mexica deities. The ceremonies at the winter solstice did not necessarily include the running ritual seen among the Mexica (James 2000, 902–903; Waters 1963, 138–141). There are suggestions that the pre-Puebloan peoples, known formerly as the Anasazi, also had ritual races, as evidence for this has been found at the ceremonial site of Chaco Canyon (Waters 1963, 43).

While observations of the Hopi date mostly from the last two centuries, many observations of the Rarámuri date from the late colonial period. Some evidence

---

[19] For a detailed study of some of these ceremonies, see Waters (1963, 97–102, 224–226, *et passim*).

links the Kachina cult to the Mexica pantheon, although the method of transmission is difficult to document. It could imply a common source, or a later Mexica export into a distant trading region (James 2000, 911–915). Traditions in each Native nation also indicate that their running practices and rituals have been in existence for many centuries.

The range of the family of Uto-Aztecan language speakers stretched from modern-day Montana, in the north, to Nicaragua, in the south. While rituals involving running were not necessarily ubiquitous among Uto-Aztecan peoples, there are some notable examples that can provide a broader cultural context within which to study the Mexica rituals. Among the Hopi and the Rarámuri, rituals involving running played important roles of cultural cohesion and of intercession with supernatural powers for rain and other benefits. The Hopi and Rarámuri running ceremonies helped to solidify the cultural identity of populations that were widely scattered. The Rarámuri peoples live in remote villages in and around the Copper Canyon region of the Mexican state of Chihuahua, whereas the Hopi live on three mesas in northeastern Arizona. Common rituals and ceremonies allow these far-flung ethnic groups to have a shared cultural experience. The running rituals played this important role for both.

Both the Hopi and the Rarámuri also saw the running ceremonies as important spiritual and religious activities. For the Rarámuri, the religious experience was connected to manipulating the supernatural. Yet for the Hopi, most of the running rituals were intimately related to agriculture, specifically seeking the two things essential for success: sun and rain. The races sought to hasten the coming of the sun and lengthening of the growing season, at the same time that running with the Kachina sought to control the rain.

While among modern Western cultures running is a pastime or a method of getting exercise, for these selected Uto-Aztecan peoples running was an essential element of daily existence. In the absence of beasts of burden, or modern vehicles, running simply was the quickest way to get around. It is a small wonder, then, that among them the act of running came to play such an important role both in daily life and in ritual lives.

### REFERENCES

Acuña Delgado, Angel. 2005. "Funciones y definición conceptual de la carrera Rarámuri en la Sierra Tarahumara." *Nueva Antropología* 19: 149–171.

Acuña Delgado, Ángel. 2006. *Etnología de la Carrera de bola y ariweta arámuris*. Mexico City: CIESAS.

Alvarado Tezozomoc, Hernando. 1992. *Crónica mexicayotl*. Mexico City: Universidad Nacional Autónoma de México.

Berdan, Frances, and Patricia R. Anawalt. 1997. *The Essential Codex Mendoza*. Berkeley: University of California Press.

Carrasco, David. 1999. *City of Sacrifice: The Aztec Empire and the Role of Violence in Civilization*. Boston: Beacon Press.

Castillo, Victor M. 1972. *Estructura económica de la sociedad mexica según las fuentes documentales*. Mexico City: Universidad Nacional Autónoma de México.

Clavijero, Francisco. 1958–1959. *Historia antigua de México*. Mexico City: Porrúa.

DiCesare, Catherine R. 2009. *Sweeping the Way: Divine Transformation in the Aztec Festival of Ochpaniztli*. Boulder: University Press of Colorado.

Hassig, Russ. 1985. *Trade, Tribute, and Transportation: The Sixteenth-Century Political Economy of the Valley of Mexico*. Norman: University of Oklahoma Press.

Hirth, Kenneth G. 2016. *The Aztec Economic World: Merchants and Markets in Ancient Mesoamerica*. Cambridge: Cambridge University Press.

Irigoyen-Rascón, Fructuoso. 2015. *Tarahumara Medicine: Ethnobotany and Healing among the Rarámuri of Mexico*. Norman: University of Oklahoma Press.

James, Susan E. 2000. "Some Aspects of the Aztec Religion in the Hopi Kachina Cult." *Journal of the Southwest* 42: 897–926.

Karttunen, Frances. 1992. *An Analytical Dictionary of Nahuatl*. Norman: University of Oklahoma Press.

Kummels, Ingrid. 2001. "Reflecting Diversity: Variants of the Legendary Footraces of the Rarámuri in Northern Mexico." *Ethnos* 66: 73–98.

Loftin, John D. 1986. "Supplication and Participation: The Distance and Relation of the Sacred in Hopi Prayer Rites." *Anthropos* 81: 177–201.

Lumholtz, Karl. 1902. *Unknown Mexico*. New York: C. Scribner's Sons.

McDougall, Christopher. 2009. *Born to Run: A Hidden Tribe, Superathletes, and the Greatest Race the World has Never Seen*. New York: Vintage.

Molina, Alonso de. 1970. *Vocabulario en lengua castellana y mexicana y mexicana y castellana*. Facsimile edition. Mexico City: Porrúa.

Nicholson, H. B. 1966. "The Significance of the 'Looped Cord' Year Symbol in Pre-Hispanic Mexico: An Hypothesis." *Estudios de Cultura Nahuatl* 6: 135–148.

Pennington, Campbell W. 1963. *The Tarahumar of Mexico: Their Environment and Material Culture*. Salt Lake City: University of Utah Press.

Pennington, Campbell W. 1970. "La carrera de bola entre los tarahumaras de Mexico." *América Indígena* 30: 15–40.

Read, Kay Almere. 1988. *Time and Sacrifice in the Aztec Cosmos*. Bloomington: Indiana University Press.

Sahagún, Bernardino de. 1950–1982. *Florentine Codex*. Edited and translated by Arthur J. O. Anderson and Charles Dibble. 13 vols. Salt Lake City: University of Utah Press.

Sahagún, Bernardino de. 1975. *Historia general de las cosas de Nueva España*. Edited by Angel María Garibay. Mexico City: Porrúa.

Schwaller, John F. 2019. *Panquetzaliztli: History as seen through the Rituals of One of the Months of the Aztec Year*. Norman: University of Oklahoma Press.

Simeón, René. 1985. *Diccionario de la lengua náhuatl*. México City: Siglo XXI.

*Tira de Pregrinacón*. Museo Nacional de Antropología de México.

Torquemada, Juan de. 1975–1983. *Monarquía indiana*. Edited by Miguel León Portilla. 7 vols. Mexico City: Universidad Nacional Autónoma de México.

Waters, Frank 1963. *The Book of the Hopi*. New York: Penguin.

Zingg, Robert. 2001. *Behind the Mexican Mountains*. Austin: University of Texas Press.

# 7

## Strategies for Confronting New Concepts in the Spanish-Latin Corpus of Ayer ms. 1478

MARY L. CLAYTON

## 1. INTRODUCTION. AYER MS. 1478. THE NEBRIJA CONNECTION

The Newberry Library's Ayer ms. 1478, known by its nineteenth-century binder's title *Vocabulario trilingüe*, is a trilingual Spanish-Latin-Nahuatl dictionary consisting of the second edition (1513 and later[1]) of Elio Antonio de Nebrija's Spanish-Latin dictionary with Nahuatl equivalents added for the majority of entries. It is anonymous, undated, and without a known place of origin. It probably dates to the sixteenth or early seventeenth century. Approximately 29 percent of entries lack Nahuatl glosses, and it contains a number of false starts and misaligned entries and parts of entries. Rosas Xelhuantzi (2017) provides a detailed and very interesting study of the physical characteristics of the manuscript, including the watermarks, which I was unable to trace. Gruda (2018, 49–51) also gives a carefully researched discussion of the watermarks. The fact that its provenance is cloudy to nonexistent before its acquisition by José Fernando Ramírez in the nineteenth century has left its date and author open to much unfounded speculation, which I will not deal

---

[1] See Vidal Díez (2007, 2015) for a discussion of evidence that the 1513 printing is the same wordlist as the 1516 printing and thus represents the earliest date of the second edition of Nebrija's Spanish-Latin dictionary. Hamann (2015, chap. 1) gives a detailed account of the various printings of Nebrija's dictionaries, especially the 1513 and following "second edition" printings. He proposes (46–47) a pirated version of Nebrija 1516, probably produced in 1520, as the source for the *Vocabulario trilingüe*. My references to these works are copied from Hamann's references.

with in this chapter. My 1989 paper established on the basis of internal evidence that the manuscript is based on the second edition of Nebrija's dictionary rather than the first, 1495, edition, as had been assumed by several scholars; that it is a copy of an earlier version that also contained all three languages;[2] that the author of the Nahuatl glosses was most likely a native speaker of Nahuatl;[3] and that nothing in the work itself ties it to Tlatelolco or to Sahagún. I argued further for a Nahuatl-speaking author in Clayton (2003).

For simplicity, I shall refer to Ayer ms. 1478, the *Vocabulario trilingüe*, as *Tri*. Having no identity for either the author or the copyist, I have named them Fernando Anónimo Tlahtolpixqui "wordkeeper" and Fernando Anónimo Tlahcuiloh "scribe" respectively, though we cannot know beyond a doubt that they were men. This naming is to remind us, if whimsically, that the author was a real person about whom we know nothing, other than that "he" was a (somewhat) bicultural speaker of Nahuatl. Here I will call the author Don Fernando.

The purpose of this chapter is to examine the author's strategies for confronting the wealth of new concepts found in the Spanish-Latin corpus of Nebrija's dictionary, which is essentially of late fifteenth-century origin with some early sixteenth-century additions. At first glance, Ayer ms. 1478 might seem to be the ideal source for the linguistic study of cultural exchange between Nahuas and Spaniards, given that the author, almost surely a native speaker of Nahuatl, has imposed upon himself the task of putting into Nahuatl the contents of the 1513 incarnation of a Spanish wordlist first published in 1495. However, it is important to realize that not all of the Spanish corpus in the dictionary had a place in this cultural exchange. Nebrija's dictionary is a dictionary of Latin accessed through Spanish for Spanish speakers. It therefore contains a mix of universal concepts, concepts from late medieval and early modern Europe, and concepts specific to classical culture. Thus, Some Spanish entries have a place in Nebrija's Spanish-to-Latin dictionary merely to serve as headwords for entries that he wanted to present in Latin.

On the other hand, since many Latin words must be translated as phrases in Spanish, many Spanish headwords are phrases that would not be in a Spanish

---

[2] See Clayton (1989, 396–399) for arguments for this claim. My comments having to do with *h* in Spanish should be ignored. At that time, the only version of the second edition of Nebrija's dictionary that I had access to was MacDonald's 1973 edition (Nebrija [1516] 1973), and I did not realize the extent to which his "transcripción crítica" respelled Nebrija's Spanish entries.

[3] Rosas Xelhuantzi (2017) makes the shockingly incorrect claim that my 1989 paper attributes the Nahuatl of Ayer ms. 1478 to Alonso de Molina! At no time would it have occurred to me that Molina could have been involved with this work, because he was a highly skilled lexicographer, and the author of the Nahuatl glosses in Ayer ms. 1478 was not.

dictionary were it not for the need to render their Latin equivalents. These particular entries can be very useful for what they tell us about how Nahuatl handles the semantic relationships that are represented by prefixes in Latin and prepositional phrases or adverbs in Spanish.

These factors play a role in the Nahuatl author's treatment of individual entries, as does his point of view as a native speaker of Nahuatl rather than of Spanish.

## 2. THE MOLINA DICTIONARIES AND THE CONCEPT OF ACTIVE AND PASSIVE DICTIONARIES

Any discussion of New World dictionaries invites comparison with Alonso de Molina's masterpieces, and we should begin by pointing out the major differences between Molina's works and the *Vocabulario trilingüe*.[4] There are important differences between assembling one's own collection of headwords, as Molina did, and taking on an existing list, as did the author of *Tri*. In addition, their goals are different, and the interplay of these two factors plus the author's Native perspective help to determine Don Fernando's approach to defining.

Molina's purpose was to make the Nahuatl language accessible to Spanish speakers so that they could use it actively. It is clear from his prefaces that he considered all three of his dictionaries to be Nahuatl dictionaries,[5] the first two (Molina 1555; Molina 1571a) accessed through Spanish, and the third (Molina 1571b)—separately foliated but bound together with 1571a with a separate title page and no unifying title page—accessed through Nahuatl. His Spanish wordlists contain concepts that may be considered universal as well as more culturally specific concepts from both the Old World and the New that he considered necessary for communication in the New World context. Although Molina used many Spanish words and phrases that

---

[4] I would like to thank my husband, Joe Campbell, for sharing his Molina and *Florentine Codex* materials with me and for writing the custom programs that have made my work on *Tri* possible. I also want to express my gratitude for his introducing me to Nahuatl and for allowing me to sit in on his SNOBOL (**St**ri**N**g **O**riented and sym**BO**lic **L**anguage) course back in the early 1970s. SNOBOL was later modified as SPITBOL (**Sp**eedy **I**mplementation of SNO**BOL**) for use on home computers. This is the programming language used for all of my data manipulation.

[5] "When I published the vocabulary of the Mexican language the first time, . . . I had no other intent than to begin to open a path, in order that in the course of time and with the diligence of other more lively minds, there would be an on-going discovery of the limitless mine (so to speak) of words and manners of speaking which this very copious and clever Mexican language has" (Molina 1571b, preface, unpaginated; translation from Clayton and Campbell 2002). He can only have been referring to the Spanish-Nahuatl dictionary of 1555.

are in Nebrija's dictionary,⁶ he rejected many others and also added many Spanish words that he needed for the New World experience, either Old World or New World concepts.

Since Molina's goal is an active, encoding dictionary to enable Spanish speakers to use Nahuatl, his Nahuatl entries are almost always translational equivalents that Spanish speakers could insert into Nahuatl sentences. Definitions or explanations would not suffice. Don Fernando, on the other hand, has considerably more latitude: he seeks only to make the Spanish entries intelligible to other Nahuatl speakers, or to himself, so that they or he can passively understand the Spanish words when they see or hear them. Since it is intended to be a decoding dictionary,⁷ he is free to provide any type of Nahuatl equivalent that he wants. They need not be translational equivalents that could be used in place of their Spanish counterparts. He is well served by this latitude, since he has taken on a preexisting wordlist and has no control over the set of words and phrases he has undertaken to define.

## 3. DEGREES OF APPROACHING FULLY NATIVE NAHUATL EQUIVALENTS

In examining Don Fernando's treatment of new concepts, I will begin by considering the differing degrees to which his Nahuatl additions approach fully native Nahuatl equivalents. I will then turn to some particularly interesting individual cases.

### 3.1.

The two weakest categories of relationship are trivial in that no Nahuatl equivalent is given. In the first instance, Nebrija's entry is omitted entirely from Ayer ms. 1478. These omissions are probably accidental and could have occurred either in the production of the Ayer copy or in an earlier version from which it was copied, with the exception of the omission of all of folios 58v and 59r of Nebrija, which must have been omitted from the first copy out of the Nebrija volume, whether it was with or without Nahuatl.

---

[6] For a highly interesting and informative treatment of the influence of Nebrija's various printings on bilingual lexicography, especially in the New World, see Hamann (2015). For some comments on my differing interpretation of Nebrija's influence on Molina, see my review of Hamann's book (Clayton 2017).

[7] I refer here to *Tri*. Nebrija's Spanish-Latin dictionary, of course, was intended to be an encoding dictionary of Latin, there being no Latin speakers who would need to decode the Spanish.

In the second instance, Nebrija's Spanish-Latin entry is present but has no Nahuatl equivalent. These blank entries comprise approximately 29 percent of the dictionary. These omissions too could have occurred either when the Ayer copy was made or at some earlier stage.

### 3.2.

In the Nahuatl entries that are furthest from being fully functional Nahuatl equivalents, the Nahuatl is a hyperonym, an underdefined explanatory equivalent. In these cases, it would appear either that the author assumes the reader doesn't need full information about the meaning of the Spanish word or that the author himself doesn't have full information. But, in fact, in a number of these cases the author is not without help: Nebrija frequently provides rather vacuous limiting or explanatory glosses for his entry words. In many cases, these are no more than hyperonyms, for example, *Anchoua pecezico* 'anchovy, a little fish' (modern Spanish *anchoa*). Nebrija gives no other Spanish meaning for *anchoua*, so there is nothing to disambiguate, and the Spanish reader could have been expected to recognize the word *anchoua* without the added *pecezico*. Thus, the gloss adds nothing to the usefulness of Nebrija's entry for the Spanish speaker. But its presence provides Don Fernando with something he can translate.

The resulting equivalents are Nahuatl words or phrases but not true equivalents, in that each refers to a broad class of objects rather than to the specific designatum. In some cases, *anchoua* among them, the same hyperonym is used for several Spanish-Latin entries. In fact, *cē michin* 'one / a certain fish'[8] is the Nahuatl equivalent for four entries:

> Aguja paladar. pescado. acus, acus, acui. cémichi. {6r1.14} 'needle fish or pipe fish'
> Alachę[9] pece. scombrus, i. halex, ecis.[10] çémichi. {7v1.11} 'herring'
> Anchoua pecezico. halecula, ę. çémichi. {17v2.10} 'anchovy'
> Centolla pescado. testudo celtina. cemíchi. {51r1.07} 'a kind of edible crab'

---

[8] Nahuatl examples in the text show my regularized spelling and my English translations of the Nahuatl, which are intended to be somewhat literal rather than artful. Complete literal entries from *Tri* are given on separate lines. These are as the scribe wrote them, except that I have sometimes added punctuation within the Latin for clarity. My English glosses for these entries translate Nebrija's Spanish. Citations for *Tri* are identified by folio, column, and entry number enclosed in braces.

[9] 'Alachę' for 'Alache.'

[10] '-ecis' for '-icis.'

Other examples of multiple uses of the same hyperonym are trees with three occurrences of *cē cuahuitl* 'a (certain) tree' and plants with five examples, four of *cē xihuitl* 'a (certain) plant,' and one using *cē* with the number classifier *-tlamantli*, *centlamantli xihuitl* 'a (certain) plant':

>Alamo blanco arbol. populus, i. çéquavitl. {7v1.17} 'white poplar'
>Alamo negrillo aʳbol. almus, i. çéquavitl. {7v1.18} 'black poplar'
>Alhostigo o alhosticigo[11] arbol. pistacius.| ij. cequávitl. {9v2.16} 'pistachio, a tree'
>Ala yerua conocida. helenium, ij. çexíutl.[12] {7v1.03} 'elecampane, horse-heal, a familiar herb'
>Almiron chicoria. intubus, i. iutibus.[13] céxivitl. {11r1.02} 'wild endive,' 'chicory'
>Apio yerua conocida. apium, ij. g. senumi.[14] çéxiuitl. {20r2.01} 'celery, a familiar herb'
>Cepa cauallo yerua. chameleon.[15] ce<n>tlama<n>tli xíuitl. {51r1.16} 'ground thistle, an herb'

And with the added modifier that this otherwise unidentified plant is fragrant or pleasant, *cē xihuitl ahhuiāc* 'a fragrant plant':

>Amoradux o axedrea. sansucus, i. amaracus. çéxivitl avíac. {17r2.16} variously identified as 'marjoram' 'summer savory' or 'winter savory'

Several month names also involve hyperonyms. These will be considered later.

Of course, not all hyperonyms have multiple occurrences. The word for 'bird' in Nahuatl is *tōtōtl*, and Don Fernando uses *cē tōtōtzintli* 'a (certain) little bird' as his equivalent in the following entry:

>Aguza nieue auezita. motacilla. sisopigis sisuras.[16] çetotoţintli. {6r1.22} (*aguzanieves* in modern Spanish) 'white wagtail'

Apparently, the Spanish disambiguating gloss *auezita* 'little bird' with its diminutive suffix *-zita* tells him that it is a small bird, and thus the Nahuatl diminutive *-tzintli*.

---

[11] 'alhosticigo' for 'alhocigo.'
[12] 'i' missing in 'çexíutl.'
[13] 'u' for 'n' in 'intibus.'
[14] 'senumi' for 'selinum.'
[15] 'chameleon' for 'chameleon.'
[16] Final 's' in Latin where there should be none.

In a few cases, Don Fernando uses a hyperonym adding *ītōca* 'its name.' For example, *centlamantli āmoxtli ītōca breuiario* 'a (certain) book, its name (is) breuiario.'

> Breuiario. breuiariu<m>. epitoma. g. çentlamántli amoxtli itoca breuiário. {32r2.17} 'breviary'

While entries with *ītōca* 'its name' might seem to provide more information, in fact they do not, since the Spanish word is the headword itself. In these cases, the Spanish word is not actually a borrowing but simply part of the explanation. There is no way to know whether Don Fernando is suggesting that the Spanish word is or should be used in Nahuatl. We turn to explanatory equivalents next.

### 3.3.

A more developed treatment of foreign concepts is the use of explanatory equivalents. These are similar to the definitions in monolingual dictionaries. They do not attempt to translate the notion under consideration so that it can be used in the target language but rather to describe it to a user so that he or she could recognize or identify this particular designatum. Explanatory equivalents occur in *Tri* for several reasons.

### 3.3.1.

The most interesting explanatory equivalents are those that Don Fernando freely creates on his own, because they show his originality in setting out the meaning of words that he can't directly translate, for example, *tepetlacalli in oncān motōcah in mimicqueh* 'stone *petlacalli* (reed chest) where are buried those who died':

> Luzillo sepultura de piedra. cippus, i. tepetlacalli ino<n>camotoca i<n> mi miq<ue>. {107r2.08} 'stone urn; stone burial vault or receptacle'

Another case is *tlohcuahuitl in īpan cochi* 'falcon-stick on which it sleeps':

> Alcandara o pecba[17] de halcones. pertieca, e. tlóquavitl inipancóchi. {8v1.12} 'a perch for falcons'

In this example, *tlohcuahuitl* 'falcon-stick' by itself would have been a good translational equivalent. Apparently, Don Fernando must have thought that his audience would need an explanation for why a falcon would have or need a stick.

---

[17] 'pecba' for 'percha.'

Don Fernando's explanation for Spanish *cura de yglesia* 'priest of a church' is *teōyōtica tētah in animameh quimmocuitlahuia* 'one's holy father who cares for (*cuitla-huia* = 'apply fertilizer to') souls'; (Spanish borrowing *anima* 'soul' with Nahuatl plural *-meh*):

> Cura de yglesia. curator a<n>i<m>arum. cu=|rio. teuiotica teta i<n> a<n>i<m>ame q<ui>n mo‖cuitláuia. {49v2.15} 'priest'

In this case, he draws his explanation from both the Latin and the Spanish of Nebrija's entry, since the Latin doesn't mention holiness and the Spanish doesn't include souls.

One of Don Fernando's more encyclopedic descriptions is for the almond tree, which he describes as *cē castillancuahuitl iuhqui cacahuatl ītech mochīhua* 'a Castile-place tree, attached to it (something) resembling cacahuatl (the fruit whose seeds are used to make chocolate) is produced':

> Almendro ~~abol~~ arbol conocido. amygda=|letum, i. cecaxtilla<n>q<ua>vitl ivhq<ui> cacavatl| itechmo|chiua. {10v2.18} 'almond, a familiar tree'

In copying from his source, the copyist of *Tri* (or of some earlier version) inadvertently returned to the wrong entry when copying the Latin, taking not the Latin for this entry, which should be *amygdalus, i*, but skipping two entries completely (*Almendra fruta del. amygdalum, i., Almendra en latin. nux longa. nux alna.*) and taking only the Latin from the third *Almendral lugar dellos. amygdaletum, i*, which he applied to the current entry. Thus, unfortunately, there is no way of knowing what Don Fernando might have said about these three missing entries, which might have been of interest. *Almendra* 'almond' was the Spanish word used for an individual cacao seed (cf. *doszientas almendras de cacao* 'two hundred seeds of cacao').[18] Molina 1571a has the entry word *cacao* followed by the explanatory gloss *almendra y moneda* 'cacao, cacahuatl seed and coin.' The Nahuatl equivalent is *cacahuatl*.[19] In his three dictionaries, Molina has fifty-seven entries that involve the word *moneda*, but only this one associates *almendra* or *cacahuatl* with *moneda*. Because of the abovementioned omission, there is no way to know what Don Fernando might have had to say about the association.

---

[18] *Florentine Codex*, bk. 9 (Sahagún [1579] 2001, II, 711).

[19] In the text, I give regularized spellings for Molina's Nahuatl words. The Spanish is rendered according to whichever dictionary I quote. Literal citations of entries from Molina's dictionaries are given on separate lines. Unless I state otherwise, citing an example from one of his sources makes no claim about whether it occurs in his other dictionaries. Slight variations in spelling and wording make it impractical to give complete lists.

Needing an equivalent for *ogaño* 'nowadays,' Don Fernando provides an adept explanation in *in xihuitl īpan ticāteh* 'the year, in it we are living':

> Ogaño aduerbio de tyempo. or|no. ixiuitl ipanticáte. {122v2.09} 'nowadays, adverb of time'

Naturally, words for Spanish garments have, in many cases, no exact Nahuatl counterparts and thus must be explained. Don Fernando deals with the concept of mourning in explaining *enlutado con xerga* as *tlīltic comaquiāni in īpampa micqui* 'one who puts on black because of a dead person':

> Enlutado co<n> xerga. sagatus, a, um. tliltic comaquiáni inipanpamíqui. {75r2.14} 'dressed in mourning with sackcloth'

In the case of friars' garments, neither the office nor the garment is native to Nahua culture. His explanatory equivalent for a friar's hood borrows the Spanish word *padre* 'father, priest,' incorporating the Nahuatl plural morpheme *-meh* while constructing the word for the garment from totally native elements, *padremeh innecuāquimiloaya* 'priests, their instrument for wrapping their heads':

> Cugulla de habito de frayle. cuculla, ę. padreme inequaquimiloáia. {49v1.09} 'hood of a friar's habit'

Don Fernando also supplies a good explanatory equivalent for another Old World garment in *cuetlaxtlaquēmitl tlāni tohmiyoh* 'a leather garment, inside [it is] furry':

> Camar<sup>r</sup>a[20] o çamarron. rheno, onis. cuetlaxtlaquémitl tlani tomío. {50r1.18} 'sheepskin jacket or vest'

Molina, in all three dictionaries, gives us the much less descriptive *ehuatilmahtli* 'skin garment' for 'çamarro,' though we should consider the possibility that he is starting with a native concept and providing the closest Old World equivalent.

3.3.2.

Other explanatory equivalents in *Tri* are translations of Spanish explanations. These are Nebrija's disambiguating or limiting glosses that actually add something to the headword, unlike the simple hyperonyms that we saw earlier. Don Fernando is able to take advantage of this type of explanation as a source of translatable material

---

[20] Another 'r' is added above and after 'r' to give 'rr.'

rather than the headword. Thus, Nebrija's explanation in *Jsla tierra cercada de agua* 'island, land surrounded by water' becomes an explanatory equivalent for Don Fernando in *tlālhuāctli āihtic* 'dry land inside water':

> Jsla tierra cercada de| agua. insula, e. tlaluactli aitic. {101v2.05} 'Island, land surrounded by water'

Likewise, Nebrija's *Clerezia ayuntamiento destos* (where *destos* 'of these' refers to the previous entry, *clerigo de missa*) is translated as *incenyeyān in tēteōyōmacani*, 'their gathering together place (their being-one place), the holiness givers':

> Clerezia ayuntamiento destos. clerus, i. iceia̵ᵉia inteteuiomacáni.²¹ {40v2.11} 'clergy, a gathering of these (priests who say mass)'

Nebrija uses true disambiguating glosses in his two *Levante* entries, *Leuante parte oriental* and *Leuante viento oriental*, 'Levant, the east,' and 'Levant, wind from the east' respectively. Don Fernando uses these disambiguating glosses as the sources for his Nahuatl equivalents: *tlālli in ompa huālquīza tōnatiuh* 'land from which the sun [(the thing) it goes along producing heat] comes out,' and *ehēcatl in ompa huālmomana tōnatiuh* 'wind/breeze, which [from] there towards here the sun spreads itself':

> Leuante parte oriental. oriens, tis. ort<us>| us. tlalli ino<m>pa oalquiça to natiuh. {104v2.07} 'Levant, the east'
> Leuante viento oriental. sobsolanus,²² i. ieecatl ino<m>pa oalmomana tonatihv. {104v2.08} 'Levant, wind from the east'

Don Fernando is seriously led astray by Nebrija's disambiguating gloss in *Vulgar cosa comun* 'ordinary, a common thing,' which he glosses *tēcemāxca* 'one's one/together-possession' 'things held in common':

> Uulgar cosa comun. vulgaris, e. tecemaxca. {156v2.28} 'ordinary, a common thing'

This is the possessed form of *āxcāitl* 'possession' combined with *cem*. Whereas the morpheme *cem/ce*, when it stands alone, means 'one' or 'a,' when it appears in prefix position, it usually means 'together, unified.' Don Fernando apparently based his Nahuatl equivalent on *cosa comun*, which he understood in the primary sense of its Latin etymon *commūnis* 'shared' rather than on Spanish *comun*, which can mean

---

²¹ 'a' crossed out and 'e' inserted above.

²² 'o' for 'u' in 'subsolanus.'

either 'shared' or 'ordinary,' the sense that Nebrija was indicating in pairing it with *vulgar*. Thus, Don Fernando used the word for 'publicly owned' rather than the word for 'ordinary.' *Tēcemāxca* is an acceptable Nahuatl word, though its meaning does not correspond to Spanish *vulgar*. Nebrija's next entry is the corresponding adverb *vulgarmente*. And here, Don Fernando derives it as an adverb, producing the somewhat improbable equivalent *tēcemāxcātica*, which doesn't mean 'in an ordinary way' but rather 'by means of public possessions':

> Uulgarmente. vulgariter. tecemaxcatica. {156v2.29} 'in an ordinary way'

### 3.3.3.

In yet other cases, Nebrija's entire Spanish entry is actually an explanatory equivalent for a Latin word for which he had no single-word Spanish translation. In these cases, Don Fernando's explanatory equivalent is simply a translation of Nebrija's explanatory equivalent. For example, *yāōquīzqueh cavallo īpan yetiyani* 'those going off to battle going on horseback' translates *Batalla de gente a cauallo*, where Nebrija provides an explanation rather than a translation for Latin *turma, -ae*:[23]

> Batalla de gente a cauallo. turma, ę. iaoquízque cavallo ipaietiáni.[24] {28r2.04} 'unit of people on horseback'

### 3.4.

A frequent and obvious means of coping with foreign concepts is simply to adopt the foreign word along with its designatum. We have already seen the Spanish borrowings *anima* 'soul' and *padre* 'father, priest' in explanatory equivalents. It is perhaps important to note that in neither of these cases does Nebrija's entry contain the Spanish word that Don Fernando borrows, indicating that these were "real words"—or morphemes—for him. He wasn't simply leaning on the Spanish to come up with an equivalent, something he tends to do far less than Molina.

Naturally, Spanish borrowings also occur in translational equivalents. Molina frequently uses *lo mismo* or its variant *lo mesmo* 'the same' to indicate that the Spanish word is used in Nahuatl as well. For example, Molina 1555 has *lo mismo* for *camisa* 'shirt.' We could take him at his word and assume that he means literally *camisa* as in Spanish, but in Molina 1571a he also has *collar de vestidura* 'collar of a garment' *iquech in camisahtli et sic de aliis*, 'its neck the camisahtli, and so on for other things,' telling us that in fact, he does know the adapted Nahuatl borrowing *camisahtli*. This

---

[23] Gruda (2018, 203) also observes that sometimes the Spanish explanation for a Latin equivalent provides the material that is translated into Nahuatl.

[24] 'n' missing in 'ipan.'

choice suggests that what he meant by *lo mismo* is that the morpheme *camisa* was borrowed—and adapted as necessary:

> Camisa de hombre. lo mismo. Molina 1555 42r 'a man's shirt'
> Collar de vestidura. yquech yn camisatli et sic de alijs. Molina 1571a 27r2 'collar of a garment'

Don Fernando does not use *lo mismo*, but he has the borrowing *camisahtli* for *camisa de varon* 'a man's shirt.' He also uses the borrowing in *Uestidura interior* 'undergarment' and provides us with a deverbal formation in *Uestido desta vestidura* 'dressed in this garment' (referring to 'undergarment'), *camisahhuah*, a preterit agentive noun 'one who has a camisahtli':

> Camisa de varon. subuculalinthea.²⁵ camisátli. {35v1.26} 'man's shirt'
> Uestidura interior. tunica. interula. camisatli. {155v1.20} 'undergarment'
> Uestido desta vestidura. tunicatus, a. camisaua. {155v1.21} 'dressed in this garment'

As might be expected, given the rich compounding and derivational nature of Nahuatl, despite Molina's use of *lo mismo*, comparatively few Spanish borrowings occur as simple Nahuatl words in either Molina's dictionaries or in *Tri*. Most are incorporated as morphemes in normally complex explanatory and translational equivalents. Don Fernando gives only seventeen tokens of bare Spanish nouns plus sixty-five that occur bare in phrases, give or take a few for differences of opinion on questions of phrase versus compound. For example, his equivalent for Spanish *missa* 'mass' is *misa*, and his equivalent for *missa dezir* 'to say mass' is *misa nicchīhua* 'mass I do it':

> Missa. res diuina. sacrificiu\<m\> christia|nu\<m\>. misa. {115r1.05} 'mass'
> Missa dezir. rem diuinam facio. missa nicchi|ua. {115r1.07} 'to say mass'

The majority of Spanish borrowings occur as morphemes in otherwise native constructions sharing the same inflectional, compounding, and derivational forms as in completely native words. The Spanish borrowing *campana* 'bell' occurs in a noun-noun compound in *campanacalli* 'bell tower' and as the object of a deverbal noun in *campanachīuhqui* 'bell maker' and *campanatzotzonqui* 'bell ringer':

> Campanario. turris cimbalaria. campanacálli. {35v1.29} 'bell tower'
> Campanero q\<ue\> las tañe & faze. cimba=|larius, ii. ca\<m\>panachiuhq\<ui\>. ca\<m\>panaţoţo\<n\>q\<ui\>. {35v2.01} 'one who plays and makes bells'

The borrowing *letra* 'letter' occurs as an incorporated noun object along with the

---

²⁵ Space omitted in 'subucula linthea.'

adverbial noun *xōchitl* 'flower, pretty thing' in the verb *niletraxōchihcuiloa* 'I decorate (flower-write) letters':

> Luminar libros. minio, as, aui. niletraxochicuilóa. {107r1.11} 'to illuminate, decorate books'

Spanish *queso* 'cheese' occurs in an adjectival function in *maxtenquilmōlli quesoyoh* 'onion-greens sauce with cheese,' using the "suffix" *-yoh*, which is the preterit of the obsolete verb *yoā* 'to have':

> Almodrote de ajos et queso. moretum,| i. maxtenquilmólli quesuio. {111r1.09} 'sauce of garlic and cheese'

Nearly all of the Spanish borrowings in *Tri* also occur in Molina, though the converse is certainly not the case. Molina uses several borrowings where *Tri* prefers to "go native." *Tri*, of course, is limited by Nebrija's corpus, whereas Molina chooses his own wordlist, though naturally many of his entries also occur in Nebrija. Among words that occur in both sources, only two Spanish borrowings occur in *Tri* and not in Molina: *madre* 'mother' and *virrey* 'viceroy.'

*Tri* uses *madre* in *cihuāmadre*, literally 'female mother,' for Nebrija's *frayla o freyla* 'nun, female friar,' and also for *monja* 'nun' in *Monia en otra manera* 'nun of another type' (to distinguish this entry from *Monia solitaria* 'a nun who lives alone' in the preceding entry):

> Frayla o freila. soror, oris. ciua madre. {87r1.04} 'nun, female friar' (two spellings)
> Monia en otra manera. soror, oris. ciua madre. {116r2.09} 'nun of another type'

In *Tri*, *visorrey* 'viceroy' is the borrowed equivalent for Nebrija's *virrey*. Note that Don Fernando doesn't borrow from Nebrija but chooses the now-antiquated form *visorrey*:

> Uirrey rey por otro. prorex, igis.[26] Visorei. {156v1.26} 'Viceroy, king in place of someone else'

A more interesting case of a borrowing that *Tri* makes extensive use of and that Molina hardly mentions is *hora*, also spelled *ora* 'hour, time,' which occurs only once each as *lo mesmo* in Molina 1555 and Molina 1571a but is thoroughly integrated in *Tri*. Don Fernando uses it in three entries having to do with time: *cē hora* 'an hour, one hour,' *ahcualli hora* 'a bad time,' and *īc cē hora* 'the first hour':

---

[26] '-igis' for '-egis.'

[27] Incorrect space after 'de' in 'desastrada.'

> Ora parte del dia natural. hora,| e. ce hora. {123v2.24} 'hour, a part of the natural day'
> Ora de sastrada.²⁷ sydus, eris. syderatio. aqualli hora. {123v2.25} 'ill-starred time'
> Prima en las oras. hora p<ri>ma. iccehora. {131v2.13} 'First in the hours, the first hour'

Don Fernando also uses *hora* as an incorporated object in three entries for types of clocks: *ātl horatamachīhualōni* 'water hour-measuring devise,' *horatōnal[ta]machihuani* 'hour sun-measurer,' and *campana horamachiyōtilōni* 'bell hour-marker.' This last word has two contiguous Spanish borrowings, but in fact *campana* is a separate word parallel with *atl* in the first example below, and the word following should be undivided *horamachiyōtilōni*:²⁸

> Relox de agua. elepsydra,²⁹ ę. atl horatamachiualóni. {137r2.14} 'water clock'
> Relox del sol. horologiu<m> solariu<m>. horatonalmachiauáni.³⁰ {137r2.15} 'sun dial'
> Relox de sombra. horologiu<m> sciotericum. campanahora machiotilóni.³¹ {137r2.16} 'sun dial'
> Relox de campana. horologiu<m> nouum. [no Nahuatl equivalent]. {137r2.17} 'clock with bells, tower clock'

While *castillan* 'Castile-place' involves the borrowing *Castilla* 'Castile,' it is not used like the other borrowings we have seen in that it does not name a denotatum but rather sets up an analogy between a native denotatum and its assumed Spanish equivalent, parallel to 'Chinese parsley' as a synonym for 'cilantro' in English. *Tri* uses more of these than Molina does, seventy-four types to Molina's fifty-two. Rather few of these correspond. Some of these are quite apt, such as *castillan ōlōtl, ōlōtōntli* 'Spanish corn cob, small corncob' for *espiga de pan* 'head of bread, (wheat)':

> Espiga de pan. spica, ę. spicus, i. spicum, i.³² castilan³³ olotl. olotóntli. {81v2.05} 'head of wheat'

---

²⁸ This equivalent was miscopied into *relox de sombra*. It actually belongs with *relox de campana*, which immediately follows it in the manuscript and which I give in the examples without a gloss, as it appears in the manuscript.

²⁹ 'e' miscopied for 'c' in 'clepsydra.'

³⁰ The copyist apparently omitted the syllable 'ta' in what should have been 'horatonaltamachiuáni.'

³¹ This equivalent was miscopied into this entry. It belongs with the following entry.

³² I give Nebrija's Latin here because the manuscript has been altered by another hand, and transcription with description of changes would be complex and somewhat dubious.

³³ One 'l' for two in 'castillan.'

Other examples signal Don Fernando's lack of understanding of the Spanish counterpart, such as *castillancapolin* 'Spanish cherry' for *avellana* 'hazelnut,' even though he gives *capolcuahuitl* 'cherry tree' for *cerezo arbol conocido* 'cherry tree, a known tree':

> Auellana. nux auellana. avellina,[34] prę|nestina. castillancapúlli.[35] {25vi.17} 'hazelnut, filbert'
> Cerezo arbol conocido. cerasus, i. capolquáuitl. {51vi.03} 'cherry, a known tree'

An interesting case involves *castillanmazātl* 'Castile-place deer' for 'beast of burden.' *Tri* follows this with *tēuctlatquimāmāni* 'one who carries royal possessions.' Punctuation in *Tri* is irregular, so it is not possible to determine whether these two words are separate equivalents or a phrase despite the period between them, but the next entry combines all of these elements and more into the longest word in the dictionary: 36 letters, 33 phonemes, and 14 morphemes. The word is *castillanmazātēuctlatquimāmāncāpixqui* 'keeper of Castile-place deer (that) are carriers of royal possessions.' Neither Molina nor the *Florentine Codex* associate mules or horses with carrying the belongings of the upper class.

> Azemila o mulo. mulus, i. castilla[36] maçátl. teuctlatquimamáni. {26vi.14} 'beast of burden or mule'
> Azemilero que las trata. mulio, onis. castilla<n>maçateuctlatquimamancapíxqui. {26vi.15} 'mule-keeper who cares for them'

This entry also involves a grammatical error: *māmāncā* would be grammatically correct if it were derived from *tlamana* 'lay out,' but our author clearly intended *māmā* 'carry,' which he has just used in the preceding entry. He treats *māmāni* as if it were a unified verb that could form a preterit by deletion of its final vowel and could add the nominalizing *-ca-*, but in fact *-ni* is a suffix and does not form a preterit. This may have been a momentary slip such as 'brang' for 'brought' by analogy to 'ring,' 'rang.'

3.5.

Of course, in interpreting foreign concepts, Don Fernando also employs fully native equivalents. *Tri*'s equivalent for *ancla de naue* 'anchor of a boat' is *tepozācalzālōlōni*

---

[34] 'avellina' for 'abellina.'
[35] 'capúlli' for 'capúlin.'
[36] 'castilla' for 'castillan.'

'a metal instrument for making a boat stick to something.' I have found no word for 'anchor' in Molina.

> Ancla de naue. anchora, e. g. ancira. tepuzacalçalolóni. {17v2.01} 'anchor'

For 'signature' *Tri* has *tlani tōcāihcuilōliztli* 'below, a name-writing.' And for 'to make verses' *nitlatamachīhuallahtōlchīhua* 'I make measured words':

> Firma de escriptura. subscriptio.| signatio. tlani tocaicuilolíztli. {86r1.17} 'a handwritten signature'
> 
> Trobar hazer v<er>sos. v<er>sificor, aris. nitlatamachiuallatolchíoa. {152r1.10} 'to be a troubador, to make verses'

Some of Don Fernando's more puzzling native equivalents have their explanation in his injudicious reliance on Nebrija's Latin. One might think that given that Don Fernando is making a Spanish dictionary for Nahuatl users, Nebrija's Latin equivalents for the Spanish headwords would be useless to him, but quite the contrary: there are clearly cases in which he bases his Nahuatl equivalent on the Latin rather than the Spanish. There may be more of these cases than we can recognize, because the only entries in which we can be sure he was relying on the Latin are those in which the Spanish meaning has changed or narrowed from Latin and he doesn't realize that. These examples are not necessarily foreign concepts, but apparently for Don Fernando they were foreign words with which he needed some help.

An interesting case is Nebrija's *abrasarse* 'to be very hot,' 'to burn oneself,' 'to get burned,' which he pairs with the Latin *in prunas delabi* 'to fall or slide down into hot coals or fire.' It is hard to imagine why Nebrija would have chosen a Latin equivalent that is so much more limited than his more general headword—or turn that around and ask why he didn't just translate the Latin more literally into Spanish. But in any case, the disparity between the Spanish and the Latin provides us a clear view into Don Fernando's strategy with this entry: he went for the Latin. *Tleco nihuetzi* translates quite literally as 'fire-place I fall':

> Abrasarse. in prunas delabi. tleco niueţi. {4v1.01} 'to get burned, to be very hot'

Nebrija's entries for *julio* 'July' and *agosto* 'August' give both the Latin month names that correspond to our modern names and also the names by which they were known in Roman times before they were renamed for Julius Caesar and Augustus Caesar. Interestingly, it is these earlier Roman names that Don Fernando uses in his Nahuatl glosses. We can be certain that he was getting his information from the Latin equivalents because the Roman names are numbers that place July as the fifth month and August as the sixth. Don Fernando glosses these as *īc mācuīltetl mētzxiuhtlapōhualōni*, 'fifth moon-year-counter' and *tlachicuacencayōtia mētztli* 'sixth moon' (more literally 'it-causes-it-to-have-six-ness moon') respectively:

> Julio mes. quintilis, is. iulius. ic macuiltetl metxihutlapoualoni. {98v2.15} 'July, a month'
>
> Agosto mes. sextilis. augustus, i. tlachicuacencayutia méṭtli. {15r2.18} 'August, a month'

For comparison, in both Spanish-Nahuatl dictionaries, Molina glosses *julio/ iulio* 'July' as both *lo mismo* 'the same' and *īc chicōntetl mētztli in cē xihuitl* 'seventh moon with reference to a year.' In the Nahuatl-Spanish dictionary, he gives only the Nahuatl phrase, which is the headword. For *agosto* 'August' in 1555 he uses both *lo mismo* and *īc chicuēyi mētztli in cē xihuitl* 'eighth moon with reference to a year.' In the two 1571 dictionaries, he uses only the Nahuatl phrase.

Don Fernando's Nahuatl *huechiliztli* 'a fall' for Nebrija's *caso* is another example of a flagrant misjudgment based on Nebrija's Latin, but only on part of it. He might have been saved by reading further. Latin *cāsus, cāsūs* 'a fall,' from *cado, cadere, cecidi, cāsum* 'to fall,' extends in meaning to 'event, occurrence accident,' and from there to 'chance, luck.' Nebrija points in this direction with his additional Latin equivalents, *fortuna, fors, forte* 'chance, luck, fortune.' In Spanish, *caso* has pretty much the same semantic range as 'case' in English. Don Fernando, however, takes the literal meaning, 'a fall,' as the basis for his Nahuatl equivalent without considering the other Latin equivalents, a step that might have gotten him a little closer to Spanish semantics:

> Caso. casus. us. fortuna. ę. fors forte. vechiliztli. {39r2.02} 'case, circumstance'

It should be noted that he uses the same Nahuatl, in a slight morphological variation, *huetziliztli*, to translate Spanish *cayda o caymiento* 'a fall, or the act of falling.' As one would expect, this entry also has *casus, us* as its first Latin equivalent:

> Cayda o camiento.[37] casus, us. occasus, us. vetilíztli. {34r2.30} 'a fall, or act of falling'

Likewise, in the case of *conuersar* and *conuersacion* 'to converse,' 'a conversation,' our author appears to have taken his meaning from Nebrija's Latin. At least by the time of Sebastián de Covarrubias (1611 [Cobarruvias Orozco 1977]), the meaning of *conversar* centered on communication and apparently differed little from 'converse' in English. But Don Fernando has translated only the Latin verb, which translates 'live with,' 'feast with,' 'spend time together,' 'dine together,' with no particular focus on communication. Thus, he gives us *tētlan ninemi* 'I live with someone' and *tētlan nemiliztli* 'the act of living with someone' for these two entries:

---

[37] 'camiento' for 'caymiento.' A 'y' is added below the line, probably in another hand.

Conuersar. conuiuo, is. conuersor, aris. tetlanninémj. {45r2.11} 'to converse'
Conuersacion. conuersatio, onis. conuic=|tus, us. tetlannemilíztli. {45r2.12} 'a conversation'

These examples are not to suggest that Don Fernando was aiming to prepare a Latin-Nahuatl dictionary. There are also examples in which he has chosen Spanish over somewhat different Latin, such as *gusano con cuernos* 'a worm with horns,' which he translates as *ocuilin cuācuahueh* 'worm head-wood-haver.' *Cuācuahueh* means 'having horns' and is the normal Nahuatl word for horned ungulates. Nebrija's Latin for this entry is simply *taurus* 'bull.' Had Don Fernando been inattentively following the Latin, he might have easily accepted this as the word to be translated.

Gusano con cueruos.[38] taurus, i. ocuili quáquahue. {92r1.07} 'worm with horns'

It would appear that our author was simply using all information available to him in determining his Nahuatl equivalents. Thus, he uses Latin equivalents much as he uses Spanish disambiguating glosses where he needs help with some Spanish entry word. In doing so, he was sometimes led astray.

## 4. INTERESTING CASES

Among Don Fernando's native equivalents for foreign concepts are a few that stand out because there are enough examples of them to suggest that they were real for him—they weren't just his attempts to capture the meaning of the Spanish—and because they occur rarely if at all in Molina and/or the *Florentine Codex*. Among these are the three cases that follow. One includes the borrowing *castillan* 'Castile-place.' The other two are completely native.

### 4.1 Castillantōchin

Among Don Fernando's uncommon words is one for which I have found no other source. Claims that something does not exist are not verifiable unless limited to a totally known and closed corpus, so I will not claim that the word is not out there somewhere else, but so far neither Google nor I have found it. The word is *Castillantōchin*, a 'castile-place rabbit,'[39] in fact, a donkey—perhaps named playfully for the shape and size of its ears. *Trī* includes seven entries involving this word, and an eighth without *Castillan*. Given its rarity, I will list all eight of them. For

---

[38] 'u' for 'n' in 'cuernos.'
[39] Gruda (2018, 111) comments on these noteworthy entries in a different context.

clarity, these examples are given in order of complexity rather than in dictionary order: *Castillantōchin* 'Castile-place rabbit'; *cuauhtlah castillantōchin* 'place of an abundance of wood ('forest, woods') 'Castile-place rabbit'; *castillantōchconētl* 'Castile-place rabbit offspring'; *castillanoquichtōchconētl* 'male Castile-place rabbit offspring'; *castillantōchpixqui* 'Castile-place rabbit keeper'; *castillantōchpepechtli* 'Castile-place rabbit pack-saddle'; *castillantōchtemalacatl* 'Castile-place rabbit stone-wheel (mill)'; and *tōchpepechchīuhqui* 'rabbit pack-saddle maker':

> Asno manso et domestico. asinus, i. castillantóchi.[40] {23r2.07} 'tame and domestic donkey'
> Asno silu<sup>e</sup>stre. onager, onagri. quahvtla castilla&lt;n&gt;tóchi.[41] {23r2.06} 'wild donkey'
> Borrico fiio de asna. pullus asini=|nus. castilla[42] tochcónetl. {31r2.15} 'donkey, son of a female donkey'
> Asno pequeño deste[43] especie. ~~asina e. ase=|~~ ~~lla, e~~ asellus, i. castillan oquich tóch conetl. {23r2.08} 'small donkey of this type' (for *asno manso e domestico* 'a domesticated and tame donkey')
> Asnero que guarda. asnos. asinarius, ij. castillantochpíxqui. {23r2.12} 'a donkey keeper'
> Albarda[X] de bestia. clitella, e. stragulu&lt;m&gt;,| i. caxtillatochpepéchtli.[44] {8r1.01} 'a packsadldle'
> Atahona de mulos. mola.[45] mulionica. castillan tochtemalácatl. {24r2.15} 'a mill turned by mules'
> Albardero. clitelarius fartor[46] tochpepechchivhqui. {8r1.02} 'a packsaddle maker'

*Tri* has three other glossed entries involving Spanish *asno*. Two of these borrow the morpheme *asno*: *asnoconētl* 'donkey offspring' and *asnomeh niquintototza* 'donkeys I drive them.' The third one merges the concepts of driving donkeys and driving mules, *asnerizo o harriero*, and uses the normal Nahuatl word for beast of burden, *mazatl*, literally 'deer': *mazāōztōmēcapixqui* 'deer-merchant-keeper.'

> Pollino hiio de asna. pullus asinin&lt;us&gt;. asnocónetl. {13or1.14} 'son of a female donkey'

---

[40] '-n' missing in 'tochin.'
[41] '-n' missing in 'tochin.'
[42] '-n' missing in 'castillan.'
[43] 'e' for 'a' in 'desta.'
[44] '-n' missing in 'castillan.'
[45] 'o' for 'u' in 'mula'; incorrect period in Latin. It is a phrase.
[46] One 'l' for two in 'clitellarius'; 'f' for 's' in 'sartor.'
[47] 'e' for 'a' in 'harriero.'

Harrear asnos. ago, is. agito, as. asnome niquintotóța. {93r2.22} 'to drive donkeys'
Asnerizo o herriero.⁴⁷ agaso, onis. maçaoztomecapíxqui. {23r2.11} 'donkey driver or mule driver'

### 4.2. XIUHTOCTLI

*Tri* offers Nahuatl equivalents for five entries involving the pomegranate, a fruit with ancient origins taken to Spain by the Arabs and from there to Mexico by the Spaniards: *xiuhtōcticātzapotl*, 'red-maize-like sapote' (two occurrences), *xiuhtōcticātzapocuahuitl* 'red-maize-like sapote tree,' *xiuhtōctzapocuauhxōchitl* 'red-maize-sapote tree flower,' and *xiuhtōctzapotocapepeyollotl* 'red-maize sapote spiderweb':

Granado arbol. malus punica. xihutucticațápotl. {90v2.16} 'pomegranate, a tree'
Granada fruta deste arbol. malu<m>| punicu<m>, i. xihutocticațápotl. {90v2.18} 'pomegranate, fruit of this tree'
Granda⁴⁸ pequeñita. citiuus.⁴⁹ xihutoctica țapoquáuitl. {90v2.17} 'small pomegranate'
Flor degranada.⁵⁰ balaustru<m>. xihutocțapoquahuxochitl. {86r2.15} 'flower of the pomegranate'
Tela de la granada entrX⁵¹ los granos. ci|cu<m>, i. xiuh~~tochica~~ᵗᵒᶜțapotocapepeiolotl.⁵² {148r2.06} 'membrane of the pomegranate between the grains'

*Tzapotl* (Spanish *zapote*, English 'sapote') is the name of several fruits and their trees,⁵³ so it is not surprising that Don Fernando applies it to this new fruit. Of greater interest is that all of these entries incorporate *xiuhtoctli*, which in one of its meanings is 'red maize.' For example, Molina (1555) has *mayz colorado. xiuhtoctlaolli*. *Xiuhtoctli* is simply 'a planted (buried) young plant stem' and *tlaolli* 'shelled corn.' None of the morphemes is directly related to color, and Molina doesn't mention color *in xiuhtoctepitl, mayz que se haze en cincuenta dias* 'corn that matures in fifty days' in Molina 1555 (or *sesenta dias* 'sixty days' in Molina 1571b). Nonetheless, each of Molina's three dictionaries has an entry equating *xiuhtoctlaolli* and *mayz colorado* 'red maize,' and Don Fernando's words for pomegranate very aptly incorporate the

---

⁴⁸ 'a' omitted in 'granda' for 'granada.'
⁴⁹ 'u' for 'n' in 'citinus.'
⁵⁰ Space missing in 'de granada.'
⁵¹ 'e' of 'entre' is obscured by a worm hole.
⁵² 'toc' is added above crossed-out 'tochica' to give 'xiuhtocțapotocapepeiolotl.' It appears to be original.
⁵³ "Zapotl" [*sic* for "tzapotl"] "is Aztec for fleshy, sweet fruit and is applied to various species, not necessarily botanically related." Schoenhals (1988, 112).

analogy between red corn kernels and the individual faceted flesh-covered seeds of the pomegranate, which do, in fact, resemble corn kernels in shape and size. And likening the membrane to a spiderweb is particularly inventive. Molina sticks with *lo mismo* 'the same' for bare *granada* 'pomegranate' and uses *granada* as a borrowed morpheme in phrases and compounds such as *granado arbol, granadacuahuitl* 'pomegranate tree' in both Molina (1555) and Molina (1571a). Neither Molina's dictionaries nor the *Florentine Codex* uses *xiuhtoctli* for pomegranate. While I am unaware of other sources, they may exist.

### 4.3. Tlatemantli

Once in each of his three dictionaries, Molina uses the deverbal noun *tlatemantli* 'something flattened, spread out,' 'paving stone' to mean 'coin,' 'money'—literally 'something spread out in a stone way' (Nahuatl has adverbial nouns.) This is the patientive noun of the causative of the verb *mani* 'lie flat, spread out,' transitive: *tlamana* 'to spread or lay something out,' combined with the noun *tetl* 'stone' used adverbially. The entries are *pieça o moneda de oro* 'piece or coin of gold' in Molina (1555, 1571a) and *pieça o tejuelo doro* in Molina (1571b), 'piece or disc of gold,' all translated with *cozticteōcuitlatlatemantli* 'yellow god-excrement thing flattened in a stone way.' Molina's dictionaries contain at least sixty-three other Nahuatl entries and glosses involving money, but only these three use *tlatemantli*. Don Fernando, on the other hand, has eighteen glossed entries involving money or coins and he uses compounds of *tlatemantli* in sixteen of these, such as *tlatemanxiquipilli* 'something flattened in a stone way bag or purse,' *teōcuitlatlatemantli* 'god-excrement thing flattened in a stone way,' and *tepoztlatemanchīuhqui* 'metal-thing-flattened-in-a-stone-way maker':

> Bolsa para dineros. loculi, or<um>. fo=|llis, is . tlatemaxiquipílli. {30v2.07} 'bag or purse for coins'
> 
> Moneda de oro. aureus, i. aureus | nu<m>mus, i. teucuitlatlatemántli. {116r1.20} 'a gold coin'
> 
> Monedero. nu<m>marius faber. mar|culus, i. tepoztlatemanchiuhquj. {116r1.22} 'one who makes coins'

His two Nahuatl equivalents not based on *tlatemantli* actually gloss two forms of the same Spanish word with the same Latin equivalent: *arrebañar dineros* and *rebañar dineros* 'to gather up or collect coins to carry them away,' both glossed with Latin *ęrusco, as, aui*. (According to Lewis and Short [1879] 1962, 60, *aerusco*,

---

[54] 'a' for 'e' in 'rebañar.'

*āre* 'to get money by going about and exhibiting tricks of legerdemain, to play the juggler.') Interestingly, Don Fernando supplies these with two different equivalents, *niteōcuitlamātataca* 'I scratch up gold with my hands; I beg for gold' and *niteōcuitlaolōloa* 'I pile up gold':

> Arrebañar dineros. ęrusco, as, aui. niteocuitlamatatáca. {22r2.06} 'to gather up coins'
> Rabañar⁵⁴ dineros. ęrusco, as, aui. niteucuitlaololóa. {135vi.26} 'to gather up coins'

*Matataca* is interesting in that in addition to its literal meaning 'to gather or scratch with one's hands,' it can mean 'to beg forcefully.' This latter meaning aligns well with the Latin *aerusco* and thus provides perhaps a closer match for Nebrija's Latin than his Spanish does. It isn't clear why, of the three glossed entries involving *dineros* 'coins,' two use *teōcuitlatl* 'gold' and the third follows his normal habit of using *tlatemantli* 'stone-flattened thing' for entries involving money.

Although both authors use *tlatemantli* for 'coin,' the usage is pervasive in *Tri*, where Don Fernando uses little else, whereas Molina prefers other native equivalents and incorporated borrowings.

These three interesting cases illustrate either Don Fernando's originality, or his exposure to different community usage.

## 5. CONCLUSION

To conclude, I would like to examine Don Fernando's treatment of month names, because his treatment tells us just how irrelevant the twelve-month European calendar was for him.⁵⁵ In addition, the month names allow us to review all of the various glossing techniques that we have seen in the preceding discussion: his entries for month names include 2 without glosses, 6 hyperonyms, 2 explanatory equivalents that contain Latin and hispanized Latin borrowings, and 2 fully translational equivalents.

For May and December, Don Fernando offers no gloss at all. We can only wonder why. In the case of May, perhaps he hesitates because he already has a fifth month.

---

⁵⁵ On the other hand, his approach to days of the week is very uniform for all days except Sunday and Tuesday, for which he provides no Nahuatl equivalents. For the other five days, he gives the Spanish day name combined with the ligature *-ti-* and the postposition *-ca*, 'by means of'; thus, for example, *lunestica*, by means of *lunes* 'Monday.'

⁵⁶ A possible comma after *mayo* is probably an incorrect period that was struck out with a diagonal line, possibly by another hand. Any punctuation within the Spanish should come after *Mayo mes*, but neither Nebrija (1516) nor Nebrija (ca. 1520) shows any internal punctuation.

Mayo,[56] mes quinto mes. maius, ii. [no Nahuatl equivalent]. {108v2.05} 'May, a month, the fifth month'

Deziembre mes. december, bris. [no Nahuatl equivalent]. {63v1.11} 'December, a month'

For February and March, he provides the hyperonym *cē mētzxiuhtlapōhualōni*, 'one / a certain moon-year counter':

Hebrero mes. februarius. cemeṯ xihutlapoalóni. {94r2.18} 'February, a month'

Março mes tercero. martiX[57] ii. cemeṯxihutlapoalóni. {110v1.22} 'March, the third month'

For November and June, Don Fernando uses *cē* plus the number classifier *tetl* 'stone,' *centetl*. However, while he uses the same hyperonym in the November entry, *centetl mētzxiuhtlapōhualōni* 'one / a certain moon-year counter,' for 'June' he omits the *-xiuh-*, leaving *centetl mētztlapōhualōni* 'one / a certain moon counter.' While this may have been a careless recopying, it might also have been just his definition of the moment.

Nouiembre mes. nouembris, is. centetl meṯxiuhtlapoalóni. {121r2.09} 'November, a month'

Junio mes. iunius, ii. centetl meṯtlapoalóni. {98v2.21} 'June, a month'

September and April are also hyperonyms, with the additional explanation that the Spanish word is its name, *ītōca*. September uses the same noun as February, March, and November, giving us *cē mētzxiuhtlapōhualōni ītōca* 'one / a certain moon-year counter its name':

Septiembre mes. september. bris. cemeṯxiuhtlapoalloni[58] itóca. {144r2.16} 'September, a month'

April uses a different construction, *cē mecatlapōhualōni ītōca*, 'one / a certain rope-counter its name':

Abril mes. aprilis. vnde aprilis, e. cemecatlapoaloni itóca. {4v1.16} 'April, a month'

The preceding glosses for month names are all hyperonyms in that they identify the month only as belonging to a certain group of objects—and not even all to the same group. So, as in the earlier cases of trees and fish, Don Fernando is satisfied with, or perhaps must make do with, very general information. For whatever reason, the objects are not an important part of his world.

---

[57] The 'us' is hidden by an ink blob.
[58] 'll' for 'l' in '-tlapoaloni.'

For October and January on the other hand, Don Fernando provides specific explanations. He tells us that October is *cē mētzxiuhtlapōhualōni ītōca october*, 'a moon-year counter its name (is) October.' And for January he uses a different explanation: *mētztli ītōca januario* '(a) moon its name (is) January':

> Otubre mes. october, is. cemeṭxiuhtlapoaloni itoca october. {125r1.03} 'October a month'
> 
> Enero mes. ianuarius, ii. meṭtli itoca januario. {74r1.11} 'January a month'

Notice that for *otubre* (modern Spanish *octubre*) he gives us the Latin *october* in his Nahuatl gloss and for *enero*, he provides *januario*, a slightly hispanized form of the Latin *ianuarius*.

Only for July and August does Don Fernando provide true translations, and these translate part of Nebrija's Latin, as we saw in section 3.5, with *ic mācuīltetl mētzxiuhtlapōhualōni*, 'fifth moon-year-counter' for July and *tlachicuacencayōtia mētztli*, 'sixth moon' (more literally 'it-causes-it-to-have-six-ness moon') for August:

> Julio mes. quintilis, is. iulius. ic macuiltetl meṭxihutlapoualoni. {98v2.15} 'July, a month'
> 
> Agosto mes. sextilis. augustus, i. tlachicuacencayutia méṭtli. {15r2.18} 'August, a month'

In conclusion, we have seen that by preparing a passive dictionary, our author has allowed himself several glossing techniques and shortcuts that were not available to Alonso de Molina. By any standard of lexicography, his is an imperfect work, but despite its imperfections, Ayer ms. 1478 provides us with a corpus of the Nahuatl language that is alive and well in what must have been an interesting time linguistically. In order to incorporate some foreign concepts, Spanish words are unapologetically woven into the fabric of the language as if they were ordinary Nahuatl morphemes. To accommodate other concepts, the rich and highly inventive morphology of Nahuatl simply describes the concept into the language unaided by Spanish vocabulary.

While we don't know the "who," "when," or "where" of this manuscript, we do know that it represents a language that is taking great social changes in stride, flexibly adapting as necessary while maintaining its unique identity.

### REFERENCES

Anonymous. n.d. (*Vocabulario trilingüe, Tri*). Dictionarium ex hisniensi in latinum sermonem interprete Aelio Antonio Neprissensi. (Sometimes transcribed as Dictionarium ex bismensi..., in either case miscopied for hispaniensi) Trilingual Spanish-Latin-Nahuatl manuscript dictionary. Ayer ms. 1478 [vault]. Newberry Library, Chicago.

Clayton, Mary L. 1989. "A Trilingual Spanish-Latin-Nahuatl Manuscript Dictionary Sometimes Attributed to Fray Bernardino de Sahagún." *International Journal of American Linguistics* 55: 391–416.

Clayton, Mary L. 2003. "Evidence for a Native-Speaking Nahuatl Author in the Ayer *Vocabulario Trilingüe*." *International Journal of Lexicography* 16: 99–119.

Clayton, Mary L. 2017. "Review of Hamann, Byron Ellsworth, *The Translations of Nebrija: Language, Culture, and Circulation in the Early Modern World*." *Dictionaries: Journal of the Dictionary Society of North America* 38 (1): 132–141.

Clayton, Mary L., and R. Joe Campbell 2002. "Alonso de Molina as Lexicographer." In *Making Dictionaries: Preserving Indigenous Languages of the Americas*, edited by William Frawley, Kenneth C. Hill, and Pamela Munro, 336–390. Berkeley: University of California Press.

Cobarruvias Orozco, Sebastián de (also spelled Covarrubias). (1611) 1977. *Tesoro de la lengua castellana o española*. Madrid: Ediciones Turner.

Gruda, Szymon. 2018. *Language and Culture Contact Phenomena in the Sixteenth-Century Vocabulario trilingüe in Spanish, Latin and Nahuatl*. Warsaw: University of Warsaw.

Hamann, Byron Ellsworth. 2015. *The Translations of Nebrija: Language, Culture, and Circulation in the Early Modern World*. Boston: University of Massachusetts Press.

Lewis, Charlton T., and Charles Short. (1879) 1962. *A Latin Dictionary Founded on Andrews' Edition of Fruend's Latin Dictionary*. Oxford: Clarendon Press.

Molina, Fray Alonso de. 1555. *Aqui comiença vn vocabulario en la lengua Castellana y Mexicana*. Mexico: Juan Pablos.

Molina, Fray Alonso de. 1571a. *Vocabvlario en lengua castellana y mexicana, compuesto por el muy Reuerendo Padre Fray Alonso de Molina, dela Orden del bienauenturado nuestro Padre sant Francisco*. Mexico: Antonio de Spinosa (bound with the *Vocabulario en lengua mexicana y castellana*, which has a separate title page).

Molina, Fray Alonso de. 1571b. *Vocabvlario en lengua mexicana y castellana, compuesto por el muy Reuerendo Padre Fray Alonso de Molina, dela Orden del bienauenturado nuestro Padre sant Francisco*. Mexico: Antonio de Spinosa (bound with its own title page following the *Vocabvlario en lengua castellana y mexicana*).

Nebrija, Elio Antonio de. 1495. *Dictionarium ex hispaniensi in latinum sermone[m]*. Salamanca.

Nebrija, Elio Antonio de. 1513. *Dictionarium ex hispanie[n]si in latinum sermonem*. Salamanca: Lorenzo Hon de Deis.

Nebrija, Elio Antonio de. 1516. *Vocabulario de roma[n]ce en latin*. Seville: Juan Varela.

Nebrija, Elio Antonio de. (ca. 1520) 1516. *Vocabulario de roma[n]ce en latin*. Seville: Juan Varela?

Nebrija, Elio Antonio de. [1516] 1973. *Vocabulario de romance en latín: Transcripción crítica e introducción*, by Gerald J. MacDonald. Philadelphia: Temple University Press.

Rosas Xelhuantzi, Tesiu. 2017. *Nahuas que saben latín: Producción intelectual indígena en el Colegio de Tlatelolco (1546–1572)*. PhD diss., Universidad Nacional Autónoma de México. http://132.248.9.195/ptd2017/septiembre/0765540/Index.html.

Sahagún, Fray Bernardino de. (1579) 1950–1982 *Florentine Codex, General History of the Things of New Spain*. Translated and edited by Arthur J. O. Anderson and Charles E. Dibble. 13 vols. Santa Fe and Salt Lake City: School of American Research and University of Utah.

Sahagún, Fray Bernardino de. (1579) 2001 *Historia general de las cosas de la Nueva España*, II. Edited by Juan Carlos Temprano. Madrid: Dastin.

Schoenhals, Louise C. 1988. *A Spanish-English Glossary of Mexican Flora and Fauna*. Mexico City: Summer Institute of Linguistics.

Vidal Díez, Mónica. 2007. *El Vocabulario hispano-latino (1513) de AE. A. de Nebrija: Estudio y edición crítica*. PhD Diss., Universidad Carlos III de Madrid. http://e-archivo.uc3m.es/handle/10016/2538.

Vidal Díez, Mónica. 2015. *El Vocabulario hispano-latino (1513) de AE. A. de Nebrija: Estudio y edición crítica*. A Coruña, Spain: Universidade da Coruña.

# 8

## Fabián de Aquino's Nahuatl *Contemptus Mundi*

BEN LEEMING

I found this exercise among the Indians. I don't know who wrote it, nor who gave it to them. It had many errors and incongruities. But truly it can be said that it was done over rather than corrected.

NOTE WRITTEN BY FRAY BERNARDINO DE SAHAGÚN AT THE
END OF A MANUSCRIPT OF NAHUATL SPIRITUAL EXERCISES, 1574
(1574, FOL. 43R; COPY MADE OF ORIGINAL BY CHIMALPAHIN)

Here is written all of the books that are named in this will:
 1. A large book of the lives of the saints
 2. A contemptus mundi in the Mexican language
 3. A large confessionario in the Mexican language

WILL OF NAHUA DON BALTASAR DE SAN JUAN, METEPEC, 1601
(AGN TIERRAS, VOL. 2222; CITED IN BÉLIGAND 1995, 6)

*ma iuh mochihua. Fabian de aquino itlatequipanol.*
May it thus be done. The work of Fabián de Aquino.

SIGNATURE OF NAHUA FABIÁN DE AQUINO AT THE END OF HIS TREATISE
ON THE FINAL JUDGMENT, CA. 1560–1580 ([CA. 1560–1600] N.D. FOL. 55R)

Each of the quotes in the epigraph above speaks to several realities many of New Spain's ecclesiastics would have preferred to ignore.[1] First, some Nahuas were in possession of unauthorized Christian devotional texts in manuscript form, texts that were deemed to be filled with "errors and incongruities." Second, Nahua elites like Don Baltasar de San Juan were amassing small libraries of religious books that included controversial Nahuatl translations of devotional literature like the *Contemptus mundi*. And third, there existed Nahuas like Fabián de Aquino who were using the alphabetic literacy taught to them by the church to compose their own religious tracts that may or may not have had the church's approval.

It was precisely these kinds of activities that were the targets of a Dominican-led campaign from the 1550s onward to crack down on the publication of Indigenous-language sermons, catechisms, and devotional materials in New Spain. Fearing the lurking influence of Erasmian humanism in some of these projects, Archbishops Alonso de Montúfar and Pedro Moya de Contreras, the Office of the Inquisition, and various Church Councils (1555, 1565, 1585) strove mightily to restrict the production of Indigenous-language religious texts and forbid outright the possession of such materials by Native people (Nesvig 2009). And yet, as the quotes just cited suggest, there was a demand for devotional aids among certain sectors of the Indigenous community. It is perhaps unsurprising that in the absence of church-approved texts, literate Nahuas would set about to create their own: copying, translating, and even composing unauthorized Nahuatl-Christian religious texts.

This chapter will present an example of the kind of unofficial religious writing certain Nahuas were circulating in manuscript form in the late sixteenth century. The text in question is an original composition that a Nahua named Fabián de Aquino redacted into a small notebook of miscellaneous Christian texts, which is today housed at the Hispanic Society of America in New York. Based on its contents and style, it can be considered a Nahuatl adaptation of a popular genre of medieval European religious writing known as the *contemptus mundi*. Devotional literature that taught Christians to nurture a "contempt of the world" was popular from the eleventh through seventeenth centuries (Howard 1974, 56). Starting in the fourteenth century, the *contemptus* tradition was absorbed by works of the *devotio moderna*, a popular form of lay piety with strong links to Christian humanism. There it received its most famous articulation in the *Imitatio Christi* (Imitation of Christ) of Thomas à Kempis, a work that often went by the name *Contemptus mundi* after

---

[1] I would like to dedicate this essay to Joe Campbell, mentor and friend. I was first introduced to Joe by the coeditors of this volume and have been the lucky recipient of his boundless generosity ever since. As a translator of colonial Nahuatl texts, I have often considered Joe my "silver bullet," and any semblance of aptitude I appear to have for the language I humbly credit to his assistance; the inevitable errors are my own.

the title to the book's first chapter. Themes common to works of the *contemptus* tradition and the *devotio moderna* included the mutable and unsatisfying nature of earthly things; the corruption of the human body through sickness, pain, and death; and punishment or reward in the afterlife (xxvi).

*Contemptus* themes have inspired memorable bursts of rhetorical creativity in medieval Christian literature. Take for, example, this brief quote from a *contemptus mundi* text written in the twelfth century by Saint Bernard of Clairvaux:

> Hear, O man, what you were before birth, what you are from birth to death, and what you will be after this life. Truly there was a time when you were not; then you were made of vile matter and rolled about in the vilest rag, you were nursed in your mother's womb on menstrual blood, and your tunic was your outer skin . . . Nothing else is man but nasty sperm, a sack of dung, food for worms. (qtd. in Howard 1969, xxx)

Or this excerpt from an anonymous poem dating to the thirteenth century:

> Tell me, O mortal man, tell me about the putridity of the worm;
> Tell me O flesh, O dust, what good is the glory of Flesh?
> O mad wretch, why do you take pride in putridity?
> Learn what you are, what you will be; remember that you will die.
> First you were sperm, then stench, then food for worms,
> Then dust, and thence nothing; what then, does a man have to be proud about?
> As the rose pales when it feels the sun draw near,
> So man will vanish: now he is, now he has ceased to be. (Howard 1974, 54)

In his Nahuatl adaptation of this genre, Aquino took up not only these same themes but also adopted the genre's propensity for vividly conceived rhetorical flourishes. The *contemptus* text he composed (like the books that Don Baltasar collected) demonstrates that certain Nahuas had taken a keen interest in literature of this sort. And they were not the only ones. Roughly at the same time that Aquino was composing his text, an effort was underway at the Franciscan Colegio de Santa Cruz in Tlatelolco to introduce the spiritual practices and key texts of the *devotio moderna* to literate Nahuas in New Spain. These efforts were part of an incipient movement that one scholar has labeled "Nahua humanism" (Tavárez 2017). From the last half of the sixteenth century to the first quarter of the seventeenth, Franciscan friars and Nahua scholars collaborated to bring to fruition Nahuatl translations of several key works of the *devotio moderna*. The analysis presented here suggests that Fabián de Aquino was familiar with European texts like those actively being translated into Nahuatl for dissemination to literate Nahua audiences. In preparation for this essay, three of these texts were surveyed as possible sources of Aquino's Nahuatl *contemptus*: à Kempis's *Imitatio Christi*, Fray Diego de Estella's *Libro de la vanidad del mundo*, and Fray Luis de Granada's *Libro de la oración y meditación*. These three works are especially suitable for consideration because each was known to have been in the possession of New Spain's Franciscans and would therefore have been available to the Nahuas they had contact with. Additionally, each was also the subject of important translation projects from the 1550s through the first decade of the 1600s, projects that set texts on a collision course with that period's anti-Franciscan, antihumanist powers. Ultimately, the works of Estella and à Kempis, while certainly analogous in some respects, were not close enough to be considered likely sources of Aquino's text. The *Libro de la oración* of Fray Luis de Granada, on the other hand, emerged as a much more promising candidate. This chapter will present evidence suggesting that Granada's work may have been the source of inspiration for Aquino's Nahuatl *contemptus mundi*. By establishing a link between Aquino and works of the *devotio moderna* and *contemptus mundi* traditions, new insights are gained into how Christian devotional literature was received by literate Nahuas outside of the great intellectual center at Santa Cruz. One of the fruits of this analysis will be to highlight the enormous linguistic creativity of one of colonial Nahuatl's most original—and heretofore-unknown—stylists, Fabián de Aquino.

## 1. FABIÁN DE AQUINO, NAHUA INTELLECTUAL

Unfortunately, we know precious little about Fabián de Aquino apart from the small notebook he filled with miscellaneous religious texts sometime in the last third of the sixteenth century. The notebook is catalogued as Hispanic Society of America Manuscript NS 3/1, *Sermones y miscelánea de devoción y moral en lengua mexicana (nahuatl)*. The catalogue description casts confusion on the author's identity by listing him as "Aquino, Fabian de, o[rder of] S[aint] Franc[is]," and then speculating that "fr[ay] Fabian" may have been "one of the Indians" who served as an informant for Sahagún's famous ethnographic project. However, while he was certainly connected to the Franciscans—probably by virtue of being a graduate of one of their schools—Aquino was most definitely not a member of the order. Some evidence from his notebook suggests he may have hailed from Tlaxcala, although this is still speculative.[2] Information about his social status is equally ambiguous.

---

[2] Only two Nahua *altepemeh* (sing. *altepetl*; Nahua ethnic state) are mentioned by name in the entire 300 folios of the manuscript; one of these is Tlaxcala. Additionally, the name of Franciscan friar Alonso de Santiago is mentioned in another part of the manuscript; Santiago was closely associated with the early history of Tlaxcala. Certain orthographic clues also point to Tlaxcala as well, such as Aquino's frequent use of the archaic preterit *-qui* suffix.

His literacy and broad familiarity with both Spanish and Nahuatl Christian literature point in the direction of a noble background, but he did not sign his name "don," which was customary among the Nahua elite.[3] Much valuable information can be gathered from the contents of his notebook, which contains dozens of individual texts either copied, translated, or composed by Aquino and perhaps two or three other unnamed Nahuas. The contents include numerous miracle stories of the Virgin Mary and the saints, a short set of confraternity ordinances, the translation of a plenary indulgence dated 1560, an explanation of the Latin mass, and numerous treatises of a devotional nature on a variety of subjects like the life of Mary Magdalene and the Discovery of the True Cross. Two of the most surprising items in his notebook are the pair of Nahuatl Antichrist plays that were the subject of previous studies by this author (Leeming 2017a, 2017b, 2022).

Aquino's leading role in filling a notebook with Christian texts clearly suggests he had access to a convent library and that he was well versed in many forms of Christian writing, from plays to hagiographies, to sermons, and to devotional literature. In short, Fabián de Aquino was a Nahua intellectual in the sense outlined by Kelly McDonough in her book *The Learned Ones*. Like the *tlamatinimeh* (sing. *tlamatini*, "one who knows, wise person") and *tlahcuilohqueh* (sing. *tlahquiloh*, "one who writes or paints") of the precontact past, Aquino acquired knowledge from the reading of *amoxtli* ("books") and fulfilled an important social role as a "producer, transmitter, interpreter, and guardian" of that knowledge (2011, 3). As a Nahua intellectual living in colonial times, he was also a cultural intermediary, standing between Indigenous and Spanish worlds and negotiating a space for ongoing autonomous existence (Yannakakis 2008, 4–14). Alphabetic literacy seems to have been his primary tool in this capacity. Aquino lived at a crucial moment for Indigenous epistemologies. Since the colonizers first set foot on Native soil, they had systematically sought out and destroyed Indigenous books and the knowledge they contained. However, at precisely the same time, the colonizers had given their colonial subjects a powerful technology for the preservation of knowledge: alphabetic literacy. That Aquino used this technology to write Christian texts highlights the inherently ambivalent nature of cultural brokerage and the ambiguity of the cultural broker's role. On the one hand, his writing affirms the continuity of certain elements of Indigenous lifeways and mental structures. For one, his role as producer and guardian of Indigenous knowledge ensures the ongoing role of the *tlamatini* and the *tlahcuiloh* in Nahua society. In a recent study (Leeming 2022, 91–117), I

---

[3] It has been suggested to me that perhaps he was a mestizo akin to Diego Muñoz de Camargo or Diego de Valadés, neither of whom used the honorific *don* despite their positions of relative privilege (William B. Taylor, personal communication, February 23, 2018).

have demonstrated the ways in which Aquino resisted certain negative stereotypes of Indigenous Christians, pushing back with subtle conternarratives that present a Nahua-centric alternative to European categories. On the other hand, as a colonial subject, Aquino necessarily had to work within certain frameworks that were nonnegotiable: Christianity, alphabetic writing, and colonial political authority to name three. McDonough describes Nahua intermediaries who worked in close collaboration with the Spanish "conservative," and she cites Nahua Jesuit priest Antonio del Rincón as an example (2014, 36). Like Rincón, Aquino chose not to outwardly resist colonial rule but to affiliate himself with the friars and engage with them and their work. Nevertheless, we must not forget that the act of carrying out this work in the Nahuatl language, "transposing" Christianity into an Indigenous "key," was in itself an assertion of some degree of autonomy. It was Christianity and alphabetic writing—two principal "technologies" of the colonizer—that were appropriated and adapted to the purposes of Nahuas like Aquino. The Nahuatl *contemptus* text presented here is one of the fruits of Aquino's masterful deployment of these two colonial technologies: a cultural hybrid, at once beautiful and disturbing, but in the end a unique work of Indigenous American literature.

### 2. NAHUA HUMANISM AND THE *DEVOTIO MODERNA* IN NEW SPAIN

Like McDonough, David Tavárez's recent scholarship has highlighted the work of Nahua intellectuals, specifically those working in collaboration with Franciscans at the Colegio de Santa Cruz to bring the *devotio moderna* to New Spain. In 2013 he announced the rediscovery of one product of this group's efforts, a work of great importance once thought to be lost (Tavárez 2013b). It is a Nahuatl translation of portions of the Proverbs of Solomon, produced by Fray Luis Rodriquez and others sometime in the 1560s. It was banned in 1577 as part of Dominican-led efforts to quash vernacular translations of the Bible (Nesvig 2009, 153). Tavárez has also written about the two surviving translations of the *devotio moderna*'s quintessential text, *The Imitation of Christ* by Thomas à Kempis, which he argues may be the work of Fray Alonso de Molina and Nahua Hernando de Ribas (Tavárez 2013a, 210). However, it is another of Tavárez's discoveries that holds particular relevance to the work of Fabián de Aquino. Recently, he identified Fray Juan Bautista's 1604 publication *Libro de la miseria y breuedad de la vida del hombre* as an unacknowledged Nahuatl translation of Fray Luis de Granada's 1554 *Libro de la oracíon y meditación* (Tavárez 2013a, 231). Granada's text was extremely popular in Spain, a much-read introduction to the methods of prayer that characterized the *devotio moderna*. However, it had aroused the suspicions of more conservative members of the Spanish church and was placed on the *Index of Prohibited Books* in 1559. It was removed from the list in 1566 after Granada made the required corrections, but it remained suspect in certain sectors of the church (Puigbó 2004, 29). In New Spain, other works of Nahua humanism included the now-lost Nahuatl translation of Estella's *Libro de la vanidad del mundo*, Fray Juan de Gaona and Hernando de Ribas's *Colloquios de la paz y tranquilidad* of 1582, and Fray Juan de Mijangos and Nahua Agustín de la Fuente's *Espejo divino* of 1607. These translation projects required massive effort by numerous Nahuas and friars over many years. Mijangos and de la Fuente's *Espejo Divino*, for example, consists of 562 pages of dense, literary Nahuatl. Texts such as these should be seen as immensely important by linguists, literary scholars, historical anthropologists, and historians of religion alike, and yet, they remain largely unstudied. Tavárez's scholarship has begun to bring attention to the efforts of this group, whom he refers to as a "Nahua-Franciscan intellectual vanguard" that was part of a global dissemination of the *devotio moderna* (2017, 9). What this activity shows is that at precisely the moment in time when ecclesiastics were cracking down on Indigenous-language writing, the cohort at Santa Cruz was creating some of the finest examples of Nahuatl religious literature ever produced in colonial times. Unlike the more well-known ethnographic work of Sahagún et al., these Nahua humanists focused not on "describing a receding Nahua idolatrous past" but instead new social reality: "an Indigenous humanist future" (9).

The broad outlines of a Nahuatl *devotio moderna* highlight the very same qualities that landed authors like Granada on the infamous *Index*. Like the works of à Kempis, Estella, Granada, and others, Nahuatl devotio writing encouraged Indigenous Christians to seek intimate spiritual union with God by rejecting the world and live a life of simple virtue in imitation of Christ. As in Europe, an essential component of this project was the translation of devotional books into vernacular languages and their dissemination among literate members of Nahua society. Opposition to these acts was strong in conservative sectors of both the Spanish and New Spanish churches (Moore 1977; Nesvig 2009). In Spain, Dominican Melchor Cano, who condemned Granada's work in 1559, wrote that "the reading of similar books in vernacular languages has done much harm to women and idiots" (Carrera 2005, 82; translation mine). Some of his Dominican counterparts in New Spain would surely have agreed, adding to his list "and Indians." Also viewed with suspicion were the various forms of mental prayer, meditation, and spiritual exercises propagated by the *devotio moderna*. Writers like Ludolph of Saxony, Thomas à Kempis, and Luis de Granada encouraged the faithful to give their imagination free reign to viscerally experience the mysteries of the faith, to project themselves into the scenes of Christ's life and passion, and in so doing to cultivate a strong emotional connection with God. In sixteenth-century Spain, those who sought out personal religious experiences using methods like these risked being accused of being *alumbrados*, Spanish mystics who periodically were persecuted as heretics (Moore 1977, 16). At the heart of this issue was power. If common laypeople could personally communicate with God through meditation and prayer, what need was there of the institutional church, the formal priesthood, the sacraments? Since the Nahuatl devotional literature authored by Santa Cruz's humanists employed the same methods to the same end, it must surely have aroused the same critiques as those raised by Cano and others in Spain. To some, the idea of an Indigenous laity in possession of devotional books written in Indigenous languages was a threat to ecclesiastical authority that led down a slippery slope toward heterodoxy. This is attested in numerous statements of the Mexican Church Councils, which declared as early as 1555: "We require and state by law that from now on no sermon be given to Indians to translate or keep in their power, and if any Indian has any it must be confiscated" (Lorenzana 1769, 144; translation mine). Yet remarkably, Bautista, de la Fuente and others plowed ahead with massive translation projects that sought to introduce to Nahuas the work of the *devotio moderna*. The work of Aquino shows that it was not only in major intellectual centers like the Colegio de Santa Cruz in which projects like these were being carried out. Making use of his contact with the Franciscans, Aquino culled texts from their libraries and filled his notebook with his own renderings of a wide variety of Christian texts. This same process was repeated all across New Spain by similarly educated, literate Indigenous Christians, not only Nahuas but Otomís, Zapotecs, Mixtecs, and Mayas. To adequately understand the multiplicity of these Indigenous "Christianities," it is necessary to bring to light through translation and analysis unique compositions like Aquino's Nahuatl *contemptus mundi*.

### 3. PRESENTATION OF THE TEXT

Aquino's untitled composition spans just six folios in Hispanic Society of America Manuscript NS 3/1 (fols. 116r–121r). There is no title or introductory statement; only a pilcrow and an ornamented capital letter "O" mark the beginning. Although there are no clearly marked sections, the text can be broken up into three distinct parts. The first section begins with the following words:

O tlacatle[4]
    tla xinechitta

---

[4] Here and in the succeeding passages, I follow the practice of William Bright (following Dell Hymes and Denis Tedlock) of presenting my transcriptions so as to emphasize the structural features of Nahuatl, such as various forms of parallelism and the use of couplets.

>     in zan iuhquin in onipactinenca in oc nitlacatl
>                                     nicatca
>         in ihcuac
>             in ayamo ticehua in notzontecon
>             in ayamo in omitl nitepeuhtoc in tecochco

(fol. 116r)

> O person!
>     Won't you please look upon me!
>     I used to go along happily while I was still
>                                     a [living] person,
>         when
>             as of yet you, my head, had not become cold
>             as of yet I was not gathered as bones in the grave.

The speaker here is a soul, recently separated from its mortal body, that cries out to the living from the depths of hell. He pleads for those who are alive to listen to his words of admonition and prepare for their own inevitable and terrifying end. In order to give a feel for the literary richness of Aquino's prose, here follows an extended excerpt of this first section of the text. After the opening lines quoted above, the soul continues to address the living, saying,

> Auh in onipactoya yn nocochiyan
>     ihuan no itech ninomatiya in cihuatl
>
> Auh in ihcuac in ohtlica niyaya
>     Ca zan no niquixcahuiaya inic oniteicelehuitinemiya
> Auh in ihcuac nitlacuaya
>     Ca zan no paquiya in nocamachal
>
> Auh in ninomatiya
>     ayc ticehuaz in notzontecon
>
> Auh
>     in nixteloloh in ixquich quipahpaquizittaya
>     in ninomatiya in nixteloloh aic pachacahuaquiz
>                                     aic chicopiniz
>
> in ixquich in nichuelittaya
>     in chalchihuitl

          in coztic tepoztli
              in iztac ihuan
                  in quetzalli
in ixquich in nictlazohtlaya yn tlalticpac intla
    ixquich oc nixpan neci

Auh cuix ma oc quihuelittaz in nixteloloh

Auh in tehuatl
    ximixmati

tlacatle
    Occenca xinechitta

tlapanahuia in tiuhqui tiyez

Auh in ixquich in tlallan onoqueh
    in azcameh
    in ocuilimeh
        ca niman mitzcuazqueh

Auh in motzontecon iihtic mocaltizqueh
    ihuan in ixquich tlallan onoqueh

Auh inin ixquich tlacatl ipan mochihuaz
    in timacehualli
    in manel titeuctli
    in manel tipilli
intla nel cenca timahuiztililoni

in ac tehuatl
    Cuix no mitzmahuiztilizqueh in azcameh
                            in ocuilimeh

ma huel ximomati
    ca titemalli
        titlacauhtoz yn tecochco occenca tlapanahuia inic
        tipotoniz

                                                      (fols. 116r–v)

I used to lie happily in my bed
    and think about women.

When I was going along the road,

likewise I devoted myself to desiring people.
When I was eating,
    likewise my jaw would rejoice.

I used to think to myself that
    you, my head, would never grow cold.

And
        my eyes used to see all joyfully!
    I used to think my eyes would never go blind,
        would never pale.

Everything that used to satisfy me,
    precious greenstone,
        gold,
            silver and
                quetzal feathers,
everything that I used to love on earth, when
everything was still visible to me—

does it still satisfy my eyes?

And you,
    take care!

O person!
    Look especially at me!

You will be likewise, but even more so!

Everything that dwells on the earth
    the ants,
    the worms,
        will then eat you,

and within your head everything that dwells in the earth
    will make their home.

This will happen to all people:
    to you, commoner,
    even to you, lord,
    even to you, nobleperson,
even though you are very worthy of honor.

> Who do you think you are?
>> Will the ants and
>>> the worms honor you also?
>
> Know for sure that
>> you are pus,
>>> you will lie rotting in the grave; how surpassingly
>>>> you will stink!

In this opening section, Aquino presents a number of themes that are characteristic of *contemptus mundi* literature. He emphasizes the impermanence of life and the illusory nature of pleasurable things (here imagined in distinctly Indigenous terms as "precious greenstone, gold, silver, and quetzal feathers"). Although they may bring joy to one's eyes, in an instant they will be swept away by death and consumed by hell's merciless fire. Here too death features prominently as the reminder par excellence of humankind's mortality, striking down all people irrespective of status: "even you lord, even you nobleperson." Like Saint Bernard's *contemptus* text, Aquino's shares the view of the human body as "nasty sperm, a sack of dung, food for worms," emphasizing the putrefaction and stench associated with decomposition.

Following these opening lines, the soul shifts from addressing the living to addressing its own mortal body, whom he blames for his present state of suffering in hell. This section consists of a long and doleful litany of regrets, each of which follows a similar pattern. The beginning of each new stanza is marked by the use of a vocative expression like *nonacayoe*, "O my body!," *nixtelolohe*, "O my eyes!," or most frequently, *iyoyahue*, "Alas!" Aquino relies heavily on repetition to convey the intensity of the soul's anguish. He often presents these expressions in pairs (*nonacayoe, nonacayoe*), triplets (*iyoyahue, iyoyahue, iyoyahue*), and even quatrains (*iyoyahue, iyoyahue, iyoyahue, iyoyahue*). In one instance, Aquino's tortured soul simply cries out, *hao, hao, hao, hao, hao, hao,* "Ow! Ow! Ow! Ow! Ow! Ow!" Each of these initial expressions is followed by a statement about the pain and suffering the soul is experiencing at the hands "the wild beasts, the *mictlan tzitzimitl*" (fol. 116v).[5] These are some of the most vivid passages ever recorded in colonial Nahuatl. Here Aquino exhibits his talent for capitalizing on the expressive range of the Nahuatl language to shock his audience and produce in them a state of terror; this will be quoted extensively in the text that follows.

---

[5] The *tzitzimitl* were frightening stellar deities associated with the liminal time between the extinguishing of ritual fires and lighting of the "New Fire" every fifty-two years. Here and elsewhere, I have left certain Nahuatl words untranslated due to the lack of correspondence between them and the English words typically used to translate them. *Mictlan*, the precontact realm of the dead, is typically translated as "hell" but will also be left in the Nahuatl.

In the second section, Aquino makes an abrupt shift in style and tone. Here he abandons the frantic cries of the damned soul and assumes the didactic, dispassionate tone of a friar or priest. Returning to directly addressing the audience, the speaker begins by stating,

    Otlacatle
        yehhuatlin in tiquilnamiquiz in cemihcac
                in ceyohual
                in cemilhuitl
        yaquine in mochipa ihuan
            in mocochian
            in moneyehuayan
    inic ahmo titlahtlacoz                                           (fol. 118v)

    O person!
        Remember these [ten things] forever
            (night,
            day)
        and always
            (in your sleeping place,
            in your living place)
    so that you won't sin.

What follows reads as if it were based on some as-of-yet unidentified Nahuatl *doctrina* or sermon. It consists of a series of ten statements about the events that will happen from the moment of death to the Final Judgment. Each statement begins with the command *xiquilnamiqui*, "remember," and then lists things like "when you die you will be covered in a ragged old cloak," "you will suffer exceedingly when your soul comes out," "God will address you [saying], 'Won't you please recount for me...'" and "God will judge you... and the devils will quickly snatch you up" (fols. 118v–120r). Notably, this section is of a far-less-Indigenous character than the first. For one, it contains very few of the markers of traditional Nahuatl verbal art such as parallelism and couplet forms. Its organization as a list of ten items is distinctly European, and each item on the list is presented in the matter-of-fact manner of many *doctrinas*. All of these characteristics support the hypothesis that for this section Aquino may have shifted into copying or translating straight from a source, as opposed to adapting or composing more freely as he seems to be doing in the first and third sections.

    Finally, in the third section of the text, Aquino leads the reader back to the terrifying vision of hell he began to create in the first. This part begins with the following enigmatic announcement:

> Izcatqui in icuepca
> > in mictlan tlahtolli
> > technonotza in tzahtziliztli
> > in tentoc in cuauhcalco
> > > in necaltzacualoyan (fol. 120r)
>
> Here is the translation of
> > the hell-words,
> > the shrieks that call out to us.
> > The jail,
> > the prison[6]
> > > is filled up [with these cries].

He then presents thirteen stanzas of text, each one set apart with a pilcrow, which contain heart-wrenching exclamations in the first-person plural. These can be interpreted as the cries of the damned, calling out for God for an end to their suffering. This section will be analyzed in greater detail at the end of this chapter.

### 4. AQUINO'S ADAPTATION OF THE *LIBRO DE LA ORACIÓN*

Aquino's Nahuatl *contemptus mundi* text shares the same overall purpose, subject matter, and spiritual methodology as Luis de Granada's *Libro de la oración*. Both works seek to engender a fear of sin and the desire to confess by presenting highly embellished descriptions of the horrors of death, Final Judgment, and hell. In terms of methodology, both texts urge the reader to meditate on the *postrimerías* (Final Things) and in so doing seek a strong emotional response that solidifies the sinner's resolve to live a life of virtue. In terms of structure, Aquino's text follows Granada's meditations for the evenings of Wednesday (which deals with death), Thursday (on Judgment), and Friday (on hell).

Like Granada's, Aquino's text adopts the methodology of the *devotio moderna* that engages the imagination and the emotions of the devotee and encourages them to project themselves into the scenes being meditated upon. In order to assist in such a task, Granada calls on each of the five senses to imagine the tortures that will be inflicted on the damned in hell. In his meditation for Friday night he writes, "Indecent and carnal eyes will be tormented with the horrible sight of the demons, ears with the confusion of voices and groans that will be heard there, noses with the intolerable stench of that filthy place, taste with rabid hunger and thirst, touch and

---

[6] "The jail, the prison," that is, hell.

all the members of the body with unbearable cold and fire. The imagination will suffer with the apprehension of the present pains, the memory with the remembrance of pleasures passed, the understanding with the consideration of the lost goods and of the evils to come" (1566, fol. 173r–v; translation mine). Aquino adopts an analogous strategy, rendering similarly frightening visions for his Nahua audience. At various locations in the text, he incorporates each of the five senses into his description of hell and punishment at the hands of demons:

*Sight*
nixtelolohe nixtelolohe:
 in niman ahtleh cenca ic limoncellos yn ihuicpa in totecuiyo. (fol. 118r)
O my eyes! O my eyes!
 There is absolutely no way you will find the favor of our lord.

*Sound*
¶ Tlahtoanie
ma xitechicneli
 ma ic timiquican in totzahtziliz-netoliniliz
 ya huel tzatzayani in totozcatecuacuil
ayoc hueli inic tiquiquinaca (fol. 120v)

O Ruler!
Grant this to us!
 Would that we might die from our shouts of suffering.
 Already our uvulas are torn.
It's no longer [even] possible for us to moan.

*Smell*
ma huel ximomati
 ca titemalli
 titlacauhtoz in tecochco
occenca tlapanahuia inic tipotoniz (fol. 116v)

Know for sure that
 you are pus,
 you will lie rotting in the grave;
how surpassingly you will stink!

*Taste*
inic techitia in eztli
  in temalli

in cuitlatli
in tepozatl (fol. 121r)

[the demons] make us drink blood,
pus,
excrement,
molten metal.

*Touch*
... in ompa in cempolihuiztitlan ...
in tetlehuatzaloyan ... in cetitlan ... (fols. 116v–117r)

... there in the place of utter perishing ...
where one is roasted ... [it is] an icy place ...

Another link between Granada and Aquino is the special attention both pay to the frightening moment of death, when the soul and the body are separated from each other. In the meditation for Wednesday night, Granada writes, "Think about the separation between the soul and the body that must then happen" (1566, fol. 137r); "What sadness the soul of the condemned will feel when it sees its body ... dirty, foul-smelling, and abominable" (1566, fol. 167r). In order to intensify and personalize this experience for the devout reader, Granada personifies the newly separated soul, giving it a lengthy monologue in which it addresses the now-defunct body. Here is an excerpt:

> [The soul will say]: "O unfortunate body! ... O beginning and end of my pains! O cause of my condemnation! O no longer companion but enemy; not helper but persecutor; not abode but chain and lasso! O unlucky taste! How much your gifts cost me now! O smelly flesh, to what torments have you brought me with your pleasures? This is the body for whom I sinned? These were the pleasures for which I was lost?" ... These and other desperate words the unfortunate soul will say to that body which in this world it loved so much. (1566, fol. 167r; translation mine)

I would like to specifically point out Granada's use here of first-person address, the repeated exclamations using the vocative, the anguished interrogative statements, and the overall dolorous tone of the soul's lament. Passages such as this, where the soul of the deceased laments its betrayal by the pleasure-seeking flesh, may have been the source of inspiration for the first section of Aquino's *contemptus* text. Whether it was the influence of Granada's *Libro de la oración* specifically or another text like it, Aquino adopts many of the characteristics of the speech just quoted. Here is an excerpt for comparison:

O iyoyahue tenacayoe
    ma ximolnamiqui ca ya tlayahualotitlan
tinechhuica

A iyoyahue
    in axcan ma ic nimochoquili in yehica: in ya nitemoznequi in mictlan

iyoyahue iyoyahue iyoyahue
    inin ca onotlahueliltic

iyoyahue iyoyahue
    ohuelnonetoliniltic

A iyoyahue nonacayohe nonacayohe
    ca ya tinechcalaquiz in incamac
        in tecuanimeh
        in mictlan tzitzimitl

O alas, O body!
    Remember that already you have brought me to the place of darkness.

Alas! Alas!
    Now may I weep because I am about to descend to *mictlan*.

Alas! Alas! Alas!
    O how unfortunate I am!

Alas! Alas!
    How very miserable I am!

Alas! Alas! O my body! O my body!
    Already you cause me to enter into the mouth of
        the wild beasts,
        the *mictlan tzitzimitl*.

Like in Granada, Aquino's lamenting soul leads the reader down an ever gloomier and more frightening path of meditation on the frailty of the flesh and the frightening moment of separation at death.

The first and third parts of Aquino's *contemptus* text are highly imaginative adaptations of a source text or texts, not translations in the strict sense. There is little doubt that Aquino was familiar with a broad range of religious literature, and while texts like his *contemptus* were surely derived from European sources, Aquino's engagement with these sources is akin to a jazz musician's improvisation based on a standard tune (Clendinnen 2014, 310). Building off his deep knowledge of the sources, he "riffs" on the themes they contain, exploiting the expressive quality of the Nahuatl language. In a sense, this serves to underscore his role as perpetuator of the traditions of the precontact *tlahcuilohqueh* and *tlamatinimeh*, whose oral performances were based on painted codices but were shaped by the inspirations of the moment and the energy of the audience. Most notably, Aquino's creative adaptation of his source text indigenizes that text for Nahua readers. In so doing, he indigenizes (or "Nahuatlizes") the message as well (Dibble 1974).

First, Aquino anchors his *contemptus* text and the message it contains in the Indigenous cultural sphere, scattering throughout references to precious materials (greenstone and quetzal feathers), a natural product associated with ritual activity (copal resin), and Native ritual practices (flaying of bodies). He also recasts demons of the European imaginary as frightening Indigenous beings *tzitzimimeh* (stellar deities associated with dangerous moments of uncertainty in the Mesoamerican calendar cycle) and *tlatlacatecoloh* (literally "human horned owls," a species of shape-shifting Native shaman with malevolent powers). Additionally, the Christian God is named using the Indigenous epithets *Tlahtoanie* ("O Ruler!"), *Tlachihuale* ("O Creator!"), *Tloquehe* ("O Lord of the Near!"), and *Nahuaquehe* ("O Lord of the Nigh!"), which were frequently applied to Nahua deities in ritual settings. Together, these linguistic maneuvers not only lend an Indigenous flavor to Aquino's *contemptus* text but subtly alter the message as well, seamlessly incorporating the foreign doctrine into the stream of Indigenous spirituality.

Aquino's linguistic improvisation is also presented in an Indigenous "time signature," unfolding according to the poetic structures common to Nahuatl oral performance. As can be seen from the examples provided, Aquino relies heavily on couplet and triplet forms and frequently employs parallel constructions of both morphological and syntactic types:

*Morphological Parallelism*
nechtzatzayanazqueh
nechitzeltilizqueh (fol. 118r)

they will tear me to shreds,
they will chop me to bits

*Syntactic Parallelism*
macamo mochihuani in dios
    inic ahmo tictlahtlacalhuitinemizquiya
    inic ahmo ticmoyolihtlacalhuitinemizquiya
    inic ahmo ticchiuhtinemizquiya

in ixquich in temamauhtih in tlahtlacolli
　　　　　　　　in oticchiuh (fol. 117v)

If only God hadn't made you,
　so that you wouldn't go on offending,
　so that you wouldn't go on provoking,
　so that you wouldn't go on committing
all the frightening sins
　that you committed

In the first instance Aquino describes the tortures inflicted on the damned by demons using a pair of terms whose morphology is closely related. Each word begins with Nahuatl's first-person object prefix *nech-* (me); is followed by a verbal stem, in this case *tzatzayana* ("to tear to shreds") and *itzeltilia* ("to chop to bits"); and finally ends with the third-person plural future suffix, *-zqueh*. In the second example Aquino crafts a triplet of phrases whose syntax bears an identical shape (*inic*+*ahmo*+verb). Note that each of the verbs in these phrases also evinces morphological parallelism (*ti*+verbal stem+*tinemi*+*zquia*). Examples like these clearly reveal Aquino to be a master of the art of Nahuatl oral performance.

However, Aquino's most creative and striking form of Nahuatl poetic structuring is his use of what is sometimes called synthetic parallelism, where vivid images are built up through lengthy repetitions of subtle variations on a theme (Schwaller 2005, 73). The example of morphological parallelism is actually part of this much longer string of phrases:

Auh nechtzatzayanazqueh
　　nechitziltilizqueh
　　　　nechmomotzozqueh
　　　　　　nechcocotonazqueh
　　　　　　　　nechxipehuazqueh
　　　　　　　　　　nechichinozqueh
　　　　　　　　　　　　nechtlehuatzazqueh
　　　　　　　　　　　　　　nechmecahuitequizqueh (fol. 118r)

And they will tear me to shreds,
　they will chop me to bits,
　　they will scratch me,
　　　they will tear me up into little pieces,
　　　　they will skin me alive,
　　　　　they will scorch me,
　　　　　　they will roast me,
　　　　　　　they will whip me.

An even more elaborate instance of synthetic parallelism comes from a passage describing what kind of place hell is. The damned soul laments, "Alas! O my body! O my body! You have thrown me into a place of danger."

    in ompa in cempolihuiztitlan
        in tetonehualoyan
            in tetzacuiltiloyan
                in texipehualoyan
                    in tetlehuatzaloyan
                        in temecahuitecoyan
                            in tecopalchipiniloyan
                                in tepiloloyan
                                    in tetecoyan
                                        in cetitlan temayaohuayan
                                        in teitziltililoyan
                                        in tepotzapazco
                                        tecuauhneloloyan
                                        in ixquich in ipan cenquiztoc in tlai-
                                          hiyohuiliztli (fols. 116v–117r)

  there in the place of utter perishing,
     where one is tormented,
         where one is imprisoned,
             where one is flayed,
                 where one is roasted,
                     where one is whipped,
                         where one is dripped with copal,
                             where one is hung up,
                                 where one is stretched out,
                                     an icy place where one is hurled down,
                                       where one is chopped into pieces,
                                     where one is placed in a metal pot
                                     and stirred with a stick;
                                     every sort of suffering lies spreading
                                        out upon it.[7]

---

[7] This passage is an excellent example of an instance where the assistance of Joe Campbell was indispensable.

There are few places in colonial Nahuatl writing where authors dared display their linguistic "chops" with such exuberance. Phenomena like the preceding are rare in the more formalized writing of the Nahuas and Franciscans of the Colegio de Santa Cruz, where couplets and triplets predominate. That Aquino would stretch this string of words from two or three to twelve is simply stunning in its creativity and its daring. Whereas much colonial Nahuatl writing bears the unmistakable stamp of the Spanish language, here we have a notable example of the preservation of Nahuatl orality and the performative nature of precontact verbal art. Passages such as these clearly mark Aquino's *contemptus mundi* as a work of Indigenous literature. Just as Granada's descriptions employ cultural references and stylistic choices intended to engage a European reader more personally and intimately, Aquino has thoroughly adopted and modified Granada's approach for his Indigenous audience.

One of Aquino's most inventive adaptations of his source text is the so-called *mictlantlahtolli* ("words or speech of Mictlan") of the final section. Mictlan (lit. "among the dead") was one of several Indigenous "otherworlds" of Mesoamerican cosmology. In their early ethnographic research, the missionary friars learned that Mictlan was an underground location that was the destination of the souls of the dead. Also, their sources told them it was a cold, desolate, and inhospitable place, which, while not perfectly aligned with the Christian understanding of hell, was deemed close enough to warrant Mictlan being chosen as the translation for the Spanish *infierno* (hell). Aquino's use of Mictlan as a stand-in for *infierno* is perfectly in keeping with Nahuatl doctrinal discourse, and along with other linguistic choices already mentioned, it contributed to the indigenization of text and message.

The section of the text under consideration here begins with the words *Izcatqui in icuepca in mictlantlahtolli*, "Here is the translation of the hell-words." While it is possible that Aquino's reference to translation could be an admission that he is translating from some unnamed source, I don't believe that is the case. I propose that Aquino's *mictlantlahtolli* is actually his imaginative "translation" of the gut-wrenching cries of the damned in hell. Like his monologue between the soul and the body, this too may have been inspired by his reading of Granada. In his Friday evening meditation ("On the Pains of Hell"), Granada writes the following: "To feel something of this punishment, imagine now that you are passing through a very deep valley which is filled with an infinite crowd of captives and wounded and sick and that all of them are shouting and crying each in their own way, men as well as women, children as well as elderly. Tell me, how would this great noise and confusion sound? What will the frightful noise of such a great number of condemned sound like?" (1566, fol. 179r; translation mine). What I am proposing is that in reading this passage (or one like it), Aquino may have pondered to himself what these poor souls were actually saying. And so, taking Granada's vivid description as his point of departure, Aquino "translated" the "shouting and crying" of the souls in hell for his Nahua reader. Here is a sample of what he wrote:

¶ Tlahtoanie
    intlacamo tiquizazqueh in quemman
        ma timiquican
        ma ticempolihuican
        ma xicmihtalhui
        ma xicmonequilti

¶ Totecuiyoe
        maca titlacatinih
            tleica in otitechmochihuili
        ma xitechmocnelili
        ma ic timiquican in totzahtziliz

¶ Jesu christoe
    ma tlazohti in moyollohtzin
    ma ic timiquican in tomauhcachoquiliz
            in tixayopatzcaliz

¶ Tlahtoanie
    ma in timiquican in toquiquinaquiliz
            tonanalcaliz
    ayoc hueli inic tiquiquinaca ets.

¶ Tlahtoanie
    ma xitechicnelli
    ma yc timiquican in totzatziliznetoliniliz
        ya huel tzatzayani in totozcatecuacuil
    ayoc hueli inic tiquiquinaca ets.

¶ Tlahtoanie
    ma xicmonequilti
    ma ic timiquican
            in totenenaliz
            in toquiquinaquilizcaltemaliz

    ayoc hueli icnohuae
            tloquehe

¶ Tlachihualehe

    ma timiquican
    inic timonepantlahntzatzayanah[8]
        inic timixpoloah
            inic timomictiah
                inic ayoc ac tlazohtli        (fol. 120r–v)

O Our Ruler!
    If we don't escape, then

        Would that we would die!
        Would that we were utterly destroyed!

        Say it!
        Wish it!

O Our Lord!

    Would that we had never been born!
        Why did you make us?
    Grant this to us:
    Would that we might die from our shouting.

O Jesus Christ!

    May you do the right thing!
    Would that we might die of our frightful weeping,
                of our tears!

O Ruler!

    Would that we might die of our moans,
                      our grunts,
    It is no longer possible for us to growl, etc.

O Ruler!

    Grant it!
    Would that we might die from our shouts of suffering.
        Already our uvulas are torn.

---

[8] Read all these as *tito-*.

> It's no longer possible for us to growl, etc.
>
> O Ruler!
>
> > Will it!
> > Would that we might die of
> > > our painful moans
> > > our house-filling groans of pain
> >
> > It is no longer possible, O compassionate one,
> > > O lord of the near!
>
> O Creator!
>
> > Would that we might die!
> > > Since we are tearing ourselves down the middle,
> > > > since we are destroying ourselves,
> > > > > since we are killing ourselves,
> > > > > > since there is no longer anyone who is precious [to you].

These words are some of the rawest expressions of emotion that may be found in colonial Nahuatl writing. Of course, there are analogues, such as some of the lines spoken by characters in certain Nahuatl religious morality plays. Consider the words of a sinner named Lucía in the *Final Judgment* play—

> ay ay
> ma centelchihualo in tlalticpactli
> > ihuan in cahuitl in ipan onitlacat
>
> ma no centelchihualo in nonantzin
> > in quin in onechchiuh (Sell and Burkhart 2004, 206; translation mine)

> Ah! Ah!
> May the earth be utterly despised,
> > and the time in which I was born!
>
> May my mother also be despised,
> she who made me!

—or in the cries of sinners who never confessed their sins in certain examples of the popular *exempla* genre, such as the "Lustful Woman" in Biblioteca Nacional de Mexico Ms. 1493:

> Yoye!
> omochiuh onocentlahueliltic

    in nitlatelchihualli,
ca aic cemihcac niyaz,
        nicalaquiz,
        niyez
in ompa in itlahtocachantzinco in Dios (Dehouve 2010: anexo CD:48; translation mine)

Alas!
How utterly unfortunate I am!
    I am a cursed thing!
For all eternity never will I go,
        will I enter,
        will I be
there in God's kingdom!

We might even find analogous material in the Indigenous *icnocuicatl*, "songs of lament," found in the manuscript *Cantares mexicanos*:

zan yehica nichoca
        nicnotlamati
        no nicnocahualoc
            in tenahuac in tlalticpac.
quen connequi moyollo ipalnemoani . . .
Dios an tinechmiquitlani. (Bierhorst 1985, 172; translation mine)

It is just because of this that I weep,
        I feel sad,
        also I am bereft]
        among others here on earth.
What does your heart require, Life Giver? . . .
God, you want me dead!

Each of these sources—doctrinal literature, Nahuatl plays, sermons, Indigenous song-poetry—can be seen as general sources of inspiration for Aquino. He was clearly drawn to the emotional intensity of a certain kind of literature and found ample means to exploit these emotions in the frightening events of the *postrimerías*. It is worth noting that there are *four* Last Things: death, judgment, hell, and heaven. Granada and others typically follow their terrifying descriptions of the three former Things with equally as vivid descriptions of the last one. This final hope of sinners, the consolation of Heavenly glory, is notably absent from Aquino's composition.

Considered along with Aquino's treatise titled "On the Terrifying Final Judgment and Eternal Punishment," cited in the epigraph and his two apocalyptic Antichrist plays, Aquino's *contemptus* reveals a pattern of preferences in the work of this Nahua writer. However, it is in Luis de Granada's *Libro de la oración* that lay the deepest roots of Aquino's inspiration. Not only does he replicate the emotional intensity and sensorial immersion of Granada's text, but he embraces the spiritual methodology of this master of *devotio moderna* writing. Drawing on Nahuatl's propensity for repetition, elaboration, and embellishment, Aquino responds to Granada's call "in order to feel something of this suffering, imagine now . . ." (1566, fol. 179r; translation mine). The "translations" of the "hell-words" he produces as a result are exceptionally moving. And if these words can move us today, surely such was the case for Aquino's sixteenth-century readership.

## 5. CONCLUSION

We return now to the opening theme, that of the existence of unauthorized texts like the spiritual exercises Sahagún corrected. Texts like these suggest that for some Nahuas the kind of rudimentary Christian instruction made available to them by the church simply wasn't enough. Some, like Don Baltasar de San Juan, whose personal collection of books contained a Nahuatl *contemptus mundi*, were clearly hungry for more advanced spiritual nourishment and so took to copying, composing, and circulating among themselves devotional writings like à Kempis's *Imitatio Christi*. However, Nahua Intellectuals like Aquino went beyond the mere copying of texts. Aquino allowed his creativity to range more freely, composing devotional materials that, while rooted in the European texts he had access to, were unique hybrid productions that astound the reader to this day. In Aquino and his notebook, we have an opportunity to observe an example of how European Catholicism was refracted through the prism of Nahua minds, splitting out a colorful array of Native Christianities of diverse hues. Although Aquino may not have been a member of the Nahua humanism centered at Tlatelolco, it is likely that he existed in an orbit just outside of that gravitational center of Nahua-Franciscan intellectual activity. Nevertheless, his *contemptus mundi* text—along with others he redacted into his notebook—suggests he engaged in his own "Nahua humanist" projects. Brushing off the friars' charges of "errors & incongruities," he took up the pen and set about producing the devotional literature that his people were demanding.

## REFERENCES

Aquino, Fabián de. (ca. 1560–1600) n.d. *Sermones y miscelánea de devoción y moral en lengua mexicana (nahuatl)* MS NS 3/1. New York: Hispanic Society of America.

Béligand, Nadine. 1995. "Lecture indienne et chrétienté: La bibliothèque d'un *alguacil de doctrina* en Nouvelle-Espagne au XVI siècle." *Mélanges de la Casa de Velázquez* 31 (2): 21–71.

Bierhorst, John, ed. and trans. 1985. *Cantares Mexicanos: Songs of the Aztecs*. Stanford, CA: Stanford University Press.

Carrera, Elena. 2005. *Teresa of Avila's Autobiography: Authority, Power and the Self in Mid-Sixteenth-Century Spain*. London: Modern Humanities Research Association and Routledge.

Clendinnen, Inga. 2014. *Aztecs*. Cambridge: Cambridge University Press.

Dehouve, Danièle. 2010. *Relatos de pecados en la evangelización de los indios de México (Siglos XVI–XVIII)*. Mexico City: Centro de Investigaciones y Estudios Superiores en Antropología Social.

Dibble, Charles E. 1974. "The Nahuatlization of Christianity." In *Sixteenth-Century Mexico: The Work of Sahagún*, edited by Munro S. Edmonson, 225–233. Albuquerque: University of New Mexico Press.

Granada, Fray Luis de. 1566. *Libro de la oración y meditación. En el qual se tracta de la Confideracion de los principales mysterios de nuestra Fe. Con otros tres breues tractados dela excellencia de las principales obras penitenciales: que son Limosna, Ayuno, y Oracion*. Salamanca: Andrea de Portonarijs.

Howard, Donald Roy, Ed. 1969. *On the Misery of the Human Condition*. Indianapolis: Bobbs-Merrill Co.

Howard, Donald Roy. 1974. "Renaissance World-Alienation." In *The Darker Vision of the Renaissance: Beyond the Fields of Reason*, edited by Robert S. Kinsman, 47–76. Los Angeles: Center for Medieval and Renaissance Studies, University of California.

Kempis, Thomas à. (1999) 187. *The Imitation of Christ*. Project Gutenberg. Translated by Rev. William Benham. Boston: Lee and Shepard. https://gutenberg.org/cache/epub/1653/pg1653-images.html.

Leeming, Ben. 2017a. "Aztec Antichrist: Christianity, Transculturation, and Apocalypse on Stage in Two Sixteenth-Century Nahuatl Dramas." PhD diss., Department of Anthropology, University at Albany, SUNY.

Leeming, Ben. 2017b. "A Nahua Christian Talks Back: Fabián de Aquino's Antichrist Dramas as Autoethnography." In *Words and Worlds Turned Around: Indigenous Christianities in Colonial Latin America*, edited by David Tavárez, 172–192. Louisville: University Press of Colorado.

Leeming, Ben. 2022. *Aztec Antichrist: Performing the Apocalypse in Early Colonial Mexico.* Louisville: University Press of Colorado. Co-published with the Institute for Mesoamerican Studies, University at Albany. IMS Monograph Series, Publication No. 16.

Lorenzana, Francisco Antonio. 1769. *Primero, y segundo, celebrados en la muy noble, y muy leal Ciudad de México, presidiendo el Illmo. Y Rmo. Señor D. Fr. Alonso de Montúfar, En los años de 1555, y 1565.* Mexico City: Imprenta del Superior Gobierno.

McDonough, Kelly S. 2014. *The Learned Ones: Nahua Intellectuals in Postconquest Mexico.* Tucson: University of Arizona Press.

Moore, John Aiken. 1977. *Fray Luis de Granada.* Boston: Twae Publishers.

Nesvig, Martin Austin. 2009. *Ideology and Inquisition: The World of the Censors in Early Mexico.* New Haven, CT: Yale University Press.

Puigbó, Armando Pego. 2004. *El renacimiento espiritual: Introducción literaria a los tratados de oración españoles (1520–1566).* Anejos de la Revista de literatura, vol. 61. Madrid: Editorial Consejo Superior de Investigaciones Científicas.

Sahagún, Fray Bernardino de. 1574. *Comiença un exercicio en lengua mexicana sacado del Sancto Evango. y distribuido por todos los días de la semana.* Ayer MS 1484. Chicago: Newberry Library.

Schwaller, John F. 2005. "The Pre-Hispanic Poetics of Sahagún's *Psalmodia Christiana.*" *Estudios de Cultura Náhuatl* 36: 67–86.

Sell, Barry D., and Louise M. Burkhart, Eds. 2004. *Nahuatl Theater.* Vol. 1, *Death and Life in Colonial Nahua Mexico.* Norman: University of Oklahoma Press.

Tavárez, David. 2013a. "Nahua Intellectuals, Franciscan Scholars, and the *Devotio Moderna* in Colonial Mexico." *Americas* 70 (2): 203–235.

Tavárez, David. 2013b. "A Banned Sixteenth-Century Biblical Text in Nahuatl: The Proverbs of Solomon." *Ethnohistory* 60 (4): 759–762.

Tavárez, David. 2017. "Nahua Humanism, Dissent, and Indigenous Publics in New Spain, 1550s–1600s." First European Nahuatl Conference, Warsaw, Poland, November 18.

Yannakakis, Yanna. 2008. *The Art of Being In-Between: Native Intermediaries, Indian Identity, and Local Rule in Colonial Oaxaca.* Durham, NC: Duke University Press.

# 9

## Nahua Notaries of Jerusalem
*Lucio Sestilio and His Partners in Crime*

LOUISE M. BURKHART

### I. NAHUA NOTARIES TAKE THE STAGE

As Nahua and other Indigenous communities adapted to Spanish colonial demands, their cultures of literacy came to focus in part around the notary. Called by the Spanish loanword *escribanoh*, or, in Nahuatl, *tlahcuiloh*, "one who writes things," the notary was an alphabetically literate official connected to the local ruling council, or *cabildoh*, in each Indigenous corporate community, and also to the local Catholic Church. While literacy remained a specialized and prestigious art concerned with keeping historical records and fulfilling ritual obligations, many new document genres, such as wills and petitions, emerged, as *escribanos* mastered the formulas and strategies required for negotiating the new political landscape, sometimes learning the Spanish language as well. Their legal and literary skills empowered them as intermediaries and power brokers between Indigenous communities and the colonial regime and also nurtured the intellectual life inscribed in Indigenous-language chronicles, religious treatises, and literary works.[1]

What Kathryn Burns calls "notarial truth" was a written construct that did not necessarily coincide with all concerned parties' views of reality (2005, 354). In

---

[1] On colonial Nahua notaries, see, for example, Haskett (1991, 110–111); Horn (1997, 63–65); Lockhart (1992); and Taylor (1996, 351–352). On notaries and other Indigenous intermediaries as power brokers in Oaxaca, see Yannakakis (2008). McDonough (2014) provides a historical sampling of Nahua intellectual culture.

Spain, concern over the corruptibility of notaries, who might be paid to produce a desired result or be angling to enhance their political power, spilled over into Early Modern literature. Spanish writers such as Miguel de Cervantes presented notaries as "stock figures of greed, eager to produce the best truth money could buy" (353; see also Burns 2010, 14, 21–22). How did the Nahuas' own literary culture characterize the notary, a figure essential to its development yet easily suspected of betraying the interests of his clients or community? How was literacy itself displayed and performed on stage? In this chapter I explore the character of Notary in colonial Nahuatl theater, focusing especially on Passion plays, where Escribanoh enjoyed his largest onstage presence.[2] Colonial notaries, being the only, or among the only, literate individuals in their communities, probably participated in creating and copying theatrical scripts and teaching nonliterate actors their lines. It is possible that they even played these or other roles themselves—a logical casting choice in instances where the character is called upon to read a lengthy document aloud. Theater provides a context in which Nahuatl literacy held a mirror up to itself.

Only one Notary character shows up in extant Nahuatl morality plays, a genre in which demons induce people to sin and dissuade them from properly confessing those misdeeds. In *The Merchant*, from 1687, Escribanoh helps a sinful merchant defraud a poor widow and her children by forging a land sale document and lying about a will, demanding a bit of property in return for his false witness (Sell and Burkhart 2004, 252–257). It is Merchant, however, who is beset by demons and consigned to afterlife punishment; Notary's obedient complicity is not punished. In a comic intermezzo adapted into Nahuatl by Don Bartolomé de Alva, a priest of Spanish and Nahua descent, around 1640, an old woman brings turkeys and money to bribe the local magistrate (*alcalde*), claiming falsely that her husband has beaten her. The magistrate has a notary, who tells him what the old woman and old man carry, as if he is a younger man with better eyesight. The magistrate orders Notary to assign lashes to the old man, increasing the number as, apparently, the old woman forks over additional coins. Later, Magistrate orders Notary to beat the old woman but immediately leaps up in a drunken rage and falls backward over his chair (Sell, Burkhart, and Wright 2008, 154–159). The outlandish humor centers on the elderly couple and the magistrate, while Notary's presence adds verisimilitude to the mock legal proceedings.

Other than these two brief appearances, all Escribanos in the extant theatrical corpus inhabit first-century Jerusalem, their presence at official proceedings making the ancient events seem more familiar and accessible. They serve masters who mandate mistreatment of Jesus Christ. They are complicit in this abuse, but, unlike Merchant's

---

[2] I capitalize Escribanoh and Notary when referring to play characters called Escribanoh in Nahuatl scripts.

abettor, they gain no illicit profit from these actions. These Notaries record and read aloud decrees aimed at Jesus's injury or destruction, whether dictated by King Herod the Great, the Jerusalem Sanhedrin, or Pontius Pilate, the Roman prefect of Judea at the time of Jesus's death. At these junctures, key actions await the oral recitation of written instructions, as audiences were reminded of the efficacy of the written word and also of its potential to legitimize dishonest testimony and to pronounce doom upon innocent sufferers. This performance convention also provided a context into which some Indigenous playwrights slotted a curious text claiming to be Pilate's actual death warrant against Jesus. This dubious but detailed pronouncement gave Notary a more noteworthy role in the events of the Passion.

The earliest Notary in the known theatrical corpus works for King Herod. He must record and, on two occasions, read out Herod's order to massacre the small children of Judea in the hope of eliminating young Jesus among the others. The original manuscript for this play is now missing, so I rely on Francisco del Paso y Troncoso's 1902 study. The manuscript stated that the play was composed for Fray Juan Bautista at Tlatelolco in 1707; both Paso y Troncoso and Fernando Horcasitas assume that this date is an error and that the play numbers among the theatrical works this Franciscan claimed to have amassed a century earlier, in collaboration with Agustín de la Fuente and other Nahua scholars associated with the Colegio de Santa Cruz (Bautista 1606, prologue; Horcasitas 1974, 281; Paso y Troncoso 1902, 77). Even if the 1707 date is correct, and this script was a later copy of a work prepared for Juan Bautista, these Notary scenes are early examples of their kind.

We first meet Escribanoh after a two-folio gap in Paso y Troncoso's source. The missing text included all but the last few words of Herod's proclamation, but fortunately that decree is repeated later in the script. We do see Escribanoh responding to Herod, as follows, in Paso y Troncoso's idiosyncratic orthography (1902, 98):

| | |
|---|---|
| ESU.O: *ka ye* kualítçin, Tlakatlé, Tlà'touanié; *ma* nik'-tlali in mo-tlà'toka Tlanauatiltçin *iniuhki* tinexmo-nauatilia, Tlakatlé, Tlà'touanié. | NOTARY: Very well, O master, let me put down your royal command, like you command me, O master, O ruler. |
| ¶ níma ki-tlaliç, **Çentensia** in Esu.°: *intla* oki-tlali *níma* ki-póuaç, ki-tekakiçtiliç. | *Then Notary will put down the sentence. When he has put it down, he will read it, he will proclaim it.* |
| ESU.O: Tlakatlé, Tlà'touanié; ka ye onik'-tlali in mo-tlà'toka Tlanauatíltçin: ma xik'mo-kakilti, ma nik'-poua. | NOTARY: O master, O ruler. I have now put down your royal command. May you listen to it. Let me read it. |
| ¶ níma ki-póuaç **Çentensia**. | *Then he will read the sentence.* |

In order to declaim the warrant to the intended victims, Notary must accompany Herod's troops to Nazareth, where the Jewish captain orders him to read Herod's *i-Amatlakuilóltçin*, "his paper writing," transcribed as follows (Paso y Troncoso 1902, 106):

ECRIVANO: *in nika* i-*pa* Altepétl **Gerosalen** ni-tlanauatia *ínik*.... nikin-titlani in no-Yaotiakáua in i-*pa* am-Amaltepéuh *ínik in ik* moxíntin–mimikiçke in amo-Pílhuan: in mokèketça, mo-uilana, in *manel ye kin* o-tlákat *íua* in aki in-*pan* tlà-'toç, *no* te-*ua onka* -miktiloç; *ínik àuel*[3] -neltiç, mo-xíuaç, in tlàtokaTlanauatili, *in nika* nik'tçonteki in Tekutlàtoloya **Gerosalen,** *ínik* moxintin -mímikiçke in Pipiltonti, *ínik no* té-*huan onka* -míkiç in aki *kin* o-tlákat, in *aço* neli Çemanáuak Tlà'-touani -yeç, *íua* -tenkíxtiç *in uel* i-*ka*, i-*panpa*, mo-tlalía 'nín Tetlatçontekiliçtlà'toli, in mo-tokayotia Çentesia: no-yoMa*tika* nik'-tlalía, in néhuatl **Rey Erodes,** *in nika* n'ok'on-pixtika in uei Altepétl **Gerosalen.**

NOTARY: Here in the *altepetl* of Jerusalem I order that....[4] I send my war captains into your *altepetl* so that all your children will die: the toddlers, the ones who crawl, and even the newborns. And anyone who speaks up for them will also be killed there with the others. So that the royal command will be carried out and done, I here pass judgment, in the court of Jerusalem, that all the children will die, so that among the others there he will die, he who was recently born, who perhaps is to be the true ruler of the world, and will save people.[5] That is precisely why this statement of judgment is being put down, which is called a "sentence." I put it down myself, I King Herod, who here am in charge of the great *altepetl* of Jerusalem.

Note that in this comparatively early play, the loanword *sentenciah*, though used repeatedly in the stage directions, does not stand alone in the oral speeches, or even in a simple pairing with a Nahuatl equivalent but is given an "it is called by name" (*motocayotia*) explanation. In no later play will a judicial *sentenciah*—a loanword attested in notarial texts by 1551 (Karttunen and Lockhart 1976, 58)—require such an explanation. Also, although both Herod and the Jewish captain depend on Notary for reading and writing, Herod gives himself credit for setting down the decree, speaking in the first person (*nictlalia*, "I put it down") and adding the emphatic *noyomatica*.[6]

A later version of this play survives, dated 1724, from Metepec, in the State of México (Biblioteca Nacional de Antropología e Historia, Archivo Histórico, Colección Antigua, vol. 872). Here Herod summons Notary with these words (15v; Sell and Burkhart 2009, 100–101):

---

[3] Read *uel* (as in the Metepec version, to be discussed shortly).

[4] Here the Metepec play has *yhuan noqualanalistica niquinmixnahuanti yn Judea tlaca*, "and in my anger I condemn the people of Judea" (Sell and Burkhart 2009, 102–103).

[5] Paso y Troncoso probably misread *temaquixtiz*, "he will save people," the term that appears here in the Metepec play, as *tenquixtiz*, from *tenquixtia*, "to declare (something)," which would require an object prefix (Sell and Burkhart 2009, 102–103).

[6] Paso y Troncoso (1902, 125), followed by Horcasitas (1974, 325), reads *noyomatica* as "with my hand" (i.e., *nomatica*) and thus infers that Herod signs the document; however, *-yoma-* does not refer to *maitl*, "hand." I thank participants in the 2018 Northeast Nahuatl Scholars conference for advising me on this construction.

| | |
|---|---|
| Tla xihualauh yn tehuatl yn ties<sup>no</sup> niman axcan oncan on xictlali yn notlatocaCatlanahuatil yn insentencia yn Judea tlaca y[n]ic quicaquisque yn itlatontequililoca ynic mochintin mimictilosque yn inpilhuan y nehuatl y nitlanahuatia Reyn erodes | Do come, you, Notary. Put down my royal command, the sentence of the people of Judea, right away, so that they will hear the judgment passed on them, that all their children will be killed. It is I who issue the command, King Herod. |

Escribanoh replies exactly as in the Tlatelolco play. However, the Metepec play revises and expands the later part of Herod's decree (16r, Sell and Burkhart 2009, 102–103):

| | |
|---|---|
| yn huel yca ypanpa yn motlalia yni tetlatzontequililistlatoli y nehuatl yn Reyn erodes y nican yn Jerosalen ynic ayac aquin yn quipanahuis y notetlatzontequinlilistlatol ynic mochicauhtias y nocapp<sup>n</sup> yhuan yn ocsequintin y notiacahuan ynic niquinmaca yn nohuelitilistlatol ynic ayac aquin quixnamiquis quixitinis yn noçentensia y nican yn ipan y huey altepetl yn Jerosalen yn omicuilo yn miquistetlatzontequilistli | That is precisely why this statement of judgment is being put down. I, King Herod, here in Jerusalem, so that no one will violate my statement of judgment, so that my captain and my other brave soldiers will be empowered, hereby grant them my authorization, so that no one will dispute or undo my sentence. The death judgment was written here in the great *altepetl* of Jerusalem. |

In these passages the word *sentenciah* is employed with confidence, interchangeably with Nahuatl words, and Herod makes no first-person claim to its production. Metepec's Notary adds authoritative verbiage to the earlier model. However, this later play leaves unspecified which actor recites the sentence to the people of Nazareth. After reading back Herod's words, Notary hands the warrant to the Jewish captain to take into the field. When the time comes for it to be proclaimed, the captain orders an unnamed individual to read it, and after it is read, the soldiers proceed to attack the children. Perhaps Escribanoh was to step in to do the reading, but the script does not say.

Herod's exchange with his deferential Notary and the authority-asserting language added to his sentence have counterparts in other eighteenth-century plays, whose casts include Notaries who hold office at the time of Jesus's death. I base this discussion on six Nahuatl Passion plays, all ultimately derived from an unknown model, perhaps composed, like the Epiphany play, early in the seventeenth century:

1. *Dominica Pasión de Ramos,* 1757 or earlier, from Tepalcingo, Morelos (facsímile in the Latin American Library, Tulane University, published in Sell and Burkhart 2009);
2. *Nican ompehua in ipasiom yn ipantzinco totecuiyo Jesu christo omochiuh,* 1732, from Amacuitlapilco, Morelos (Archivo General de la Nación, Indiferente Virreinal exp. 040, caja 6610);

3. *Pasion Domini nustri Jesu Xpo secudu Matheo*, from Axochiapan, Morelos, dated 1732 (Biblioteca Nacional de Antropología e Historia, Archivo Histórico, Colección Antigua, vol. 464);
4. *La Passion de Nrō Senōr Jesu christo*, undated, in the Berendt-Brinton Linguistics Collection at the University of Pennsylvania (Kislak Center for Special Collections, Van Pelt-Dietrich Library Center, Ms. Coll 700, item 200); I refer to this as the Penn play;
5. *Nica pehua yn itlasomahuispasiōtzi y t.º Jesu Xp̄o*, 1750 or earlier (Princeton Mesoamerican Manuscript no. 13, Department of Rare Books and Special Collections, Princeton University Library); I refer to this as the Princeton play;
6. Incomplete Passion play, San Simón Tlatlauhquitepec, Tlaxcala, undated (Archivo de la Fiscalía, published in Sell and Burkhart 2009 and Macuil Martínez 2010).

English translations and paleographic and standardized transcriptions of these plays can be viewed on my collaborative digital project "Passion Plays of Eighteenth-Century Mexico." For a more extensive analysis of the plays, see Burkhart (2023).[7]

The three plays from Morelos were confiscated in 1757 by the parish priest of Jonacatepec, Fray Miguel de Torres, presumably in compliance with the decree issued that year by Archbishop Manuel Rubio y Salinas, in which he demanded the suspension of Indigenous Passion plays and confiscation of all scripts.[8] In response to this suppression effort, some non-Indigenous people wrote plays in Spanish, in order to keep the popular practice going. That is how Fray Antonio de Victoria, the Mexican Inquisition's commissary for Chalco, accounted for four Spanish-language plays swept up during a 1768 Inquisition investigation that probed Indigenous and non-Indigenous Passion performances.[9]

---

[7] I thank Nadia Marín-Guadarrama for photographing the Amacuitlapilco and Axochiapan plays, and the AGN and BNAH for permitting this photography. I also acknowledge the National Endowment for the Humanities, an independent federal agency, for grant funding in support of the development of this digital project, and a fellowship supporting my book project. I also thank the Kislak Foundation and the John W. Kluge Center, Library of Congress, for fellowship support.

[8] Torres attached a note to the Axochiapan script referring to six scripts; notes in his hand appear on the other plays.

[9] Archivo General de la Nación (AGN), Ramo Inquisición, vol. 1072, leg. 5. I am grateful to Daniel Mosquera, my principal collaborator on the Passion Plays of Eighteenth-Century Mexico project, for sharing his facsimiles and transcriptions of the AGN material, including his table comparing the four Passion plays side by side. Leyva (2001) has published the play from Ozumba; much of the case's accompanying documentation is in Ramos Smith et al. (1998). English versions of the Spanish plays and accompanying reports can be found on our website. Victoria's statement explains that Rubio y Salinas issued his decree: "para

Some Passion play Escribanos, like their offstage counterparts, were called upon to record legal testimony from witnesses. As Caiaphas and Pilate interview the *testigos*, they may pause one to three times to ensure that Notary is accurately recording the proffered lies and hearsay. These perfunctory exchanges resemble that between Herod and Notary quoted earlier, including Notary's use of the polite vocative, a courtesy his employers do not extend to him. Here are examples:

| | | |
|---|---|---|
| Amacuitlapilco (34r) | Cayfas = ye oniccac yuhqui xictlali amapan xiquicuilo[10] ess.ⁿᵒ ess.ⁿᵒ = Ca ye cualitzin tlatohuanien ma yuhqui nictlali | CAIAPHAS: I have heard it. Put it down like this, write it on the paper, Notary. NOTARY: Very well, O ruler. Let me put it down like this. |
| Penn (23v) | Caifas Ca ye onicac iuhqui xictlali iuhqui xicicuilo escribano = escribano ca ye cual[i] tlatohuanie Ca ye onictlali = tlacuilos | CAIAPHAS: I have heard it. Put it down like this, write it down like this, Notary. NOTARY: Very well, O ruler. I have put it down. *He will write something.* |
| Axochiapan (29r) | pilato = yuqui xictlali yn iteyxipāhuiloca yn xpo escribano ess.ⁿᵒ = Ma yoqui mochihua yn quexquich tlatoli quitenehua yn testigos ynnic tlaneltilia | PILATE: Write it down like this, the accusations against Christ, Notary. NOTARY: May it so be done, all the words that the witnesses utter, as they testify. |
| Princeton (33v) | Pilato = escribano yuh xiquiCuilo yuh xictlali escribano = Ma ⁱᵒqui niquicuilo nopiltzine pilatoe | PILATE: Notary, write it down thus, put it down thus. NOTARY: Let me write it down like this, O my noble, O Pilate. |

que no se les permitiessen a los indios estas representaciones, pero como ya estos indios avian tomado por diversión annual en las quaresmas, los que llaman en los pueblos gentes de razon tomaron a su cargo representar la Passión, y traduciéndola del idioma mexicano en nuestro castellano la representan en algunos pueblos con grave escándalo, irrisión y desprecio" (so that the Indians were not allowed these representations; but because this [practice] had already been repeated as annual entertainment during Lent, those called people of reason in the villages took charge of representing the Passion and, translating it from the Mexican language [Nahuatl] into our Castilian [tongue] represent it in some towns with serious scandal, derision and contempt) (1951; transcription and translation by Daniel O. Mosquera). In spite of Victoria's characterization, the Spanish-language plays are too different from the extant Nahuatl plays to have been translated from them.

[10] *amapan xiquicuilo*: a different hand crossed these words out and wrote in *yohqui oquito*, "like he said it."

These interactions highlight Notary's compliance and the susceptibility of written proceedings to false testimony. If Jesus can fall victim to a colonial judicial system, so can anyone else.

Notary enjoys a longer time on stage when he reads Pilate's death warrant against Jesus. Here is this scene in the play from Axochiapan:

[34v–35r] pilato = ESC.ⁿᵒ xiquinpohuili ȳ sentensia ma mochi tlacatl quicaquican ynic ynyollo pachihuisque ynic onictlatzontequili yn Xp̄o

PILATE: Notary, read them the sentence. Let everyone hear it so that they will be satisfied as to how I passed judgment on Christ.

ESCⁿᵒ—ca ye qualitzin nopiltzintzin notlatohuanie

NOTARY: Very well, O my noble, O my ruler.

Sentencia
Yn nehuatl ponsio pilato presidente yn nican Jerusalen ytencopa yn notlatocauh yn sesar sunpe Agusto o ixquich nixpa oquis yn cauhsas yn probansas yn inneteylhuil yn intlaytlaniliz yn Judiosme yn quiteyxpanhuique yn Jesus yn itoca Xp̄o yn oquitoque ynic tetlapololtitinemi yn nican Jerosalen auh ca oniquitac yn ixquich yn cauhsas yn probansas yn iteixpanhuiloca notencopa omecahuitecoc otlayyohuiltiloc auh ámo yc yyolo opachiuh ocsepa oquitoque ynic miquis ynic miyec tlacatl ytech mixcuitis ca senca quimatataca ynic quimamasohualtisque auh ca onicceli yn intlaʸᵗˡᵃnilis auh ȳmac onicauh yn yehuanti ypan quichihuazque yn quenin quinequis yn inyolo omochiuh ynin Sentensia nican ynpa altepetl Jerosalen ypan metztli marso ytlamia

Sentence
I, Pontius Pilate, president here in Jerusalem by order of my ruler, Caesar, always venerable.[11] Before me have passed all the actions and evidence, the accusations and demands of the Jews who have accused Jesus, who is called Christ, who they have said is such a troublemaker here in Jerusalem. And I have seen all the actions and evidence that speak to the complaints made against him. By my order he was flogged and tormented. But they were not satisfied with that. Again they said that he is to die, so that many people will take an example from him. They strongly insist that they will stretch him by the arms. And I have accepted their demands. And I have left him in their hands. They will do to him as their hearts desire. This sentence was issued here in the *altepetl* of Jerusalem at the end of the month of March.

Tepalcingo's very similar version (Sell and Burkhart 2009, 234–235) specifies the date as March 25 and names Tiberius as the Roman emperor, or Caesar, in question. Consistent with Gospel accounts, Pilate speaks of his examination of Jesus and the flagellation he ordered, which failed to quell the demands for Jesus's death. A long tradition in Europe had placed the Crucifixion on March 25, so that detail does not point to any particular source tradition.

Although its immediately preceding dialogue precisely parallels that of the Tepalcingo play, and closely resembles Axochiapan's, the Amacuitlapilco script directs Escribanoh to read the death sentence but does not include the words. It

---

[11] *semper augustus*.

appears he was to recite from a document not incorporated into the script itself. At the very end of the Amacuitlapilco script, a different copyist began to inscribe a death sentence, but as he got no farther than *yn Nehuatl PonÇion* 'I, Pontius' (57r), it is impossible to determine what he had planned to write. It is possible that a new, more elaborate death sentence had already come into circulation among Nahuatl-speaking communities, as early as 1732, the date on both the Amacuitlapilco and Axochiapan scripts. As will be seen in the next section, this text was definitely circulating before 1750.

The extant portion of the Tlatlauhquitepec play ends before Pilate orders the crucifixion. But its Escribanoh does read a "Sentence of Lashes," a few lines in length, ordering Christ's flagellation (Sell and Burkhart 2009, 158–159):

| | |
|---|---|
| [12v] [Pilato:] Escribano xicpoa yn[in] nosentencia Yc mecahuitecoz Ynon acualtlachihuani tlaca[tl] Yc mixcuitizque occequintin tlacâ Yn itlachihual Escribano: Ca ye cuali tlacatle tlatohuaniê | [PILATE:] Notary, read this sentence of mine, by which that evildoer is to be flogged, so that other people will take an example from his deeds. |
| Escribano: Ca ye cuali tlacatle tlatohuaniê | NOTARY: Very well, O master, O ruler. |
| Sentençia de âsotes | Sentence of Lashes |
| Jesus Nazareno acualtlachihuani Yeyca yc teilhuilo ypanpa Yn toteopixcatlatocahuan Ynic amo quimocacanequi Yn itenahuatiltzin yn Moyses Xictlatotomican, Yhuan XicYlpican Temimiltitech Çenca chicahuac = xicmecahuitequican Yca huitzilitlacotl ma yuh neltiloz = Presidente Poncio pilato | Jesus the Nazarene, evildoer, because testimony has been made on his account to our high priests that he does not want to obey[12] the laws of Moses, unbind him and tie him to a very strong stone column. Flog him with thorny sticks. Let it be carried out in this way. President Pontius Pilate. |

The reference to violating the laws of Moses probably came into the Tlatlauhquitepec play from the new version of Pilate's death warrant that seems also to have affected the Amacuitlapilco script. While death sentences, like that of Axochiapan, were the longest speeches that Notaries gave in any play, this imported proclamation gave them a speech that vied with Judas's soliloquy—a Hamlet-worthy expanse of anxious wishy-washiness—to be the longest single speech in the performance. The Princeton and Penn plays both feature a version of this document. Two versions in Spanish were confiscated in 1768 in the course of the Inquisition investigation mentioned earlier. Though collected as loose sheets, one accompanied a Passion play from Amecameca and the other belongs with the play confiscated from Ozumba (AGN, 197r–198r, 244r[13]). Another of the Spanish-language plays, from Tenango,

---

[12] Translation tentative.

[13] All following citations to the AGN are to the Passion play Inquisition case, volume 1072, file 5.

scripts a short distillation of this text (AGN, 273v). I turn now to this document and its Mexican exemplars.

### THE DEATH WARRANT FROM L'AQUILA

In the Gospels Pilate orders Jesus flogged but, finding him innocent, orders no further punishment. He turns Jesus over to the Jews who are clamoring for his crucifixion, washing his hands to signify cession of his responsibility. Only one of the four Gospel accounts (John 19, 19–22) names Pilate as the person who places on the cross the signboard reading "Jesus of Nazareth, the King of the Jews." Christian apocrypha offering additional details about the Roman prefect's actions, including the judgment he utters against Jesus, go back at least to the fifth century *Acta Pilati* (Quasten 1983, 1:116). Coming late to this tradition was a Renaissance-era fabrication purporting to be the actual death sentence decreed by Pilate, in which he orchestrates many details of Jesus's death. Although this warrant lists representatives of the Jewish high priests and the Twelve Tribes of Israel as witnesses, it nevertheless moves more responsibility for Jesus's death onto the Roman prefect relative to the Jewish leaders. Thus, while hardly contradicting European anti-Semitism, it also implicates Rome's colonial government in actively programming Jesus's final agony rather than simply relinquishing him to a mob.

Early propagators of this text claim it was discovered in 1580, written in Hebrew on sheepskin, in the ruins of an ancient house in L'Aquila, in the kingdom of Naples, near the ancient city of Amiternum, Pilate's supposed birthplace (Beskow 1983, 19). Neapolitan jurist Camillo Borello soon proclaimed it inauthentic, but his 1581 commentary, which included the decree in Italian, was not published until 1588. By then the text was in wide circulation, having been published in French and German in 1581 (Berliner 2003, 50–52; Beskow 1983, 19–20).[14] Also in 1581, a version arrived at the court of Philip II, where it inspired Spanish translations by, among others, the Hieronymite friar Rodrigo de Yepes, who appended his to a 1583 treatise about Palestine (Beskow 1983, 20; Yepes 1583, 86r–88r). Two other versions relevant to the eighteenth-century Mexican context are a copy in garbled Italian (as if transcribed by a Spaniard) held by the Archivo General of Simancas, Spain (Sutcliffe 1949), and a similar Spanish version translated or copied by Domingo Valentín Guerra, archbishop of Segovia from 1728 until his death in 1742 (Guerra n.d., 284v–288r; Santos Otero 1956, 566–569[15]). The death sentence document from Ozumba

---

[14] For a German trajectory, see Fabricius's 1719 version, itself an exact reprint of an earlier text (487–493); Donehoo (1903, 333–337) has an English translation.

[15] Santos Otero cites a 1786 published version of Guerra's text.

refers to a "Carta de 4 de septtiembre eCritta al secrettario grahan [*sic*], secretario de Las Lenguas de su mag<sup>re</sup>" ("letter of September 4 written to Secretary Gracián, Secretary of the [Interpretation of] Languages of His Majesty"; AGN 198r). This seems a deliberately vague way to describe a dubious document, as neither the year, nor the Majesty, nor the Secretary Gracián is specified; direct descendants of Diego Gracián de Alderete, whom Charles V installed in 1527, served in this office with only occasional interruptions throughout Spain's Hapsburg era (Cáceres Würsig 2004, 611–612). However, this statement suggests another Spanish trajectory, as neither Yepes nor the Simancas and Guerra versions mention such a date or Secretary Gracián.

I have found no evidence that the L'Aquila death warrant circulated in New Spain before the mid-eighteenth century, although it could have been imported earlier. Nor have I yet found much evidence of its influence on European Passion plays.[16] But at least in the cases of the Penn and Princeton plays, probably the Tlatlauhquitepec play, and possibly the Amacuitlapilco play, Nahuas translated this account into the archaic, Stage Two Nahuatl used in Nahua theater and employed it in the scene where the Notary, on Pilate's order, reads Jesus's death warrant, either including it within the script, as in the Penn and Princeton texts, or using a separate document, as, apparently, in the Amacuitlapilco play. While the Penn play's death sentence shares some divergent details with the Spanish one from Amecameca, no two versions match up exactly. Rather, the four versions demonstrate that a number of variations on the L'Aquila text were circulating in New Spain in the mid-eighteenth century, rendered in Nahuatl or Spanish according to the needs of local *pasioneros*.

While the Ozumba and Amecameca death sentences are loose sheets that could have been brandished as props during a performance, stage directions do not actually state that they are to be read. All extant Nahuatl versions specify that the Escribanoh reads the *sentenciah* aloud. The Spanish play from Tenango, dated 1766, does include its brief death sentence within the script and also retains the Nahua convention of having a notary read the sentence. However, this occurs, here and in two of the other Spanish plays, after an at least semiliterate Pilate signs the document and Christ kisses it, actions omitted in the Nahuatl plays (AGN 217v, 273v,

---

[16] A scribe reads Pilate's death sentence in all versions of the Oberammergau Passion play. In his 1750 revision, Rosner replaced a brief statement referring to the flagellation and Christ's innocence with a 259-word decree that specifies details of the Crucifixion; this was shortened in the nineteenth century (1974, 232). This change may have been influenced by the L'Aquila text, but Rosner did not follow that model closely. Spanish Passion plays could include a substantial death sentence, such as the ninety-three-line one in Alonso del Campo's play from the 1480s (Torroja Menéndez and Rivas Palá 1977, 174–176), but I have not found L'Aquila-influenced examples.

292v).[17] The non-Indigenous authors of these plays elided or reduced the role of Notary and did not grant him a monopoly on literacy. Clearly, Nahuas found these characters more important than did non-Indigenous *pasioneros*, probably because of the roles real-life notaries played in *cabildoh* and church affairs and other aspects of daily life in the colonial *altepetl*.

Here are Pilate and Notary in the Princeton Passion play:

| | |
|---|---|
| [39v][18] Pilato= escriVano xiquinpohuili yn sentensia ynic onitlatzontec ynic omotecpa yn caosas | PILATE: Notary, read them the sentence, as I have ordered things, as the legal actions have been set in order. |
| escribano = ca ye Cuanlitzi tlatohuanie ca nican catqui yn amatl | NOTARY: Very well, O ruler. Here is the document. |
| quipohuas yn amatl yn iscriVano auh yn xp̄o san yonpan quiquisquitiyes yn pilato = aᵘh yntla ontla Omopoh yn sentencia mochitin Jodinme tlancahuatzazq̄ = nima hualmotemouis nimā quimoquechpanoltilisq̄ [40r] Cruz nima calaquisque | *Notary will read the document. And as for Christ, Pilate will just be holding onto him there. And when the sentence has been read all the Jews will raise a clamor. Then the cross will be lowered. Then they will make him carry it on his shoulders. Then they will go inside* |
| Yn nehuatl y niponsio pilato y niCan nipresidente yn ipan huey altepetl tlatocayotl roma yntencopa y notlatocauh tiVerio sesar enperador nohuiyā Cm̄c tlatohuani y niman amo panahuiloni yntoca Conles lusiano marso misorio bale notalio ahu in itlatocopa yn Jodea goVernador yntoca quinto fabia ytech pohui yn tlatocayotl Jerusalen auh yn galilea tlatohuani herodes Ahu in nican Jerosalen nehuatl nipresidenten niponsio pilato ahu in huehuenyntin teopixque Anas Cayfas auh yn yahuitiacahuan yntoca quinto cornelio yhuan sexto robilo ynnoncan | I, Pontius Pilate, I am President here in the great *altepetl*[19] kingdom of Rome by authority of my ruler Tiberius Caesar, Emperor, ruler everywhere in the world, unsurpassable. The names of the Consuls are Luciano, Marso Misorio, Bale Notalio, and from the kingdom of Judea, the governor, his name is Quinto Fabia, he pertains to the kingdom of Jerusalem,[20] and the ruler of Galilee is Herod. And here in Jerusalem I am the President, I, Pontius Pilate, and the high priests are Annas and Caiaphas, and the war captains, whose names are Quinto Cornelio and Sexto Robilo.[21] I pass judgment on people there in the |

---

[17] Leyva (2001, 92–93n22) speculates that the L'Aquila death warrant may have been newly imported to New Spain at the time of the 1768 investigation, as it was not used in the 1766 Tenango play. However, the Tenango play's short death sentence tracks closely with L'Aquila. Also, the 1750 date on the Princeton play evidences that the L'Aquila text was being used in Nahuatl plays by that time.

[18] I have removed a symbol resembling "=" that the copyist frequently placed between words or phrases.

[19] A reference to Jerusalem may have been omitted here.

[20] In Yepes, "Consules del pueblo Romano Lucio Pisano, Mauricio Scaurio, Procōsules Lucio Balena Balestina: Publico Gouernador de Iudea Quinto Flauio so el regimiento y gouierno dela ciudad de Hierosalē" (1583, 87v).

[21] In Yepes, "Cōnsules Romanos y de la ciudad de Hierusalem Quinto Cornelio Sublena y Sexto Ponpilio Rusto" (1583, 87v).

nitetlatzontequiliya yn huey teuhtlatoloyan
nictlatzontequilia ihuan niquixnahuatia
ynic miquis yn Jesus yn quitocayotia yn
masehualti Xp̄o auh oniquitac yn ixquich
yn prosensas yhuā yn probansas Ahu in
Xp̄o honpa ychan y nasaret yen ca senca
quixnamiqui yn itenahuatil yn muysen yhuā
no quixnamiqui yn huey enperador auh ca
ynca y nonsentencia nictlatzŏtequiliya yhuā
[40v] yn iuh nictenquixtiya ca ynic miquis
yntech cruz mamasohualtilos ynca yn Clabos
ytech sasalolos yn iuh chihualo yn aquique
tlatlacohuanime yehica ca miyequinti
oquinechico oquinsentlali yn mocuiltonohua
tlaca yhuā in motolinia tlaca auh hamo
onnŏotlacahualtiani ynic tlaacomătinemi y
noyan Jodea quimotocanyotitinemi ypiltzi
D.ˢ yhuā rey de ysrael ynic quimamauhtiya
quimilhuiya xixitinis yn amoteocal hierosalen
yhuā ynic senquiscacuali teopătli yhuān
amo quimocuitiya yn itlacalaquil ynic
macos yn sesar nohuiyan omotlapalo ynic
ohualcalac yn itic altepetl Jerosalen soyatl
ymac ohualonotiya yhuā miyec Cuauhxihuitl
omotzotzolo ynic otla[pa]nahui yhuan
miyequitin masehualti yn oquihualcaque
yhuān ōcan ocalac yn senquiscacualcan teopa
ynpapă ynic niquinahuatia y nohueytiacahuā
Sĕtonrio publico cornelio ynic yehuātin
quihuicasque yn Xp̄o quihualteyntitisque
yn ipa altepetl Jerusalen ylpitias auh
quimaquitiyas chichiltic tilmatli yhuān
icpac onmatias huisyahuali yehuatl yn huel
tecoco huistli yhuā ynoma quiquechpanotias
yn icuauhnepanol ynic nexcuitili [41r]
yes ynic ayac yuhqui quichihuas yhuā no
nicnequi quinhuicasque omentin ichteque
teychtacamictiyani auh ca onpan quisasque
yn tlatzacuiltiloya yntocayocan galiola yn
axcan ye ytocayocan antoniyana auh ynhuā
quihuicasque yn Jesus yn opan tepeticpac yn
onpa techihuililoyan Jostitia yntocayocan
CalVario yn ōca mamasohualtilos auh yn
inacayo yntech pilcos y Cruz motlalilis
yetlamantli tlatoli yn ocan motenehuas
yn itlatocatocan yehuatl nebreo yhuan
yn engriego yhuā latin yn iquicuiliuhtos
omochiuh yni sentensia ypan

great court, I pass judgment on and I condemn
to death Jesus, whom the *macehualtin* call
Christ. And I have seen all the proceedings and
evidence. And Christ's home is over in Nazareth.
He greatly contradicts the laws of Moses and he
also contradicts the great emperor. And with
my sentence I pass judgment on him and so I
proclaim that he is to die. He will be stretched by
the arms on a cross, he will be attached to it with
nails, as is done to those who are sinners, because
he assembled, he gathered together, many people,
rich people and poor people. And he does not
want to stop stirring things up everywhere in
Judea. They go around calling him the child of
God and the king of Israel. And he threatens them,
he tells them that the great *altepetl* of Jerusalem
will fall into ruin along with its supremely good
temple, and he does not acknowledge the tribute
that is to be given to Caesar. He dared to enter
inside the *altepetl* of Jerusalem with palm fronds
in his hand, and many tree branches were waved
as he triumphed. And many *macehualtin* came to
stand and there he entered the supremely good
place, the temple. Therefore, I command my great
warriors, centurion Publico Cornelio, that they
take Christ, that they show him to people in the
*altepetl* of Jerusalem. He will go tied up. And he
will put on a red mantle, and on his head will
be laid a circlet of thorns. They are very painful
thorns. And he will carry on his own shoulders
the wooden cross, so that it will be an example
so that no one will act like this. And I also want
them to bring two thieves, murderers. And they
will come out there at the gate called Galiola,
which now is called Antoniana. And they will
take Jesus with the others over on the top of the
hill, the place where justice is done to people, the
place called Calvary. There he will be stretched by
the arms. And his body will hang on the cross. It
will be placed in three languages, his royal name
will be said there, in Hebrew and Greek and
Latin it will lie written. This sentence was made
in the year 2187 and the 25th day of the month
of March. And I command that no one shall dare
to dispute this justice as I have adjudicated it, as I
have put it down, so that it can be executed with
my words of judgment and the commands of the
rulers, the Romans.

| | |
|---|---|
| matlactzonXihuitl yhuan sentzoxihuitl yhuan chicnauhpohualxihuitl yhuan chiconxihuitl auh tlapohua meztli marso senpohuanli yhuan macuinlitonali yhuan nitlanahuatia yniC ayac motlapalos quixnamiquis ynin Jostisia yniC onitlatzōtec ynic onictlali ynic huel neltiyas ynca y nontetlatzotequililistlatol yhuā yn intenahuatil yn tlatoque romanos ahu in aqui quixnamiquis yn notetlatzontequililistlatol ypa machos ca quixnamiqui yn roma tlatocayotl auh yn testigos omochiuhque yn ipan yn sentensia matlactli yhuannome yntech oquisque yn matlactlamatli omonec yn itlacamecayo yn israel ymixpa omochiuh ometin tlacuiloque ynic se ytechpa yn ebreos ytoca matheo bereto ahu in itechcopa tlatocayotl Roma yehua no moteneuh prisindente ytoca losio textillo | And anyone who disputes my words of judgment, on him it will be made known that he disputes the kingdom of Rome. And they who became witnesses on the sentence are twelve, who came from the twelve lineages of Israel. It was made before two notaries, the first from the Hebrews, whose name is Matheo Bereto, and from the kingdom of Rome, the president who has also been mentioned, his name is Losio Textillo. |

The Nahua redactor retained some of the armature of officials' names found in the L'Aquila warrant. His names correspond roughly to those in Yepes's and Guerra's Spanish versions. However, he omits the sixteen fanciful names of Jewish witnesses found at the end of Yepes's publication, retaining only that of the Roman notary's Hebrew counterpart, to whom he assigns the name Matheo (or Mateo) Bereto, giving him a recognizable first name. This man, Notanber in Yepes's account (1583, 88r), has a different name in every source.[22] However, all European variants agree on the name of one Roman notary, whether given the Latin form Lucius Sextilius or modernized into Italian or Spanish as Lucio Sextilio. Princeton's closing phrase echoes Yepes's "por el imperio y presidente de Roma, Lucio Sextilio, Amasio Chilion" (1583, 88r).[23] Changing Sextilio to Textillo creates a name that reads as "milled" or "crumbled" in Nahuatl (*textilo* is the passive form of *texti*, "to become flour, to be crumbled"). Both Nahuatl versions omit the second Roman notary. He appears as Aman Strenileo in Borello's Italian (Berliner 2003, 52), Amasio Chilio in Guerra (n.d., 288r), and, without his partner, as Amassio Lillio in the death sentence document from Ozumba (AGN 197r).

---

[22] Guerra and the Simancas manuscript have fourteen Hebrew witnesses, Borello's Italian text seventeen, Fabricius's German version eighteen. Borello has two Hebrew notaries, Rotam and Barta; Guerra has one, named Nitanbarta; the Simancas document has Nastan Restena, and Fabricius has Natani and Bertoch (Berliner 2003, 52; Fabricius 1719, 493; Guerra n.d., 288r; Sutcliffe 1949, 437).

[23] In Borello, "Per l'imperio, e Presidente di Romani" (Berliner 2003, 52).

In addition to its lists of officials' names, the L'Aquila warrant wields a legitimating armature of dates in six different year counts, beginning with the reign of Tiberius Caesar (year 17) and then veering into fantasy (Sutcliffe 1949, 438–439). The Nahuatl versions retain just one count, deriving from the Hebrew count of years since the creation of the world, an anachronistic inclusion in the European texts (438–439). The Princeton play's 2187 bears a vague similarity to Yepes's corresponding formula, 4 × 1187 (1583, 87v), but we may wonder how people in the 1700s understood this futuristic year.

Pilate refers to Christ's followers as *macehualtin*, using the Nahuatl term for the commoner class that by this time was well established as a term for Indigenous people and thus implied Indigenous as well as nonelite status; contemporary Nahuatl speakers retain this usage. This term likely translates *plebe*, "common people," which Yepes (1583, 87v) and Guerra (n.d., 286r) employ in this context, in contrast to the more derogatory *turbe* or *turba*, "throng," of the Italian texts (Berliner 2003, 51; Sutcliffe 1949, 437). Nahuatl Passion play scripts typically identify not just Jesus's followers but Jesus himself as *macehualtin*: the allusion to interethnic conflict and oppression added here to the decree is a standard motif in the dramas.

The Penn play more clearly links Pilate's alleged notary Lucius Sextilius with the play's own Notary, placing the name Lucio (or Lesio) Sestilio not just in its original context near the end of the proclamation but also at the very beginning and end of the speech. The repetition of the name suggests that the writer meant to adopt it for his character. With this impressive name, Notary could be more easily imagined as an authentic historical/mythological figure just like the nefarious President he serves.

Here is the Penn death sentence in full:

[32v] Pilato auh in axcan escribano ma xiquinpohuili in Sentencia Yn iuhqui onictzonthec onicthecpan

Escribano = ca ye cuali tlatohuanie ma nicpohua = Lesio sestilio =

Y Nehuatl y niponcio Pilato nipreciden[te] nican ypann in tlathocamahuisaltepetl Jerusalen inic oncan nithetlatzonthequilia in hueican thecpan theuctlatholoyan nictlatzonthequilia ihuan niquixnahuatia in imiquis in Jesus Yn quithocayotia masehualtin nasareno in ompan ichan Galiliea Ye ic tlacomanthinemi ihuan quixnamiqui in ithenahuatil in moices ihuan in huei enperador thiverio Sesar auh ca yca i noSentencia nictzonthequi ihuan nicthenquixtia inic micquis ica Clabos

PILATE: And now, Notary, read them the sentence, as I have adjudicated it, as I have set it in order.

NOTARY: Very well, O ruler. Let me read it. LUCIO SESTILIO

I, Pontius Pilate, I who am President here in the royal, honored *altepetl* of Jerusalem, such that I pass judgment on people there in the great palace, in the court, I pass judgment on and I condemn to his death Jesus, whom the *macehualtin* call Nazarene, whose home is over in Galilee. So does he go around stirring things up and contradicting the laws of Moses and the great emperor Tiberius Caesar. And with my sentence I pass judgment on him and I proclaim that he is to die. With nails his body crustitech thepoSCuaminalos Salolos inninacayo in iuh chihualo in aquique tlatlacoleque Yeica Ca oquinSentlali yhuan oquinhualhuicac miequintin motholinicatlaca ihuan mocuiltonohuanime auh inin tlacatl auh amo motlacahualtisnequi inic tlacomanthinemi noyan Judea quimothoyotitinemi[24] ypiltzin Dios ihuan ^(Rei) isreael auh quinmomauhtia quimilhuia ca xixitinis in huei altepetl [33r] Jerusalen ihuan iSenquiscaCualcan theopan ihuan amo ^(quimo)cuithia inic macos in itla^(ca)laquil i^n Sesar ihuan huel omotlapalo Ynic ohualcalacac in nican huei althepepan Jerusalen Soyatl oquihualquitzquilia Yhuan Cuauhxihuitl omotzetzelo yn iuhqui Yc ontlapanahui inic ohualcalac in oncan hueican theeopan Salomon auh ca nicnahuatia in achto notheyecancauh itoca quinto Cornelio inic quihuicasque in itec in omotheneuh huei altepetl Jerusalem auh inic huicos ilpitias yhuan quimaquitias xocohuitzcorona ihuan yahtias in queni omecahuitecoc nothencopa ihuan quimaquitias in itlaquen Ynic yximachos auh huel inonma quiquechpanos in Crus Ynic ythech mamaSohualthilos Yhuan quihuicasque omentin in ichteque teichthacamictianime ca sa no in oquic[25] tlatzonthequililoque Ynic inneixcuiltil mochihuas in ixquich tlacatl acualtlachihualeque ihuan Sa no iuh[?]qui Yhuan nitlanahuatia ica in noSenthencia Yntla ye oquitheithitique nohuian ipan altepetl Jerusalen inin tlacatl quiquixtisque in que nin? Sa no iuhqui tlacpac Onictheneuh ne altepetl Jerusalen in oncan ytlatzacui[33v]lotitlan pagora auh yn axcan ythocayocan antoniana ic tzatziualotias quitecaquisthilitiasque in ixquich ytlatlacol in iuh tecpanthiuh in ipan noSentencia quihuicasque in onpa tzompantepec quithocayotia Calvario Ynic onpa chihuililos Justicia yn iuh chihualo in ocsequinthin tlahueliloque inic onpa mamaSohualilos ithech in Crus quequechpanos in iuh ye omitho auh inn inacayo ithech pilcas in Crus auh in ocsequin Sa no iuh chihualosque Yn ithech in crus nictlalis in itlathocatoca Yn iuhqui axcan mocaquis Yetlamantli tlantholi in

will be pierced with metal on the cross, it will be attached, as is done to those who have sins, because he gathered together and accompanied many poor people and rich people. And this person, and he does not want to stop stirring things up everywhere in Judea. They go around calling him the child of God and the king of Israel. And he frightens them, he tells them that the great *altepetl* of Jerusalem will fall into ruin along with its supremely good temple, and he does not acknowledge the tribute that is to be given to Caesar. And he really dared to enter here in the great *altepetl* of Jerusalem carrying palm fronds, and tree branches were waved, as if he triumphed, as he entered there in the great place, the temple of Solomon. And I command my first Leader, whose name is Quinto Cornelio, that they take him into the said great *altepetl* of Jerusalem. And as to how he will be taken, he will go tied up and he will go wearing a crown of thorns, and he will go along in the manner that he was flogged by my orders, and he will go wearing his clothes so that he will be recognized. And he will carry on his own shoulders the cross on which he will be stretched by the arms, and two thieves, murderers, will go along with him, who have also been judged, so that he will become an example to every person, they who have bad deeds. And likewise, I command with my sentence that when they have shown him everywhere in the *altepetl* of Jerusalem, they will take this person in the manner that I stated above out of the *altepetl* of Jerusalem there at its gate Pagora. And it is now called Antoniana. Thus, it will go being cried out, they will go announcing all his sins as they go set in order in my sentence. They will take him over to Skull Hill, the place called Calvary, so that justice will be done there, as it is done to other scoundrels, so that there he will be stretched by his arms on the cross that he will carry, as has already been said. And his body will hang on the cross. And the others will have it done to them the same way. On the cross I will place his royal name, like it will be heard now in three languages, in Hebrew, Greek, and Latin language, so that

---

[24] Read *quimotocayotitinemi*.

[25] Transcription tentative

| | |
|---|---|
| ipan ebreo y Griego yhuan latin tlantholi ynic nochintin quitasque ihuan quitosque ynin Jesus nasareno yntlathocauh in Judiosme inic nochintin casicamathisque Yhuan quiximatisque ihuan nitlanahuatia ynic neltias Y notetlatzonthequililistlatol yn saso aquin Camo huel quixnamiquis i noJusticia auh in thestigos omochiuhque in imixpan Omochiuh in Sentencia ca matlactetl omomentin yn ithech oquisque in itlacamecayo yn isreael auh in oquichiuhque omentin tlacuiloque ynic se ithechpa in ebreos in itoca [34r] taberto auh ithechpa in Roma tlathocayotl ihuan in onictheneuh precidencia ytoca lucio Sestilio in ipan in intlapohual Yn Romanos yhuan ebreos in itzinpeuhayan Cemanahuatl macuili xiquipili ihuaⁿ matlacpohuali on macuili tonali mani metztli marso Otlathocatia tiverio lucio Sestilio | all will see and will say that this is Jesus the Nazarene, ruler of the Jews, so that all will understand it perfectly and will recognize him, and I command that my words of judgment be executed. No one whatsoever shall dispute my justice. And they who became witnesses, before whom the sentence was made, are twelve, who came from the lineages of Israel. And two notaries made it, such that from the Hebrews his name is Taberto and from the kingdom of Rome and the presidency that I have mentioned, his name is Lucio Sestilio. In the count of the Romans and the Hebrews since the beginning of the world 40,405 days, in the month of March. Tiberius was ruling. Lucio Sestilio |

This death sentence's redactor reduced the number of official names, retaining, in addition to Pilate and his notary, only Tiberius, the centurion Quinto Cornelio, and the Hebrew notary, now named Taberto. In Yepes, Pilate orders that "*mi primer centurion Quinto Cornelio*"[26] take Jesus "publicaměte por la ciudad de Hierusalě" (1583, 87v; italics added); that *publicamente* seems to be the source for the Princeton play's change of his name to Centurio Publico Cornelio, which the writer treats as multiple people. In the incomplete play from Tlatlauhquitepec, which terminates before the point at which a death sentence would have appeared, Caiaphas calls upon *titeyaoyacanqui Quinto Cornelio*, "you war leader Quinto Cornelio," to lead the soldiers who will arrest Jesus (Sell and Burkhart 1989, 144–145), a clue, like the reference to the "laws of Moses" mentioned earlier, that an adaptation of the L'Aquila warrant once formed part of this play. This character is consistently named Centurion in some Passion plays (e.g., Tlatlauhquitepec, Princeton) and Teyacanqui, "leader of others," in some (e.g., Tepalcingo, Penn), whereas in the Axochiapan and Amacuitlapilco plays Centurion and Teyacanqui are colleagues.

The Penn death sentence specifies that its date is counted from the creation of the world, like the Hebrew year count in the European sources, but collapses the Roman and Hebrew counts into one, and gives a date in days rather than years. While the number given bears no particular resemblance to any of the dates in other versions—these seem, indeed, to have varied with the whim of the redactor—the juxtaposition of Roman and Hebrew suggests this death sentence's shared derivation

---

[26] *Mi primer* is *presente*, "current," in Borrero's Italian (Berliner 2003, 51).

with the sentence from Amecameca, where the statement, cognate with European sources, that the decree is to be "executada con todo Rigor, segun los decretos, y Leyes Romanas, y hebreas" (executed with full rigor, according to the Roman and Hebrew decrees and laws) is followed immediately by "Anò de la Crea.ⁿ de Mundo Cinco mìl doscientos, y treinta y tres. Dia veinte y cinco de Marzo" (year of the creation of the world 5233, 25th day of March; AGN 244r).[27] Some Nahua translator shifted from laws to calendars to provide more context for the following date.

The Penn and Amecameca sentences share other details not found in any of the other versions. For example, they specify that the temple is that of Solomon. They, as well as the short death sentence in the Spanish play from Tenango, proclaim that Christ is to be marched to Calvary in his own clothes,[28] so people will recognize him. This reflects Matthew 27:31 and Mark 15:20, where, after having been dressed in a *chlamydem coccineam* (scarlet robe) while he is mocked by the soldiers, Jesus is dressed again in his own clothes prior to the crucifixion. In Guerra (n.d., 287r) and the Ozumba Sentencia (AGN 197r), Jesus remains "vestido de purpura," consistent with the Italian versions (Berliner 2003, 51; Sutcliffe 1949, 437), and turning up as *quimaquitiyas chichiltic tilmatli*, "he will put on a red (chili-colored) mantle," in the Princeton death sentence.

Pagora, the name of the gate through which Jesus is to be marched, also links the Penn and Amecameca death warrants. In the Amecameca text, however, *puerta* has become *puente*, "bridge," indicating a somewhat divergent path through copyists' hands. The Princeton play's Galiola is, conversely, not far from the Ozumba version's Galora, but this name too has diverged from European sources. Yepes gave this name as Golgotha; it would make sense for the gate to face that hill. However, Borello's Italian has Zagarola (Berliner 2003, 52; this name is retained by Fabricius 1719, 491). This name became Giancarola in the Simancas document and Sagarda in the manuscript version of Guerra (n.d., 287r; regularized as *sagrada*, "sacred," in Santos Otero [1956, 568]). Zagarola could have been truncated to Garola, and then switched around to Galola or Galora and even Pagora, especially as it passed into, and perhaps back out of, Nahuatl. The second name for this gate is Antoniana in all versions, deriving from the Antonia fortress, site of Pilate's praetorium. The retention of these gate names in the Nahuatl versions is a curious detail, as the stagings of the crucifixion make no mention of gates.

We can find many other interesting similarities and differences among the diverse death warrants. For present purposes, however, the key issues are, first, that Nahuas

---

[27] The Tenango Sentencia has 3,993 years (AGN 273v).

[28] Amecameca: "seanle pu[est]as sus Vestiduras"; Tenango: "con sus propias vestiduras" (AGN 244r, 273v).

participated in the dissemination of the L'Aquila text by slotting it into Passion plays as a speech made by Notary. They eliminated many of the fanciful dates and officials but retained a year or day count and, at the least, the names of notaries, Emperor Tiberius, and a centurion. Nahua redactors dropped the story of the document's discovery but retained most of the details of Christ's alleged misdeeds and the directions for the crucifixion. Within the play, the extended death sentence recaps events already enacted—the triumphal entry into Jerusalem, the accusations leveled against Jesus and his teachings—and foretells what is about to unfold as players act out the crucifixion. It is somewhat adapted to fit its performance context. Escribanoh becomes a narrator of sorts, encapsulating the complete drama into a written summary, in a manner analogous to the actions of his real-life counterparts as they transcribed oral testimony into written records and prescribed future legal actions.

## 2. COMPLICIT, BUT HONEST, ESCRIBANOS

Nahuatl theatrical scripts document an Indigenous performance genre that took hold in the sixteenth century and confronted various attempts at suppression and control later in the colonial era. The ability to read, copy, and perform these texts into the mid-eighteenth century depended on the retention of alphabetic literacy in Nahuatl among at least some members of a community, including those men who held office as notaries for the church or the *cabildoh*. The onstage performance of document creation and the use of written texts as props reinforced the importance of the Nahuatl-language literacy on which the performance itself depended. Stage literacy accomplishes this end in a rather ironic manner, as all the testimonies and judgments Notaries record have hurtful purposes. Yet the key event in Christian mythos—Jesus's death on the cross—hinges on the availability of a cooperative Notary who will record and read out the instructions, a pause in the action that in some cases expanded to accommodate a large portion of the L'Aquila death sentence. Notaries are important; world-changing events can rely on a sheet of paper. Nahuas who participated in or viewed these performances had no reason to doubt that this detail of the enactment was historically accurate.

Notaries are also predictable. Stage notaries are uniformly obedient and efficient, acquiescing to their assigned tasks and transcribing promptly and accurately whatever is dictated to them. They treat their evil employers with deference. Thus, these stage notaries contradict the stereotype of the corrupt and venal functionary, promoting a positive view of notarial honesty even as the characters serve evil ends. A presumption of honesty and respect was vital if nonliterate Nahuas were to trust notaries to record their testaments and other transactions exactly as dictated, even statements that might ramble on as long as the L'Aquila death warrant. Hence, the

Nahua Notaries of Jerusalem demonstrate to their audiences that however egregious the circumstances, a proper notary will keep his own opinions to himself and obediently write down whatever he is called upon to write. On that trust the business of the *altepetl*, as well as the performance of plays, depended. Whether Nahuas in the audience viewed Lucio Sestilio and his confreres as collaborators with a callous colonial regime or as low-level functionaries forced to facilitate evil acts, what they saw on stage gave them no reason to question the accuracy of what notaries put on paper. And like the retention, recopying, and circulation of their scripts over periods of many decades, these performances reminded all viewers of the importance of paper and writing to the survival of Nahua language and cultural expression throughout the era of colonial rule.

## REFERENCES

Bautista, Fray Juan. 1606. *A Iesu Christo S. N. ofrece este sermonario en lengua mexicana.* México: Diego López Dávalos.

Berliner, Rudolf. 2003. "Das Urteil des Pilatus." In *Rudolf Berliner (1886–1967): "The Freedom of Medieval Art" und andere Studie zum christlichen Bild*, edited by Robert Suckale, 43–59. Berlin: Lukas Verlag.

Beskow, Per. 1983. *Strange Tales about Jesus: A Survey of Unfamiliar Gospels.* Philadelphia: Fortress Press.

Burkhart, Louise M. 2023. *Staging Christ's Passion in Eighteenth-Century Nahua Mexico.* Denver: University Press of Colorado.

Burns, Kathryn. 2005. "Notaries, Truth, and Consequences." *American Historical Review* 110 (2): 350–359.

Burns, Kathryn. 2010. *Into the Archive: Writing and Power in Colonial Peru.* Durham, NC: Duke University Press.

Cáceres Würsig, Ingrid. 2004. "Breve historia de la secretaría de interpretación de lenguas." *Meta* 49 (3): 609–628.

Donehoo, James DeQuincey. 1903. *The Apocryphal and Legendary Life of Christ.* London: Macmillan.

Fabricius, Johann Albert. 1719. *Codex Apocryphi Novi Testamenti, Pars tertia.* Hamburg: Schiller & Kisner.

Guerra, Domingo Valentín. n.d. *Libro de varias noticias y apuntaciones que dexó escritas, en latín, español, francés e ytaliano, Domingo Valentín Guerra, obispo de Segovia.* Biblioteca Nacional de España, Biblioteca Digital Hispánica. Accessed May 29, 2018. http://bdh-rd.bne.es/viewer.vm?id=0000145015&page=1.

Haskett, Robert. 1991. *Indigenous Rulers: An Ethnohistory of Town Government in Colonial Cuernavaca*. Albuquerque: University of New Mexico Press.

Horcasitas, Fernando. 1974. *El teatro náhuatl: Épocas novohispana y moderna*. Mexico City: Universidad Nacional Autónoma de México.

Horn, Rebecca. 1997. *Postconquest Coyoacan: Nahua-Spanish Relations in Central Mexico, 1519–1650*. Stanford, CA: Stanford University Press.

Karttunen, Frances, and James Lockhart. 1976. *Nahuatl in the Middle Years: Language Contact Phenomena in Texts of the Colonial Period*. Berkeley: University of California Press.

Leyva, Juan. 2001. *La Pasión de Ozumba: El teatro religioso en el siglo XVIII novohispano*. Mexico City: Universidad Nacional Autónoma de México.

Lockhart, James. 1992. *The Nahuas after the Conquest: A Social and Cultural History of the Indians of Central Mexico, Sixteenth through Eighteenth Centuries*. Stanford, CA: Stanford University Press.

Macuil Martínez, Raul, trans. and ed. 2010. *La pasión de Tlatlauhquitepec: Obra de teatro Tlaxcalteca en náhuatl del siglo XVI*. Tlaxcala, Mexico: Gobierno del Estado de Tlaxcala, Instituto Tlaxcalteca de la Cultura.

McDonough, Kelly S. 2014. *The Learned Ones: Nahua Intellectuals in Postconquest Mexico*. Tucson: University of Arizona Press.

"Passion Plays of Eighteenth-Century Mexico." Accessed July 31, 2023. https://passionplays ofeighteenthcenturymexico.omeka.net.

Paso y Troncoso, Francisco del. 1902. "La comedia de los Reyes." In *Biblioteca Náuatl*, vol. 1. Florence: Salvador Landi.

Quasten, Johannes. 1983. *Patrology*. 4 vols. Allen, TX: Christian Classics.

Ramos Smith, Maya, Tito Vasconcelos, Luis Armando Lamadrid, and Xabier Lizárraga Cruchaga, eds. 1998. *Censura y teatro novohispano (1539–1822): Ensayos y antología de documentos*. Mexico City: Consejo Nacional para la Cultura y las Artes, Instituto Nacional de Bellas Artes, Centro Nacional de Investigación e Información Teatral Rodolfo Usigli, and Escenología.

Rosner, Ferdinand. 1974. *Passio Nova: Das Oberammergauer Passionsspiel von 1750*. Edited by P. Stephan Schaller. Bern and Frankfurt: Herbert Lang.

Santos Otero, Aurelio de. 1956. *Los evangelios apócrifos*. Madrid: La Editorial Católica.

Sell, Barry D., and Louise M. Burkhart, eds. and trans. 2004. *Nahuatl Theater*. Vol. 1, *Death and Life in Colonial Nahua Mexico*. Norman: University of Oklahoma Press.

Sell, Barry D., and Louise M. Burkhart, eds. and trans. 2009. *Nahuatl Theater*. Vol. 4, *Nahua Christianity in Performance*. Norman: University of Oklahoma Press.

Sell, Barry D., Louise M. Burkhart, and Elizabeth R. Wright, eds. 2008. *Nahuatl Theater*. Vol. 3, *Spanish Golden Age Drama in Mexican Translation*. Norman: University of Oklahoma Press.

Sutcliffe, Edmund F. 1949. "An Apocryphal Form of Pilate's Verdict." *Catholic Biblical Quarterly* 9 (4): 436–441.

Taylor, William B. 1996. *Magistrates of the Sacred: Priests and Parishioners in Eighteenth-Century Mexico*. Stanford, CA: Stanford University Press.

Torroja Menéndez, Carmen, and María Rivas Palá. 1977. *Teatro en Toledo en el siglo XV: "Auto de la Pasión" de Alonso del Campo*. Madrid: Anejos del Boletín de la Real Academia Española.

Yannakakis, Yanna. 2008. *The Art of Being In-Between: Native Intermediaries, Indian Identity, and Local Rule in Colonial Oaxaca*. Durham, NC: Duke University Press.

Yepes, Rodrigo de. 1583. "Tractado y descripcion breue y cõpendiosa dela tierra sancta de Palestina." Madrid: Juan Yñiguez de Lequerica. Biblioteca Nacional de Portugal, Biblioteca Nacional Digital. http://purl.pt/26496/1/index.html#/1/html.

# 10

## Nahua Curing through Graphic Communication
*Ritual Paper Figures and Cosmic Balance*

ALAN R. SANDSTROM AND PAMELA EFFREIN SANDSTROM

### 1. ENCOUNTERING THE MASTERS

Contemporary Nahuatl speakers in the southern Huasteca learn to cut elaborate figures from paper for curings, cleansings, and other rituals by undergoing long apprenticeships to master specialists versed in local Indigenous religious beliefs and practices. In our contribution to this volume on Nahua culture and language, we demonstrate how these ritual paper figures constitute a system of semasiographic communication. By recording information through pictographs, this graphic communication system parallels but does not reproduce spoken language. In fact, the similarity of ritual strategies deployed by neighboring Otomí (Ñähñu) and Tepehua (Hamasipini) speakers demonstrates that the paper figures transcend ethnic and linguistic boundaries in their ability to transmit information directly to ritual participants. A Nahua curer (*tlamatiquetl*, "person of knowledge," or *pahchiuhquetl*, "medicine person," in Nahuatl, *curandero/a* in Spanish) dedicates offerings to a multitude of spirit entities embodied in paper and laid out precisely in elaborate arrays. After chanting at length over the images, he or she spreads out the offerings of food and drink (and depending on the context, the blood of sacrificial fowl) over the entire display.

Nahua religion is pantheistic, we argue, and the exquisite cut-paper figures manifest the ubiquitous sacred force that people reverently call Totiotzin, "Our

Honored Divinity."[1] As revealed in their paper cuttings, Nahua religious practitioners temporarily extract different facets of Totiotzin on behalf of a patient-client or an entire community. Similar to the pictographs of the ancient codices, the paper cuttings serve to embody abstract concepts, encoding meaning through their iconographic content and particular arrangements. Our analysis is based on data gathered through long-term ethnographic field research among Nahuatl speakers in a setting where both the language and the ritual paper-figure complex are very much living traditions. Getting to know people who speak the Nahuatl language in daily interaction and who engage with an Indigenous spirit pantheon through presumably ancient ritual procedures is a profoundly moving experience that is hard to match. A bit of personal history will help set the stage for our account.

Typical of what happens to most ethnographers, our introduction to the Nahua occurred by serendipity. As a graduate student in anthropology at Indiana University in 1970, Alan was chosen to participate in a summer field school in Mexico and found himself dropped off in Amatlán, Ixhuatlán de Madero, a remote village of 600 people (about 80 percent of whom were monolingual speakers of Nahuatl) located in the hilly tropical forests of the Huasteca region of northern Veracruz. The initial stay in Amatlán (a pseudonym adopted to protect the privacy of community members) lasted only two months, but it was a life-changing experience for which he felt entirely unprepared. Alan knew little Spanish and no Nahuatl and had never lived far from the urban amenities that North Americans take for granted. He returned to the university that fall, chastened but determined to overcome shortcomings, and was surprised and delighted to discover that a professor in the Department of Spanish, Joe Campbell, had begun a study of the Nahuatl language. At first there was little field material to work with, but Joe insisted on employing what was at the time relatively new technology to help with the work. The effort was intense, as enormous computers that produced much noise and heat, using IBM cards to process operations and store data, were frequently declared to be "down," halting all progress. But it soon became clear that in addition to uncovering the structure of the language, Joe had a true passion for engaging firsthand with the Nahua people in Mexico. Alan was fortunate to join him in traveling to Tepoztlán, Morelos, and other communities where Nahuatl was (and still is) spoken. Following this brief apprenticeship, Alan returned to Amatlán in 1972 to conduct dissertation research knowing far more Nahuatl than

---

[1] As we explain elsewhere, without intending any disrespect (see Sandstrom and Sandstrom 2022b: xiii, 44n88), we prefer to put the Nahuatl names of spirit entities in lowercase italics unless they are directly addressed in chants or traditional stories to avoid fixing their identities as proper nouns, a common convention in naming the ancient Aztec deities. We capitalize and set in regular roman font the name of the most sacred Totiotzin, however, because of its universal nature encompassing everything in the cosmos.

Spanish. In 1975, Pamela joined in the ethnographic enterprise. Since then, the two of us have returned to Amatlán many times to continue what has amounted to a collaborative long-term research effort.

We have been privileged to witness and learn about many features of the culture of our Nahua colleagues, particularly their sophisticated religious beliefs and ritual practices. The religion called *el costumbre* in the local dialect of Spanish (using the article *el* in place of *la*, typically, thus marking the practice as their own) exhibits many enduring elements rooted in Nahua history, including ritual paper cutting. Indigenous practitioners continue to create figures out of paper in order to address spirit entities in elaborate crop-increase ceremonies and in ritual cleansings and curings to deal with illness, misfortune, and affliction. They typically cut the images from inexpensive mass-produced paper purchased in regional markets in place of the handmade bark paper (*amatl* in Nahuatl, *amate* in Spanish) manufactured and employed in the pre-Hispanic era, although the *amate* paper is still produced in Indigenous communities in the Sierra Norte de Puebla and on a limited scale in the Huasteca region. The ritual specialists use scissors to cut the paper into elaborate shapes, but in the past people employed obsidian blades to cut it into strips and banners to adorn temples and clothe priests, statues, and deity impersonators (*ixiptla* or *teixiptla*).[2] The *costumbre* practitioners may produce anthropomorphic images by the thousands for a single ritual offering, distinguishing individual spirit entities by iconographic cuts that reveal their place in the Nahua pantheon.[3]

After years of research, our conclusion is that the *costumbre* religion is a form of pantheism (Sandstrom and Sandstrom 1986, 249–280), an idea anticipated in the work of Hermann Beyer ([1910] 1965) and Eva Hunt (1977), and more fully developed by John Monaghan (2000) and especially James Maffie (2014). Pantheism, with its foundation in philosophical monism, differs from theistic religions based on philosophical dualism (such as Christianity) that insist on conceiving a creator deity separate from the creation or distinguishing the ontological status of ideas separate from their representations. For dualists, signifiers are distinct from what is signified, whereas in a monist's universe, signifier and signifed are isomorphic. The diversity that humans perceive as a kaleidoscope of beings and things is an illusion; viewed from the outlook of pantheism and monism, beings and things present

---

[2] Bassett (2015, 45–88) summarizes more than a century of scholarship on the subject of Aztec concepts of divinity and deity impersonators; Maffie (2014, 113–114) discusses the ontological status of the *ixiptla-teixiptla*.

[3] Information on the contemporary ritual use of paper by Nahua, Otomí, and Tepehua *costumbre* practitioners can be found in Dow (1986); Gessain (1938); Sandstrom (1978, 1981, 1986, 1991, 2003); Sandstrom and Sandstrom (1986, 2003, 2021, 2022a, 2022b); and Williams García (1963).

aspects, manifestations, or unfoldings of a single seamless totality. To reiterate, this encompassing principle is called Totiotzin, a Huastecan Nahuatl possessive honorific form of the classical concept of *teotl* or *tiotl*. The Spanish friars equated this divine force with the Christian God, but Nahuas then held (as they do now) a very different conception of divinity.

In such a universe, there is no absolute or exclusive good and evil (a dichotomy that is foundational to theistic religions), because these incompatible opposites are equally part of the divine. Threat and danger to human life are to be found in everything that disrupts the balance and equilibrium of the sacred cosmos. But these disruptions are no more evil than a virus or an earthquake. The entities portrayed in paper thus evoke the multiple aspects of Totiotzin rather than constitute a distinct set of spirits, beings, or deities. The paper images are concrete elements brought into physical existence by the ritual specialist in order to address specific problems such as preventing disease or curing affliction. The spirit entities thought to cause disease are conceived as disruptions—breaks, disturbances, interferences, or fractures—in the integrity of the cosmos. These polluting agents (characterized by the Nahua concept of *tlazolli*—refuse, trash, or disordered matter) are the source of human suffering and cosmic imbalance, poisoning bodies and social relations alike.[4]

The set of paper cuttings we illustrate and discuss was produced in 2007 by Encarnación Téllez Hernández, a respected ritual specialist known by his nickname Cirilo, who lived in Amatlán until his death in 2012. The task of such a person of knowledge is to set right the relations between the complex of spirit entities (again, the many aspects of Totiotzin) and the dependent human community. Rituals specialists accomplish this goal by engaging these elusive beings in systems of reciprocity—a form of social exchange, in which food offerings, tobacco, incense, music, and chanting are dedicated with the expectation that spirit entities are social beings who will respond with what people need for their lives and thus fulfill their end of the bargain. It takes years of training under a master for ritual specialists to achieve the status of recognized persons of knowledge who have the ability to assemble a clientele with confidence in their efficacy.

While we focus here on the cuttings of one prominent master, at least five additional ritual specialists were also resident in Amatlán during the years of our fieldwork, and many others live in communities throughout the region. The question arises of how representative is the sample presented here for the ritual paper-figure complex as a whole? If the paper cuttings are pictographs, to what degree are the meanings

---

[4] Mesoamerican conceptions of pantheism and monism are the focus of a growing body of literature that spans disciplinary boundaries. In Sandstrom and Sandstrom (2022a; 2022b, 59–71), we synthesize the key sources that have helped inform our reading of the Nahua view of divinity that underlies the ritual paper complex.

shared throughout the region? Even at this point in our research, which spans decades, we cannot fully answer these questions. Early on, we published a book comparing Nahua, Otomí, and Tepehua cuttings based on the limited sample available for study (Sandstrom and Sandstrom 1986). To our knowledge (aside from our own work among the Nahua), no other systematic studies have been published. It is our current understanding that *costumbre* practitioners and their followers throughout the Huasteca share beliefs about spirit entities that fall into several broad categories: the ubiquitous damaging or disease-spreading winds and death-dealing underworld entities that are sometimes implicated in sorcery attacks; the fertile seeds, earth, and water-related entities; celestial or meteorological-related entities such as the sun, stars, good gentle winds, clouds, and flags or banners; and various types of guardians and witnesses. Individual ritual specialists develop their own distinctive styles of portraying and presenting these entities, but they must conform to the culturally determined expectations of their followers. We have observed that masters invest considerable time and effort in training apprentices to carry on their ritual procedures, which creates localized designs and particular lineages of practice. We do not have sufficient information on the complex of *costumbre* paper cutting to be able to determine the degree to which people can decipher the images from different traditions, or whether variations in portrayal reveal some degree of competition among groups within the system. For our recent study of Nahua pilgrimage rituals and Nahuatl chanting (Sandstrom and Sandstrom 2022b), it was only after having spent many years in the field that were we able to acquire a systematic collection of images along with detailed information on their meaning and use.

## 2. READING THE PAPER FIGURES

To calm disturbances in the cosmic order, ritual specialists chant before elaborate altars and dedicate offerings to spirit entities in an effort to engage them to support and fulfill human needs and desires. They identify each by name, welcoming them to partake of the offerings and share in the general camaraderie of the ceremonial event. Words alone, however, are not enough. Master paper cutters must also give form to each spirit entity, and no offering is complete without the requisite images. For crop-fertility or rain-petition rituals and observances geared to the calendrical planting seasons, they cut a pantheon of figures evoking the sacred water, seeds, the earth's revered hills, Catholic saints, clouds, ritual implements such as walking sticks, and the altar itself. In Cirilo's lineage of practice, these paper creations are laid out precisely in units of twenty paired (i.e., twofold) figures in two overlapping rows on rectangular paper sheets called *petates*, a Spanish borrowing from the Nahuatl *petlatl* (sing.), the name for a woven palm sleeping mat. These *petates* with their paper figures are produced in great numbers. They are bundled in the order in which they will be used in rituals and finally laid out on top of and beneath the altar table in neat rows. This altar arrangement, replete with floral adornments and food offerings, including animal blood spread liberally over the paper figures, is called a *mezah* (in the Huastecan Nahuatl orthography), a borrowing of the Spanish word *mesa*, meaning both the table proper and the ritual offering laid on it (Monaghan 2003; Sullivan et al. 2016, 310; Sandstrom and Sandstrom 2022b, 17).

Cleansing-curing rituals such as we describe here, which aim either to cure a patient or prevent polluting forces from disrupting a ritual event, follow a similar plan but with several important differences. The paper figures evoke disease-causing winds, frightening underworld characters, and fearsome entities associated with bones, graveyards, sorcerers' malign intentions, and death. In Cirilo's customary way, the array of these dangerous figures are also laid out on *petates* but in units of twelve rather than twenty. These cuttings on paper beds, along with a set of large-scale paper figures of malevolent spirit entities associated with *mictlan* (literally, "place of the dead"), are laid on the bare earth directly, not on a raised platform. This display of dreaded entities also receives offerings of raw egg, food items, bottled beverages, cane alcohol (*aguardiente*), and tobacco. It is likewise called a *mezah* in Nahuatl, even though no actual altar table is involved. Offerings to these entities, however, are fewer in number and less abundant, and the procedure takes on a more somber air. The careful layout of assemblies of cut-paper figures in rituals designed to ensure crop yields or for various cleansing-curing procedures clearly constitutes the core feature of Nahua *costumbre* practice.

Following Elizabeth Boone, we make the case that the Nahua paper figures are a contemporary instance of a system of graphic communication that was widespread among the Indigenous people of pre-Columbian Mesoamerica and beyond, which likely traces to the pre-Classic Olmec period.[5] Boone writes that we lack a name for such a graphic system and suggests analysts call it "X," which she defines as "the practice and materiality of recording and interpreting knowledge of a specific nature by means of graphic or tactile marks that are made on or in a permanent or semipermanent substance (the permanence depending on the durability or fragility of the medium). The marks are conventionally understood within their societies to signify objects, events, identities, temporalities, relations, and other concepts and things" (2011b, 379). In short, this form of writing is not a "glottographic" system comprised of conventional symbols that approximate speech but is instead "pictographic"—a system that communicates directly to the observer through signs

---

[5] Boone (1994, 14–15), Houston (2004, 284), and Whittaker (2009, 2021) summarize what is known about pre-Hispanic Nahuatl writing.

or imagery. For the most part, the contemporary Nahua paper cuttings are iconographic in that they resemble what they are meant to convey and thus are recognizable to readers.

People who live in societies with alphabetic writing tend to believe that their type of glottographic communication is the advanced endpoint of a long evolutionary process that begins with pictography. This frankly ethnocentric viewpoint is expressed in the work of historian I. J. Gelb ([1952] 1963: 190), for whom writing always refers to graphic systems that reproduce spoken language. This conception is an example of presentism that falsely diminishes alternative communication systems according to Boone (1994, 4–13).[6] In contrast to alphabetic writing, pictographs can convey "meaning directly to the reader/viewer by means of graphic marks that signify within the conventions of its own system" (2016, 31). Like writing, pictographs have the ability to record across space and time the specific kinds of information and understandings that are important to people operating in a culture (2011b, 379, 381).

Boone claims that "pictography easily conveys a great range of data and thought, including entities, qualities and states of being, places, abstract concepts, actions and events, temporalities, appellatives, and the sounds of language" (2016, 34). Often overlooked, pictographs offer certain distinct advantages over writing. For one, they can be read by people who do not share a common language. The Aztecs could read Mixtec pictographs, for example, even though their languages were unrelated (1994, 19). Picture writing arguably has the potential to elicit a wider range of knowledge, emotion, and interpretations than writing tied to speech. Writing systems tend to be linear in presentation so that they can mimic language, while picture writing can be arranged in any number of ways to enhance whatever is being recorded. Finally, pictographic systems tend to combine aesthetic expression and communication in a way that is rarely achieved through alphabetic writing systems alone.

The ancient pictographic systems of Mesoamerica are examples of a broader form of communication that Gelb ([1952] 1963: 11–13) called "semasiography" to distinguish graphic expressions from alphabetic systems based on spoken language. Gelb derived the term from the Greek *sēmasía*, referring to "meaning or signification," plus *graphē*, "writing" (190–191). Though the technical term is not widely used today even among linguists, we adopt it, shorn of its unilineal bias, in the analysis that follows. "Semasiographic systems of communication," as defined by

---

[6] Marcus (1992, 17) defines true writing as signs reproducing spoken language, but at the same time she asserts that "the differences between Near Eastern and Mesoamerican writing that have lowered Gelb's opinion of the latter have more to do with the *functions of early writing in the two areas* than with the level of cultural achievement" (19; emphasis in original).

Boone (1994, 15), "convey ideas independently from language and on the same logical level as spoken language rather than being parasitic on them as ordinary scripts are. They are supralinguistic because they can function outside of language." Gordon Whittaker (2021) illustrates convincingly that many Aztec pictographs did convey meaning by referring to the sounds of speech, but the overwhelming majority of these signs communicated directly to the reader and not through spoken language. Examples of semasiographic communication are found in virtually all cultures throughout the world, not least in Europe despite its long tradition of literacy founded on alphabetic writing.

Boone distinguishes two types of semasiographic systems: conventional and iconic. In conventional systems, meaning is encoded in arbitrary signs or symbols. Examples in the European tradition include systems for presenting mathematical equations, scientific rendering in chemistry, and musical or choreographic notation. In iconic systems, signs convey meaning directly because they resemble what they are meant to represent. Examples include international road or airport signs, and the many functions shown on computer screens, keyboards, and other machines (Boone 1994, 16). In European history, the stained-glass windows of medieval cathedrals are models of iconic semasiography where artists rendered biblical themes in spectacular, emotion-laden displays. The illuminated windows were created to inform a largely illiterate population for whom written accounts would be meaningless. Contemporary case examples of semasiography's ingenuity and appeal include graphic novels or comic books that, like technical manuals, artfully integrate pictures and words in ways that often equal or surpass information conveyed by writing alone.

In Mesoamerica, pictographs were made into permanent fixtures when they were carved into monuments or used to embellish architecture.[7] Messages were also conveyed in books made from deerskin or bark paper that included historical accounts, almanacs, calendars, divination manuals, or treatises on natural history. Mesoamerican pictographs were generally rendered without depth or dimension, and the area around the figures was likewise flat; incidentally, most alphabetic writing systems share the same features of two-dimensionality on a flat ground. The pictographs resembled what they were meant to portray: human beings were rendered with unmistakable heads, torsos, arms, and legs and so were recognizable to people from different cultural traditions and historical eras. They were not, however, realistically portrayed or designed to create the illusion of three-dimensional space, as found in representational art. Thus, "figures are arranged to display the most

---

[7] Wright-Carr (2017) documents how Otomí craftsmen incorporated semasiographic messages in the stonework of sixteenth-century churches in Mexico.

characteristic features of the different parts, which means that heads and limbs in profile extend from torsos that are usually frontal" (Boone 2011a, 200).

It is our contention that the anthropomorphic cut-paper images featured so prominently in Nahua rituals derive from this ancient, widespread semasiographic system. Boone points out that a "complex pictographic image is also accretive and agglutinative, being composed of multiple visual elements that are added to a core" (2016, 33), as we similarly have described the paper figures with their core-adjunct composition (Sandstrom and Sandstrom 1986, 272–275). Boone could be referring to the layout of the paper figures during performance of a cleansing-curing ritual when she writes (2011a, 197) that extant pictography of past Mesoamerican cultures "employed figures and symbols to encode semantic meaning that relied on spatial arrangements of these figures to provide relational syntax." The images become meaningful and efficacious when laid out in patterned arrays for particular purposes, while chanting by the ritual participants conveys supplemental information. For the contemporary Nahua, however, the pictographs depicted in cut paper do not merely *symbolize* the spirit entities but rather *embody* them, thus providing viewers with unmediated access to the divine.

Picture writing among the Aztecs (just as for today's paper cutters) "allowed individuals to convey information across time and space," and it was part of the information technology "in which their societies invested prodigious amounts of cultural and human energy" (Boone 2011b, 380). Accordingly, semasiographic systems "not only functioned to record information and ideas, they also were significant sites of discourse between people. They set the stages and became the foundations of ceremonies and other actions on which their societies depended" (388). Of course, the application of semasiography to Mesoamerican graphical systems is not without controversy. The monumental work by Katarzyna Mikulska (2015) on deciphering the Mesoamerican graphic communication system expressed in the divinatory codices covers the extensive scholarly debates over definitions of writing and other systems of recording information. An edited volume by Mikulska and Jerome Offner (2019) offers a cogent rethinking of the complexities underlying Indigenous graphic communications systems. Our documentation of one master ritual specialist's lifelong practice of ritual paper cutting for cleansing-curings gives witness to a hitherto little-known Mesoamerican pictographic system that, we argue, exemplifies insights from Boone's analysis of the ancient documents and inscriptions. Cirilo's command of the enormous amount of information contained in this pictographic system powerfully and yet parsimoniously communicates his shared monistic conception of the fundamental nature of reality.

A few preliminary observations may help confirm the relationships between the paper figures of contemporary *costumbre* religious practice and the Indigenous

Mesoamerican tradition of picture writing. Gelb notes that "both the old Mexican writings and the more modern writings of the American Indians frequently employ a method of coloring the signs" ([1952] 196: 19). In semasiographic communication systems, color is one means to convey information. Color in alphabetic signs, by contrast, is more typically a decorative technique that rarely conveys meaning. We will see that certain images of the malevolent winds are created from paper of various colors, whereas those without color identifiers are sometimes blackened with charcoal from the fireplace to link them to polluted, disordered places. And unlike signs in alphabetic writing, semasiographic signs do not need to be presented in a specific order to convey meaning (193). Laying out the paper images in a cleansing-curing array presents a multidimensional message to people, without the requirement of any narrative line. The following statement by Isabel Laack (2019, 193) about the importance of seeing as a Nahua cultural value applies to the pre-Hispanic pictographic system but equally so to the contemporary ritual paper-figure complex:

> The pictorial writing system by itself strongly emphasized the act of seeing. While it tells us little about the thoughts, ideas, and motivations of the protagonists, it strongly presents visual aspects of individual identities, places, or situations. The Central Mexican pictorial sources place particular emphasis on the attire, ceremonial implements, adornments, and paraphernalia of deities and deity impersonators, sometimes depicted elaborately, sometimes abbreviated.... These rich associations with qualities, emotions, activities, cognitive concepts, and cosmic relationships can be quickly perceived and imagined by a literate Indigenous reader of pictorial writing and much more easily than if they had been recorded in alphabetic writing.

The well-ordered display of disease-causing agents cut from ephemeral paper holds the same power for people who behold the drama of a cleansing-curing performance enacted on their behalf.

### 3. SPIRIT ENTITIES AND THEIR EMBODIMENTS

In the discussion that follows, we focus on the set of dangerous entities whose images are the focus of Cirilo's general cleansings to prevent disease as well as rituals aimed at healing or curing particular ailments. This type of ritual is called *ochpantli* in Nahuatl (from the verb *ochpana*, "to sweep") and *barrida* in Spanish, meaning "sweeping." For the Nahua *costumbre* practitioners of Amatlán, cleansings and curings are essentially identical procedures and the concepts are interchangeable. The specific goal of cleansing-curings is to banish disease-causing agents and remove obstacles to health and well-being from a person's body, a designated place, or a particular event. Some degree of variation can be observed in the arrangements of the offerings by different ritual specialists. In our case study of Cirilo's practice over nearly four decades, his layouts have varied only in minor ways, as the following selection of photos will illustrate. The cuttings are produced as two-ply anthropomorphic figures from *papel de china* (colored tissue paper) or *papel revolución* (off-white newsprint). When color is deemed important, the two layers are usually the same, although Cirilo would occasionally layer together different colors of paper. As we have noted, the ritual specialist methodically and respectfully lays out these embodiments of malevolent forces in a fixed pattern with certain ones placed atop *petates* and others laid directly on the earth.

The cleansing-curing procedure usually takes place in the ritual specialist's *xochicalli* ("flower house"), either a purpose-built shrine or just a corner of the practitioner's dwelling, or it may be performed in a client's house. For community-wide rituals aimed at ensuring a good harvest or for pilgrimages, the cleansing typically precedes the major ritual action and occurs outdoors, often in the dead of night. After chanting over the array, the practitioner casts the offerings directly onto the paper figures. Following a brief interval during which time the spirits are said to consume the food and drink, the sodden figures are gathered up, formed into a neat bundle, and hidden far off in the forest so as not to infect others. While chanting, the ritual specialist names the spirit entities portrayed and directs each to find their image, accept the offering, and once satiated, to leave the patient.

Cirilo is seated just outside the frame of the picture (in figure 10.1), facing the incense brazier, his arrangement of cut-paper figures and offerings at the ready: an egg, cups containing coffee and pieces of bread, and bottles of Coca Cola and cane alcohol. Beeswax-colored paraffin candles (left) and tallow candles (right) have been placed on bundles of palm-and-marigold adornments that serve as brooms to sweep the ritual participants. After the cleansing, the clients will take the sacralized paraffin candles home to burn on their home altar. Four large paper figures of a spirit entity from the underworld called *tlacatecolotl* ("man owl") stand at the base of the array. Cirilo has marked them with charcoal from the fireplace and placed lighted cigarettes in their mouths as a tobacco offering.[8] On top of these underworld figures Cirilo has arranged four small figures with their hands folded across the mouths and held in place by a drop of a plant-based glue; we surmised at the

---

[8] Sandstrom (1989, 359–361) describes this cleansing-curing procedure that took place in September 1985 (not, as stated, in 1986); see additional photos and a diagram of the preliminary cleansing array (1989, 365–369, 372; 2003, 54, fig. 3) and drawings (1989, 371, figs. G–H) of two distinctive paper cuttings that we now recognize as *tlacatecolotl*. At the time, Cirilo identified each as an *ehecatl* (dangerous wind), associating them with *diablos* ("devils") and cats (sing., *mizton*, in the Huastecan Nahuatl orthography, following Sullivan et al. 2016).

**Figure 10.1.** Cirilo performed a cleansing-curing ritual for a client in September 1985 whose immediate family members had been ill. His divination procedure, involving casting kernels of maize, determined that neighbors' invidious gossip had caused agents of disease to infect the patients. Photo by the authors.

time that these invoked the trouble caused by gossip. A marigold-decorated loop called *xochimecatl* ("flowered vine") or *rosario* ("rosary" in Spanish) surrounds the array and serves to contain these malignant winds. Also encircling the display are paired cuttings of a type of wind tied onto packets of leaves from a species of the *amatl* tree (family Moraceae, genus *Ficus*), placed neatly at intervals. Years later Cirilo identified these generalized winds as "soldiers."[9] At the periphery of the array are piles of intricate cuttings called *tlacotontli* ("something cut smaller") produced from colored paper, which we will discuss later in the chapter.

In the photo, Cirilo has just finished laying out his cut-paper figures along with floral adornments and items for the offerings and is about to begin chanting over the display. The array in figure 10.1 is similar to those of figures 10.2 and 10.3, but a close comparison presents some striking differences. The photos document the layout we have observed frequently in Cirilo's repertoire, with the rectangular *petates* at the center holding an assortment of twelve white and twelve colorful paper figures of the winds. Often, these cuttings are referred to collectively by the Nahuatl

---

[9] See further discussion of this class of winds in Sandstrom and Sandstrom (2022b, 224).

NAHUA CURING THROUGH GRAPHIC COMMUNICATION    241

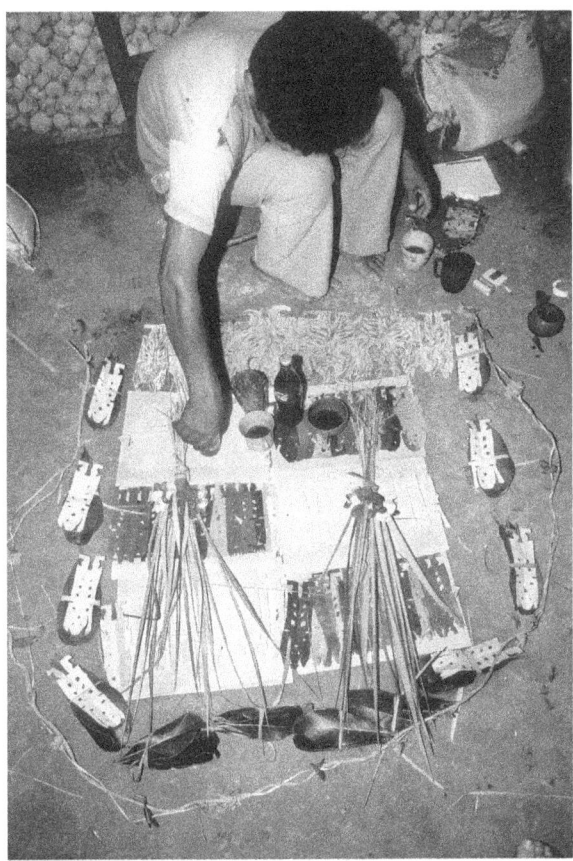

Figure 10.2. In May 1986, Cirilo performed an elaborate cleansing-curing ritual for us and our three-year-old son to protect us from harm on our return to the US after a nine-month stay in the village. Photo by the authors.

term *ehecatl* (plural, *ehecameh*), meaning "wind(s)" but implying "bad wind(s)," and *malos vientos* or *malos aires* when speaking Spanish. The four *petates* in figure 10.1 show the white- and colored-paper cuttings alternating in an X-shaped pattern that is reversed in the other photos, but we do not know if this variation is intended or even significant. Several prominent piles of the elaborate *tlacotontli* cuttings can be seen positioned around the arrays in figures 10.1 and 10.3 (but they are absent in figure 10.2). Visible in figures 10.1 and 10.2 (but missing from figure 10.3) are the cuttings of soldier winds tied onto the packets of leaves encircling the array. Another notable difference in figure 10.2 is Cirilo's creation of six instead of four *petates* for the central component, although these rectangular beds holding white and colorful winds are juxtaposed in the same alternating pattern.

Another cleansing performed by the ritual specialist in 2007 further illustrates a high degree of continuity alongside the variations. After he laid the body of the

**Figure 10.3.** In this photo (also taken by the authors in May 1986), Cirilo is shown chanting over another array in a cleansing-curing episode that preceded a crop-increase ritual hosted by a family to ensure a productive rainy-season planting.

sacrificed fowl atop the offerings and placed lighted candles around the display in figure 10.4, Cirilo proceeded to distribute the remaining offerings of raw egg, bread soaked in coffee, soft drinks, beer, and cane alcohol over the entire array. Although this array (like the previous, in figure 10.3) did not include soldier winds tied on leaf packets, each of the *tlacotontli*—something-cut-smaller figures piled on bunches of herbs outside the flowered loop—received a share of the libations. The procedure this time, however, was unusual in our experience in that it featured a blood offering, which we had never before observed for a cleansing-curing episode, even though the precious substance is a prominent component of the *mezah* altar offering for many Nahua and Otomí *costumbre* practitioners.[10]

---

[10] In Sandstrom (2003, 57), the statement that the dangerous assembly of winds never receive blood "for fear that it would add to their strength" must stand corrected; see our further analysis of blood offerings in Sandstrom and Sandstrom (2022b, 103).

**Figure 10.4.** In this 2007 cleansing-curing ritual for a young female client with a chronic condition, the photo shows Cirilo's layout after he had sprinkled the blood of a chick over the charcoal-blackened figures of winds from the underworld. Photo by the authors.

Figure 10.5 summarizes the range of variations that we have observed from 1973 to 2007 in Cirilo's orderly configurations of the infectious wind spirits, offerings, and implements. The detail (labeled A) shows the layout for a cleansing conducted in March 1973 prior to a major community-wide crop-increase ritual that featured eight *petates* of the winds at the center surrounded by twelve charcoal-blackened cuttings of the *tlacatecolotl*–man owl paper figure. The array included the *tlacotontli* and soldier winds in full force and contained many multiples of the cuttings of these two types of dangerous winds. As part of Cirilo's training in the ritual techniques, the 1973 ceremony was conducted jointly by Cirilo and his mentor, the Otomí master Evaristo de la Cruz, who had traveled to Amatlán from Cruz Blanca, a small hamlet in the vicinity of the multiethnic municipal head town of Ixhuatlán de Madero, close to the Puebla border.[11] The layouts labeled B, C, D, and E document, respectively, the variations shown in photos in figure 10.1 (1985), figure 10.2 (1986), figure 10.3 (1986), and figure 10.4 (2007).

---

[11] The description of this twelve-day *xochitlalia* observance and preliminary cleansing in Sandstrom and Sandstrom (1986, 39–43) includes a diagram (following page 39) of the cleansing array recorded in our fieldnotes, but we have no photographs of the proceedings.

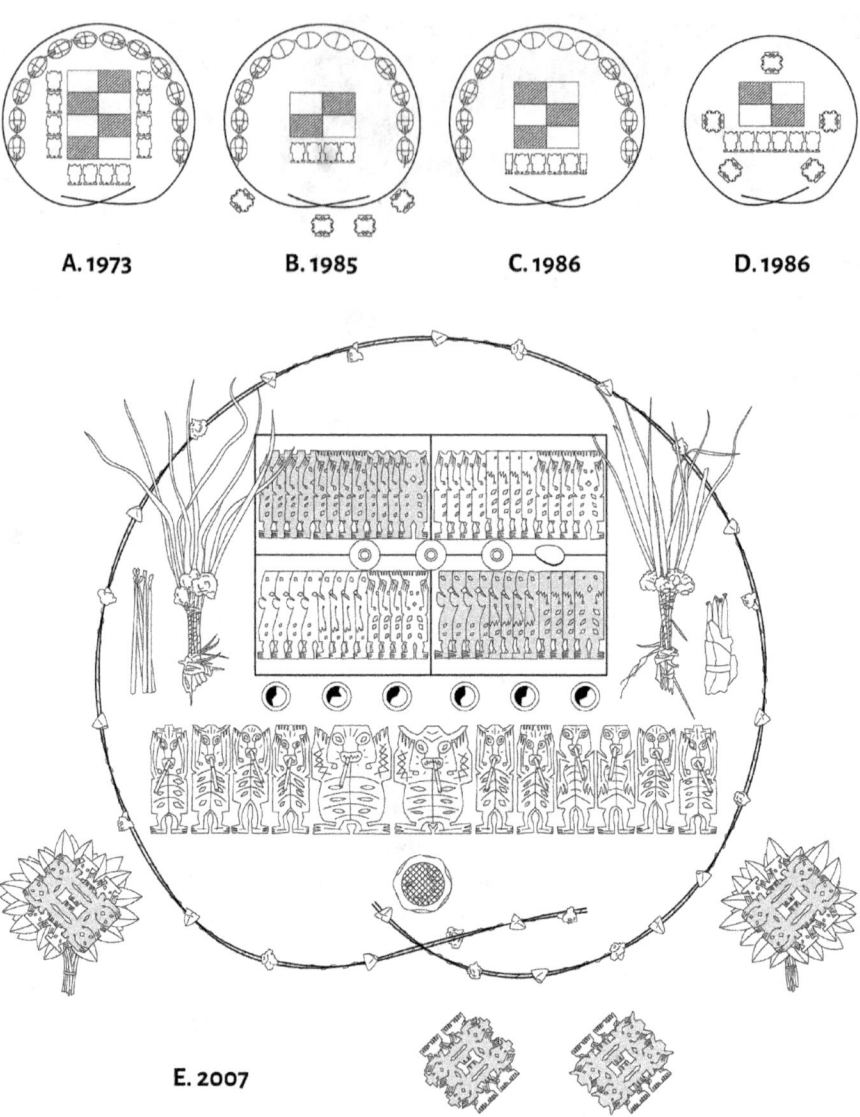

**Figure 10.5.** A rendering of the variations in ritual specialist Encarnación (Cirilo) Téllez Hernández's standard arrays for cleansing and curing. The diagram drawn by Michael A. Sandstrom is adapted from his drawings that accompany descriptions of cleansing-curing procedures to counteract sorcery (Sandstrom and Sandstrom 2021, 96, fig. 3.3) and to deflect polluting agents from *atlatlacualtiliztli* rain-petition rituals (2022b, 121, fig. 6.2).

At the center of the array are typically four (or as we have observed, sometimes six or eight) rectangular paper *petates* holding paired cuttings of different sets of the winds (whose individual identities we discuss in the following section). At the base of the display are numbers of charcoal-blackened paper images associated with death and the underworld. These fearsome entities typically have lighted cigarettes placed in their mouths as a tobacco offering. The whole tabular array is encircled by the vine-and-marigold loop that not only imprisons the wind spirits that come to partake of the offerings but plays an important role in cleansing the participants. As part of Cirilo's standard routine, groups of people step into and out of the loop in unison, as it is raised seven times and lowered seven times over them. Just outside loop may lie four (or more) piles of the highly infectious *tlacotontli* figures. When not omitted altogether, these cuttings lie atop bundles of herbs, packets of earth from the patient's house floor, or a container of water from their place of bathing. Inside the loop are palm-and-marigold brooms that the curer uses to sweep the ritual participants and rid their bodies of lurking disease agents. Bundles of beeswax-colored paraffin candles (left) and tallow candles (right) are added to the display. The ritual specialist arranges bottled drinks along with cups containing coffee and bread on top of the paper figures, and places lighted candles around the periphery. During the course of the ritual, he takes up the copal-incense brazier positioned at the base of the display and chants at length, naming the spirit entities and directing them to partake of the offerings that he spreads out over the entire array.

The arrangement of paper figures, whether for a cleansing-curing episode prior to a major public observance or for a client to prevent or cure disease, presents a pictorial summation of the precarious nature of reality. Understood as an orderly but nonhierarchical whole, it is a statement that outlines the elements of disease, disorder, and death that have power to afflict human beings and the entire cosmos. Each of the cut-paper images embodies a type of disruption, interference, or obstacle to maintaining the delicate equilibrium between the entire world and the human community. People depend on a near-constant round of rituals to achieve and maintain this balance. Repeated cleansing episodes within larger ritual events address these negative forces directly, without ambiguity, and through chanting the ritual specialist admonishes the disruptive spirit entities to vacate the area. The physical presence of the paper figures communicates a significant amount of information to ritual participants who are able to read (with greater or lesser facility) their iconographic content and thereby enrich and deepen their own experience of the ritual proceedings.

## 4. FACING THE FORCES OF DISEQUILIBRIUM

The ritual paper figures created for cleansing-curing procedures are but a portion of Cirilo's repertoire, refined and amplified over more than four decades. In our study of Nahua pilgrimage rituals (Sandstrom and Sandstrom 2022b), we illustrate and discuss the iconography of several ritual specialists' cuttings, showing how the pairing of headdress and body designs yield a practitioner's design vocabulary. Here we offer a brief summary of the graphic-design principles of one master and the messages they convey. We begin by focusing on a complete set of Cirilo's paper figures produced in 2007 to analyze what constitutes his basic cleansing array.[12]

The first ritual paper cutting we examine is *tlacatecolotl* in Nahuatl (*hombre búho* in Spanish), which we translate as "man owl" (figure 10.6). According to people we talked to, this spirit entity leads the souls of the dead who reside in the underworld. The name *tlacatecolotl* is a compound of *tlacatl* ("man," "human being") and *tecolotl* ("owl"), a bird associated with darkness and death among many Indigenous people in Mesoamerica. His consort's name includes *cihuatl*, meaning "woman" (or "wife" in its possessive form); as one might expect, the Nahua spirit pantheon reflects human marital relations. To reinforce the connection with souls of the dead, these dual aspects of *tlacatecolotl* are portrayed with rib holes, a convention revealing skeletons. Both have jagged, dangerous-looking teeth and the male figure has pronounced animal horns and the suggestion of a tail. By associating these cuttings with animals, the ritual specialist is linking them to wild, untamed creatures of the tropical forest. Unlike her mate, man owl woman lacks a headdress. In Cirilo's design scheme, a pair of figures with and without headdresses that share a name indicates opposite gender (and presence or absence of headgear in some cuttings in his repertoire appears to reveal binary oppositions other than gender). Additional variations on the horned-headdress designs can be made out in the photos.

Cirilo establishes the uncontrolled and dangerous nature of these and other underworld figures by blackening them with charcoal from the fireplace before lining them up at the base of his cleansing array. This treatment links the creatures with disorder and pollution. People say that they "do whatever they want," unconstrained by human values and posing a constant danger to everyone. The dual-aspect figure

---

[12] Sandstrom and Sandstrom (2022b, 22–23, 181, 365) explains how we commissioned Cirilo and his colleagues to produce a complete set of paper cuttings similar to what he would prepare for a major pilgrimage, and we describe in detail their materials and methods of manufacture (2022b, 87–88, 207–225). Note that each paper figure illustrated is actually doubled, cut from two layers of paper; the labels identify the number of such paired cuttings in Cirilo's standard array. Graphic artist Ana Laura Ávila-Myers created the vector drawings from photographs of the originals.

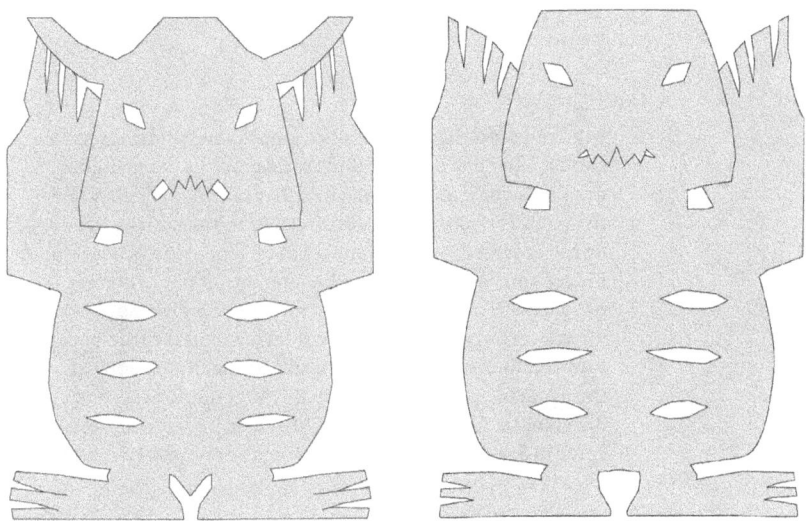

**Figure 10.6.** *Tlacatecolotl* and *tlacatecolotl cihuatl* (two large white paired cuttings, blackened with charcoal). Cirilo's cuttings of man owl and man owl woman over the years have featured various horned headdress designs and vary somewhat in size. Figures he cut in 2007 (here reproduced from Sandstrom and Sandstrom 2022b, 210–211, table 6.1, 212, figs. 00-01 and 00-02) measured 17–17.5 × 23.5–24 centimeters.

of *tlacatecolotl* is sometimes associated with another malevolent character named *tlahueliloc*, Nahuatl for "wrath" or "anger" (or poetically, "wrathful one"), who exemplifies personal disorderliness and social discord. Spanish missionaries over the centuries have tried to convince people that man owl is equivalent to the Christian Devil, and several people in Amatlán articulated this belief when we asked about it. However, the Indigenous conception shares few characteristics that this embodiment of evil holds for Christians. For instance, during Carnival (*nanahuatilli* in Nahuatl, *el carnaval* in Spanish), masked dancers called *mecos* (from *chichimecos*, referring to the hunter-gatherer peoples of the north) go rampaging through the village, playfully causing mayhem and breaking rules of decorum. People say the *mecos*, along with souls of the dead, are led by *tlacatecolotl*.[13] Neither purely evil nor even necessarily the opposite of good (again, these categories reflect a decidedly Euro-American view of the world), they are social beings who may enter into exchanges with humans. When someone is feared to be dying, for example, they can be convinced to save the person's life (Sandstrom and Sandstrom 2021). With this description of only the first

---

[13] Báez-Jorge and Gómez Martínez (2001) link the figure of *tlacatecolotl* (styled Tlacatecolotl) to the pre-Hispanic trickster deity Tezcatlipoca, Smoking Mirror.

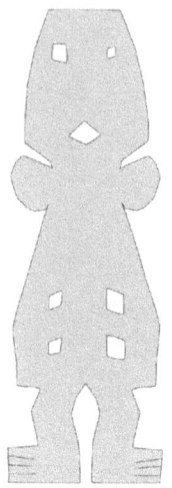

**Figure 10.7.** *Miquiliztli ehecatl* (four paired cuttings in four colors, plus four paired white cuttings). This paper-figure design, accompanied by the next five cuttings (figures 10.8 to 10.12), is relatively small compared to the cuttings of the horde of large-bodied winds lined up alongside man owl and his consort, as we will describe. The sets of paper cuttings produced in multiples from white newsprint measure 5–5.5 × 17.5 centimeters, and those cut from colored tissue paper measure 6–6.5 × 18.5–19 centimeters; the dimensions of the available paper sheets probably account for these size differences. These images are illustrated in grayscale and color in Sandstrom and Sandstrom (2022b, 209–211, table 6.1, 212–215, figs. 00-03 to 00-08).

prominent figures deployed during a ritual cleansing, already one can appreciate that the paper pictographs contain a great deal of information and emotional content to be interpreted by the participants. Seeing the blackened figures surrounded by their minions carries a powerful, even terrifying, message.

One member of the group Cirilo identified as *miquiliztli* or *miquiliztli ehecatl*, meaning "death" or "death wind" (*viento de muerte* in Spanish), although some people also call it simply *ehecatl* (figure 10.7). Death wind is embodied in the form of four anthropomorphic images, identical to one another and their counterparts cut from white paper except for color: yellow and red (usually associated with the sun), black (earth), and green (water). The range of colors probably indicates that the menace of death comes at a person from many directions. Telltale rib holes associate this entity with skeletal bodies of the dead, and its truncated wing-like arms allow it to take flight, like the wind. This terrifying creature infests the whole cosmos and particularly likes to attack unsuspecting people as they walk along trails. Like man owl, death is dangerous although not evil as it, too, enters into exchanges with human beings.

According to the ritual specialist, death likes to travel around with the generalized bad winds but particularly likes the company of *miccatzitzin ehecatl*, or "corpses wind" (*viento de cadáveres* in Spanish) (figure 10.8). Cirilo said it comes from the buried bones of dead people and stated that the position of the figure's arms pointing downward associate it with *tlalli* (the earth), *mictlan* (the place of the dead), and *miquiliztli* (death itself). In white and colored embodiments, its hands are

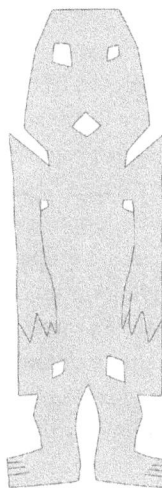 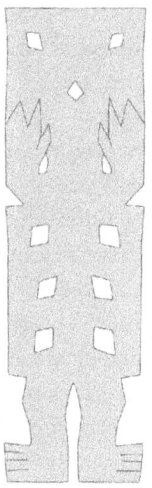

**Figure 10.8.** *Miccatzitzin ehecatl* (four paired cuttings in four colors, plus four paired white cuttings).

**Figure 10.9.** *Ehecatl* (four paired cuttings in four colors, plus four paired white cuttings).

wing-like because it too is a dangerous wind that flies about sickening people and causing tragedy to strike. Cirilo cut these figures in two shades of red paper, along with black and yellow. The two diamond-shaped cuts near the tops of the legs are probably rib holes. One can imagine the nightmare-like associations that people have when contemplating corpses wind.

Cirilo identified the next generalized wind simply as *ehecatl* ("bad wind" or "bad air," *mal aire* in Spanish), giving it no other special designation (figure 10.9). Its rib holes, like the others, are a clear indication of the spirit entity's dangerous nature. The creature travels around at night searching for victims to sicken or kill. Nighttime in Nahua culture is thought to be a dangerous period when the protective sun departs, leaving people vulnerable to attack. Stars are seen by many people as guardians who watch over humanity until the sun's return. Shooting stars are their arrows, aimed to kill or immobilize dangerous spirit entities. The upraised hands of this paper figure are cut out of its block-like square head (or perhaps headdress). It appears in the usual mix of white newsprint and four colors of tissue paper (purple, yellow, green, black) to indicate the wide range of places where it threatens. Cirilo stated that this figure is the rather sociable companion of death and corpses wind, since the three spirit entities like to travel around together.

Before we describe the next three figures, it is important to emphasize how clearly the paper figures reveal a form of duality that is at the heart of Nahua metaphysical thought (and see further discussion, below). Many images, like man owl and man owl woman, are manifested as male-female binaries, whereas others may reveal some essential polarity or opposition by distinguishing their salutary-benevolent versus dangerous-malevolent natures. A paper figure embodying bad winds as bringers of suffering, for instance, stands in opposition to good winds that blow in the rain-producing clouds that fertilize the milpas. The cross is one such multivalent icon, an embodiment of the life-giving sun and, by associating the sun with Jesus, one of the most powerful and positive manifestations of Totiotzin for the Nahuas today. However, we see also an example of the anti-cross embodied in this cutting of *caruz ehecatl*, "cross wind" (figure 10.10). Its name *caruz* is the Nahuatl pronunciation of the Spanish *cruz*, while its full name in Spanish is *mal aire de la cruz* (literally, "bad air of the cross"). The cross as portrayed in this cutting comes from beneath the earth (not from the sky), and like all harmful winds, it causes illness and affliction. Cirilo specified that the paper figure reveals the male aspect of this spirit entity, but he did not point out its female counterpart. The typical square shape of the body depicts a common item of apparel for Nahua—the *jorongo* (also *poncho* in other Spanish dialects). The figure is cut with rib holes and its headdress prominently features a cross shape. Its colors of purple, black, yellow, and green (in addition to its replicas in white) convey the message that it is ubiquitous.

An excellent example of Nahua spirit entities' ambiguous nature (especially from the Euro-American perspective) is found in the malevolent figure *tlalli ehecatl* ("earth wind"), *viento de la tierra* in Spanish (figure 10.11). The sacred earth, which supports the revered mountains, is one of the most powerful and beneficent entities in the Nahua pantheon. People often simply refer to the earth as "Dios/*dios*" (or "God/god"), but when speaking Nahuatl they understand this supreme being as Totiotzin/*totiotzin*, sacredness itself, as we have emphasized. To indicate its central importance, people readily acknowledge that from the earth comes all wealth, water, fertility, maize, and the very possibility of life. And yet here is earth wind, which causes disease and adversity. It is cut with the customary rib holes and has a modified headdress closely resembling that of the beneficent earth spirit, depicting tree trunks emerging from the top of the head. It is cut in its different aspects in red, purple, blue, and yellow paper, underscoring its ties to the earth (the purple color) and its ubiquity (the other colors). Again, the white versions are also prominently on display.

The figure called *atl ehecatl* ("water wind"), *viento de agua* in Spanish (figure 10.12) embodies the malevolent side of the precious liquid sought by Nahua farmers

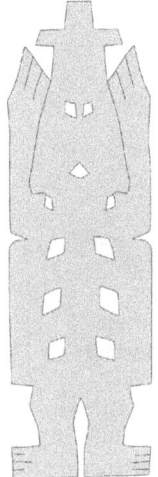 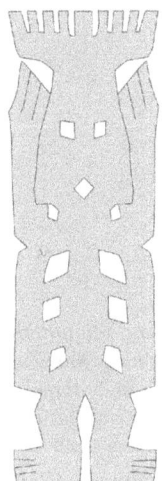 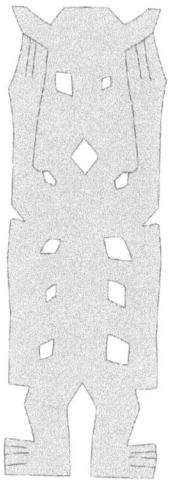

**Figure 10.10.** *Caruz ehecatl* (four paired cuttings in four colors, plus four paired white cuttings).

**Figure 10.11.** *Tlalli ehecatl* (four paired cuttings in four colors, plus four paired white cuttings).

**Figure 10.12.** *Atl ehecatl* (four paired cuttings in four colors, plus four paired white cuttings).

during pilgrimages to sacred mountains. This malevolent entity, an embodiment of the self-same water that is crucial to the survival of slash-and-burn horticulturalists, appears to be the antithesis of *apanchaneh*, the water dweller who sprinkles rainwater on the fields. However, the situation is more complex and the character of this water spirit, like all Nahua spirit entities, is decidedly ambiguous. In the myths told about *apanchaneh*, she is quite capable of destructive and seemingly unfair behavior. She punishes an innocent man when his wife gives away the fish he has caught, she demands the life of a man's guiltless son when he injures her children the fish, and she punishes all humanity by withholding her bounty because of the disrespect of a few. The aspect of *apanchaneh* embodied in this paper figure, sometimes referred to simply as "bad water," is invoked in cleansing-curing rituals to deflect attacks on people while they are bathing in the arroyo. The creature is said to be attracted to situations in which people exhibit envious behavior, and it also causes them to listen to bad counsel, leading to disastrous decisions. Its paper image features headgear that links it unmistakably to water iconography, but also, resembling the animal horns of man owl, associates it with untamed, wild places. Rib holes are evident, and the figure is cut from yellow, green, red, and purple paper as well as white to point out its wide dispersal.

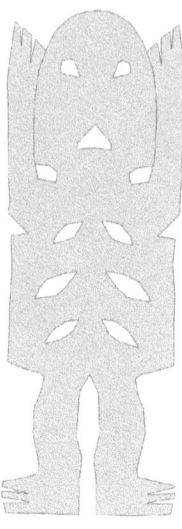

**Figure 10.13.** *Miquiliztli ehecatl* (two large white paired cuttings). Along with the five pairs of winds flanking the male-female *tlacatecolotl* duo at the bottom-center of the array shown in figure 10.5, these paper figures of *muertito* or "little dead one wind" are narrow and tall; cut from white newsprint, they measure 8–8.5 × 23.5–24 centimeters.

Thus far, the assembly includes six distinct wind spirits (death, corpses wind, the generalized bad wind, cross wind, earth wind, and water wind) who appear in color and white sets of four cuttings each, for a total of forty-eight two-ply figures. Cirilo reassembled them into four groups of twelve cuttings, neatly laying them on four (or more) paper *petates* and arranging them into a grid pattern at the center of the array (as the photos and diagrams show). We can see that it is the ritual specialist's strategy to force these exemplars of disorder into an orderly arrangement, an island of order in the disrupted world of disease-causing agents that demonstrates the state of equilibrium and universal basis for health and well-being.

Cirilo duplicated all but one of the cuttings we have examined in a larger format in white paper as if to reiterate—much like repetition in chanting—their constant threat and ever-present danger. Their white color may be associated with the cold rain and storms originating in the north, but it is unambiguously the color of bones, linking these figures with the underworld and death. He produced twofold pairs of cuttings of corpses wind and cross wind, specifying that the larger cross comes "from below." He also cut large versions of earth wind and water wind, but not the generalized bad wind. Only one large *ehecatl* (figure 10.13) has a unique design (compare that of *miquiliztli*, death itself, figure 10.7), which he distinguished also in name by referring to it in Spanish as *muertito*, or "little dead one wind." The other oversized cuttings of the dangerous winds each resemble their aforementioned namesakes.

He explained that this aspect of death wind travels around at night as a companion of cross wind and corpses wind. The cutting reveals the standard iconography

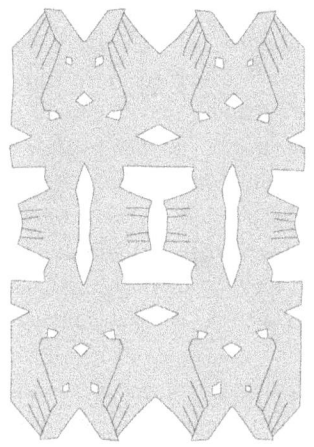

**Figure 10.14.** *Tlacotontli* (multiple paired cuttings in assorted colors). We illustrate 14 different designs in color in Sandstrom and Sandstrom (2022b, 211, table. 6.1, 215–216, figs. 00-09 to 00-21), and elsewhere show them folded to illustrate how these double-layered images are cut (2021, 95, fig. 3.2). Conjoined as four anthropomorphic figures attached at the feet and the sides, the individual units are much smaller than other winds, only about 6 × 9 centimeters. When the four figures are opened, the cuttings measure 12–12.5 × 17.5–18.5 centimeters.

of death with rib holes, although he gave it upraised arms unlike the smaller images of death with their wing-like protuberances. Altogether, he placed five pairs of the oversized cuttings in a row alongside man owl and his consort, directly on the earth (as figure 10.4 and figure 10.5 illustrate). The lineup of this malignant horde at the base of the array, where the ritual specialist sits before its entirety, makes it appear as if they are faced off against one another. Their size and precise arrangement likely indicates the relative importance of these *ehecameh*, or dangerous winds, in the Nahua pantheon. But even so, being smaller does not necessarily reduce their power, as the next class of fearful beings demonstrates.

An important part of many cleansing-curing arrays is the series of diminutive cuttings called *tlacotontli* (figure 10.14) that we pointed out earlier in the photos (figures 10.1 and 10.3) and the diagram (figure 10.5) and translated as "something cut smaller." Cirilo fashioned them from a range of colors of tissue paper (but notably, not white paper). We illustrate only a single example here, one that features a forked headdress, although Cirilo created as many as fourteen such images for his standard cleansing, all somewhat similar except for their headdress designs and colors. The cuttings embody an unusually powerful set of infectious winds, composed as a unit of four, tiny anthropomorphic figures conjoined at the feet and sides. Over the years, we have observed these paper figures employed in many rituals to address a client's concerns but were never able to identify them individually by name. Rituals specialists seemed always reluctant to speak about them and simply acknowledged that they are particularly strong. Our friends in Amatlán identified this class of figures as *tlacotontli*, but from our perspective an ambiguity exists in how the term is applied or generally understood. According to one person, *tlacotontli* refers to an abbreviated preventive cleansing ritual designed to deflect or thwart sorcery or envy. However, the term has been translated as meaning "to cut," "to burst or wreck," or "to destroy" (in Spanish, *cortar*, *reventar*, or *destruir*), which seems to apply to the dangerous spirit entities embodied in the paper cuttings, not the ritual per se. Over the centuries, the word has perhaps changed meaning, and it is possible that the paper cuttings take their name from the ritual of which they are a part. In the sixteenth century, Fray Alonso de Molina ([1571] 1944) defined the meaning of the word *tlacotontli* in one sense as "something cut down to size or made smaller."[14] While we translate the name of this category of entities as "something cut smaller" in English, this part of Molina's definition of the term could apply equally to the cleansing-curing ritual and the entities addressed.[15]

Eventually, we did learn that the ritual specialist deploys the diminutive but powerful figures to ward off the malevolent intentions of a *tetlachihuihquetl* (sorcerer) (Sandstrom and Sandstrom 2021). A sorcerer may be envious of offerings made during ritual proceedings or be paid by a disgruntled person to cause trouble. Sorcery is rarely discussed among the Nahua, especially not with outsiders, and ritual specialists do not normally try to halt the activities of sorcerers themselves. Instead, they work to intercept the dangerous spirit entities that malevolent practitioners send out to disrupt, destroy, and kill. Despite their small size, these lacelike cuttings reveal entities that are regarded as extremely dangerous—nothing to be trifled with.

One day a ritual specialist quietly informed us that the four-figure cutting forms a malignant family composed of a father, mother, and two children. The full set of these cuttings that Cirilo prepared for his standard cleansing-curings presents headdress designs that distinguish among them (with recognizable icons of cross, earth, water, vegetation, etc.), but surprisingly, Cirilo was adamant that they do not have individual names. He started to attribute other generalized names to the sample of cuttings, such as *xochiehecatl* ("flower wind") but then stated that they really do not have separate designations. The *tlacotontli* are the only paper figures we have seen not specifically identified by name. Cirilo said that they are very bad winds that have the power to break things, even massive trees, as they move along. Our close examination of the iconography of these images reveals that although they share elements of the iconography of other dangerous winds, perhaps the message they present, collectively, is of a force and counterforce too ubiquitous and wild to contain.

## 5. DUAL-ASPECT MONISM

Because they are entirely inimical to human welfare, the *tlacotontli* cuttings and the whole horde of *ehecameh* present a puzzle. Perhaps they are best seen as simply the antithesis of more salutary spirit entities—the malevolent face of beneficence in the Nahua form of duality (McKeever Furst 2001). They appear to be negations of the life-affirming spirit entities addressed in the round of crop-fertility and rain-petition rituals, and as such, they counteract the benefits accruing to human beings that flow from the earth, water, seeds, good winds, and sun, and thereby threaten life, inviting death. These embodiments of destruction engage in constant struggle with forces that preserve humanity's place in the cosmic order. Like envy, they undo people's work. And yet, disruption and danger are as much a part of the sacred cosmos as their opposites. Stasis is not an option. In the pantheistic religious system, the interplay between human cooperative action and nonhuman agency becomes evident during ritual performances.

This essential tension is what philosopher Maffie terms "agonistic *inamic* unity." He coins the mixed Nahuatl-English phrase to define ancient Aztec process metaphysics (a "world in motion") as "the continual and continuous cyclical struggle (*agon*) of paired opposites, polarities, or dualities" (2014, 137). *Inamic* is a Nahuatl word derived from the verbs *namiqui* and *namictia* meaning "his, her, or its equal" or, simply, "its match." Much has been written about the Mesoamerican abstract concept of "twoness" as epitomizing wholeness or completion (Monaghan 1998, 142–143). Maffie (2014, 143–148) offers numerous examples from classical Nahuatl to illustrate how that vocabulary brings together and orders complementary pairs, a relational activity that describes dual facets of one sacred reality, what he terms "dual-aspect monism" (2014, 169–172) and "unified twoness and twofold oneness" (2014, 433). As he explains this dynamic, we can see that it applies equally well to the Nahua today: "The cyclical, back-and-forth tug-of-war between *inamic* partners combined with the alternating, temporary dominance of one *inamic* over its partner constitutes and hence explains the genesis, diversity, movement, and momentary ordering of the cosmos. Each moment in this back-and-forth, cosmic tug-of-war consists of the temporary dominance of one or the other *inamic* within a pair, and therefore represents a temporary imbalance between the two" (Maffie 2014, 138, italics added). The purpose of Nahua ritual cleansings and curing procedures is to bring this counterpoint into balance, albeit temporarily. The paper images created for cleansing-curing rituals do not appear individually but form a collectivity, ordered on the earth's surface by the ritual specialist—a sort of pas de deux that

---

[14] Our translation of the Spanish original: "cosa circuncidada, o cortada, cosa abreviada" (Molina [1571] 1944, 119).

[15] For glosses of *tlacotontli*-related words, see Sandstrom and Sandstrom (2022b, 281n16). Karttunen (1983, 256) defines the verb *tlacotōnaltia* as "to prohibit someone from doing something," which would seem to confirm our interpretation.

brings together contrastive parties or things. Participants stand around facing the display, gazing upon its symmetry, holding ritual items in their arms, stepping into and out of the flowered loop repeatedly—actions that rid their bodies as well as the objects they carry of adhering bad winds.

We doubt most people could identify all of the individual cuttings accurately. Only the ritual specialists possess such systematic knowledge. However, Nahuas who have seen these impressive arrays on many occasions throughout their lives know it to be a concentration of cosmic forces. Much as a magnifying glass concentrates sunlight, the *mezah* draws these beings from the distant and dangerous periphery to a central place.

### 6. VISUALIZING NAHUA SPACE-TIME

To recap our understanding of dual-aspect monism, a key operating principle that is perhaps difficult to conceive for people whose experiences lie outside the Nahua worldview and religiophilosophical foundation is that the cut-paper figures are not *representative* or *symbolic* of the disease-causing winds; they *embody* them fully. By cutting the images according to legible-yet-adaptable iconographic standards, ritual specialists allow the divine cosmos to unfold or reveal itself through the particular shapes, layers, and colors of each paper figure. In this sense, the cutouts of *tlacatecolotl* and *tlacatecolotl cihuatl* reveal the actual presence of man owl in dual aspects and, in turn, manifest Totiotzin. What properly cut images do is *unconceal* (using Maffie's felicitous expression) various aspects of the overwhelming power of Totiotzin. The danger posed by the array of wind spirit images during cleansing-curing rituals is far more than symbolic—it is a palpable threat. Paper images are contagious, and (not unlike our understanding of pathogens) even touching one can leave a vulnerable person infected. The malevolent entities are actually present in their images, and their threatening character is felt strongly by everyone who participates in the rituals.

These dangerous entities do not seem to have personal histories. With the possible exception of the man owl–man owl woman duo, there seem to be no stories associated with them and they do not play a part in oral narratives; corpses wind, for instance, has no adventures that people could recount. Many of the disease-causing winds are the wandering souls of people who died violent deaths or who were neglected by their kinsmen during *xantolon*, or Day of the Dead observances. It is as if in their wanderings the winds have become anonymous vehicles of disorder and disequilibrium, devoid of personality. The virulent wind spirits are indeed an aimless horde, dangerous if not intentionally malicious. By contrast, the entities that do have histories and play roles in riveting accounts that people enjoy telling involve the many aspects of water, fire, and sacred maize, as well as the earth, thunder, lightning, and other entities that feature prominently in the body of Nahua Oral Tradition.

The way ritual specialists arrange the cleansing-curing *mezah* is also revealing of Nahua worldview. Unlike the altar tabletop used for crop-fertility/rain-petition horticultural rituals, the array is laid directly on the earth—an apparent horizontal, two-dimensional plane. But a closer look discloses unexpected complexity. At the center of the display are the colorful paper figures on *petates* juxtaposed with more *petates* of their counterparts in plain white paper. The rectangles are arranged to form an X-shape, which creates a repeating quincunx design that reproduces the earth's surface, *tlaltepactli*, where humans live out their lives. The colorful figures and their twin images in white are arranged on paper *petates* above the lineup of larger-scale images flanking man owl and man owl woman. The display shows the variegated surface of the earth overlying the bleak underworld, home to figures of death the color of bones, all of them blackened with charcoal. The white figures on the *petates* are invaders of the human social realm, and it is up to the ritual specialist to arrange them in an ordered grid and return them to the underworld where they belong and pose less of a threat.

Using computer-aided design tools, anthropologist Susan Gillespie (2007) has ingeniously demonstrated how ancient Aztec and Maya two-dimensional art may have been understood by people at the time to be folded up in such a way to represent multidimensionality, much like a pop-up book. The *mezah* for curings and cleansings is designed in a similar way, and we can surmise that people skilled in interpreting the layout see a hidden third dimension that models the interface between the human and underworld realms. It is tantalizing to posit the visual parallels in the *mezah* arrays of *costumbre* practitioners and the vivid painted images of the Mictlantecuhtli-like figures in the sixteenth-century *Magliabechiano* and *Tudela Codices* (Boone 2020, 123, fig. 6.25; 132, fig. 6.31). The supernaturals receiving the priests' blood offerings in these works are depicted as a fearsome clawed figure standing atop an eight-panel base of alternating skulls and crossbones in a design that suggests its three-dimensionality. The scene closely mirrors the layout of alternating *petates* of these agents of death in the photos and diagrams, and their iconographic features, particularly of *tlacatecolotl*, are recognizable in the renderings. It seems to us plausible to conclude that the contemporary system of graphic communication among *costumbre* practitioners is the enduring descendant of Aztec pictography. Further systematic study of the lineages of practice of these master paper cutters and their repertoires of ephemeral paper figures may reveal many fascinating correspondences within the Aztec corpus.

We have so far not uncovered evidence that the images laid out for cleansings, curings, and horticultural rituals constitute a fully formed narrative—at least, not a narrative imposed by the ritual specialists. The paper figures instead constitute the widest spectrum of misfortune originating from all realms and conditions. They convey chaos, disease, and death from the water, earth, air, and dead bodies, and they are universal in their threat. From the range of possibilities, participants undoubtedly create private narratives involving their own extended family members, their children, and themselves. By gazing upon the array, they look deep into the contingencies of their own lives and address the fears born of experience and their own imaginations. Herein lies the incredible communicative power of the paper images to illuminate these forces and render them manageable through the efforts of skilled specialists.

To summarize, the layout properly and consistently arranged gives physical form to the inchoate fears and emotional states of people who live in a world constantly threatened by dissolution, breakdown, and destabilizing forces due to its inevitable disequilibrium. Nahua ritual specialists present a visual reality that far surpasses anything that could be expressed by words alone. Like the stained-glass images that impressed the people of medieval Europe and affect people even today, the paper figures encapsulate meaning the Nahua would find difficult to express through other means. A person does not have to know the specific identity of each figure to perceive the power that it embodies. Equally important, a person does not have to know its name to understand its relevance for his or her own life. Each one is a physical manifestation of something very real that poses a concrete threat to existence. The purpose of cleansing-curing rituals is to shine light on these shadowy forces and to offer a means for dealing with them. They are indeed a powerful form of pictography—signs that engage people simultaneously on intellectual and visceral levels.

The cleansing array—along with chanting, dedication of offerings, candle-lit ambience, copal incense, music, and other ritual attentions—is part of a dramatic performance that allows people to experience and participate in unseen workings of the cosmos that have critical relevance to their daily lives. As the focus of these activities, the sacred cut-paper figures constitute a semasiographic system with counterparts throughout North and South America. These systems include the quipu system of the Inca, the *uchu* dolls of the Cuna, Hopi *katsintithu* (kachina), sand paintings of the American Southwest, pottery decorations, ceramic and rubber figurines, petroglyphs, and certainly the codices of ancient Mesoamerica. Paper figures are pictographs in that they are two-dimensional, iconographic images used to encapsulate and convey meaning to people in a specific cultural context. Existing alongside language, they cannot be reduced to speech acts alone. By their rich iconographic content and orderly arrangement in purposeful ritual contexts, the paper pictographs are the focus of people's attention during dramatic ritual performances. Seen in this wider context, the ritual paper complex of the *costumbre* religion in Mesoamerica today becomes less mysterious and more the outcome of a logical evolution of ritual practices recorded during (and undoubtedly predating) the sixteenth century.

**REFERENCES**

Báez-Jorge, Félix, and Arturo Gómez Martínez. 2001. "Tlacatecolotl, señor del bien y del mal: La dualidad en la cosmovisión de los nahuas de Chicontepec." In *Cosmovisión, ritual e identidad de los pueblos indígenas de México*, edited by Johanna Broda and Félix Báez-Jorge, 391–451. Mexico City: Consejo Nacional para la Cultura y las Artes, Fondo de Cultura Económica.

Bassett, Molly H. 2015. *The Fate of Earthly Things: Aztec Gods and God-Bodies*. Recovering Languages and Literacies of the Americas. Austin: University of Texas Press.

Beyer, Hermann. (1910) 1965. "El ídolo azteca de Alejandro de Humboldt." In *Obras completas*, tomo 1: *Mito y simbología del México antiguo*, vol. 10 of *El México antiguo*, edited by Carmen Cook de Leonard, 390–401. Mexico City: Sociedad Alemana Mexicanista. Translation of "Das aztekische Götterbild Alexander von Humboldt's." In *Wissenschaftliche Festschrift zur Enthüllung des von Seiten Seiner Majestät Kaiser Wilhelm II. dem Mexikanischen Volke zum Jubiläum seiner Unabhängigkeit gestifteten Humboldt-Denkmals*, edited by Ernst Ludwig Maximilian Emil Wittich. Mexico City: Müller Hermanos, 1910.

Boone, Elizabeth Hill. 1994. "Introduction: Writing and Recording Knowledge." In *Writing without Words: Alternative Literacies in Mesoamerica and the Andes*, edited by Elizabeth Hill Boone and Walter D. Mignolo, 3–26. Durham, NC: Duke University Press.

Boone, Elizabeth Hill. 2011a. "Ruptures and Unions: Graphic Complexity and Hybridity in Sixteenth-Century Mexico." In *Their Way of Writing: Scripts, Signs, and Pictographs in Pre-Columbian America*, edited by Elizabeth Hill Boone and Gary Urton, 197–225. Washington, DC: Dumbarton Oaks Research Library and Collection.

Boone, Elizabeth Hill. 2011b. "The Cultural Category of Scripts, Signs, and Pictographs." In *Their Way of Writing: Scripts, Signs, and Pictographs in Pre-Columbian America*, edited by Elizabeth Hill Boone and Gary Urton, 379–390. Washington, DC: Dumbarton Oaks Research Library and Collection.

Boone, Elizabeth Hill. 2016. "Pictorial Talking: The Figural Rendering of Speech Acts and Texts in Aztec Mexico." In *Sign and Design: Script as Image in Cross-cultural Perspective (300–1600 CE)*, edited by Brigitte Miriam Bedos-Rezak and Jeffrey F. Hamburger, 31–50. Washington, DC: Dumbarton Oaks Research Library and Collection.

Boone, Elizabeth Hill. 2020. *Descendants of Aztec Pictography: The Cultural Encyclopedia of Sixteenth-Century Mexico*. Austin: University of Texas Press.

Dow, James W. 1986. *The Shaman's Touch: Otomí Indian Symbolic Healing*. Salt Lake City: University of Utah Press.

Gelb, I. J. (1952) 1963. *A Study of Writing: A Discussion of the General Principles Governing the Use and Evolution of Writing*. 2nd ed. Chicago: University of Chicago Press.

Gessain, Robert. 1938. "Contribution a l'étude des cultes et des cérémonies indigènes de la région de Huehuetla (Hidalgo): Les 'muñecos' figurines rituelles." *Journal de la Société des Américanistes* n.s. 30: 343–371.

Gillespie, Susan D. 2007. "Different Ways of Seeing: Modes of Social Consciousness in Mesoamerican Two-Dimensional Artworks." *Baessler-Archiv: Beiträge zur Völkerkunde* 55: 103–142.

Houston, Stephen D. 2004. "Writing in Early Mesoamerica." In *The First Writing: Script Invention as History and Process*, edited by Stephen D. Houston, 274–309. New York: Cambridge University Press.

Hunt, Eva. 1977. *The Transformation of the Hummingbird: Cultural Roots of a Zinacantecan Mythical Poem*. Ithaca, NY: Cornell University Press.

Karttunen, Frances. 1983. *An Analytical Dictionary of Nahuatl*. Austin: University of Texas Press.

Laack, Isabel. 2019. *Aztec Religion and Art of Writing: Investigating Embodied Meaning, Indigenous Semiotics, and the Nahua Sense of Reality*. Numen Book Series, Studies in the History of Religions, vol. 161. Leiden, Netherlands: Brill.

Maffie, James. 2014. *Aztec Philosophy: Understanding a World in Motion*. Boulder: University Press of Colorado.

Marcus, Joyce. 1992. *Mesoamerican Writing Systems: Propaganda, Myth, and History in Four Ancient Civilizations*. Princeton, NJ: Princeton University Press.

McKeever Furst, Jill Leslie. 2001. "Duality." In *The Oxford Encyclopedia of Mesoamerican Cultures: The Civilizations of Mexico and Central America*, vol. 1, edited by Davíd Carrasco, 344–345. New York: Oxford University Press.

Mikulska, Katarzyna. 2015. *Tejiendo destinos: Un acercamiento al sistema de comunicación gráfica en los códices adivinatorios*. Zinacantepec, Mexico City: El Colegio Mexiquense; Warsaw, Poland: Universidad de Varsovia, Instituto de Estudios Ibéricos e Iberoamericanos.

Mikulska, Katarzyna, and Jerome A. Offner, eds. 2019. *Indigenous Graphic Communication Systems: A Theoretical Approach*. Louisville: University Press of Colorado.

Molina, Alonso de. (1571) 1944. *Vocabulario en lengua castellana y mexicana*. Colección de incunables americanos, 4. Madrid: Ediciones Cultura Hispánica.

Monaghan, John. 1998. "The Person, Destiny, and the Construction of Difference in Mesoamerica." *Res: Anthropology and Aesthetics* 33: 137–146.

Monaghan, John. 2000. "Theology and History in the Study of Mesoamerican Religions." In *Supplement to the Handbook of Middle American Indians*, vol. 6, *Ethnology*. 24–49. Victoria R. Bricker, gen. ed., John D. Monaghan, vol. ed. Austin: University of Texas Press.

Monaghan, John. 2003. "Shamanism, Colonialism, and the *Mesa* in Mesoamerican Religious Discourse." In *Mesas and Cosmologies in Mesoamerica*, edited by Douglas Sharon, 141–148. San Diego Museum Papers, 42. San Diego: San Diego Museum of Man.

Sandstrom, Alan R. 1978. *The Image of Disease: Medical Practices of Nahua Indians of the Huasteca*. Monographs in Anthropology 3. Columbia: University of Missouri-Columbia, Museum of Anthropology.

Sandstrom, Alan R. 1981. *Traditional Curing and Crop Fertility Rituals among Otomí Indians of the Sierra de Puebla, Mexico: The Lopez Manuscripts*. Indiana University Publications, Occasional Papers and Monographs, no. 3. Bloomington: Indiana University Museum.

Sandstrom, Alan R. 1986. "Paper Spirits of Mexico." *Natural History* 95 (1): 66–73.

Sandstrom, Alan R. 1989. "The Face of the Devil: Concepts of Disease and Pollution among Nahua Indians of the Southern Huasteca." In *Enquêtes sur l'Amérique moyenne: Mélanges offerts à Guy Stresser-Péan*, edited by Dominique Michelet, 357–372. Études Mésoaméricaines, vol. 16. Mexico City: Instituto Nacional de Antropología e Historia, Consejo Nacional para la Cultura y las Artes; Centre d'Études Mexicaines et Centraméricaines.

Sandstrom, Alan R. 1991. *Corn Is Our Blood: Culture and Ethnic Identity in a Contemporary Aztec Indian Village*. Civilization of the American Indian Series, vol. 206. Norman: University of Oklahoma Press; 2012 Internet Archive edition available at https://archive.org/details/cornisourbloodcu00sand/.

Sandstrom, Alan R. 2003. "Sacred Mountains and Miniature Worlds: Altar Design among the Nahua of Northern Veracruz, Mexico." In *Mesas and Cosmologies in Mesoamerica*, edited by Douglas Sharon, 51–70. San Diego Museum Papers, 42. San Diego: San Diego Museum of Man.

Sandstrom, Alan R., and Pamela Effrein Sandstrom. 1986. *Traditional Papermaking and Paper Cult Figures of Mexico*. Norman: University of Oklahoma Press; 2012 Internet Archive edition available at http://archive.org/details/traditionalpape00sand/.

Sandstrom, Alan R., and Pamela Effrein Sandstrom. 2003. "The Shaman's Art." In *Personal Encounters: A Reader in Cultural Anthropology*, edited by Linda Walbridge and April K. Sievert, 163–170. New York: McGraw-Hill.

Sandstrom, Alan R., and Pamela Effrein Sandstrom. 2021. "Sorcery and Counter-sorcery among the Nahua of Northern Veracruz, Mexico." In *Sorcery in Mesoamerica*, edited by Jeremy D. Coltman and John M. D. Pohl, 69–113. Boulder: University Press of Colorado.

Sandstrom, Alan R., and Pamela Effrein Sandstrom. 2022a. "Cut-Paper Figures and Nahua Conceptions of the Divine: Art and Revelation in Pantheistic Religion." *Estudios de Cultura Náhuatl* 64: 15–62.

Sandstrom, Alan R., and Pamela Effrein Sandstrom. 2022b. *Pilgrimage to Broken Mountain: Nahua Sacred Journeys in Mexico's Huasteca Veracruzana*. Denver: University Press of Colorado.

Sullivan, John, et al. 2016. *Tlahtolxitlauhcayotl: Chicontepec, Veracruz*. Zacatecas, Mexico: Zacatlan Macehualtlallamiccan, Instituto de Docencia e Investigación Etnológica de Zacatecas (IDIEZ); Warsaw, Poland: University of Warsaw, Faculty of Liberal Arts.

Whittaker, Gordon. 2009. "The Principles of Nahuatl Writing." *Göttinger Beiträge zur Sprachwissenschaft* 16: 47–81.

Whittaker, Gordon. 2021. *Deciphering Aztec Hieroglyphs: A Guide to Nahuatl Writing*. Oakland: University of California Press; London: Thames and Hudson.

Williams García, Roberto. 1963. *Los Tepehuas*. Xalapa, Mexico: Universidad Veracruzana.

Wright-Carr, David Charles. 2017. "Signs of Resistance: Iconography and Semasiography in Otomi Architectural Decoration and Manuscripts of the Early Colonial Period." *Visible Language* 51 (1): 58–87.

# 11

## Five Centuries of Self-Determination

· *Indigenous Intellectuals and Nahuatl Language in Mexico*

KELLY S. MCDONOUGH

Since the earliest days of conquest and colonization, Nahuas have deftly negotiated complex situations and subjectivities, often in unequal social, political, and economic conditions. They have done so as creative problem solvers who have strategically held fast to cultural traditions of their own, appropriated and adapted those of others, and developed new practices that responded to changing times. The introduction of the technology and practice of alphabetic writing provided Nahuas with a new tool to defend their memories, identities, and territories in new contexts. Their embrace of alphabetic writing, evident in the myriad examples of Nahuatl-language texts from the past five centuries, makes clear that that Nahua intellectuals—creators, guardians, and disseminators of knowledges—engaged a broad range of issues through an equally wide variety of genres in their written work. A recurring concern has been a tenacious commitment to protecting and revitalizing their native language. This chapter dips into distinct historical time periods to consider how the Nahuatl language has served as a mechanism and symbol of self-determination; as a conduit to the past, present, and future; and as a source of pride and dignity in often-oppressive environments.

### 1. COLONIAL PERIOD: ENGAGING NEW WORLDS, APPROPRIATING NEW TECHNOLOGIES

There is a tendency to believe that Spaniards successfully imposed the Castilian language on Indigenous peoples of what is today called Mexico from the earliest days of the Spanish invasion. This is far from the truth; New Spain (colonial Mexico) was always a plurilingual space. Nahuatl, the common language of the Aztec (Mexica) Empire, was in fact the semiofficial language in both religious and secular spaces until the late eighteenth century. Not surprisingly, the Spanish Crown wished for Indigenous subjects to learn the Castilian language and European customs (Heath 1972, 14).[1] But Catholic priests, those who were ultimately made responsible for such instruction, were far more concerned with evangelization than they were with Hispanization. And they realized quickly that instruction in the Faith was far more efficient when Castilian was bypassed altogether; instead of teaching Native people the Castilian language, priests learned Indigenous language(s) of the local populations in order to preach and teach in that language. For example, at the Colegio de Santa Cruz de Tlatelolco, the well-known school for sons of Indigenous nobles established by the Franciscans in 1536, Native students studied topics such as music, rhetoric, and grammar in Nahuatl and Latin. Castilian had little representation in the curriculum.[2]

Scholars such as cultural studies theorist Walter Mignolo have drawn our attention to how Indigenous languages were co-opted as vehicles for religious conversion and cultural assimilation projects, and how these processes oppressed Native ways of thinking and being (2003). For instance, Catholic friars did not study and document Indigenous languages and cultures to preserve or promote them; they did so to monitor and mold Indigenous subjectivities. Along similar lines, sociologist Rolando Vázquez has posited that the translation and alphabetic recording of Indigenous oral knowledges and pictographic writing was "the demise of these living oral traditions" (2011, 32). As for Vázquez's theory, I firmly disagree. In my view, alphabetic and oral traditions are mutually constitutive intellectual modalities. Though in Spanish circles alphabetic writing was understood as superior to orality, this does not mean that Indigenous peoples felt the same. Moreover, there is no evidence that the Native people fell silent and ceased to transmit oral knowledges in their own spaces.

It is true that preinvasion Indigenous writing systems (semasiographic inscriptions, in the case of Nahuas) gradually ceded to alphabetic writing. In less than 100 years after initial encounters with Europeans, those who knew how to read the painted *amoxtli* (Native codices) became fewer and far between. But the hegemony

---

[1] See *Recopilación de leyes de los reynos de las Indias: Mandadas imprimir, y publicar por la Magestad Católica Del Rey Don Carlos II, Nuestro Señor* (1681, lib. VI, tít. 1, ley 18, 1550): "Que donde fuere posible se pongan escuelas de la lengua Castellana, para que la aprendan los Indios."

[2] On the Colegio de Santa Cruz de Tlatelolco, see Hernández and Máynez (2016).

of the Roman alphabet does not mean, as some would have it, that Native thought unequivocally ceded to European thought, or that Indigenous memory was completely erased. Indeed, anthropologists Bryan Pfaffenberger and William Schaniel, among others, have convincingly argued that one can adopt a technology without adopting the worldview of the culture that originally created said technology (Pfaffenberger 1992, 511; Schaniel 1988). As for Nahuas specifically, as ethnohistorian Justyna Olko observed, "they did not see it [alphabetic writing] as something imposed and culturally alien but used it both to preserve their tradition and to negotiate successfully or even challenge the Spanish administrative, judicial, political and religious arrangement, its institutions and functionaries" (2014, 194).

Consider the letters that Nahua nobles of the Central Valley wrote to the king of Spain in the mid-sixteenth century. Primarily concerned with requesting/confirming privileges and contesting new policies that rescinded noble exemption from tribute, these letters are overwhelmingly written in Castilian, though several were drafted in an erudite Latin (e.g., those of Don Pablo Nazareo de Xaltocan).[3] Some were even penned in Nahuatl, as is the case for the 1554 letter written to King Phillip II by Indigenous nobles of Tenochtitlan including Don Esteban de Guzmán, and Don Pedro Moctezoma Tlacahuepantli, along with several *alcaldes* and *regidores* (judges and council members of the Indigenous municipal council).[4] In this letter, they decried that Spaniards consistently mistreated Native nobility and were meddling in Indigenous politics. Why send a letter to the king in Nahuatl? Surely Nahuas knew he did not understand their language. It is likely that Nahuatl was symbolically deployed as a means to channel Indigenous pride and autonomy. Without denying their identity as vassals to the Spanish Crown, Nahuas conveyed they had their own complete and complex language capable of communicating important issues, including diplomatic negotiations between nations.[5]

The most well-known example of intellectual work in the Nahuatl language during the colonial period is the *Florentine Codex*, a sixteenth-century collaboration between the Franciscan friar Bernardino de Sahagún and Nahua scholars including Antonio Valeriano. Alonso Vegerano, Martín Jacobita, Pedro de San Buenaventura, Diego de Grado, Bonifacio Maximiliano, Mateo Severino, and a

---

[3] Transcriptions of Don Pablo Nazareo de Xaltocan's Latin letters can be found in Pérez-Rocha and Tena (2000).

[4] See a transcription of this letter in Pérez-Rocha and Tena (2000, 191–197).

[5] As an anonymous reviewer cogently pointed out, Nahuas were not alone in writing to the Hapsburg kings in their own languages. For example, the Aragonese petitioned the king in the Catalan language in order to similarly assert their unique (non-Castilian) identity and local autonomy. On Early Modern Indigenous petitioning in the Atlantic world, see Masters and Dixon (2022).

host of unnamed Nahua elders. The twelve-book multilingual and multimedia encyclopedic work is the most comprehensive extant source treating Indigenous life before Spanish invasion and the first decades of colonial life.[6] While those reading this edited volume are likely quite familiar with the *Florentine Codex*, it bears revisiting Sahagún's belief that language was the key to understanding the culture. In his words, the project was similar to "a dragnet to bring to light all the words of this language with their exact and metaphorical meanings, and all their ways of speaking, and most of their ancient practices good and evil" (see the prologue in Sahagún et al. 1950, "Introduction & Indices," 47). By compiling an exhaustive *calepino/vocabulario* (dictionary/glossary) in Nahuatl, Sahagún hoped to gain a clear understanding of preinvasion religion so he could easily identify and eradicate idolatrous behaviors and teach others to do the same. Additionally, he wished to document certain aspects of the culture he admired, a means to refute erroneous depictions of Indigenous cultures as "uncivilized" in preinvasion times. Without losing sight of the more nefarious designs of the project, we should not overlook the fact that the "dragnet" also, unwittingly, preserved knowledges that might otherwise have been lost (Mignolo 2003, 199). Nahua collaborators surely had their own reasons for contributing to the project as well, although there is no record of their thoughts on the work. If we consider our own delight (and struggles) as scholars immersed in our areas of expertise and interest, it is fair to assume that Nahuas too enjoyed moments of deep satisfaction throughout their years of scholarly inquiry. For along with learning more about their own language and culture, they were also learning about Spanish ways of understanding and engaging the world around them.

Nahuas also used the alphabet to record the histories of their respective *altepetl* (sociopolitical and territorial units). The Nahuatl-language annals genre, an extension of the preinvasion *xiuhpohualli* (year-count) tradition, documents yearly inventories of political, economic, environmental, and social events that held meaning for the *altepetl* (Townsend 2009, 2017). Common topics that appear in the annals include transfers of power, public works, territorial disputes, and climactic phenomena, among others. Nahuatl annals provide a relatively uncensored view of the annalists' micropatriotic perspectives and sensibilities since they were produced with minimal outsider oversight or interference. Furthermore, as historian James Lockhart has observed, when compared to other Nahuatl mundane manuscripts of the time, it appears that writers of the annals "were freer to express personal or factional opinion in addition to representing the altepetl" (1992, 376). In this way, annals can be considered unique sites of Nahua self-representation.

---

[6] Scholarship on the *Florentine Codex* is vast; a good starting place is León-Portilla (1999).

Whereas most Nahua annalists were anonymous, three are well known. In the late sixteenth and early seventeenth centuries, Don Domingo de San Antón Muñón Chimalpahin Quauhtlehuanitzin (Chimalpahin) compiled the histories of his birthplace (Amaquemecan, Chalco) along with a lively, detailed account of his adopted homeland, Tenochtitlan (Lockhart 1992, 387). During this same time period, Don Hernando de Alvarado Tezozomoc of Tenochtitlan wrote Nahuatl annals (*Crónica mexicayotl*) and a Spanish chronicle (*Crónica mexicana*), both focusing on the lineages of the Mexica, his people.[7] Tezozomoc's works are especially appreciated for the elaborate speeches preserved within them (Lockhart 1992, 389–390). Don Juan Buenaventura Zapata y Mendoza of Tlaxcala crafted his annals during the mid-to-late seventeenth century. Evincing protoethnic pride, Zapata referenced only Nahuatl sources (unlike Chimalpahin, who referred to both Spanish and Nahuatl sources) and refused Spanish loanwords commonly found in other Nahuatl sources of the same time period (Lockhart 1992, 392; Townsend 2010, 154–157).

During the seventeenth and early eighteenth centuries, many Nahua communities faced the possibility of their lands and communities being legally subsumed, fragmented, or eliminated. In response, they brought forth, in alphabetic and graphic form, stories of their collective past related to the lands in question (Wood 2003, 108–124). These manuscripts, today called *títulos primordiales* (Primordial Titles), were strategic tools used in response to ongoing policies of *congregación* (forced Indigenous relocation), and *composición* (formalized distribution and titling of land). Since Indigenous peoples did not usually hold legal titles to their lands, *títulos primordiales* were meant to prove possession of them since "time immemorial." Detailed descriptions of the landscape and boundaries are accompanied by what Lockhart has called "ritual signatures" and ceremonies of possession, oftentimes witnessed by neighboring Indigenous communities. These signatures and ceremonies include naming and altering the landscape, feasting, and playing musical instruments at certain geographic locations (Lockhart 1991, 39–64). *Títulos primordiales* are identifiable by their stock set of storylines, including preinvasion and colonial encounters—pacific and otherwise—with neighboring Indigenous communities, Spaniards, deities, and saints. Narrations of conversion to Catholicism are a mainstay. Once they had accepted the new religion and recognized the king of Spain as their ruler, *títulos primordiales* usually explain their rights to the land were confirmed by Spanish authorities. Therefore, any move to disenfranchise the Indigenous community in question would be a crime against the king's loyal,

---

[7] Whether the author of the *Crónica mexicayotl* is actually Tezozomoc is still up for debate. Schroeder (2011) argues that it is Chimalpahin's work, whereas Peperstraete and Kruell (2014) see both Tezozomoc and Chimalpahin's hands in the text.

tribute-paying, Christian vassals. The *títulos primordiales* found in archives today were submitted to the court system as Indigenous communities appealed for justice. That said, ethnohistorian Stephanie Wood has convincingly argued that these manuscripts were directed first and foremost to the Indigenous communities themselves (1998, 220–222). They tend to read as if an elder were addressing his or her community, with a scribe recording their words.[8] In the *título primordial* from San Matías Cuixinco, for example, the elder warns the People that Spaniards were coming to take their lands. But if the community knew their history and relationship to the land, they say, the People could hold strong. "Huel monema yhuehue yn ilama yn itlatol," the elder states: "it is truly your inheritance, the knowledge and words of the elders" ("Título primordial de San Matías Cuixinco," ca. 1700s, 336f).

Nahuas not only produced original materials in Nahuatl; they also translated Spanish materials to their maternal language. Scores of Catholic doctrinal materials translated from Spanish to Nahuatl are attributed to European/criollo priests. But we know that these works were only made possible by the mostly unacknowledged Nahua apprentices and scholars who collaborated with the friars; Mark Christensen has rightly called the Indigenous collaborators "ghostwriters" (2013).[9] A notable seventeenth-century translator of Spanish to Nahuatl was Texcocan parish priest Bartolomé de Alva Ixtlilxochitl (younger brother of Fernando de Alva Cortés Ixtlilxochitl, the Texcoco historian). Alva's only original Nahuatl-language publication was a confessional manual, *Confesionario mayor y menor* (1634), belonging to the extirpation of idolatries genre (Schwaller 2014, 48–51). He is better known, however, for his translations of Golden Age Spanish drama to Nahuatl, including works by Lope de Vega Carpio and Pedro Calderón de la Barca (Sell, Burkhart, and Wright 2012).[10] The result of Alva's creative curiosity allowed Nahuas to return the gaze to Spaniards when viewing those plays in their own language.

Although for lack of space I won't discuss Nahuatl-language mundane documents (petitions, complaints, wills), suffice it to say that such materials are evidence of how Nahuas attended to the business of daily life and eventually death in their own language well into the colonial period, evidence of tenacious resistance to Hispanization.[11]

---

[8] The Nahuatl language does not mark gender in the same way that Spanish does. Because of this, it is unclear if the speakers are male or female unless they are directly identified as such.

[9] Tavárez details the Nahua scholars who did in fact receive recognition for their important contributions to religious works translated to Nahuatl with Franciscans (2013, 205–210).

[10] Plays translated by Bartolomé de Alva include *The Great Theater of the World*, by Pedro Calderón de la Barca; *The Mother of the Best*, by Lope de Vega, and *The Animal Prophet and the Fortunate Patricide*, attributed to both Lope de Vega and Antonio Mira de Amescua (Sell, Burkhart, and Wright 2012, xvii–xviii).

[11] On Nahuatl mundane documents, see Anderson et al. (1976).

## 2. INDEPENDENCE PERIOD: SALVAGE SCHOLARSHIP

It was not until the late eighteenth century that the church and crown (in the midst of Bourbon Reforms) achieved consensus that Castilian should be the common language of New Spain (Lorenzana y Buitrón 1770, 47).[12] That is, Indigenous peoples were not pressured to assimilate into Spanish-speaking subjects until at least 200 years into colonial rule. In fact, somewhat ironically, it was not until the newly formed Republic of Mexico won its independence from Spain in 1821 that Spanish was codified in the republic's first constitution as the official language of the land. With a gradual transition to Spanish as the common language of both religious and secular spaces, Nahuatl-language texts became increasingly scarce.[13] That said, Nahuatl-language use, alphabetic writing, and scholarship did not completely cease. Faustino Galicia Chimalpopoca, the nineteenth-century Nahua polymath, was a pivotal political figure, attorney, and professor of law as well as of the Nahuatl and Otomí languages, and salvage-scholar of colonial Nahuatl texts.[14] What I mean by "salvage-scholar" is that in a society bent on eliminating Indigenous languages and Indigenous ways of being, Chimalpopoca tirelessly worked on locating and depositing Indigenous language materials (primarily in Nahuatl but in other Indigenous languages as well) into the National Museum (today called the National Museum of Anthropology) in Mexico City before they were discarded, destroyed, or sold to private investors and foreigners. Indeed, much of our access today to colonial sources in Nahuatl is due to Chimalpopoca's actions, without which the materials would surely have been lost.

Along with salvage-scholar activities, Chimalpopoca served as the personal Nahuatl teacher and interpreter for Emperor Maximilian I and presided over the Junta Protectora de las Clases Menesterosas (Council for the Protection of the Impoverished) during Maximilian's short-lived Second Empire. Chimalpopoca transcribed and translated an exceptionally wide variety of texts, including pictographic representations of ritual time, ceremonies, and natural cycles; ecclesiastic works; *títulos primordiales*; and historical annals. He also published original materials, scattered in archives in Mexico, the United States, and Paris, such as philological studies of Nahuatl texts; a catechism in Nahuatl with a Spanish translation, *Devocionario para oir misa en lengua Mexicana: Dedicado á los indios* (1848); a

---

[12] For a more detailed discussion of Lorenzana's thoughts on Indigenous languages and Castilian, see Mignolo (2003, 61–63).

[13] Melton-Villanueva's (2016) study of 150 Nahuatl-language last wills and testaments from nineteenth-century San Bartolomé Metepec in the Toluca Valley gives evidence of Nahuatl as the language of life and death in this village well into the nineteenth century.

[14] On Chimalpopoca, see Martínez Díaz (2022); McDonough (2014, 88–115); and Segovia-Liga (2017).

surprisingly accessible treatise on the vigesimal numeral system used by Nahuas: *Disertación hispano-nahua-latina sobre el origen y modo de contar de los indios nahuacenses* (1858); and a bilingual pamphlet seeking donations for the Virgen of Guadalupe, *El centavo de Nuestra Señora de Guadalupe* (1869a). He was also author of three original works on Nahuatl grammar: (1) *Silbario de idioma mexicano* (1849, 1859), comprising an introduction to Nahuatl vocabulary, fragments of Nahuatl language texts with lessons, a brief religious text, and a *huhuehtlahtolli*-style (ritual elder-speech) exhortation of proper behavior of girls and boys; (2) *Epítome o modo fácil de aprender el idioma náhuatl* (1869b), a grammar focusing on verbs and geared toward teaching nonnative speakers; and (3) a glossary of Nahuatl terms, *Vocabulario correcto conforme a los mejores gramáticos en el mexicano o Diálogos familiares que enseñan la lengua sin necesidad de maestro* (1869c). Finally, although it is unclear whether it is an original work or a translation of something prior, he is also responsible for what appears to be a treatise on Aristotelian logic in Nahuatl (this text yet awaits study by a much more ambitious Nahuatl scholar, particularly one versed in ancient philosophy).[15]

Among Chimalpopoca's papers held in the Colección de Documentos Históricos at the Biblioteca Nacional de Antropología e Historia in Mexico City is an untitled and undated manuscript he wrote in Spanish, likely directed to one of the scholarly associations he belonged to. In it, he vehemently criticizes society's views on Indigenous languages, alluding to the "civilizing" and assimilative projects of nation building: "Because unfortunately, we Mexicans have misunderstood in thinking that, since we were free and we could wear gentlemen's [European style] pants, not only should we cease to speak our native language, but we should eradicate it altogether. What would people think of a man in [European] pants who spoke 'that' language? I am deeply saddened by this viewpoint, because the true history of Mexico is marked in her language, in Nahuatl."[16]

In Chimalpopoca's estimation, language policies and practices of Independent Mexico were systematically erasing knowledges of the past that were embedded in Indigenous languages. Although assimilative processes—bolstered by intense discrimination—succeeded in diminishing the general use of Indigenous languages

---

[15] See Sepúlveda y Herrera (1992) for a listing of documents penned by Chimalpopoca held at the Biblioteca Nacional de Antropología e Historia in Mexico City.

[16] "Porque por desgracia nosotros los mex.(icanos) desde que mal entendimos, que ya eramos libres y podiamos vestir pantalones, no solo no debiamos hablar la lengua mexicana sino obvidarla del todo; por que ¿qué se diria de un Señor de pantalon hablando en tal idioma? Lo siento en extremo porque la verdadera historia de Mexico esta marcada en su idioma o en la lengua náhuatl." Original orthography preserved.

during the nineteenth century, these languages and knowledges were not completely suppressed, much to the chagrin of many. Consider, as but one example, ethnologist Nicolás de León's report on the state of Indigenous languages in the early twentieth century: "As an ethnologist, the loss [of Indigenous languages] gives me great pain. But as someone devoted to the betterment of my country, I would wish for their complete extinction: the greatest obstacle to the progress of Mexico is its diversity of languages. Once they are extinguished, the Indian will fall in with less resistance to national progress" (1905, 181).[17] De León's comments give insight to ideological context in which Chimalpopoca labored. Yet he persisted in viewing his language as a priceless window to the magnificent past of Mexico that could and should inform its present as well as its future.

### 3. TWENTIETH CENTURY: STORIES AND SELF-DETERMINATION

Like many other Indigenous peoples across space and time, Nahuas have kept their language and culture alive by creating, guarding, and transmitting stories. Knowledges of the relationships between humans and other-than-humans (deities, plants, or animals) have been passed down through oral, written, and embodied stories in Nahua communities for centuries, if not millennia. Though oral knowledges can be difficult to trace due to its ephemeral nature, twentieth- and twenty-first-century anthropologists and linguists recorded and transcribed copious amounts of Native voices. The academic obsession with collecting and scrutinizing Indigenous words and thoughts is, of course, not without problems. But the mining of what many academics viewed as simply "data" has fortuitously left Indigenous communities with a rich cache of ancestral voices. Such archival materials, though written, can be approached in the spirit of listening, or in Kanaka Maoli scholar Noelani Arista's words, "ear witnessing" (2020, 46). A return to Nahuatl-language materials with such a reframing yet awaits, but I am confident that this approach will be rewarding to scholars and Indigenous communities alike. I am aware of the fact that the vast majority of anthropological and linguistic archival materials were mediated by outsider academics. But my concern here is not about encountering a "pure, untainted" Indigenous voice (as if that ever existed). Instead, it is to carefully eye- and earwitness that which has actually survived in archives made by and for dominant culture, especially since for many Indigenous communities these materials are the only written record of their past. To discard this vital connection to previous generations because of mediation seems unwarranted.

---

[17] "Si como etnologista me duele esa pérdida [de los idiomas indígenas], como amante del engrandecimiento de mi patria quisiera su completa extinción: el obstáculo mayor para el adelantamiento de México es la diversidad de idiomas: extinguidos ellos, el indio concurrirá con menor resistencia al progreso nacional."

Consider the mediated work of Doña Luz Jiménez (1897–1965), a Nahua woman from Milpa Alta. Along with being model and muse to many of Mexico's most prominent twentieth-century painters, such as Diego Rivera, Fernando Leal, David Siqueiros, John Charlot, she shared her words and knowledges with anthropologist Fernando Horcasitas, and linguist Benjamin Whorf, among others. Doña Luz's decades-long collaboration with Horcasitas resulted in two posthumous publications in Nahuatl and Spanish: *De Porfirio Díaz a Zapata: Memoria náhuatl de Milpa Alta* (1968) and *Los cuentos en náhuatl de doña Luz Jiménez* (1979, with Sarah O. de Ford). Doña Luz narrated stories in Nahuatl, and renarrated a Spanish version of the same story, while Horcasitas transcribed her words. In *De Porfirio Díaz a Zapata*, Doña Luz details her community's experience with government-sponsored assimilative education for Indigenous children as well as the violence and displacement they experienced due to the Mexican Revolution. Along with this historical content, this slim volume shows the triangulated nature of Nahua identity. There is no solitary or authorial *yo*: all of experiences, actions, and knowledges recorded are in relation to others. This is similar to *Los cuentos en náhuatl de doña Luz Jiménez*. Whether focused on topics of medicine, ceremony, or past events, all the stories in *Los cuentos* either explicitly focus on relationships or implicitly draw the reader/listener to consider them. The stories are entertaining, to be sure. Yet they are also what Dian Million (Athabascan) has deemed theories, since "they posit proposition and paradigm on how the world works" (2011, 322). Nahuas knew (and know) how to read and listen to such Nahua theories. What could be gained if others learned to do so as well?

Adding to her already-lengthy and impressive resumé, Doña Luz is also one of the few women who wrote for the short-lived midcentury Nahuatl-language newspaper *Mexihkatl itonalama*. Circulating primarily in the states of Mexico, Morelos, and Puebla from May to November of 1950, *Mexihkatl itonalama* was financed and edited by anthropologist/historian Robert Barlow. Miguel Barrios Espinosa, a Nahua from Hueyapan, served as the director of the publication, and Valentín Ramírez, another native speaker of Nahuatl, was secretary. Barrios Espinosa and Ramírez contributed to the periodical (the former more so than the latter), along with some thirty other Nahuas. The majority were men, although several Nahua women—Rakel Ramires, Franciska Rio, and Masedonia Mendosa—appear in later issues. Doña Luz contributed two *sasanilli* (stories): "Tewewentsin ihuan tetepeh" ("The Old Man and the Mountain") and "Tlohkenawake" ("Lord of the Near and the Nigh").

According to the trilingual introductory material (Nahuatl, Spanish, and English) to the compilation of the thirty-four issues of *Mexihkatl itonalama*, the primary goal was "to stimulate the reading and writing of the Nahua language amongst the two million natives who speak it; to this end, it publishes materials on customs, traditional feasts, dances, songs, and plays and news items, climatic and social. Likewise, it popularizes pre-Hispanic customs, with the aim of showing that despite the Conquest, there still exists an intimate link between the past and present." (*Mexihkatl itonalama* 1950).

The first issue of the run began with a notice that the newspaper was concerned with publishing the knowledges and practices of Nahuas in Nahuatl. This notice is followed by an exhortation to Nahua readers that they must know (or learn) their language and teach it to their children. If they lost their language, it continued, they would bring shame upon themselves, as it was the legacy of their revered ancestors such as Nezahualcoyotl, Cuauhtemoc, and other *tiaxca* (learned elders). This call is followed by an explanation of the orthography that would be employed. The editorial team noted that in the Spanish language, *c* and *q* are used, but in *Mexihkatl itonalama* they would use *k*; likewise, for the Spanish *s* and *ce*, they would employ *z*; and for long vowels *h*; and for *hu*, *w*.[18] The simple explanations for these choices was that "inin totlahtolokse: Tleca tikihkwiloskeh kemen kaxtillan?" ("Our language is different: why should we write as it is done in Spain?"). Through the publication's contributors' chosen orthography, they turned their gaze away from dominant culture, and toward themselves and their own history. Though brief, the introduction packs a punch: it evinces pride, dignity, and self-determination. It presents a distinctively Nahua way of thinking and being in the world and frames their vehicle for communicating these things as a precious resource.

The content of *Mexihkatl itonalama* includes, among other topics, news reports, poetry and *kwikatl* (song), riddles, local customs, *huhuehtlahtolli* (elder speech), short stories, essays on Mexican colonial history, descriptions of artefacts and codices, infrastructure building projects, introductions to Nahuatl orthography and vocabulary, census data, and contacts in several cities to study the language. News reports range from local theft and accidents to changes in administration at the Universidad Autónoma de México (UNAM) and visits from foreign dignitaries. On the latter, it is mostly female visitors from the United States who are reported; perhaps solo female travelers were a novelty at the time. News reports are not restricted, however, to local or even national events. Nahuas who contributed news items were very much interested in what was happening around the world.

---

[18] Linguist Magnus Pharao Hansen calls this orthography "Americanist." See his detailed discussion of Nahuatl orthographies here: https://nahuatlstudies.blogspot.com/2016/07/how-to-spell-nahuatl-nawatl-nauatl.html.

The Korean War is discussed several times (along with an introduction to war-related Nahuatl neologisms). News from other countries such as Peru, South Africa, England, Russia, Guatemala, Venezuela, Japan, and the Philippines figure as well, with one of the more curious entries (at least to this reader) being a notice of the marriage of Japanese emperor Hirohito's daughter. For reasons unknown, Issue 22 goes back in deep time to discuss the Norman/French-English Battle of Hastings in 1066.

The editorial team of *Mexihkatl itonalama* was intent upon teaching their readers about Indigenous colonial history. Issue 3 describes the lives of two of Moteuczoma II's children: Tecuichpo, later known as Isabel Moctezuma, and her brother Don Pedro Moctezoma. In Issue 8, there is a summary of the renowned Nahua annalist Chimalpahin's record of the hanging of Africans who had supposedly planned a rebellion in Mexico City. Since the newspaper was produced in Azcapotzalco (Tepanec territory), it is no surprise that Tepanec history appears more than once. Issue 10 regales the reader with tales of the Tepanec empire, and Issue 12 discusses Tezozomoc, the Tepanec *tlatoani* (ruler) of Azcapotzalco during the fourteenth and early-fifteenth centuries. Other historical figures populating the corpus include Cuauhtemoc and his son, Don Diego de Mendoza Austria y Moctezuma, as well as La Malinche. History in *Mexihkatl itonalama* moves beyond the colonial period with discussion of the nineteenth century, particularly Indigenous contributions to the fight against French invasion in the Battle of Puebla (Cinco de Mayo) in 1862. As in the News Reports section, the historical offerings are not confined Mexican affairs: Simón Bolívar, for example, found his way to the pages of Issue 9.

Robert Barlow died in January 1951, less than a year after the debut of the inaugural issue. While Barlow's death meant the end of both intellectual and financial support for the project, Nahuas, of course, continued thinking about themselves and their relationships to local and global contexts. Other grassroots revitalization projects were regularly in the works over the next several decades, although publication of written materials in Nahuatl—whether for lack of funding or interest—did not seem to be the highest priority. But with a confluence of Indigenous activism (on local, national, and global scales) and neoliberal-multicultural policies, by the 1980s writing in Indigenous languages in Mexico was on the cusp of what many refer to as a renaissance.

## 4. LATE TWENTIETH- AND TWENTY-FIRST CENTURIES: MARKING PRESENCE IN THE PRESENT

Though the Mexican government had invested a significant amount of money and effort in projects aimed at assimilating Indigenous populations to dominant culture's norms, by the last quarter of the twentieth century it was clear that forced homogeneity did not unify the nation. Taking a different tack, neoliberal-multicultural policies instead promoted cultural diversity. Scholarship, prizes, and other resources were directed toward Indigenous peoples to support linguistic and cultural projects, and by the 1990s publication outlets for written Indigenous language materials appeared on the horizon. What eventually became clear, however, was that the state was interested in Indigenous artisanal products and anything ostensibly *folklórico* but not Indigenous economic and political critiques, nor Indigenous demands for rights. That is, along the lines of what anthropologist Charles Hale theorized as the *indio permitido*, Indigenous people were now "allowed" to speak, but only in acceptable forms and on certain topics (2006).

In his study of Nahua literature produced between 1985 and 2014, literary scholar Adam Coon noted that although literary styles and political strategies varied, nearly all Nahua writers of this time period were focused on contesting ingrained and erroneous ideologies and discourses that framed Nahuas as "not present in the present" (2015, ix). Although this "vanishing Indian" trope in Mexico differed from that north of the Río Bravo, the rationale was the same. If Indigenous people were "absent," their land and resources would be freely available to the larger population. Additionally, the state would be absolved of its responsibility to contemporary Indigenous communities. By imagining Indigenous peoples as frozen in the deep past, desirable aspects of their culture could be selectively appropriated and inserted into the national imaginary. Writing became a way for Indigenous peoples to register themselves in the present; with the pen, Nahuas continued their centuries-long fight against erasure and protected their territories, their cultures, and their right to self-representation.

Nahua writer and political figure Natalio Hernández Hernández (Lomas del Dorado, Veracruz) is one of the leading figures of the so-called Nahuatl literary renaissance. As a poet and essayist, Hernández brought forceful truth-telling to Indigenous and national conversations. In his earlier poetry, for example, in the poem "Na noquia ni tlacatl" ("I Also Am a Human Being") (2005a), Hernández states: "sequi coyome quihtohua niyolcatl / samolhui nitlachixtoc; / ni tlahtoli amo melauac / noquia nipia notlalamiquilis / nipia nonemilis" ("Some *ladinos* say I am an animal / that my existence has no purpose. / This opinion is mistaken: I have my own wisdom, my own path in life"). In another poem, "Na ni indio" ("I Am Indian") (1991), he appropriates and rehabilitates the racial epitaph of *indio*. Each stanza begins with the affirmation of "I am Indian." The poem begins with the origin of the term (Columbus's mistaken identification of the land and the people he encountered), followed by a condemnation of Indigenous suffering and discrimination meted out by dominant culture. The poem then shifts to an embrace of self and closes with a condemnation of the negative ways in which whites and mestizos have interpreted and framed Native peoples and their cultures.

As Coon reminds us, Hernández and fellow cofounders of Escritores en Lenguas Indígenas A.C. (ELIAC; National Association of Writers in Indigenous Languages) in Mexico City lobbied tirelessly in the 1990s for "constitutional reform that would recognize Indigenous linguistic and cultural rights" (2015, 250). The 2003 passage of Article 2 ("Ley general de derechos lingüísticos de los pueblos indígenas"), which promised a series of reforms meant to validate and promote Indigenous language use in Mexico, was due in no small part to Indigenous activists like Hernández who raised their voices in unison, demanding change. As time progressed, Hernández moved away from outright critique of dominant culture and shifted toward exploring intercultural understanding. For example, in his book of poetry *Semanca huitzilin* (*Hummingbird of Harmony*) (2005b), he plants seeds of reconciliation.[19] Regardless of the tenor or the topic, Hernández's many decades of public reflection in the Nahuatl language is a powerful act. Writing in his language, Hernández has emphasized that his people are still here in the present, and despite centuries of oppression their language and knowledges have not been taken from them.

Nahua muralist, dramaturge, bilingual teacher, cultural promoter, and cofounder of ELIAC Ildefonso Maya Hernández (1936–2011) was known for directing powerful criticism toward the church, the state, and Indigenous people themselves. Regardless of the medium, he tended toward a realist sensibility. In his 1987 play *Ixtlamatinij* (*The Learned Ones*), for instance, Maya places the Nahua world, flaws and all, on the center stage. Centered on a multigenerational Nahua household, this play introduces us to Epitacio, a bilingual educator (one of the few jobs available to Indigenous men beyond fieldwork and the military). He returns to his family's rural village to celebrate *Xantolo* (All Saint's Day) and manages to wreak havoc in less than twenty-four hours. He belittles traditional culture, flaunts his cash, drinks to excess, and disrespects his elders by pressuring them to assimilate to mestizo ways. By the end, Epitacio realizes his errors and the family is united, though fragilely. The storyline, not unfamiliar to Indigenous audience members (the play was presented in a series of Indigenous communities where similar scenarios were unfolding in real time), was meant to prompt serious conversations about interfamilial challenges. Through the character of Epitacio, Maya hoped audience members would consider how they (or other Indigenous peoples) had been co-opted as part of the colonizing project. In what ways were they participating—often unknowingly—in the cultural extermination of their own people?

---

[19] On Natalio Hernández Hernández and his body of work, see Coon (2015, 54–157).

Literary production by Nahuas has flourished in the twenty-first century. *Xochitlahcuilo* (flower-writer/poet) Gustavo Zapoteco Sideño (Guerrero/Morelos), for example, has amassed a formidable collection of Nahuatl-language poetry and essays, which he self-translates. Zapoteco Sideño treats a broad range of topics in his work, although ceremony, elder knowledge, and critique of multiple injustices are the most prevalent. In his book of poetry entitled *Cuicatl pan tlalliouatlmej (Song-Poems from the Sugarcane Fields)* (2004), these injustices are encapsulated not only in word but also in images via photographs taken by Zapoteco Sideño's brother Noé Zapoteco Sideño. On the book cover, the poverty and harsh conditions of Indigenous daily life confront the reader through a photograph of a seven-year-old Nahua boy covered in ash, sitting in the back of a truck on his way from harvesting in the sugarcane fields. More recently, Zapoteco Sideño has begun to write about the omnipresent violence of narcotrafficking in his region, although in a recent conversation he mentioned he has some concerns about publishing this work lest it draw the attention and ire of the wrong people. As Coon has observed, Nahuas are also increasingly using their language in new media such as Facebook. In his study of the use of Facebook (or *ixamoxtli*, in Nahuatl) by Nahua author, television host, and musician Mardonio Carballo, Coon sees new media as an important tool used "to strengthen Nahua and Indigenous kinship ties in Mexico City, strengthen Nahuatl, and protest social injustices" (2019, 229). Scores of other Facebook pages dedicated to Nahuatl language and culture, as well as Twitter and YouTube channels, are also active spaces of exchange, language promotion, and cultural revitalization.

### 5. LOOKING TOWARD THE FUTURE: THE NEXT GENERATION

In this final section, I introduce two young Nahua intellectuals. Eduardo de la Cruz Cruz and Gladiola Villegas Gómez. Of the many young Nahua intellectuals I have encountered, these two strike me as unique among their peers for their creativity and drive. If at times it seems that the future of Nahuatl is bleak, these young visionaries inspire optimism.

Eduardo de la Cruz Cruz (MA) is a Nahua teacher, scholar, and writer from Tecomate, Chicontepec, in Veracruz. He began working at Instituto de Docencia e Investigación Etnológica de Zacatecas (IDIEZ; Zacatecas Institute for Teaching and Research in Ethnology) in 2009 as a research assistant for the institute's monolingual dictionary project *Tlahtolxitlauhcayotl* (2016) and as a language instructor. After a few years working at IDIEZ, he began to crave a change in the instructional model. Instead of just teaching the language, de la Cruz wanted to see the curriculum rooted in, and springing from, the study of his culture. He began to work with his colleagues at IDIEZ to develop what he calls *ce tlamachtiliztli ica ce tlalneltoquilli*, a mode of teaching that incorporates Nahuatl cultural beliefs and practices. As opposed to grammar drills, IDIEZ has always had real-life scenarios at the heart of their curriculum. But de la Cruz's dream was to see even the simplest introductory lessons contextualized in rain-petitioning ceremonies, the preparation of ritual altars, planting and harvesting corn, traditional dance and theater, or embroidery. With this in mind, since 2011 IDIEZ has systematically reorganized its curriculum to teach the language from within authentic cultural contexts.

His scholarly works reflect his deepening expertise in Nahua cultural practices, all of which he deems ceremonial practices. In his view, Nahua life *is* ritual life; for him, there is no separating the quotidian and the sacred. For his master's thesis, entitled "Mocencuiltihualtoc mopatla tequitiloni, campeca huan tlaneltoquilli tlen quimanextia toquiztli pan macehualtlallamiccayotl" ("Continuities and Change in the Techniques, Customs, and Concepts Related to the Cultivation of Corn in the Nahua World Over Time"), he studied the ceremonies surrounding *maiz* in his village. Since 2015 he has published two single-authored Nahuatl-language books and three more in collaboration with others among other publications.

In our conversations, de la Cruz stated that is pleased with the headway he and the IDIEZ team are making in forging meaningful community relationships between scholars and the larger Nahua community in Chicontepec. After years of effort, stakeholders are finally in a position to truly reciprocate with Nahuas in Chicontepec who have supported their teaching or scholarship in one way or another. De la Cruz recognizes that many scholars (Indigenous and non-Indigenous alike) have benefited from Nahuas in their professional work. So, from his perspective, it is only right that they give back, or better yet, work *with* the people. What does "giving back" mean for de la Cruz? For one, he and his colleagues return to the community regularly to share updates on the type of work they are involved in and to consult community members on future efforts. Nahua scholar Abelardo de la Cruz de la Cruz (PhD) from Tepoxteco and de la Cruz have given workshops to discuss orthographic conventions employed by IDIEZ and distributed de la Cruz's books to the bilingual schools in the region that either have no materials in Nahuatl or only have materials that do not reflect the local variant. Prior to the pandemic, de la Cruz piloted a summer workshop in Tecomate that taught oral history collection, video editing, and English to Nahua students (the latter at the request of Nahua parents in the community).

Another commitment spearheaded by de la Cruz in the past few years has been a yearly community workshop called "Xiquixmati totlahtol" ("Learn About / Know Our Language"). At these workshops de la Cruz organizes expository competitions wherein local Nahuas narrate life histories and elder teachings and share entertaining-didactic stories in their language. The workshops have a clever byline:

"Ica totlahtol no hueli tictlanih ce tlamantli" ("With Our Language You Can Win/Gain Something"). The more obvious reference is to the workshop's awards of coveted home appliances such as blenders, microwaves, and stoves, as well as gas tanks, construction tools, and school supplies. But the byline also hints at the nonmaterial gains of speaking one's language in community: remembering one's past and teaching each other through traditional story. More recently, de la Cruz has begun organizing the annual Colloquium on Nahuatl Language and Cultural Studies, specifically designed as a space for young Nahua scholars to present their work and network with each other. I once asked de la Cruz if he considered himself to be an "intellectual," or an *ixtlamatini*. He laughed and said he doesn't even call himself a "Maestro" which is technically his professional title, since he holds a master's degree. "I am just a teacher," he said. "I am satisfied that people in my community recognize me and say 'oh, that one, he is interested, he is concerned about our people and our language.' That is more than enough for me."

I asked him why he was so committed to revitalizing and strengthening his language and culture, unlike so many of his peers. He thinks his passion is directly connected to the time he spent at his grandfather's side as a child. His grandfather rejected dominant-culture interventions that had infiltrated the Huasteca, such as the use of chemical fertilizers in the milpa. Nor did he attend the local Catholic Church on Sundays; instead, he lit a candle for Chicomexochitl (Lord Seven-Flower, deity of rain and fertility). He prayed for a good harvest and for the well-being of his family. "Malhuilli," he would say to de la Cruz while lighting the candle: "this is sacred."

As a participant in a joint project of the Getty Museum in Los Angeles and University of California, Los Angeles (UCLA), de la Cruz was recently recorded reading the Nahuatl portion of Book 12 of the *Florentine Codex* out loud. We spoke about the original Nahua scholars who had worked with Sahagún. He said, "In many ways, I am like them; I have become an intermediary." When asked if working with outsiders troubled him at all, he explained that his vision for his language, culture, and people in general is an expansive one of increased vitality. And for this vision to manifest, he said, he would need a team with diverse skills and perspectives. Therefore, as opposed to begrudging non-Nahua interest in Nahuatl, he is grateful. De la Cruz holds great respect for John Sullivan, the founder and Director of IDIEZ, for his unfailing commitment to the language and culture. But he most admires how Sullivan's goal had always to make himself obsolete in the operation by carving a path for Nahua leadership. Now director of IDIEZ (since 2020), de la Cruz is poised to steer the institute toward more integrated community-engaged teaching and scholarship.

Although Gladiola Villegas Gómez has had a different career trajectory from de la Cruz, hers is no less promising. Villegas is a young Nahua woman from Chalingo,

Huatla, in the state of Hidalgo, and is an emerging powerhouse in Indigenous higher education. She holds a bachelor's degree in English and a master's degree in education. She has served as the Languages Coordinator at the Universidad Politécnica in Huejutla, Hidalgo, where she also taught English as a Second Language. At that institution, she estimated that 70 percent of her students were native speakers of Nahuatl. Bypassing Spanish altogether, she used Nahuatl language and culture to teach English, and vice versa. It was one of the few times, Villegas said, that she has seen native speakers with an advantage in the university classroom. Normally, Villegas noted, when Indigenous students arrive at the university, they often believe that they must deny their language and culture. They internalize the message that their own traditions and knowledges are inferior and must be replaced by the Western knowledges valued in the university setting. But Villegas always wondered: What would happen if the Indigenous students felt pride in their language and culture? What if at the university they could master an area of study—say, agro-industrial engineering or nursing—and then complement this with knowledges from their home communities? Villegas is convinced that soon entrepreneurs and business leaders will also realize that Indigenous people who deftly dwell (cognitively and otherwise) in multiple worlds are the key to more creative solutions to our ever-increasing and shared problems. Since 2019, Villegas has operated her own online language school, the International Language Institute, where she teaches English and Nahuatl. She also collaborates with IDIEZ in curriculum design and has taught their advanced Nahuatl course for their summer intensive program. Add to this, she regularly offers free English and Nahuatl courses for Nahua children in her region. Most recently, she has begun writing short stories in Nahuatl.

Her views on the importance of her language and culture are informed by the affective ties to her family, and the enormous amount of optimism and fortitude she exhibits is homegrown. Her father, Mario Villegas Cortázar, is a well-regarded Nahuatl-language activist, court interpreter, writer, and radio announcer. He has long believed that the state is not the place to look to for social, political, and economic change for Indigenous peoples of Mexico. Instead, he sees more possibilities in collectively building a critical mass of world citizens who no longer accept stereotypes and myths of Indigenous peoples—first in individual households, and then at grassroots local levels. A poignant reminder that Nahuatl language and culture has always been about relationships, Gladiola Villegas teared up in our interview, saying, "It's the language I spoke with my grandparents, If I forget my language, I won't remember what they told me. I won't remember them, and I won't know who I am."

Through their language, Nahuas create, cultivate, and imagine their relationships to past and present, to their ancestors and kin, to outsiders, and to other-than-humans. In alphabetic writing or otherwise, they have recorded their histories, demanded and protected rights, satisfied curiosities, and taught their own people and others who they really are. Nahuatl is the lens and conduit through which they meet, interpret, and shape the world around them. And for the intellectuals discussed in this chapter, this has been something worth defending. I do not mean to suggest that to be Nahua one must speak their language: that is a tall order for a People who have been systematically prohibited from doing so for hundreds of years. Nor am I implying that alphabetic writing is any more important than other modalities of knowledge work. But the legacy of these intellectuals remains a viable way back for Nahuas who have become disconnected from their language and culture. Some ties, after all, can never be broken.

### REFERENCES

Anderson, Arthur J. O., Frances F. Berdan, James Lockhart, and Ronald W. Langacker. 1976. *Beyond the Codices: The Nahua View of Colonial Mexico*. Berkeley: University of California Press.

Arista, Noelani. 2020. "Ka Waihona Palapala Mānaleo: Research in a Time of Plenty. Colonialism and the Hawaiian-Language Archives." In *Indigenous Textual Cultures: Reading and Writing in the Age of Global Empire*, edited by Tony Ballantyne, Lachy Paterson, and Angela Wanhalla, 39–70. Durham, NC: Duke University Press.

Christensen, Mark Z. 2013. *Nahua and Maya Catholicisms: Texts and Religion in Colonial Central Mexico and Yucatan*. Stanford, CA: Stanford University Press.

Chimalpopoca, Faustino Galicia. n.d. "Untitled manuscript." Colección de documentos históricos de Faustino Galicia Chimalpopoca, Colección Antigua, núm. 254. Mexico City: Biblioteca Nacional de Antropología e Historia.

Chimalpopoca, Faustino Galicia. 1848. *Devocionario para oir misa en lengua mexicana: Dedicado á los indios*.

Chimalpopoca, Faustino Galicia. 1858. *Disertación hispano-nahua-latina sobre el origen y modo de contar de los indios nahuacenses*.

Chimalpopoca, Faustino Galicia. 1859. *Silbario de idioma mexicano: 1839–1849*. Mexico City: Tipografía de Manuel Castro.

Chimalpopoca, Faustino Galicia. 1869a. *El centavo de Nuestra Señora de Guadalupe*.

Chimalpopoca, Faustino Galicia. 1869b. *Epítome o modo fácil de aprender el idioma náhuatl o lengua mexicana*. Mexico City: Tipografía de la V. de Murguía è hijos.

Chimalpopoca, Faustino Galicia. 1869c. *Vocabulario correcto conforme a los mejores gramáticos en el mexicano o Diálogos familiares que enseñan la lengua sin necesidad de maestro*.

Coon, Adam. 2015. "Iajki Estados Onidos (She Went to the U.S.): Nahua Identities in Migration within Contemporary Nahua Literature, 1985–2014." PhD diss., University of Texas, Austin.

Coon, Adam. 2019. "From Facebook to Ixamoxtli: Mardonio Carballo's Activism through Social Networking." In *Indigenous Interfaces: Spaces, Technology, and Social Networks in Mexico and Central America*, edited by Jennifer Gómez Menjívar and Gloria Chacón, 227–252. Tucson: University of Arizona Press.

Cruz Cruz, Eduardo de la. 2016. "Mocencuiltihualtoc mopatla tequitiloni, campeca huan tlaneltoquilli tlen quimanextia toquiztli pan macehualtlallamiccayotl." MA thesis, Universidad Autónoma de Zacatecas, 2016.

Hale, Charles R. 2006. *Más que un indio (More than an Indian): Racial Ambivalence and Neoliberal Multiculturalism in Guatemala*. Santa Fe, NM: School of American Research Press.

Heath, Shirley Brice. 1972. *Telling Tongues: Language Policy in Mexico, Colony to Nation*. New York: Teachers College Press.

Hernández, Esther, and Pilar Máynez. 2016. *El Colegio de Tlatelolco: Síntesis de historias, lenguas y culturas*. Mexico City: Grupo Destiempos.

Hernández, Natalio. 1991. "Na ni indio / I Am Indian." In *Corn Is Our Blood: Culture and Ethnic Identity in a Contemporary Aztec Indian Village*, by Alan R. Sandstrom, xviii–ix. Norman: University of Oklahoma Press.

Hernández, Natalio. 2005a. "Na noquia ni tlacatl / I Also Am a Human Being / You también soy un ser humano." In *Words of the True Peoples: Anthology of Contemporary Mexican Indigenous-Language Writers / Palabras de los seres verdaderos: Antología de escritores en lenguas indígenas de México*, edited by Carlos Montemayor and Donald H. Frischmann, 2:158–59. Austin: University of Texas Press, 2005.

Hernández, Natalio. 2005b. *Semanca Huitzilin / Colibrí de la armonía / Hummingbird of Harmony*. Translated by Donald H. Frischmann. Mexico City: CONACULTA.

Jiménez, Luz. *De Porfirio Díaz a Zapata: Memoria náhuatl de Milpa Alta*. Translated and edited by Fernando Horcasitas. Mexico City: UNAM, 1968.

Jiménez, Luz. *Los cuentos en Náhuatl de doña Luz Jiménez*. Translated and edited by Fernando Horcasitas and Sarah O. de Ford. Mexico City: UNAM, 1979.

León, Nicolás. 1905. "Las lenguas indígenas de México en el siglo XIX: Nota bibliográfica y crítica." *Anales del Instituto Nacional de Antropología e Historia* 2 (2): 180–191.

León-Portilla, Miguel. 1999. *Bernardino de Sahagún: Pionero de la antropología*. Mexico City: UNAM.

Lockhart, James. 1991. *Nahuas and Spaniards: Postconquest Central Mexican History and Philology*. Stanford, CA: Stanford University Press.

Lockhart, James. 1992. *The Nahuas after the Conquest: A Social and Cultural History of the Indians of Central Mexico, Sixteenth through Eighteenth Centuries*. Stanford, CA: Stanford University Press.

Lorenzana y Buitrón. 1770. "Cartas pastorales y edictos del Illmo. Señor D. Francisco Antonio Lorenzana y Buitón, Arzobispo de México." http://cd.dgb.uanl.mx//handle/201504211/10602.

Martínez Díaz, Baruc. 2022. "Un intelectual indígena del México decimonónico: La vida y la obra de Faustino Chimalpopoca Galicia." *Estudios de Cultura Náhuatl* 63: 103–133.

Masters, Adrian, and Bradley Dixon. 2022. "Indigenous Petitioning in the Early Modern British and Spanish New World." In *Petitioning in the Atlantic World, c. 1500–1840: Empires, Revolutions and Social Movements*, edited by Miguel Dantas da Cruz, 105–136. Cham: Springer International Publishing, 2022.

Maya Hernández, Ildefonso. 2007. *Ixtlamatinij / The Learned Ones*. In *Words of the True Peoples: Anthology of Contemporary Mexican Indigenous-Language Writers / Palabras de los seres verdaderos: Antología de escritores en lenguas indígenas de México*, edited by Carlos Montemayor and Donald Frischmann, 3:230–81.

McDonough, Kelly S. 2014. *The Learned Ones: Nahua Intellectuals in Postconquest Mexico*. Tucson: University of Arizona Press.

Melton-Villanueva, Miriam. 2016. *The Aztecs at Independence: Nahua Culture Makers in Central Mexico, 1799–1832*. Tucson: University of Arizona Press.

*Mexihkatl itonalama*. 1950. Mexico City: Azkapotzalco.

Mignolo, Walter. 2003. *The Darker Side of the Renaissance: Literacy, Territoriality, and Colonization*. Ann Arbor: University of Michigan Press.

Million, Dian. 2011. "Intense Dreaming: Theories, Narratives, and Our Search for Home." *American Indian Quarterly* 35 (3): 313–333.

Olko, Justyna. 2014. "Alphabetic Writing in the Hands of the Colonial Nahua Nobility." *Contributions in New World Archaeology* 7: 177–198.

Peperstraete, Sylvie, and Gabriel Kenrick Kruell. 2014. "Determining the Authorship of the *Crónica Mexicayotl*: Two Hypotheses." *Americas* 71 (2): 315–338.

Pérez-Rocha, Emma, and Rafael Tena. 2000. *La nobleza indígena del centro de México después de la conquista*. Mexico City: Instituto Nacional de Antropología e Historia.

Pfaffenberger, Bryan. 1992. "Social Anthropology of Technology." *Annual Review of Anthropology* 21 (1): 491–516.

*Recopilación de leyes de los reynos de las Indias: Mandadas imprimir, y publicar por la Magestad Católica del Rey Don Carlos II, Nuestro Señor*. 1681. Madrid: Ivlian de Paredes.

Sahagún, Bernardino de, et al. 1950. *General History of the Things of New Spain; Florentine Codex*. Translated by Arthur J. O. Anderson and Charles E. Dibble. Santa Fe, NM: School of American Research.

Schaniel, William C. 1988. "New Technology and Culture Change in Traditional Societies." *Journal of Economic Issues* 22 (2): 493–498.

Schroeder, Susan. 2011. "The Truth about the *Crónica Mexicayotl*." *Colonial Latin American Review* 20 (2): 233–247.

Schwaller, John F. 2014. "The Brothers Fernando de Alva Ixtlilxochitl and Bartolomé de Alva: Two 'Native' Intellectuals of Seventeenth-Century Mexico." In *Indigenous Intellectuals: Knowledge, Power, and Colonial Culture in Mexico and the Andes*, 39–59. Durham, NC: Duke University Press.

Segovia-Liga, A. 2017. "'The Rupture Generation': Nineteenth-Century Nahua Intellectuals in Mexico City." PhD diss., Leiden University, Leiden, Netherlands.

Sepúlveda y Herrera, Ma. Teresa. 1992. *Catálogo de la colección de documentos históricos de Faustino Galicia Chimalpopoca*. Mexico City: INAH, 1992.

Sell, Barry D., Louise M. Burkhart, and Elizabeth R. Wright. 2012. *Nahuatl Theater: Spanish Golden Age Drama in Mexican Translation*. Norman: University of Oklahoma Press.

Sullivan, John, Eduardo de la Cruz Cruz, Abelardo de la Cruz de la Cruz, Delfina de la Cruz de la Cruz, Victoriano de la Cruz Cruz, Sabina Cruz de la Cruz, Ofelia Cruz Morales, Catalina Cruz de la Cruz, and Manuel de la Cruz Cruz. 2016. *Tlahtolxitlauhcayotl; Chicontepec, Veracruz*. Warsaw, Poland: University of Warsaw, Faculty of "Artes Liberales; Instituto de Docencia e Investigación Etnológica de Zacatecas."

Tavárez, David. 2013. "Nahua Intellectuals, Franciscan Scholars, and the 'Devotio Moderna' in Colonial Mexico." *Americas* 70: 203–235.

"Título primordial de San Matías Cuixinco." ca. 1700s. Tierras, vol. 2819, exp. 9, fols. 40r–87v (359f–392v). Archivo General de la Nación, Mexico City.

Townsend, Camilla. 2009. "Glimpsing Native American Historiography: The Cellular Principle in Sixteenth-Century Nahuatl Annals." *Ethnohistory* 56 (4): 625–650.

Townsend, Camilla. 2010. "Don Juan Buenaventura Zapata y Mendoza and the Notion of a Nahua Identity." In *The Conquest All Over Again: Nahuas and Zapotecs Thinking, Writing, and Painting Spanish Colonialism*, edited by Susan Schroeder, 144–180. Portland, OR: Sussex Academic Press.

Townsend, Camilla. 2017. *Annals of Native America: How the Nahuas of Colonial Mexico Kept Their History Alive*. New York: Oxford University Press.

Vázquez, Rolando. 2011. "Translation as Erasure: Thoughts on Modernity's Epistemic Violence." *Journal of Historical Sociology* 24 (1): 27–44.

Wood, Stephanie. 1998. "The Social vs. Legal Context of Nahuatl *Títulos*." In *Native Traditions in the Postconquest World: A Symposium at Dumbarton Oaks, 2nd Through 4th October 1992*, edited by Elizabeth Hill Boone and Tom Cummins, 201–231. Washington, DC: Dumbarton Oaks Research Library and Collection.

Wood, Stephanie. 2003. *Transcending Conquest: Nahua Views of Spanish Colonial Mexico*. Norman: University of Oklahoma Press.

Zapoteco Sideño, Gustavo. 2004. *Cantos en el cañaveral / Cuicatl pan tlalliouatlmej*. Mexico City: CONACULTA, 2004.

# Index

Alderete, Diego Gracián de, 217
allophones, 6–7
alphabetic: education, 13; literacy, 9, 11–12, 15, 17, 180, 183, 225; systems, 235; writing, 6, 9, 11–12, 14, 17, 23, 184, 235–36, 238, 265–67, 269, 271, 282–83
Alva, Bartolomé de, 14–15, 208, 270
Alvarado Tezozomoc, Hernando de, 14
Amacuitlapilco, 211, 214–15, 217, 223
Amatlán, 230–32, 238, 243, 247, 254
Amecameca, 215, 217, 224
Amith, Jonathan, 17
ancestors, 21, 24, 35, 57, 78, 275, 282
Anderson, Arthur, 18, 75
Andrews, Richard, 9–10, 137$n10$
Aquino, Fabián de, 14, 22–23, 179–84, 186, 190–97, 199–200, 203–4
Arista, Noelani, 273
Arreola, José María, 91–94, 96–97, 100, 107–8, 110
Aubin, Joseph, 16
authority, 23, 87, 100, 123, 218; administrative, 85, 109$n47$; constitutionalist, 130; ecclesiastical, 186; institutional, 9; political, 184; religious, 4; vice-royal, 90$n9$
Axochiapan, 212, 214–15, 223
Ayotitlán, 21, 101, 106–7, 110
Azcapotzalco, 86$n3$, 276

Barlow, Robert, 17, 123, 274, 276
Barrios Espinosa, Miguel, 274
Bautista, Juan, 14, 184, 186, 209
Bautista, Paulina, 99, 101–3, 186
Beekman, Christopher, 32–33, 35, 38
Berdan, Frances, 18
bilingualism, 4, 17, 117
bilinguals, 4, 19, 90, 127–29
blood, 142, 242–43; offerings, 258
Boas, Franz, 38, 40
Boone, Elizabeth, 234–37
borrowing, 117, 159, 163–66, 170, 234
Boturini Benaducci, Lorenzo, 16
Brunk, Samuel, 119–20
Buenaventura, San, Pedro de, 14, 267
Burns, Kathryn, 207

Calderón de la Barca, Pedro, 270
Campbell, Lyle, 33, 40, 43, 45
Campbell, R. Joe, 18, 30–31, 40, 43, 45, 137$n10$, 139$n14$, 155$n4$, 180$n1$, 198, 230
Canger, Una, 6, 30, 35, 39–40, 43, 46, 48–49, 94$n16$, 104, 106
Cano, Melchor, 185–86
Carballo, Mardonio, 279
Carochi, Horacio, 5, 7, 15, 76, 140
Castilian, 5, 7, 266–67, 271; language, 265–66
Catholic Church, 13, 87

caves, 62, 66–67, 69–70, 72–73, 75
celebrations, 92, 140, 144
ceremonies, 133, 135, 142–44, 148–49, 231, 237, 243, 269, 271, 274, 279–80; marriage, 138; rain-petitioning, 280; religious, 22, 133, 135, 142–44, 148; water, 147
Cervantes, Miguel de, 208
chanting, 229, 232, 237, 239–40, 242, 245, 252, 259
Chichimec, 46, 66; migrations, 49
Chicontepec, 35, 279–80
children, 70, 87, 108, 123, 130, 251, 275; mestizo, 4; of Moteuczoma II, 276; place of origin, 76
Chimalpahin, Domingo Francisco de San Antón Muñón, 14–15, 67–68, 269, 276
Chimalpopoca, Faustino Galicia, 16, 20, 271–73
Cholula, 59, 63–64, 123
Christ, Jesus, 23, 185, 201, 209, 213–16, 218–19, 221, 223–25, 250; mistreatment of, 208
Christensen, Alexander, 32–33, 35, 38
Christensen, Mark, 270
Christianity, 3–5, 14, 184, 186
Christian texts, 180, 183, 186
Cirilo, 232–34, 237–50, 252–55
Clairvaux, Saint Bernard of, 181
cleansing-curing rituals, 234, 237, 240–41, 243, 251, 255–57, 259
cleansings, 229, 238–39, 241, 243–45, 248, 256, 258
Cline, Sarah L., 118
cognates, 32, 45, 148, 224
coins, 173–74
Colegio de Santa Cruz de Tlatelolco, 12–13, 15, 22, 87, 154, 181–82, 184–86, 199, 204, 209, 266
Colima, 21, 87, 89, 91–92, 95–96, 100–101, 108–11; dialect of Nahuatl, 108, 111
colonial: administration, 4, 15, 85–86; period, 5, 12, 14–17, 19, 31, 33, 49, 89–90, 118, 135–37, 140, 183, 185, 265, 267; subjects, 183–84
colonization, 117–18, 121, 265
colonizers, 183–84
communities, 17, 99–100, 107, 118–20, 122–23, 125, 127, 130, 208, 230, 232, 269–70, 280–81
conquest of Mexico, 3, 5–6, 11, 13, 17, 134, 140, 142, 265–66, 268, 275
contact, 17, 29–30, 33, 35, 37, 46–47, 49, 86, 91–92, 182, 186
Coon, Adam, 277–79

Cora, 33, 37, 45–46
Corachol, 29, 32, 35, 46–47
Cortés, Hernán, 121, 134
Cortés y Zedeño, Jerónimo, 89$n8$, 101, 104, 107, 110
Cortina-Borja, Mario, 31
couplets, 56–63, 66, 69–72, 74–75, 78–79, 98, 196, 199
couriers, 133–37, 144
cross, 216, 218–19, 222, 225, 250, 252
crucifixion, 214–17, 224–25
Cruz, Evaristo de la, 243
Cruz Cruz, Eduardo de la, 279–80
Cruz de la Cruz, Abelardo de la, 280–81
Cuauhtinchan, 65–66
culture, 13–14, 18, 20, 22, 55, 58, 145–46, 235–36, 266–68, 273, 277–79, 281–83
curings, 229, 231, 238, 244, 258

Dakin, Karen, 18, 20, 32, 35, 42–43, 45, 47–48, 62$n13$, 75, 123
death, 181, 190–92, 194–95, 203, 232, 234, 245–46, 248–49, 252–54, 256, 258–59
deities, 21, 138–40, 144, 190$n5$, 196, 232, 238, 269
demons, 192–94, 196–97, 208
devotional books, 185–86
dialect diversification, 42, 142–43, 148
dialects, 21, 39, 43–44, 47–49, 86, 89, 101, 103, 106–9, 111; in contact, 86
Dibble, Charles, 18, 75
dictionaries, 5–6, 16, 22, 154–55, 157, 160–61, 167, 169, 172–73
diphrases, 21, 57–60, 62–63, 67, 69, 72–73, 75–76, 78–79, 137; definition of, 55; function of, 56
donkeys, 171
Durán, Diego, 4, 14, 134

elders, 59–60, 106, 268, 270, 278
Escritores en Lenguas Indígenas A.C. (ELIAC), 278
Estella, Diego de, 182, 185
ethnohistory, 24, 33, 117; methods, 119; sources, 39; theories, 30; tradition, 116
European contact, 29, 35
Europeans, 11, 30, 134$n2$, 191, 266–67, 272
European sources, 181, 195, 204, 221, 223–24
evil, 193, 225, 232, 247–48, 268

family, 17, 31, 38, 92*n14*, 149, 278, 281–82
festivals, 133, 140, 143–44. *See also* ceremonies
food, 57, 64, 181, 190, 239; offerings, 229, 232, 234
Franciscans, 4–5, 98, 182, 184, 186, 199, 209, 266, 270*n9*
Fuente, Agustín de la, 185–86, 209

Galicia Chimalpopoca, Faustino. *See* Chimalpopoca, Faustino Galicia
Gamio, Manuel, 120–21
Gante, Pedro de, 4–5, 12, 267
Gaona, Juan de, 185
Garibay, Ángel María, 15, 18, 79
Gibson, Charles, 18
Gillespie, Susan, 258
glottal stop, 7, 137*n10*
glottography, 6, 11
goddesses, 67, 142
gods, 72, 76, 79, 98, 102*n33*, 104, 139, 144, 147–48, 185–86, 191–92, 197; as bearers, 144; communication with, 57; impersonators, 142–43, 148, 231, 238; responsibilities, 139; supplication, 147. *See also* deities
Gracián de Alderete, Diego. *See* Alderete, Diego Gracián de
Grado, Diego de, 267
Granada, Luis de, 23, 182, 184–85, 192, 194–95, 199, 203–4
greetings, 21, 77, 92, 99, 101–3, 107–8, 111
Guadalajara, 89–91, 99, 102–3, 106
Guanajuato, 32–33
Guerra, Domingo Valentín, 216
Guerrero, 17, 35–37, 102–3, 122, 125; central, 35, 37, 118; northern, 106, 120

Hale, Charles, 277
Haskett, Robert, 18, 118
Hasler, Juan A., 30, 39, 41–42
healers, 21, 106–7, 110
hell, 10, 187, 190–93, 199–200, 203
Hernández Hernández, Natalio, 277–78
Hidalgo, 282
hill, 30, 32, 44, 60, 62–63, 70, 107, 219, 224, 233; and water, 60
Hill, Jane, 30
Hispanization, 266, 270
historiography, 116–17, 122; indigenist, 120; national, 119, 121; political, 116

history, 13–14, 18, 24, 30–32, 39–41, 115–17, 119, 121–22, 268–70, 275–76, 282; of Mexico, 16, 272
honorifics, 56, 109*n46*, 140, 183*n3*
Hopi, 22, 31, 145, 147–49, 259; religion, 148; rituals, 147
Horcasitas, Fernando, 209–10, 274
Horn, Rebecca, 18
Huasteca, La, 29, 32, 35–37, 41, 118, 229, 230–31, 281
Huasteca Nahua, 35
Huichol, 33, 37, 45–47
Huitzilopochtli, 133, 136, 138–40, 143–44
hyperonyms, 22, 157–59, 161, 174–75

identity, 23, 125, 234, 238, 259, 265, 267
Indianism, 121
Indians, 3, 5, 13, 16, 119, 121, 145, 179, 186, 273
Indigenous: activism, 276; activists, 278; agency, 15; agriculturalists, 120; Christianities, 186; Christianity, 14, 186; Christians, 184–86; communal lands, 16; communities, 119–21, 180, 207, 231, 270, 273; communities, contemporary, 277; corporate community, 207; cultural sphere, 196; cultures, 115, 268; cultures erased, 16; daily life, 279; demands, 277; elite, 12–13, 15, 266–67; epistemologies, 183; graphic communications systems, 237; higher education, 282; histories, 116; identity, 119; intellectuals, 15; languages, 3–7, 9, 13, 19–20, 90, 116–17, 119, 123–27, 129, 266, 272–73, 276, 278; languages, geographical distribution, 118; languages, speakers of, 47, 125, 127; linguistic and cultural rights, 278; literature, 199; oral knowledges, 266; otherworlds, 199; peoples, 116, 119, 122, 127, 130, 265–66, 269, 271, 273, 277–78, 282; political institutions, 118; population, 4, 12, 19, 126, 129; population loss, 125, 128; population of Morelos, 21, 116, 128; scribes, 17, 87; struggles, 119; students, 12, 282; subjectivities, 266; subjects, 266; suffering and discrimination, 277; temporality, 196; towns, 21, 116; viewpoints, 116; women, 13. *See also* Indians
Instituto de Docencia e Investigación Etnológica de Zacatecas (IDIEZ), 19–20, 279–82
Ixtlilxochitl, Bartolomé de Alva. *See* Alva, Bartolomé de
Ixtlilxochitl, Fernando de Alva, 14

Jacobita, Martín, 267
Jalisco, 33, 47, 87n6, 101–2; northern, 90; southern, 87, 91, 100, 108–11
Jerónimo, 14
Jerusalem, 210–11, 214, 218–19, 221–22, 225–26
Jews, 214, 216, 218, 223
Jiménez, Francisco, 5
Jiménez, Luz, 120, 274
Johansson, Patrick, 18
justice, 219, 222–23, 270

Karttunen, Frances, 17, 117–18, 137n10, 256
Kempis, Thomas à, 180, 182, 184–85, 204
Klein, Sarah, 18
Klor de Alva, Jorge, 18
Knight, Alan, 121

Laack, Isabel, 238
land: of the dead, 74–75; legal titles, 269; relationship to, 270; rights, 269
landscape, 21, 57–58, 61, 64, 269
Langacker, Ronald, 33
language: acquisition, 4–5; contact, 30–31, 35, 39, 49, 117; and culture, 268, 273, 281–83; decline, 20; documentation of, 6; histories of, 116; nature of, 9–10; policies, 90, 272; preservation of, 17; regularity, 9; shift, 21, 106, 116–19, 126; substitution, 109; universals, 8, 10; vitality, 108–9; written, 17, 119
language revitalization, 19
Lasso de la Vega, Luis, 14
Lastra de Suárez, Yolanda, 38, 101
Latin, 3, 8, 12, 154–58, 168, 170–71, 173–74, 219, 266
laws, 119, 130, 186, 224, 271
Lehmann, Walter, 40
León-Portilla, Miguel, 18, 122
literacy, 11, 118, 183, 207–8, 218, 236; alphabetic, 15; institutions of, 9
literature, devotional, 180, 183, 204
loanwords, 32, 37, 117, 210
Lockhart, James, 9–11, 17–19, 117–18, 268–69
Looper, Matthew, 32
Lope de Vega Carpio, 270
López Austin, Alfredo, 18
Lumholtz, Carl, 145

Macri, Martha, 32
Manzanilla, Linda, 35–36
Mason, Alden J., 40

Maximiliano, Bonifacio, 267
Maya, 121, 127, 146, 186, 258
Maya Hernández, Ildefonso, 278
McDonough, Kelly, 16, 183–84
Mendieta, Jerónimo de, 3–4, 14
Mendosa, Masedonia, 274
merchants, 137–38, 140, 142
Merrill, William, 32
Mesoamerica, 20, 23, 29–30, 32, 63, 145, 235–36, 246, 260; cultures, 146
Mesoamerican: concept of "twoness," 256; graphical systems, 237; linguistic groups, 29
messengers, 134, 144–45; New Fire, 136; of victory, 135
mestizo, 13–14, 118–19, 121–22, 125–26, 147, 183n3, 278
Metepec, 179, 210–11
Mexica, 10, 22, 30, 37, 133–37, 140, 142, 144–46, 148, 269; calendar, 138; deities, 139, 148; migration, 138–39, 143; pantheon, 149; people, 63; ritual calendar, 144; rituals, 133, 149; sacrificial system, 144; society, 22, 144
Mexican Nationalism, 16, 120
Mexico, 4–5, 13, 15–16, 18, 20–21, 31–33, 39–41, 43, 129–30, 133, 140–41, 145–46, 230, 271–74, 276–78; central, 3, 29, 35, 38–39, 109; colonial administration, 86; de-indigenization, 116; Indianism, 121; modern, 21; national historiography, 119; north-central, 38; northwestern, 39, 144; southeastern, 33; southern, 3, 40; western, 101, 109; western colonial, 86
Mexico City, 12, 86–87, 97, 115n1, 271–72, 276, 278–79
Mictlan, 75, 195, 199
Mignolo, Walter, 266
migration, stories, 67
migrations, 32, 35, 37–39, 41–42, 61–63, 86, 143–44; rural-to-urban, 124
Mijangos, Juan de, 185
Mikulska, Katarzyna, 237
Miller, Wick, 31, 35
Million, Dian, 274
Millón, Roberto, 121
Mira de Amescua, Antonio, 270n10
Molina, Alonso de, 4–5, 16, 22, 30–31, 60, 94, 97–98, 107, 139, 154–56, 160–61, 163–70, 172–74, 176, 184, 255
Molina glosses, 169
Montúfar, Alonso de, 180

Morelos, 21, 31, 39, 115–31, 230, 274; ethnic composition, 122
Moteuczoma, 3, 134
mother, 70–71, 74, 77–79, 105, 143, 165, 202
Moya de Contreras, Pedro, 180
Muñoz Camargo, Diego, 14, 59–60, 183*n3*

Nahua: children, 4, 282; communities, 29, 129, 269, 273, 280; culture, 14–16, 20, 121, 161, 229, 238, 249, 280; culture, ancient, 18; dialects, 21, 33, 39–42, 44; dialects, Central, 33, 49; dialects, Eastern, 35, 37, 39, 44–48; dialects, Western, 30–31, 35, 37–39, 42, 44–47, 49; history, 13–14; humanism, 181, 184–85, 204; intellectuals, 14, 17, 22, 24, 182–84, 204, 265, 279, 283; language/languages, 20–21, 30–32, 40, 49, 226, 275; languages, early history of, 20, 29; languages, variants, 21, 30, 39–42; migration, 29; pantheon, 231, 250, 254; religion, 13; scholars, 181, 209, 267, 281; way of thinking, 275; writers, 14, 204, 277
Nahuatl: after the conquest, 17; alphabetic, 12, 14; annals, 268–69; arrival in central Mexico, 33; central, 3, 30, 39, 86–87, 89, 94–96, 100, 104, 107, 109–10; classical, 6–7, 9, 12, 19, 57, 109, 256; colonial, 182, 190, 199, 202; colonial theatre, 208; dialects, 86, 110; diversification, 31–32, 40; grammars, 5, 9, 272; as lingua franca, 3, 85; literacy, 14, 16–17, 85, 208; literary, 185; in Morelos, 122, 124; native speakers, 8, 12, 19–20, 22, 154–55, 274, 282; oral performance, 196–97; origins of, 24; poetic structuring, 197; revitalization, 20; texts, 13, 15–16, 70, 142, 271; Tuxpan, 97, 100, 106; Western, 21, 86, 89, 106, 108–9; written, 20, 86, 117
Nahuatl speakers, 11–12, 19, 86, 91, 103, 118, 120, 124–28, 130, 144–45, 221; in Ayotitlán, 106; bicultural, 154; contemporary, 229; distribution of, 124; early colonial, 139; monolingual, 128–29; in Morelos, 127; in Tehuipango, 128
Native languages, 5, 8, 110, 265, 272. *See also* Nahuatl
Nebrija, Antonio de, 22, 156–57, 162–63, 165, 168–69, 174; dictionary, 12, 22, 153–54, 156–57; Latin, 22, 168–70, 174, 176
New Spain, 4–5, 87, 180–81, 184–86, 217–18, 266, 271
notaries, 23, 207–8, 211, 215, 217, 220, 223, 225–26

Oaxaca, 38, 118
Ochpaniztli, 22, 142–44
offerings, 20, 23, 80, 229, 231, 233–34, 240, 243, 245, 255, 259; blood, 258; tobacco, 239
Offner, Jerome, 237
Olko, Justyna, 19–20, 267
Olmos, Andrés de, 5, 13, 97
Otomí, 85, 186, 233, 242, 271
Ozumba, 215–16, 220, 224

Panquetzaliztli, 22, 133, 140, 142–44
pantheism, 231–32
Paso y Troncoso, Francisco del, 209–10
Peñafiel, Antonio, 123
Pfaffenberger, Bryan, 267
Pharao Hansen, Magnus, 30, 33, 40, 42, 49, 275*n18*
phonemes, 6–7, 87, 110, 167
pictographs, 135, 229–30, 232, 235–37, 259
pictography, 235, 238, 258–59, 266
Pipil, 3, 33, 40–41; speakers, 37
place-names, 57–58, 60, 66–67, 79, 87; archaic, 37; pre-Hispanic Nahua, 21
Pochutec, 37–38, 41, 45–46
Pomar, Juan Bautista, 14
pomegranate, 172–73
porters, 22, 133, 136–38
power, 4, 63*n18*, 72, 89, 186, 238, 245, 254–55, 257, 259, 268
prayers, 71, 102, 106–7, 110, 147–48, 184, 186; healing, 107–8, 111
priests, 3, 5, 12–13, 15, 91, 100, 135–36, 138–40, 142–44, 160–61, 163, 258, 266; parish, 212; village, 120; young, 137
proto-Nahua, 43, 46–47
proto-Uto-Aztecan, 33, 43–44

Quetzalcoatl, 78

Rafaela Villanueva, 99
Ramires, Rakel, 274
Ramírez, Valentín, 274
Rangel, Alonso de, 5
Rarámuri, 22, 145–49
religion, 13, 148; *el costumbre*, 231, 260
religious texts, 12, 15, 22, 180, 182, 272; in nahuatl, 15, 22; production of, 12–13
Restall, Matthew, 18
Revolution, Mexican, 21, 90, 100, 116, 122, 126, 131, 274; in Morelos, 116, 119–21, 127

Ribas, Hernando de, 184–85
Rincón, Antonio del, 5, 7, 184
Rio, Franciska, 274
Ríos, Gerardo, 120
ritual specialists, 23, 139, 232–33, 237, 239, 241, 245–46, 248, 252–59
Romero, José Rubén, 18
Rubio y Salinas, Manuel, 212
Ruvalcaba, Melquiades, 91, 96, 99, 101, 104
Ryesky, Diane, 123

Sahagún, Bernardino de, 13, 18, 30, 70–71, 133–34, 136, 139–40, 154, 179, 182, 185, 267–68, 281; ethnographic work, 185
San Andrés Ixtlán, 91–94
San Buenaventura, Pedro de, 267
Sánchez, Mateo, 14
Sandoval, Carlos, 20
San Juan, Baltasar de, 179–80, 204
Santos, Miguel, 15
Schaniel, William, 267
Schroeder, Susan, 18
scribes, 11, 86, 109
semasiography, 235–37, 259
sermons, 12–13, 15, 183, 186, 191, 203
Severino, Mateo, 267
Siméon, Rémi, 16
sins, 44, 191–92, 202, 208, 222
Sotelo Inclán, Jesús, 120
space, 55, 57–58, 61, 68–70, 75, 79, 105$n$40, 109, 144, 235, 237, 266, 273; conceptual, 56, 68, 70, 80; mythical, 71, 80; plurilingual, 266
Spain, 172, 184–86, 208, 269
Spaniards, 3–4, 6–9, 12–14, 117, 123, 140, 154, 172, 265, 267, 269–70
Spanish: ancestry, 146; authorities, 3, 91, 269; borrowings, 22, 117, 163–65; language, 199, 207, 275; missionaries, 12, 247; mystics, 186; priests, 4, 6, 12, 15; speakers, 110, 127, 154–57
Spanish Flu, 129–30
speech acts, 99, 101–3, 107–8, 259
spirit entities, 23, 229–35, 237–39, 245–46, 248–51, 255, 257–58; dangerous, 249, 255
spoken language, 90, 119, 126, 129, 229, 235–36
Stubbs, Brian, 32
Suárez, Jorge, 101
Suchitlán, 89, 91–96, 107
Sullivan, John, 18–19, 281

Taibo II, Paco Ignacio, 130
Tavárez, David, 184–85
Téllez Hernández, Encarnación. *See* Cirilo
Templo Mayor, 136, 143
Tenango, 215, 217–18, 224
Tenextepango, 122, 124–25
Tenochtitlan, 3, 6, 61, 72, 85$n$1, 133, 136–38, 140, 142–44, 267, 269
Teotihuacan, 29, 35, 49, 63, 72$n$39, 92
Tepalcingo, 211, 214
Tepehua, 229, 233
Terraciano, Kevin, 18
Tetelcingo, 120, 125
Tezozomoc, Hernando Alvarado, 14, 269$n$7
Tlacopan, 143
Tlajomulco, 87, 89–90
Tlatelolco, 6, 15, 22, 86–87, 138, 143, 154, 181, 204, 209, 211
Tlatlauhquitepec, 215, 217, 223
Tlaxcala, 39, 86, 182, 212, 269; early history, 182$n$2
toponyms, 21, 59–68, 75; Weyéwa, 58
Torres Nila, Álvaro, 33
Townsend, Camilla, 18
Tutino, John, 18
Tuxpan, 91–93, 96, 99, 101–2, 106, 110; dialect, 104, 110

underworld, 69, 239, 243, 245–46, 252, 258
Uto-Aztecan: language family, 22, 145; languages, 3, 29, 31–32, 43, 45, 145; peoples, 31–32, 35, 145, 147, 149; speakers, 149

Valadés, Diego de, 183$n$3
Valeriano, Antonio, 267
Valiñas Coalla, Leopoldo, 31–32, 35, 38–39, 42$n$3, 91$n$12, 93$n$15, 100–104, 108, 110
Van Young, Eric, 119
Vázquez, Rolando, 266
Vegerano, Alonso, 267
Veracruz, 35, 78, 118, 127, 279
Victoria, Antonio de, 212
Villanueva, Rafaela, 99
Villegas Cortázar, Mario, 282
Villegas Gómez, Gladiola, 279, 281–82
Voegelin, Charles F., 31
Voegelin, Florence M., 31
von Mentz, Brígida, 30, 123

war, 55–56, 86, 128, 135, 144
warriors, 90*n9*, 133, 136, 142–44
water, 57, 59–61, 66–67, 69–70, 72–73, 75, 144–45, 148, 162, 245, 248, 250–51, 256, 258–59
Whittaker, Gordon, 30, 39, 49, 236
Whorf, Benjamin Lee, 40–41, 43
Wichmann, Søren, 32
winds, 93, 107, 162, 240–43, 245, 248–50, 252–54, 256–57
Womack, John, 120, 122, 126–27, 130
Wood, Stephanie, 18, 270

Xoxocotla, 122, 125

Yáñez Rosales, Rosa, 15, 21, 33, 100, 104
Yaqui rebellion, 130
Yepes, Rodrigo de, 216–18, 220–21, 223–24

Zapata, Emiliano, 119–20, 122–23, 269; as Indigenous community leader, 121; manifestos, 120
Zapata y Mendoza, Juan Buenaventura, 15
Zapatista movement, 19, 115–16, 119–22, 126
Zapoteco Sideño, Gustavo, 279
Zongolica region, 118, 120, 127

# About the Authors

**Galen Brokaw** is professor of Latin American studies and Hispanic studies at Montana State University. He is the author of *A History of the Khipu* (Cambridge UP, 2010) and coeditor with Jongsoo Lee of *Texcoco: Prehispanic and Colonial Perspectives* (University Press of Colorado, 2014) and *Fernando de Alva Ixtlilxochitl and His Legacy* (University of Arizona Press, 2016).

**Louise M. Burkhart** is professor emerita of Anthropology at the University at Albany, State University of New York, where she taught for thirty-two years. She has authored, coauthored, or edited eleven books on colonial Nahuas' engagement with Christianity, as inscribed in doctrinal and devotional literature. Her research on Passion plays also includes the book *Staging Christ's Passion in Eighteenth-Century Nahua Mexico* (University Press of Colorado, 2023) and the digital project "Passion Plays of Eighteenth-Century Mexico."

**Mary L. Clayton** holds a PhD in linguistics from the University of Texas at Austin. She taught in the Department of Spanish and Portuguese at Indiana University, directing the program in Hispanic Linguistics for many years. After publishing on phonological theory, including two articles in *Language*, she turned to Nahuatl, coauthoring two papers with her husband, R. Joe Campbell, and publishing on the *Vocabulario trilingüe* and related topics in *IJAL*, *Dictionaries*, and *International Journal of Lexicography*.

**Karen Dakin** obtained her PhD in linguistics from the University of Wisconsin–Madison. She is a research professor at the Instituto de Investigaciones Filológicas of the Universidad

Nacional Autónoma de México. She has published research on Nahua philology, including etymologies based on comparative evidence but principally work on the historical developments in and the diversification of Nahua languages from proto-Uto-Aztecan.

**Pablo García Loaeza** teaches at the Cannon School. His research has focused on Latin American literature, especially of the colonial period. He is coeditor of *History of the Chichimeca Nation: Don Fernando de Alva Ixtlilxochitl's Seventeenth-Century Chronicle of Ancient Mexico* (University of Oklahoma Press, 2019) and *The Conquest of Mexico: 500 Years of Reinventions* (University of Oklahoma Press, 2022).

**Ben Leeming** is chair of history at the Rivers School in Weston, Massachusetts. Since completing his PhD in anthropology, Leeming is also a practicing ethnohistorian whose independent scholarship focuses on early colonial Mexico and the missionary Nahuatl writings of Franciscans and Nahuas. Leeming's most recent work is an NEH-funded project to translate a very early collection of sixteenth-century Nahuatl sermons composed by Franciscan friar Bernardino de Sahagún and several anonymous Nahua collaborators.

**Magnus Pharao Hansen** is a linguistic anthropologist and assistant professor at the University of Copenhagen. He studies the social, historical, and geographical variation of Nahuatl, as well as its cultural contexts and political implications. He is the author of *Amapoualistle: Lecturas en Náhuatl de Hueyapan Morelos* (Fondo Editorial del Estado de Morelos, 2017) and *Nahuatl Nations: Language Revitalization and Semiotic Sovereignty in Indigenous Mexico* (Oxford University Press, forthcoming).

**Kelly S. McDonough** (Anishinaabe [White Earth Ojibwe] and Irish descent) is associate professor of Latin American literary and cultural studies and Indigenous studies in the Department of Spanish and Portuguese at the University of Texas at Austin. She is the author of *The Learned Ones: Nahua Intellectuals in Postconquest Mexico* (University of Arizona Press, 2014) and *Indigenous Science and Technology: Nahuas and the World Around Them* (University of Arizona Press, 2024)

**Mercedes Montes de Oca Vega** is a full-time researcher at the Universidad Nacional Autónoma de México. Her primary field of study is colonial Nahuatl, mainly its semantic, pragmatic, and discursive aspects. She has published a book and several chapters on *difrasismos*, a salient lexical feature of ancient Mesoamerican discourses. She has also published several articles on the Nahuatl used for evangelization. Her other interests include colonial Zapotec and the discursive aspects of Uto-Aztecan languages.

**Alan R. Sandstrom** has conducted long-term ethnographic research in Amatlán, the pseudonymous Nahua community located in the tropical forests of northern Veracruz, Mexico, since his first visit there in 1970. Professor emeritus of anthropology at Purdue University Fort Wayne, he is a sociocultural anthropologist whose research interests and publications focus on cultural ecology, cultural materialism, economic anthropology, Native Americans, and religion and ritual.

**Pamela Effrein Sandstrom** is associate librarian emerita and former head of reference and information services at Helmke Library, Purdue University Fort Wayne. She has applied optimal foraging theory to the study of citation patterns in human behavioral ecology and has written about ethnographic methods in library and information science. A coresearcher in the ongoing fieldwork with the Nahua, she is currently engaged with preserving access in archives and other repositories generated by anthropologists.

**John F. Schwaller** is emeritus professor of history at the University at Albany (SUNY) and research associate in history and Latin American studies at the University of Kansas. He is known for his work on the church in colonial Mexico, on Nahuatl, and on the Mexica. For years he served as an academic administrator, eventually as president of SUNY Potsdam. He currently is editor of the journal the *Americas* and was editor of *Ethnohistory*.

**Rosa H. Yáñez Rosales** is associate professor of linguistics and Mesoamerican studies at the Universidad de Guadalajara. Her research focuses on issues of linguistic historiography, language policies in Mexico, Nahuatl dialectology, and Nahuatl legal and evangelization documents from western Mexico. She is the editor of *Escribiendo desde el occidente colonial: Paleografía, traducción y vocabulario de 20 documentos en náhuatl, 1557–1737* (Universidad de Guadalajara, 2022).

www.ingramcontent.com/pod-product-compliance
Lightning Source LLC
Chambersburg PA
CBHW070803040426
42333CB00061B/1837